ALL OUR YESTERDAYS

90 YEARS OF BRITISH CINEMA

Edited by Charles Barr

BFI Publishing

First published in 1986 by the
British Film Institute
21 Stephen Street
London W1P 1PL

In association with The Museum of Modern Art, New York

Copyright © British Film Institute 1986

Reprinted 1992

British Library Cataloguing in Publication Data

All our yesterdays: 90 years of British cinema.
  1. Moving-pictures—Great Britain—History
  I. Barr, Charles   II. British Film Institute
  791.43'0941   PN1993.5.G7
ISBN 0–85170–179–5

Cover design: Christie Archer

Printed in Great Britain by The Trinity Press, Worcester

ALL OUR
YESTERDAYS

ᴐ **Quarter Library**

᠁ must return this item on or before the date on
r receipt.
ɔu return this item late you will be charged a fine
᠁ may be able to renew this item by using the
wal Hotline (0113 283 6161), or the Library
᠁ ᴐue.

ᴐ᠁ **Due**	᠁

CONTENTS

Cover: *Peeping Tom*

PREFACE AND
ACKNOWLEDGMENTS

The immediate occasion for the production of this book is the lengthy and ambitious retrospective, British Film, presented by the Department of Film at the Museum of Modern Art (MOMA) in New York between 1984 and 1987. The first part of this was devoted to the films produced, over a forty-year span, by Michael Balcon: in conjunction with this, MOMA published, in 1984, *Michael Balcon and the Pursuit of British Cinema*, a book comprising essays by Geoff Brown and Laurence Kardish, shorter contributions by David Puttnam and Adrienne Mancia, and a substantial apparatus. The second and larger part of the retrospective, under the general title of 'Traditions', constitutes, in the words of the Michael Balcon book (p. 9), 'an extensive and critical ninety-year history, tracing the specific traditions and illuminating the various aspects that collectively distinguish British film.'

All Our Yesterdays, although not so closely tied to the event itself as the Balcon book was, has been produced in collaboration with MOMA, by whom it is partly funded. It respects the imaginative design of part 2 of the retrospective in its planning and structure: that is, it brings together a number of *diachronic* studies of particular 'traditions' and other aspects and strands of British national cinema, tracing them through the decades. The commissioning of the volume, linked to MOMA's unprecedently ambitious attempt, in partnership with the National Film Archive in London, to get an overall perspective on ninety years of British cinema in its full continuity and diversity, seemed to us to offer the opportunity to produce a book which was significantly different in form from other surveys, and which would have a currency going beyond the context of the New York event itself.

The core of the book, in terms of its conception, is the set of five essays that explore the connections between cinema and other media:

theatre, literature, Music Hall, broadcasting. These are supplemented by four other sections, all but one of them also diachronically organised, which deal with

the film industry, and its relations with the state;
two modes and conceptions of cinema, broadly distinguishable as the realist and the non-realist;
divergent strands: independent cinema, animation, representations of Scotland (as an example of 'the regional'), 'underworld' films;
a set of shorter case studies: of three films, three stars, two directors, and one organisation.

These shorter items, in the final section, are included in order to vary the book's otherwise homogeneous format, and to give space for a number of more detailed studies than can easily be accommodated within the wider-ranging essays. They represent a set of personal enthusiasms, rather than being commissioned in the service of an overall design: the only criterion was that they should, at least implicitly, incorporate their own justification for their presence in this kind of survey book, by engaging with some clearly pertinent or exemplary element in British cinema. The obviously uncomprehensive spread of items in this section, ranging from Denis Gifford's interview with Lewin Fitzhamon, director of *Rescued by Rover* in 1905, to Peter Hutchings' account of Hitchcock's final film in Britain (*Frenzy*, 1972), serves to stress the open-endedness of the project – clearly these nine essays could be replaced by nine others on different topics, or by eighteen, or by ninety. Likewise, the long essays do not claim or aim to be *comprehensive* either within their own spheres or in the way they interlock with each other to cover the field. They are designed to open up, in an informed and accessible way, a plurality of overlapping perspectives on British film history. The book's content is discussed further in the general Introduction that follows.

I am extremely grateful to Mary-Lea Bandy and her colleagues at MOMA for making the project possible, and for their informed encouragement at every stage; to the staff of the National Film Archive, in London, who have been centrally involved in planning and servicing the whole MOMA season, as well as arranging a lot of film viewings for contributors to this book – it is particularly pleasing that one of the Archive officers working most closely with MOMA, Elaine Burrows, has made her own contribution in the chapter on British animation; to the staff of the British Film Institute's Library,

Information and Stills departments, for comprehensive support; to David Wilson and Geoffrey Nowell-Smith of BFI Publishing, who have guided and co-ordinated all aspects of the project; to Elaine Burrows, Andy Medhurst and Caroline Merz for substantial help with the Appendices; and, not least, to individual contributors, who have worked to some demanding deadlines.

Stills by the National Film Archive/Stills Department.

This book is dedicated to the memory of Thorold Dickinson (1903–1984): British film-maker, critic and teacher.

C.B.

Charles Barr

INTRODUCTION: AMNESIA AND SCHIZOPHRENIA

> I do not think the British are temperamentally equipped to make the best use of the movie camera.[1]

As a provocative starting-point for thinking about British cinema, these words by Satyajit Ray (1963) at least make a change from the François Truffaut remark that has become so tediously familiar. In the course of his book-length interview with Alfred Hitchcock (1966), Truffaut suggested that there was 'a certain incompatibility between the terms "cinema" and "Britain"'.[2] Roy Armes' very useful *Critical History of British Cinema* uses this remark as its epigraph,[3] and it is a striking fact that virtually no one who writes about British cinema finds it possible to do so without quoting, or coining their own version of, some such sweepingly dismissive, or at best severely limiting, verdict on an entire national output. Being so prevalent and deep-rooted, this phenomenon has, I think, to be noted (and thus incidentally repeated) at the start of an enterprise like this book, if only to try to pin down and interrogate what it is that switches so many people off the subject, and to sketch out something of the broad critical context within which – and to some extent against which – the book is operating.

In 1968, Pauline Kael wrote in the *New Yorker* that

> The English can write and they can act (or at least *speak* beautifully, which is enough to cripple us with admiration), but they can't direct movies.... Compared with the motion picture art of Sweden or Italy or Japan or France or pre-Nazi Germany, English films have always been a sad joke.[4]

For her fellow-American Dwight Macdonald (1972):

I

The British over-use the close-up – they're not a very visual race, at least in our time – they douse their movies with close-ups the way people with defective taste-buds use ketchup.[5]

Nor is this quasi-racist kind of critical line confined to Americans, Frenchmen, Indians, and other outsiders: the natives adopt it as well, providing support for Gilbert Adair's contention (1985) that 'the history of the British cinema is that of an inferiority complex'.[6] James Park declares in the first sentence of his 1984 book *Learning to Dream: the New British Cinema* that 'the history of British cinema is one of unparalleled mediocrity',[7] while for David Shipman, reflecting upon his researches for the second and concluding volume of *The Story of Cinema* (1983):

It is one of the curiosities of film history that American films, when they seem to change with the passing of years, become either better or worse, while on re-examination British films, if they change at all, only become worse.[8]

Nevertheless, a number of writers have, since the 1960s, found the re-examination of British cinema to be worth embarking upon. In a formulation as resonant as Truffaut's, Alan Lovell had characterised British cinema, in the title of a 1969 essay, as 'The Unknown Cinema';[9] in the same year Peter Wollen, in *Signs and Meaning in the Cinema*, turned aside from discussing the now well-mapped landscape of American cinema to remark that, in contrast, 'the English cinema remains utterly amorphous, unclassified, unperceived'.[10] Unquestionably it has, since then, become much more thoroughly known, classified, and perceived. Many of the specific gaps Lovell pointed to have been filled: there have been substantial studies of the documentary movement, Hammer, Ealing, Humphrey Jennings, and other individuals, films and studios, to say nothing of various wider-ranging surveys: in some academic and critical quarters, British cinema has become as serious an object of study as Hollywood or European. Yet the impact of this work has, to date, been distinctly limited. As evidence, consider three of the most ambitious film-publishing ventures of the past decade: David Shipman's film history just referred to, the two-volume *Cinema: A Critical Dictionary* edited by Richard Roud (1980), and the Macmillan *Dictionary of Films* and *Dictionary of Film-makers* (both 1984).[11] All three enterprises are designed, with evident success, to take their place on library shelves as standard works of reference, and all three approach the British cinema in a resolutely old-fashioned way, offering nothing, in terms of selection, judgment and method, that could not have been written in the 1960s. In the case of the two multi-author dictionaries, the Roud one in particular, this creates a striking dichotomy between the handling of Hollywood and non-English-speaking cinema on the one hand, which is often ambitious and sophisticated, and of British on the other, which is considerably less so. It is as though the proliferation of work on British cinema existed somewhere on the margins, outside the mainstream of real film history and criticism, as a branch of sociology, or of cultural analysis, or of an insular national history – or as a curious specialised area for a minority of film buffs.

It seems more profitable to try to explain this marginalisation than simply to deplore it: there are good reasons for it.

The most distinguished spread of contributions both to the Roud and to the Macmillan dictionaries are those written, mainly on Hollywood topics, by the English critic Robin Wood. Now an expatriate, Wood was based in England, writing and teaching, for most of the 1960s and 1970s, and became an exceedingly influential figure in the transformation of film culture during this time, in Britain particularly but also in North America. Through his rigorous auteurist analyses, including books on Hitchcock, Hawks, Penn, Bergman, and Satyajit Ray – respected art-house directors and commercial Hollywood ones, approached with equal seriousness – he helped to change the terms in which cinema, and especially Hollywood cinema, was viewed. For British cinema, Wood has consistently expressed a low regard, on the rare occasions when he has referred to it at all. His first and most important book *Hitchcock's Films* (1965) wrote off the pre-1939 British work *en bloc* with a daunting sternness, as low-pressure apprentice work compared with the mature American films.[12] In 1974 he told *Framework* magazine in an interview:

My own reluctance to confront the British cinema is simply attributable to my sense that its achievement is so limited and so much less interesting than that of other countries.[13]

It is an attitude broadly shared by other important figures who began writing at the same period, notably David Thomson (author of *A Biographical Dictionary of the Cinema*), V. F. Perkins (author of *Film as Film*), and *Movie* magazine as a whole, in which both Perkins and Wood were prominent.[14] The importance of this mid-1960s period can hardly be exaggerated: it saw the foundation of academic film study in Britain, and a huge expansion of published criticism, and it set new terms for approaching popular cinema, film authorship, and close textual analysis. Both explicitly and implicitly, British

3

cinema was discounted as a rewarding object of study, put down in relation to Hollywood on one side and European art cinema on the other, as being conditioned (geographically, historically, culturally) to dither between the two, lacking the characteristic strengths of either. The classic statement of this position is found in the editorial on 'The British Cinema' in the first issue of *Movie*, in 1962, which was billed as being 'written by V. F. Perkins on behalf of the editorial board':

> The British cinema is as dead as it was before. Perhaps it was never alive.

An elaborate chart set out, on two halves of the same page, the editors' judgment of the talents of all practising Hollywood and British directors, grading them in a series of six categories: almost all the British were huddled in the two lowest ones, creating a spectacular, eloquent, and polemically very effective asymmetry.

Of course, *Movie* was not the whole of British film criticism. Much of the polemical thrust of that first editorial was in fact provoked by the admiring treatment which the new British cinema of the early 1960s was attracting in certain quarters, including the weighty British Film Institute publication *Sight and Sound*. *Movie* reported, with derision, the current view that 'We have had a breakthrough, a renaissance, a New Wave', and opposed it effectively, not so much (after that first issue) by writing negatively about British films as by writing positively about others. Such British films as did occasionally get praised were presented as being marginal and atypical, exceptions which, in the true sense of the term, proved the rule – they tested and bore out, by their demonstrable difference, and by the fact that they seemed to lead nowhere, caught in a cinematic cul-de-sac, the 'rule' that certain notions and practices of cinema were somehow embedded in Britain which were inimical to the kind of high achievements of skill and moral seriousness valued by *Movie*. Historically, in terms of the publications and influence that followed, *Movie*'s project can be shown to have had a decisive conviction and (relative) staying-power, and one effect of this was that the case against British cinema so sweepingly stated by Truffaut, Kael *et al* was able to go virtually by default: compared with Hollywood, and with other serious national cinemas, British cinema stayed 'unknown', and not worth knowing.

One way of representing this line is as a by-product of the influence of the French magazine *Cahiers du Cinéma*, a magazine strongly present in the background to *Movie*: it had, through Truffaut and others, been celebrating Hawks, Hitchcock, and other Hollywood

4

directors for a decade before *Movie* first appeared, and it had no time at all for British cinema (with the significant exception of Joseph Losey, refugee from America). It is, however, more revealing to place *Movie* in the context of a series of native film magazines that have successively represented, as *Movie* did for a time in the 1960s, the 'leading edge' or growth point of film criticism in Britain. Over a period of some fifty years, there was always, in fact, one particular magazine that could be convincingly identified in this way, particularly in retrospect. Dates and titles can be set out schematically as follows:

1927	*Close-Up*
1932	*Cinema Quarterly*
1936	*World Film News*
1940	*Documentary News Letter*
1947	*Sequence*
1949	*Sight and Sound*
1962	*Movie*
1971	*Screen*

The dates given are those of the respective first issues, except in the case of *Sight and Sound* and *Screen*, where they denote a change of editor and of orientation. From the late 1970s, it ceases to be so easy to pick out a single magazine.

Of these magazines, *Close-Up* belongs to the early years of the Film Society movement, and the discovery by a generation of intellectuals of the cinema as an art form. *Cinema Quarterly* is closely associated with the British documentary movement: John Grierson helped to found it, and wrote for it, and there is a strong continuity in organisation, personnel and policy between it and the next two magazines listed, *World Film News* and *Documentary News Letter*, which are in effect succeeding versions of the same magazine. *Sequence* was started at Oxford University before moving its base to London: its dominant figures were Gavin Lambert and Lindsay Anderson, and it published thirteen issues between 1947 and 1951, by which time its writers had gained a more prominent critical platform on *Sight and Sound*, Lambert having been appointed editor in 1949. *Sight and Sound* had been published continuously from 1932, and was taken over as the British Film Institute's house magazine when the Institute was founded in 1933, but for a long time it kept a low critical profile, and only in the 1950s can it be said to have represented, as it did through Anderson especially, the 'leading edge' of British film criticism. *Movie*, like *Sequence*, came out of Oxford, having its roots in the University-based magazine *Oxford Opinion*: by the end of the 1960s it had become intermittent in publication, and generally less of a force. *Screen*, like *Sight and Sound*, was transformed by a change of policy and editor after many years of intellectually unambitious, classroom-oriented existence: the first issue edited by Sam Rohdie in 1971, which was also the first in the familiar austere 1970s format, embodied in its very different, structuralist, way as strong a statement of opposition to prevailing orthodoxies as did the first issue of *Movie*.

A strong recurring feature within this influential succession of magazines is a hostility to the established practices of British film journalism and/or of British film-making, particularly when the one operates in chauvinistic support of the other. *Close-Up* attacked the optimism and general 'hype' that surrounded the expansion of British film production following the 1927 Films Act: a thoroughly representative example is the 1929 survey of seven new British films by Hugh Castle, a regular contributor. On *Master and Man*:

> Really British. Another endurance test. . . . One realises, on seeing it, how weary, stale, flat and unprofitable seem to be all the products of the British cinema.[15]

Cinema Quarterly and its successors stood, virtually by definition, for forms of British cinema opposed to the commercial mainstream. Harry Watt, a junior director within the GPO Film Unit in the 1930s, describes in his autobiography how 'we all had to work on *World Film News*', and refers to Hitchcock as 'the only British feature director we respected'.[16] The war years saw a degree of consensus, in criticism as elsewhere, with *Documentary News Letter* getting behind the propaganda work of British film-makers, while being continuously critical of the limited vision of government and film industry. The post-war critical euphoria that saw British cinema, after its important war-time development, as being ready to challenge the world commercially and artistically, was attacked by *Sequence* in a series of robust polemics: 'British Cinema: the Descending Spiral' is an indicative title.[17] *Movie*'s hostility to the native product has already been described.

The orientation of the most recent of the seminal critical magazines, *Screen*, has been rather different. It has gone in for no apocalyptic dismissals of British cinema (only of mainstream British criticism) but has increasingly fostered a productive and sympathetic engagement with it. It is, at the same time, notable that *Screen*'s decisive initial impact upon film culture in the early 1970s came from a particular set of analytical and theoretical texts, some translated from the French, others written by Stephen Heath, Colin MacCabe and Laura Mulvey: these dealt almost exclusively with American films, and not at all with British. Meanwhile, the apocalyptic tendency surfaced again in two shorter-lived but dynamic small magazines from the same period. The third issue of the Cambridge-based *Cinema* (1969) carried a black-bordered obituary by Tom Nairn:

10 April 1969
Deceased at the Paramount, Piccadilly, London W.1.
THE BRITISH CINEMA

– the occasion was the premiere, and journalistic celebration of, Richard Attenborough's film of *Oh! What a Lovely War*. The third issue of *Monogram* (1972) addressed itself to recent British cinema rather in the same spirit that *Movie* had done ten years earlier, and delivered, in the long article 'Between Style and Ideology' written by its editor Thomas Elsaesser, a comparably magisterial negative verdict.

Tracing this particular succession of film magazines does have the effect of pointing to the existence, in Britain, of a tradition of lively engagement with issues of film criticism and aesthetics. It has been a compact tradition, generally manifested in terms of a dialectic between an orthodoxy and an articulate opposition (which may become the next orthodoxy). In fact, this critical work has had a consistently greater prestige internationally than British cinema itself has done, and the very prestige of this tradition has, with a certain irony, helped to keep the prestige of British films at a low level, as a result of the consistent way in which the most progressive and interesting elements in this criticism have – at least until recently – been actively hostile, or at best indifferent, to the work of the commercial mainstream of the British cinema.

This kind of cultural self-laceration is hardly unique. A similar process operated for a long time in America (perhaps still does, in a reduced way), with the Hollywood product past and present being extensively patronised by the country's own intelligentsia. Robin Wood has remarked on the novelty value he had as a visiting lecturer in Canada in the 1960s, as an English-speaking critic who attended seriously to Hollywood cinema:

I was invited over there ironically enough primarily to lecture on the American cinema, the assumption being that there were plenty of people in North America who could talk about European art movies, but almost nobody who was qualified or particularly interested in discussing Hollywood movies.[18]

But Robin Wood did at least exist, to be imported, and it is clear to the point of truism that American cinema had long since been 'taken seriously' by critics abroad, as by popular audiences worldwide, right from the time when national cinemas first began to be distinguished. In a 1922 essay entitled 'Americanitis', Lev Kuleshov generalised from his several years' experience of audience response to films in both pre- and post-revolutionary Russia, in these terms:

1. Foreign films appeal more than Russian ones.
2. Of the foreign films, all the American ones and detective stories appeal most.[19]

Compare the recognition of national cinematic identities recalled from his formative years by another future film-maker, Satyajit Ray:

In the 1930s there used to be two cinemas next to each other in the heart of Calcutta's theatreland. The first one, as you came up the side street that contained them, showed only British films, while the other specialised in the American product. I was at school then and had already become something of a film addict. On Saturday afternoons I used to turn in at the side street and make a beeline for the second cinema, casting a contemptuous sidelong glance at the first one *en route*.

We did not think much of British films at that time. Word had got round over the years that the art of film making had somehow eluded the British.[20]

Kuleshov's essay went on to analyse what was special about the American product:

The success of American motion pictures lies in the greatest common measure of film-ness, in the presence of maximum movement and primitive heroism, in an organic relation to contemporaneity.

Secondly, due to conditions of life in their country and their particular commercial methods, Americans are able to show more plot in a film of limited length and strive to attain the greatest number of scenes and the greatest impression with the least expenditure of film stock.[21]

Ray, looking back from the 1960s, reflected upon his gut response to the British product (contrasted with the American) in terms that are virtually a negative image of Kuleshov's:

8

The main stumbling block in the path of the British film makers was, one suspects, the very fact of their being British. I do not think the British are temperamentally equipped to make the best use of the movie camera. The camera forces one to face facts, to probe, to reveal, to get close to people and things; while the British nature inclines to the opposite; to stay aloof, to cloak harsh truths with innuendoes. You cannot make great films if you suffer from constricting inhibitions of this sort. What is more, the placidity and monotony of habit patterns that mark the British way of life are the exact opposite of what constitutes real meat for the cinema. The cinema revels in contrasts and clashes – however small and subtle. The calm has to be ruffled, the patterns disturbed and tensions created – and these have to be revealed in audible speech and visible action, to provide the basic raw material for the director to work upon. These were lacking in the British scene. Or if they existed, then the creative imagination and daring to turn them into the stuff of cinema was lacking.[22]

This is quite a complex and searching piece of writing, an unusually thorough articulation of a not uncommon feeling: as such it provides a particularly useful text to consider and interrogate in the context of this book.

First, an apparent paradox. During the cinema's ninety-year history to date, two film-makers above all others have attained worldwide recognition to the extent of becoming, at different periods, virtually synonymous with the notion of popular cinema – Chaplin and Hitchcock. Both were Londoners by birth, upbringing, and cultural formation. True, Chaplin didn't involve himself in cinema until he had been working for some time in America, and Hitchcock moved to America at the age of 40, eventually becoming an American citizen; but these two do create difficulties for the thesis that the British are 'temperamentally unsuited' to cinema. So does a man like the much less celebrated James Whale, who went more or less straight from a career in English theatre to direct the first two films in Universal's Frankenstein cycle of the 1930s, full-blooded Hollywood genre films whose cinematic and iconographic power has been unusually pervasive and enduring, and which embody Kuleshov's concept of *film-ness* in exemplary fashion. They are, in fact, extremely 'British' films in personnel (not only Whale but most of the actors, especially in the second film *The Bride of Frankenstein*: Colin Clive as the Baron and Boris Karloff as the Monster are common to both); and the literary source was of course British as well, as *The Bride* reminds us by inserting a prologue in which Mary Shelley starts to narrate to her fellow-authors the story of this

9

putative sequel to her original novel. Mary is played by (British) Elsa Lanchester, who doubles the role with that of the female created in the laboratory in the film's climax – thus very appositely enacting the notion of the author projecting herself into her own creation, her own fantasy.

The standard explanation for this 'paradox' would be that the occasional imaginative director like Whale had to go to Hollywood in order to be able to tap this vein of creative fantasy; that the Britain of the 19th century may have been conducive to a dynamic popular art which the cinema would seize upon for source materials and for narrative models (cf. the very title of Eisenstein's essay 'Dickens, Griffith and the Film Today'), but that 'the British scene' had since changed, becoming stagnant and placid. Hitchcock's British work, on this reading, was of a low-pressure, muted kind compared with his later American films: he was working uneasily against the British grain, within a commercial cinema whose norms were, in Ray's word, 'innocuous', at the period of, significantly, the rise of the documentary film movement and of a dominant critical ethos which overlapped with and supported it.

'The documentary film,' John Grierson wrote, 'was an essentially British development. Its characteristic was the idea of social use. . . . If it came to develop in England there were good reasons for it.' The primary reason was this: 'It permitted the national talent for understatement to operate in a medium not given to understatement.'[23] As a critic, Grierson was keen to persuade even Hitchcock to embrace this idea of direct 'social use', imploring him in 1930 (following *Blackmail* and *Murder*) to 'give us a film of the Potteries or of Manchester or of Middlesbrough, with the personals in their proper place and the life of a community instead of a benighted lady at stake.'[24] Ray, in the essay already quoted, provides an echo of Grierson's claim for the documentary as being characteristically British: 'One possible reason why the British took to documentaries was that it involved a legitimate process of dehumanisation'[25] – rather a chilling sentiment, though a consistent one.

For Ray, predictably, and indeed by common consent, British cinema came into its own in World War Two. In these years, to adapt Grierson's phraseology, the life of a community *is* at stake, inescapably and dramatically, and the classic feature films of this period (*In Which We Serve, Millions Like Us, Fires Were Started, The Way to the Stars, San Demetrio London*) do 'put the personals in their proper place', subordinating individual desire and ambition to the team and the job, either after a struggle or after no struggle at all. Audience pleasure comes from the maintenance of group effort and from the very neatness of the narrative devices which subdue or sublimate individual drives. Choking back, or snapping out of, grief for the death of a loved one becomes – in all five of the films named, and many others – a central and very moving motif. Such films could be grouped together as achievements of a national cinema to be proud of.

It is impossible to exaggerate the centrality of this period to any reading of British film history, from whatever critical perspective: several of the essays that follow make this point independently. By the end of the war, a positive reading of 'mainstream' British cinema for the first time became convincingly available, both in Britain and abroad. It was a cinema unproblematically British in personnel (after a decade of foreign infiltration that was resented by many[26]), it dealt with current realities of British life, it was on the whole intelligently supported by the state, was popular with British audiences,[27] and earned respect abroad. As in politics, so in cinema, a productive coalition had been formed out of previously opposed factions: documentary personnel had been integrated into the industry. A lesson widely drawn was that British cinema had embraced its true vocation, the most noble vocation of cinema itself: realism. Lindsay Anderson has recalled the values he had soaked up by the time he returned to England from war service in 1945: 'I had all the conventional upper-middlebrow ideas about "good cinema", realism (good) and commercialism (bad).'[28] Of the characters in *The Way to the Stars*, released in that same year of 1945, the influential *Observer* critic Caroline Lejeune wrote in a review full of admiration and pride that: 'These people are real people, and like real people they do not make much of their private emotions.'[29] Significantly, these people include Americans as well as British, brought together at a wartime flying base, and one senses a special satisfaction in the spectacle of Americans being absorbed into this regime of reticence and under-statement: British realism could perhaps subdue American brashness on a wider front.

Cinematically as in other ways, the war seemed to have validated precisely those qualities of restraint and stoicism which might previously (as they did to observers like Ray) have appeared insipid. It had, in addition, opened up access to a rich historical and cultural *heritage* – in a sense, had only re-opened it, since the cinema has already tried from time to time to exploit this heritage in seeking out prestige material with export potential. Geoff Brown and Brian McFarlane demonstrate in their respective essays later in this book how far back into the silent period goes the strategy of making respectful film versions of classic plays and novels, while the same man who directed many of these, Maurice Elvey, had made a gallant effort in World War I to recall historic campaigns in an inspirational way with his biopic of *Nelson*. As the basis for any sustained success these strategies were handicapped in two main ways: first, and obviously, by the lack, in the formative silent period, of the prestige weapon of the educated English voice on the soundtrack to deliver the words of Shakespeare or Dickens, or striking patriotic addresses; second, and more radically, by the regular lack of any 'organic relation to contemporaneity'. Whatever the precise interpretation one gives to this phrase of Kuleshov, which seems to refer to thematic and stylistic factors together, a film like Laurence Olivier's *Henry V* (1944) has clearly got it, both in its unforced exploitation of parallels between then and now (the invasion of Europe; the unity-in-diversity of soldiers from all parts of the kingdom; the set-piece of the King going among his subjects, so evocative of all those images of King and Queen visiting blitzed London) and in its delight in the process of 'making cinema' for a confined wartime audience, knowingly bursting the bounds of Shakespeare's 'wooden O'.

Henry V is the culmination of a wartime series, almost a genre in itself, of 'heritage' films, which include – among many others – *This England*, *The Young Mr Pitt*, and the Nelson film of this war, Churchill's own favourite, *Lady Hamilton*; also, incorporating literature as well as history, *A Canterbury Tale*, short films like Jennings' *Words for Battle*, and even Carol Reed's film of the H. G. Wells novel *Kipps*. Whatever their merits, and they are an uneven lot, none of these was simply recreating a bit of heritage in an inert, Trooping-the-Colour manner, and *Henry V* achieved a very superior status as a high-quality British product. It made an encouraging impact abroad as well as at home, most importantly in America.[30]

If one looks at these two major (and overlapping) developments together, it can be appreciated how British cinema could seem to have been definitively appropriated for realism and for 'quality'. At last there was a national cinema able to exploit effectively those two distinctive objects of pride, British understatement and the rich British heritage, which had previously appeared rather intractable material for films. Hence the euphoria of the mid-1940s period, which saw a more cohesive and enthusiastic support for British cinema from the 'serious' end of British criticism than at any time before or since. The newly won status of cinema in national life was evidenced in a variety of ways in these years: extraordinarily high attendance figures; a proliferation of polls, film annuals, and books-of-the-film; the institution of the Royal Film Performance (1946 onwards); and an impressive number of ambitious publications. These included the *Penguin Film Review* (nine issues between 1946 and 1949); Roger Manvell's best-selling 1944 Penguin book called simply *Film*; a handsome multi-author volume on *20 Years of British*

Film, 1925–1945; the beginning of Rachael Low's magnificent enterprise *The History of the British Film* (first volume published 1948); and the survey *The Factual Film* which provides Andrew Higson, in a later section of this book, with the title for his chapter 'Britain's outstanding contribution to the film' – documentary being identified as such, as *The Factual Film*'s very premise.[31]

The notions of cinema generally, and of the renascent British cinema within it, that were current at this time and in publications like these, have been illuminatingly analysed by John Ellis in *Screen* magazine, in an article whose 145 footnotes testify to the thoroughness of its coverage.[32] Manvell, Caroline Lejeune and Richard Winnington are probably the three critics of the period whose work is most familiar to us now, being accessible in book form (which in itself indicates their special status); Ellis shows how widely their attitudes were shared within contemporary journalism. There was a general optimistic support for British cinema provided that it stayed true to its vocation of realism and quality, and an excitement at the prospect of extending the successes already achieved in the American market. Along with *Henry V*, David Lean's work of the mid-1940s was particularly important. *Brief Encounter* represented sensitive realism; *Great Expectations*, culture. Winnington ended a review of the latter film in *Penguin Film Review* by saying: 'It is a landmark in the history of British films. . . . Cineguild have made the first great challenge to the world on behalf of Britain. They have made the first big attack.'[33]

Cinematically as in other ways, the post-war years were to be perceived as a steady process of disappointment and anti-climax, a falling off from a lost Golden Age of purposeful austerity. Those who championed a cinema of realism and quality were for the most part disillusioned by what they saw as betrayal or vulgarisation of those principles, and by a loss of impetus in the work of those, especially in the documentary movement, who stayed true to them. Those who, like *Sequence* magazine, were more sceptical about the whole ideology of documentary, restraint, and the great challenge to the world, did not identify an alternative tradition to be enthusiastic about, though they admired Jennings for his 'poetry', and some other isolated British films. The same sort of process would continue to operate, creating the familiar stale perspective on British cinema which I can, myself, recall from the time of starting to learn about film history, around 1960. There was an established view of the correct path for British cinema, and a set of films to go with them, a list mainly from the 1940s, but brought up to date with more recent ones, including some from Ealing, Free Cinema, and Woodfall. If you found the package unconvincing (especially in comparison with

13

certain areas of non-British cinema and the kind of critical exploration of them that was developing), then you basically wrote off the
British cinema.

Into the gap between these two attitudes there fell, as one can now
begin to see, a rather richer and more diverse British cinema – a
cinema partly of unfamiliar films, partly of more familiar ones seen in
a fresh light.

Another of the special things about the mid-1940s period was the
genuine interest shown by some government ministers in films and
film policy, notably Sir Stafford Cripps (Chancellor of the Exchequer, 1947–1950) and Harold Wilson. Wilson's work as President
of the Board of Trade (1947–1951) involved him closely in the
organisation of the film industry, and his interest in cinema was more
than merely dutiful. In June 1948, he spoke to the House of
Commons as follows:

> We are getting tired of some of the gangster, sadistic and
> psychological films of which we seem to have so many, of diseased
> minds, schizophrenia, amnesia and diseases which occupy so much
> of our screen time. I should like to see more films which genuinely
> show our way of life, and I am not aware . . . that amnesia and
> schizophrenia are stock parts of our social life.[34]

This is a beautiful distillation of a recurring theme – in two connected
ways. First, there is the desire, expressed by an authoritative, school-
teacherish voice, for social realities to be treated in a sensibly
straightforward manner. Second, there is the reluctant awareness of
just how strong the darker forces are, not only in meretricious
Hollywood but in Britain. Wilson evokes an underside of 1940s
British cinema which is disturbingly 'other' and startlingly prolific.
For him, it merits discouragement and shame, and both at the time
and retrospectively criticism has indeed been ashamed of it. From
another perspective, it sounds rather thrilling, opening up an
alternative British cinema which deals with 'our social life' (including
such issues, here, as post-war readjustment, and the black-market
economy) in an oblique and displaced manner rather than head-on,
through structures of genre and fantasy – rather in the same way that
Gainsborough, Ealing's less respectable sister, was handling issues of
class and sexuality in a series of historical melodramas (from 1944)
which were like a parodic undermining of the serious 'heritage' films:
these were, again, more popular with audiences than with critics.

The second of Robert Murphy's two essays in this volume, 'Riff-
Raff', deals with precisely Wilson's range of films, indicating their
quantity and vitality and providing a context for them. The second of

Julian Petley's essays, 'The Lost Continent', incorporates Gains-borough melodrama within a broad survey of 'non-realist' traditions, linking Gainsborough's output with that of, for instance, Hammer Films from the late 1950s onward. He too stresses the sheer quantity and range of films in question. It is not a coincidence that Murphy and Petley have also written the two essays on the British film industry, in terms of its economic organisation and of its relations with government respectively: to have an informed sense of the history overall is, necessarily, to be aware of significant patterns in the type of films produced and to perceive gaps in the charts that have been conventionally drawn. Petley uses a cartographical metaphor for his title and his conclusion:

> One suspects that if the institution of the British cinema could be radically reconceptualised and wrested from the grasp of the still tenacious realist aesthetic, then the films discussed in this chapter would look less like isolated islands revealing themselves, and more like the peaks of a long submerged lost continent.

It is a notion which, broadly speaking, informs this book. A number of writers express it independently in different ways, either explicitly or implicitly. Both John Caughie and Andrew Higson discuss the tradition of British realism as a critical construction. Andy Med-hurst, writing on the links between cinema and Music Hall tradi-tions, traces another strand in the non-respectable underside of British cinema. Several of the shorter essays, that of Peter Hutchings most explicitly, are written from a similar perspective.

It is not simply a matter of counting titles, of drawing compen-satory attention to a range of films often omitted from the histories[35] (Gainsborough, Hammer, *Carry On* films, gangster films) which are significant quantitatively, commercially, and sociologically – though they are certainly all those things. It is not the case that there is a Great Tradition of British cinema from which this mass of films deviate, or to which they are alien. Possibly the conventional binary opposition of realist and non-realist is a too rigid one: at any rate, the terms of its application to British films needs reworking.

The case of Michael Powell and Emeric Pressburger, and their shifting critical status, is instructive. As a director/writer/producer team, they made eighteen films together between 1939 and 1957. Reviewing *A Matter of Life and Death* on its release in 1946, Richard Winnington criticised them in terms that were confidently Grierson-ian (or, in anticipation, Wilsonian): 'It is even further away from the essential realism and the true business of the British movie than their two recent films *I Know Where I'm Going* and *A Canterbury Tale*.'[36]

Others besides Winnington have, from a variety of perspectives, characterised their work as aberrant, whether as a continuing un-British embarrassment or (particularly in more recent years) as a rare bright thread in a drab and prosaic national cinema. *Sequence* had little time for their work, nor fifteen years later did *Movie*, which in its initial 1962 issue placed Powell as a director in the next-to-bottom of its categories, as being something less than 'talented'. In 1966, however, *Movie* printed a supportive though isolated article by the maverick critic Raymond Durgnat (of whom more below):[37] this helped to encourage a gradual rediscovery of their work and of such dazzling films as the wartime *A Canterbury Tale*, the post-war melodrama *Black Narcissus*, and the film which Powell directed in 1960 after the partnership broke up, *Peeping Tom* – an idiosyncratic and self-reflexive horror film which the critical establishment received at the time with devastating hostility. This process of rediscovery was charted, and also consolidated, by the British Film Institute publication *Powell, Pressburger and Others*, edited by Ian Christie in 1978, and they have now become thoroughly established as the British film-makers who appeal to those who don't much like British cinema, admired for going against that cinema's norms ('I distrust documentary, always have' – Powell, 1971[38]).

The real question, as hinted already, is whether those norms have been perceived accurately. In many ways the difference, the aberrancy, of Powell and Pressburger has been exaggerated. To return to the key period of the mid-1940s: far from being opposed in structure (fantasy vs realism), *A Matter of Life and Death* and *Brief Encounter* (1945) can be grouped together as instances of a spectacular shift which occurs in British films around this time from the public sphere to the private, with a stress on vision and fantasy. *A Matter of Life and Death* announces in an opening title that it will be set 'inside the mind' of the David Niven character, and contains a celebrated shot taken from behind his closing eyelid; the house of another character (Roger Livesey) incorporates a camera obscura at the top of it, and when we first see him he is manipulating its lens in order to get an image of the outside world 'as in a poet's eye'. But the modes of subjectivity and cinematic self-reflexivity which Powell and Pressburger are here foregrounding with characteristically flamboyant devices (and these help to explain their lack of appeal to *Movie*, which liked the impersonality of classic Hollywood) are equally operative, though less flamboyantly so, in *Brief Encounter*, and also in Ealing's *Dead of Night*, another film of 1945. *Brief Encounter*'s narrative is the extended reverie of its heroine, and *Dead of Night*'s narrative is the extended dream of its hero; both films have an artful circular construction, folding back upon themselves.

Because of the particular status that both Lean and Ealing have in British film history and in critical discourse about it, these films are worth looking at further.

Brief Encounter, based on Noël Coward's story of an unconsummated love affair, has always been a central point of reference, celebrated by one generation for its (or its characters') adult sobriety and restraint, rejected by the next for – the obverse side of these qualities – abject inhibition.[39] Coward's biographer accurately reflects a critical consensus in claiming that 'Lean's technique set a pattern of post-war realism in the English cinema which was to be followed for some years to come',[40] but its enduring fascination surely comes from the way in which, handling its very 'British' material, it enacts processes of fantasy which are basic to cinema. It is not the documentation of a failed love affair but the intricately constructed narrating or imaging of one. Laura Jesson says a tense farewell to a male acquaintance at a railway station and returns home, in a trance-like state, to her children and sedate husband: after dinner, with a Rachmaninov concerto playing on the radio, she settles back in an armchair to recount to herself the story of her secret romance. We look over her shoulder, and for long seconds the first image of the recounted story is superimposed, precisely as if she were watching, or summoning up, her own story on a cinema screen. Like the audience in the cinema (and she is depicted as a regular filmgoer herself) she is losing herself in reverie. She could perfectly well be fantasising parts or all of the ostensible flashbacks that follow, not that it matters: whether or not we want to say that they represent things that really, within the fictional world of the film, 'happened' to her, they are playing out impulses, fantasies and conflicts from within her, and, through her, projecting them for the audience. Every element in the film is shaped by a subjective logic: Laura's world of trains and shadows, coincidence and repetition, is structured not as documentary surface but as the projection of psychic states.

Dead of Night, likewise, plays with the processes of cinematic narration and fantasy. A character, in what will later be revealed as a recurring dream, comes to a country house full of guests and listens to a succession of uncanny stories narrated by them: these are realised in a series of episodes by a quartet of Ealing staff directors. The two most powerful are the work of, respectively, Alberto Cavalcanti and Robert Hamer: a ventriloquist finds that his partner/dummy is acquiring a murderous life of its own, and a smooth young accountant entering into a society marriage is haunted by demonic impulses emanating from the glimpsed depths of an antique mirror. In Freudian terms these are clearly stories of the return of the repressed: elements in the psyche that have been rigidly kept down find their way back to confront the repressor in a monstrous externalised form.

Who, here, are the repressors? First, the characters, complacent in their assumption of rational male control over their worlds. Behind them, the actors and the associations they bring with them: Michael Redgrave (ventriloquist) had just been in *The Way to the Stars*, playing one of those 'real' people – an archetypal Battle of Britain hero-pilot – whom C. A. Lejeune endorsed for not making much of their private emotions, while Ralph Michael (accountant) had been Ealing's standard level-headed wartime hero in a succession of films like *San Demetrio London*, controlling sexual and other tensions out of existence. Behind them, the studio: Ealing had been the dominant studio for war-effort production, absorbing documentary ideas and personnel (Cavalcanti himself among them) and making films for – to appropriate Grierson's phrase again – social use: Michael Balcon, who ran the place, made these policies quite explicit. *Dead of Night* lifts the lid on forces of sex, violence and fantasy which Ealing's wartime project had kept almost out of sight.

Ealing's subsequent output can best be read as an extension of these forms of conflict: between ventriloquist and dummy, between rationalist/realist surface and the depths of the mirror world. It is a conflict that operates both within particular films and between different strands of the studio's output – social realism vs melodrama, benevolent comedy vs subversive comedy – and it is Robert Hamer, director of the mirror story, who carries forward those energies most strongly, in the London melodrama of *It Always Rains on Sunday* (1947) and the black comedy of *Kind Hearts and Coronets* (1949). Like David Lean, Ealing remained respectable: elements of nightmare, excess and subjectivity, however powerfully rendered, are manageably contained within the films, and can thus be recuperated by a criticism anxious to celebrate sobriety and objectivity (or, as in Ealing's case, 'harmless' fantasy). This was and is harder to do with Powell and Pressburger, or with Gainsborough's period films, or with, for instance, the exhilaratingly *noir* gangster film which Cavalcanti left Ealing to direct, *They Made Me a Fugitive* (1947), undoubtedly one of those which Harold Wilson, who named no names, was signalling his disapproval of to Parliament. But it is difficult to characterise all this product as being somehow less integral to, or worthy of, British cinema. When the attic room is unlocked and the mad aunt let out, we find that she is as sane as you or me, indeed perhaps wiser in her enigmatic way.

Although critical shorthand may still tend to associate British cinema most strongly with documentary, and with a related conception of the medium as transparent, it can in fact be just as convincingly associated with the opposite conception, that of self-reflexivity. It would be hard to find, anywhere, three directors who more rigorously inscribe the processes of looking, dreaming, and fantasising into the very texts of their films (usually at the start) than do Lean, Powell and Hitchcock; and it would be hard to select more complex and imaginative films about filming than, for the silent period, Anthony Asquith's *Shooting Stars* (1927) and, for the sound period, *Peeping Tom*, both of which use the studio as a main setting and incorporate films within the film in outstandingly artful ways. British cinema is (like silent German) rich in examples of meta-cinema: films which embody a reflection on the processes and functions of making, and watching, films, whether they do so directly, like these two, or less directly, like *Brief Encounter* or *Dead of Night*, or Seth Holt's *Taste of Fear* (1962, for Hammer), or Maurice Elvey's *The Clairvoyant* (1935), or Hitchcock's *Number 17* (1932), or G. A. Smith's *Grandma's Reading Glass* (1900), or a whole range of other films directed by Powell and by Hitchcock.

Obviously, a book like this has to come to terms somehow with the figure of Hitchcock, who is discussed within several different contexts, including those of literary and theatrical adaptation. How far his career can actually be counted to the credit of his native country and cinema, rather than, by an unkind logic, to their *dis*credit (on the grounds that he had to abandon them in order to realise his potential) is still a matter of critical debate. His work, like that of Fritz Lang, falls into two such neat halves, before and after the move to Hollywood, that the temptation to compare the halves and express preferences is hard to resist. Referring in 1983 to the re-release of Hitchcock's second version of *The Man Who Knew Too Much*, Robin Wood still speaks the language of his book of 1965: for him, the American remake is 'self-evidently superior to the British original, though a few diehard British critics refuse to see this' – which leaves me happy, at least on this occasion, to be a diehard British critic.[1'] While it would be difficult, and indeed pointless, to argue for the 'superiority' of the British work as a whole over the American, it does stand in need of fresh analysis, given the terms in which its partisans have tended to characterise it: that is, as ingenious, agreeably unpretentious, and, in comparison with the overblown and glossily fabricated Hollywood films, decently realistic. The *locus classicus* for this kind of comparison is Lindsay Anderson's characteristically forceful article first published in *Sequence* in 1949: it established a line on Hitchcock that would remain dominant in Anglo-Saxon criticism for more than a decade.[42] The terms of the opposition were, of course, just waiting to be turned round, as they duly were by Wood and others, and deployed at the British films' expense, modest British realism being recognised as something very limiting (as indeed it was by Anderson, who was making no great claims even for Hitchcock's British work).

These films, in fact, though they lack the richness of *mise en scène*, and of character creation and acting, that were so important to Robin Wood and to *Movie*, are rich in precisely those elements which make Hitchcock so important to a new and very productive school of structuralist and psychoanalytic criticism. The same elements that have drawn Laura Mulvey and Raymond Bellour into detailed analyses of, for instance, *Notorious* and *North by Northwest*, as films exemplifying and exploiting in particularly subtle ways the mechanisms of classical Hollywood narrative, are strikingly present in the British films, in the process, as it were, of being developed and co-ordinated.[43] Some of the silent films are, already, powerful Oedipal stories with highly sophisticated narrative structures. The 1928 film *Champagne* is exemplary: it opens with a strongly marked *look*, aligning spectator with (male) character, and expressing a fantasy or desire which is then worked through in a narrative tightly controlled in terms of structure and point of view. Exactly the same formula could be used to summarise *Young and Innocent* (1938); Hitchcock's British work consists of a series of busy variations worked on this basic structural model, always involving (apart from some interruption in the early years of sound) play with point of view and fantasy. Increasingly, Hitchcock makes a point of showing us characters asleep or otherwise unconscious, at significant stages of the narrative, as if to convey all the more strongly the oneiric, subjective logic of the action (*The 39 Steps, Young and Innocent, The Lady Vanishes*).

This is not the place to develop an extended *auteurist* analysis. The point to make is, again, the intensely 'interior' quality of a particular set of British films; the question to ask is how Hitchcock relates to the cinematic context within which he was working.

Partly through his own retrospective testimony, he is commonly seen as having learned a lot, in his formative years, from German and Soviet and American cinema, and something from London theatre, but nothing from British cinema since there was nothing there to learn from. It is convenient to represent the period of his non-directing apprenticeship by the figure of Cecil Hepworth, whose name remains familiar as an important pioneer film-maker, one who was still active in the 1920s: his autobiography has long been a privileged document of the silent years in Britain, as have a number of the films, including *Rescued by Rover* (1905) and *Comin' thro' the Rye* (1923). In his autobiography (*Came the Dawn*, 1951), Hepworth was still ready to advocate the frontal style of film-making characteristic of early cinema:

Smoothness in a film is important and should be preserved, except when for some special effect a 'snap' is preferred. The 'unities' and the 'verities' should always be observed, to which I should add the 'orienties'. Only the direst need will form an excuse for lifting an audience up by the scruff of the neck and carrying it round to the other side, just because you suddenly want to photograph something from the south when a previous scene has been taken from the north.[44]

It is an extraordinary credo to be expressed in 1951, as it already was for 1923. In holding out against the editing strategies that had become established in and beyond Hollywood by 1920, including, specifically, the use of reverse-field cutting or shot/reverse-shot, and by continuing, as in primitive cinema, to regard the scene rather than the shot as the basic unit, Hepworth was refusing precisely those elements of 'film-ness' which Kuleshov had been struck by in American cinema and had encouraged the young Soviet cinema to adapt for its own dynamic purposes. *Comin' thro' the Rye* follows Hepworth's own principles laboriously, with extremely stodgy results (as Brian McFarlane's essay notes): it was the main attraction of a promotional 'British Film Week' (not the last event of its kind) held in 1923 under Royal patronage, which unsurprisingly fell somewhat flat.

So much, then, for the state of pre-Hitchcock British cinema. Yet even then there was more to it than *Comin' thro' the Rye*. Three people already active who plainly had a rather different concept of film structure and psychology than did Hepworth are the directors Maurice Elvey (see McFarlane again) and Jack Cutts, and the prolific writer Eliot Stannard, who would become Hitchcock's regular script collaborator. All three are important subjects for further research. The established place of Cutts in film history is to act as fall guy for Hitchcock, with whom he had a brief collaboration and rivalry within Michael Balcon's Gaumont-British company: John Russell Taylor, in *Hitch*, simply dismisses him as 'by all accounts not much of a director';[45] but the silent work of his that is available is by no means negligible. His first film *The Wonderful Story* (1921) is already far in advance of Hepworth in its organisation of narrative and cinematic form, while *The Sea Urchin* and *Triumph of the Rat* (both released in the same year, 1926, as the first films directed by Hitchcock) function in some ways very much in the early Hitchcock manner, not least in their intermittent foregrounding of the camera's presence and of the act of looking. Hitchcock was obviously something special but he was not exactly operating in a vacuum. At the end of the silent period, he would share the status of promising young British director with

Anthony Asquith: though Asquith's career would soon lose momentum, *Shooting Stars* makes his status at this time understandable, and further undercuts the over-simple retrospective view of Hitchcock as a solitary representative of real cinema working away in a hostile context.

Hitchcock's crucial breakthrough of the 1930s into a new generic format, a distinctive type of adventure story with which he quickly became identified and which was to prove marketable in, and transplantable to, America, is attributable, ironically, to the period of his deepest and most undignified immersion in what one might term the Britishness of British cinema. In 1932, at a low and rather directionless stage of his career, he was constrained by his then employers, British International Pictures, to prepare an ultra-cheap all-studio film to meet quota requirements, a 'quota quickie', a film of the play of the novel *Number 17*. It is clear from accounts given both by him and by his co-writer Rodney Ackland that, fed up with this banal assignment, he let himself go and played around freely, even flippantly, with the mechanical plot devices and two-dimensional characters available. 'It reflected a careless approach to my work,' he told Truffaut, in apology for the film's quality.[46] Carelessness can be liberating: in this wildly surreal and inventive film, all the constituent elements of the 'Hitchcock thriller' fall into place with a satisfying neatness. These include the first true Hitchcock 'Maguffin' (the object, in itself unimportant, around which the plot revolves: here, a diamond necklace); the formation of the couple in the course of an ordeal and a journey; and the creative use of manifestly unrealistic, dreamlike settings. *Number 17* shows Hitchcock not transcending rubbishy material (or failing to transcend it) but drawing important strengths from strong basic structural and generic elements, found on his own humble doorstep. This is symptomatic of the processes by which his next few films, the more famous British thrillers, were to be shaped – note, for instance, the anchoring of *The 39 Steps* in a London neighbourhood Music Hall, presented as a site of unrestrained energies (expressing sexual and class tensions) out of which the narrative is very specifically generated. It is worth noting, too, that Michael Powell had his cinematic formation not only, like Hitchcock, in Europe (Hitchcock's first two films were shot in Munich, Powell worked as assistant to Rex Ingram in Nice), but also in British quota production of the 1930s. The relation of these two to the bulk of routine indigenous 30s cinema is, for all the clear differences in the material, like that of the major practitioners of the Western to the enormous and unregarded volume of B Westerns, and singing Westerns, produced by Hollywood at the same period: that is, the relation is an organic one.

None of this is meant to suggest that British cinema is just like Hollywood after all, or that its genres are anything like as fertile, or that Satyajit Ray was altogether wrong in those antagonistic generalisations about it which were rooted in, precisely, his memories of the 1930s. The burden of Ray's case was, to recapitulate, that 'the camera forces us to face facts, to probe, to reveal, to get close to people and things, while the British nature inclines to the opposite, to stay aloof'. I hope this argument can, by now, be seen in a wider perspective.

Rather than talking of 'the British nature', which implies something immutable and homogeneous, and elides all kinds of class and regional and other variations, it seems better to use the term culture, as Daniel Snowman does in his historically based comparative study *Britain and America*, published in 1977. Ray's point about British nature/culture is partly to do with space and distance. Snowman takes as a key difference in the two cultures their differing valuations of 'the virtue of self-restraint, which was taken in Britain to imply that you did not encroach upon the territory – including the psychic and social territory – of others'.[47]

This translates neatly into the handling of *cinematic* territory. Snowman's point can be illustrated in Hepworth's extreme reluctance to interfere with the spatial coordinates of characters and of spectators; in the 'aloof' observational style of classic British documentary, and of the areas of feature production most influenced by it; and in many of the distinctive modes of British television. It is illuminating to place Frank Capra's *Why We Fight* series, shown to military and civilian audiences in World War II, alongside British documentary of the time. The seven-film series represents the colonisation, in America, of documentary by feature-film know-how – the reverse of the dominant process in Britain. This contrast functions at the level of formal construction. Not only do Capra and his team impose a Hollywood-style rapid pace and emotive musical score, but they have none of the normal inhibitions of (British-style) documentary about encroaching upon 'real' people's space. Thus in *Battle of Britain* (1943) we see through Hitler's eyes in a point-of-view shot as he looks across the Channel to Dover, and various 'documentary' re-enactments are staged with no attempt at observational verisimilitude but in the style of dramatic fiction, with free use of close-up, cross-cutting, and point of view. It is a formal contrast comparable to the one which we currently take for granted in the respective dominant institutional modes of British and American television – for instance at the more ambitious end of soap opera, between the high-key, seasonally produced and heavily scored *Dallas* and *Dynasty*, and the low-key, continuous *Brookside* and *Coronation Street*, whose only music (outside the credit sequences) comes from

23

diegetic sources. Central to this difference is the formal one between film and video: unlike the American, the British programmes are on video, shot largely in continuity with multiple cameras, which automatically limits the degree of possible encroachment on the characters' physical (and psychic) territory. It still makes sense for TV's continuity announcers to invite us to join them in 'going over' to one of these places to see what is taking place there 'today', as though the characters have an autonomous life going on in real time upon which we eavesdrop – a convention that would not be possible if the mode of shooting were not so securely observational in style.

However, this line which runs through British cinema so consistently, and passes so naturally into television (Marshall McLuhan's 'cool' or low-intensity medium which the British are, in the common stereotyping, supposed to be as good at as they are indifferent at cinema), is, as we have seen, only half the story. It is as though a social world were distinguished from an imaginative world, with different rules governing them. The social world elicits the 'aloof', objective look, which can be (Ray's term) dehumanised, but can also enact a moving respect and concern for people; the imaginative world is viewed from a different position and its rules are those of subjectivity and stylisation. Hence the need to hold in the mind together, as 'British cinema', the modes of observation and interiority, of transparency and self-reflexivity, of sobriety and excess; Grierson and Loach, but also Powell and Hitchcock; and, in production and criticism alike, an instrumentalist indifference to the medium as such, but also a passionate interest in it.

The two modes or sides may coexist, or the one may be seen as reacting against and challenging the other's dominance, as in the mid-1940s with the shift from public space to private space, and again a decade later: see David Pirie's persuasive reading of Hammer horror as a sort of equal and opposite reaction against a prevailing blandness.[48] But above all they interact and interpenetrate, all the time and in a variety of ways. To say this risks merely being platitudinous, since it can be argued that all cinema (at least outside animation) is founded on a dialectic between documentary and fantasy, objective and subjective; but the British versions of the dialectic are distinctive ones.

Back to Ray again. He found frustrating the paucity, in British life, of the overtly dramatic material which can constitute 'real meat for the cinema'.

The cinema revels in contrasts and clashes – however small and subtle. The calm has to be ruffled, the patterns disturbed and tensions created – and these have to be revealed in audible speech and visible action, to provide the raw material for the director to work on. These were lacking in the British scene.

Variations on this notion of the essence of the medium have been suggested by Hitchcock and by Arthur Penn. Hitchcock, talking to Truffaut: 'That's a fundamental of film direction. . . . People don't always express their inner thoughts to one another; a conversation may be quite trivial, but often the eyes will reveal what a person really thinks or feels.'[49] Penn to Joseph Gelmis: 'Film is the exquisite medium for expressing ambivalence. A man says one thing, but his eyes are saying another thing.'[50]

That kind of formula is, for me, particularly evocative of the way much of British cinema operates. It provides a useful handle for grasping some of its less fashionable aspects, films, and periods, and incidentally a vindication of them as being, in their own way, cinematic: even the notorious mainstream of 1950s cinema, in all its stiffness, narrowness and class-boundedness, need not be altogether a cause for embarrassment. Often there is an eloquent and poignant disjunction between surface drama, as observed in talk and action, and interior drama, which may be conveyed through the eyes (cf. Hitchcock and Penn) and/or through expressive gaps in the film's narrative structure, creating a strong sense of something *other* that is being repressed, or sought in vain. Such films as the courtroom drama *Carrington V.C.* (directed by Anthony Asquith, 1954) and *The Spanish Gardener* (1956) are powerful illustrations of Raymond Durgnat's point that 'though it is often said that British films avoid erotic themes, many of them deal very movingly with its frustration, or tepidity, or absence.'[51] Compare Andy Medhurst's argument that certain films from the 1950s cycle of World War II films such as *The Dam Busters* (1955) can be 'recast . . . as films about repression rather than as hopelessly repressed films';[52] also his discussion in this volume of *The Blue Lamp* (1950), in the context of Dirk Bogarde's career. The relation of such films to the later horror cycle, and indeed to the later 'New Wave' cinema, has to be seen, in fact, as more complicated than one of straight difference, the bland giving way to the full-blooded. The earlier films may express tensions eloquently; the later ones are not free from stiffness and inhibition. David Thomson's characterisation of Hammer horror as the work of men who 'did the garden at weekends' is neat, but not as limiting as he may intend it to be.[53] It is precisely from the interaction between 'British' sedateness and the shocking forces which disrupt it that these films' power is generated.

It is, essentially, this conception of British cinema that one finds in Raymond Durgnat's *A Mirror for England* (1970), a book too idiosyncratic to be smoothly absorbed into the critical and scholarly tradition, but one which has had a pioneer's influence through its liberating refusal to be held back, by restricting notions of what was worthy (cf. *Sight and Sound*), or of what was cinematic (cf. *Movie*), from an energetic exploration of the full diversity of the British product (mainly post-war). The kind of cinema thus opened up, one of repressions, conflicts, pleasures, and of often subtle responsiveness to extra-cinematic pressures, was clearly susceptible to more systematic analysis in ideological and psychoanalytic terms, and this is what it has increasingly been getting in a variety of publications ranging from the BFI's *Gainsborough Melodrama* to Jeffrey Richards' book on the 1930s, *The Age of the Dream Palace,* as well as in the magazines *Screen, Framework,* and *Monthly Film Bulletin,* all of which from time to time give sustained analytical attention to British films.[54] These three belong to a cluster of alert magazines which contrast with the earlier one-at-a-time succession traced at the start of this essay; they differ from those predecessors likewise in their less impatient and less prescriptive accounts of what British cinema has been like, and should be like.

Harold Wilson didn't like the idea of a British cinema that dealt with amnesia and schizophrenia, but these are two powerful and apt metaphors. First, for the psychic experience of many British protagonists and British films, both within and beyond the period of post-war dislocation and readjustment with which Wilson was concerned. Second, for the mental processes of a criticism continually struggling, or refusing, to come to terms with the teasing diversity of British cinema. This book, while not claiming to 'remember' every significant item (how can it, when *White Corridors* is not even mentioned?) does attempt to consolidate the work already under way of rescuing important elements from a collective amnesia, and to make sense of the inter-relationship of different layers and currents within a cinema which criticism has sometimes caused to seem schizophrenic, but which is more appropriately if less dramatically described in terms of dialectic and plurality.

Notes

1   Satyajit Ray, *Our Films, Their Films,* Bombay, Orient Longman, 1976, p. 144.

2   François Truffaut, *Hitchcock,* London, Secker & Warburg, 1968, p. 100.

3   Roy Armes, *A Critical History of British Cinema,* London, Secker & Warburg, 1978.

4   Pauline Kael, *Going Steady,* British edition, London, Temple Smith, 1970, pp. 180–1.

5   Dwight Macdonald, interviewed in the American magazine *Film Heritage,* Spring 1972 – on John Schlesinger's *Midnight Cowboy.*

6   Gilbert Adair and Nick Roddick, *A Night at the Pictures,* London, Columbus Books, 1985, p. 14.

7   James Park, *Learning to Dream,* London, Faber, 1984, p. 13.

8   David Shipman, *The Story of Cinema* (volume 2), London, Hodder and Stoughton, 1983, p. 558.

9   Alan Lovell, 'The British Cinema: the Unknown Cinema', seminar paper for British Film Institute, March 1969.

10   Peter Wollen, *Signs and Meaning in the Cinema,* London, Secker & Warburg/BFI, 1969, p. 115.

11   Richard Roud (ed.), *Cinema: A Critical Dictionary* (2 volumes), London, Secker & Warburg, 1980; Christopher Lyon (ed.), *The Macmillan Dictionary of Films* and *The Macmillan Dictionary of Film-Makers,* British editions, London, Macmillan, 1984.

12   Robin Wood, *Hitchcock's Films,* London, Tantivy Press, 1965: see in particular p. 29.

13   *Framework,* issue 1 (Warwick University, 1974), p. 35. The magazine subsequently moved its editorial base to the University of East Anglia (1979), and from there to London (1984).

14   David Thomson, *A Biographical Dictionary of the Cinema,* London, Secker & Warburg, 1975; V. F. Perkins, *Film as Film,* Harmondsworth, Penguin, 1972.

15   *Close-Up,* July 1929, p. 45.

16   Harry Watt, *Don't Look at the Camera,* London, Elek Books, 1974, pp. 98, 121.

17   *Sequence* 7 (1949): the author is Lindsay Anderson. A selection from *Sequence,* edited by Brian McFarlane, is to be published by the British Film Institute in 1986.

18   *Framework,* no. 1 (1974), p. 3.

19   Lev Kuleshov, *Kuleshov on Film* (ed. Ronald Levaco), Berkeley and Los Angeles, University of California Press, 1975, p. 127.

20   Ray, *Our Films, Their Films,* p. 144.

21   Kuleshov, *Kuleshov on Film,* p. 128.

22   Ray, *Our Films, Their Films,* p. 144.

23   John Grierson: from an article in *Fortnightly Review,* August 1939, quoted by Forsyth Hardy in the introduction to his edition of *Grierson on Documentary,* London, Faber, 1946, p. 5.

24 John Grierson, *Grierson on the Movies* (ed. Forsyth Hardy), London, Faber, 1981, p. 110 – review originally published in *The Clarion*, October 1930.

25 Ray, *Our Films, Their Films*, p. 145.

26 For three bitter references to the number of non-British personnel working in the British film industry, see the Hugh Castle article referred to above (*Close-Up*, July 1929); Graham Greene's review of *The Marriage of Corbal* in the *Spectator*, 5 June 1936, reprinted in the collection of Greene's film reviews, *The Pleasure Dome* (ed. John Russell Taylor, London, Secker & Warburg, 1972, p. 78); and the 1939 article from the trade paper *Kinematograph Weekly* quoted by Raymond Durgnat in *A Mirror for England* (London, Faber, 1970, p. 5).

The changes precipitated by the war were welcomed in these terms by Carol Reed (*Sunday Express*, 10 May 1942): 'British pictures are at last British. The Continental element, for which you only had to have a foreign name, or to have been someone in Vienna, has disappeared. . . . What happened? The young men in our studios, the young women, the new blood, came in. Under the pressure of war, these people, the real, undiscovered makers of movies, from English towns and counties, have moved up to recognition. They have been making films as English as oak.'

27 For material on the experience of cinema-going in wartime London, and details of audience polls which testified to the enhanced popularity of British films and actors, see Guy Morgan, *Red Roses Every Night*, London, Quality Press, 1948.

28 Review reprinted in C. A. Lejeune, *Chestnuts in her Lap*, London, Phoenix House, 1947, p. 151.

29 Lindsay Anderson, *About John Ford*, London, Plexus, 1981, p. 13.

30 See Robert Murphy, 'Rank's Attempt on the American Market' in *British Cinema History* (ed. James Curran and Vincent Porter), London, Weidenfeld and Nicolson, 1983, pp. 164 ff.

31 Roger Manvell, *Film*, Harmondsworth, Penguin, 1944; Rachael Low, *The History of the British Film 1896–1906*, in collaboration with Roger Manvell, London, Allen & Unwin, 1948; (six subsequent volumes, as sole author); The Arts Enquiry, *The Factual Film*, London, PEP/Oxford University Press, 1947.

32 John Ellis, 'Art, Culture and Quality: Terms for a Cinema in the Forties and Seventies' in *Screen*, vol. 19, no. 3, Autumn 1978, pp. 9–49.

33 *Penguin Film Review*, no. 2, January 1947, p. 19.

34 Hansard, 5th series, vol. 452, column 775, 17 June 1948, part of a debate on the film industry. The passage is quoted by Paul Foot in *The Politics of Harold Wilson*, Harmondsworth, Penguin, 1948, p. 73. On Wilson and the film industry see also the interview with him by Margaret Dickinson and Simon Hartog in *Screen*, vol. 22, no. 3, 1981, pp. 9–24.

35 Hammer Films are simply not referred to in Alexander Walker's informative and authoritative *Hollywood England* (London, Michael Joseph, 1974), even though the book's sub-title is 'The British Film Industry in the Sixties' and Hammer was the commercial success story of that period. More recently they and their contemporaries in the horror field

go unmentioned in the three works of the 1980s referred to above, the Shipman history and the Macmillan and Roud dictionaries. In making points about critical selectivity, one is emphatically not just fighting old battles or pushing at an open door.

36 Review in *News Chronicle*, 22 November 1946: reprinted in Richard Winnington, *Drawn and Quartered*, London, Saturn Press, 1948, p. 69.

37 'Michael Powell' by O. O. Green (Raymond Durgnat) in *Movie*, no. 13, 1966: reprinted under Durgnat's own name in *Movie Reader* (ed. Ian Cameron, London, November Books, 1972) and in *Powell, Pressburger and Others* (ed. Ian Christie, London, BFI, 1978).

38 Powell interviewed by Kevin Gough-Yates in the booklet *Michael Powell: in Collaboration with Emeric Pressburger* produced to accompany a National Film Theatre season of their films in 1971 (p. 5).

39 On the shifts in attitude to *Brief Encounter*, see Durgnat, *A Mirror for England*, pp. 180–1.

40 Sheridan Morley, *A Talent to Amuse*, London, Heinemann, 1969, p. 309.

41 Robin Wood, 'Fear of Spying', in *American Film*, November 1983, p. 29.

42 Lindsay Anderson, 'Alfred Hitchcock', in *Sequence*, issue 9, Autumn 1949, reprinted in *Focus on Alfred Hitchcock* (ed. Albert La Valley, New Jersey, Prentice-Hall, 1972).

43 See Laura Mulvey, 'Visual Pleasure and Narrative Cinema' in *Screen*, vol. 16, no. 3, Autumn 1975; Raymond Bellour, *L'analyse du Film*, Paris, Editions Albatros, 1979, and also items in various issues of the American journal *Camera Obscura*, particularly issue 3/4, 1979.

44 Cecil Hepworth, *Came the Dawn*, London, Phoenix House, 1951, p. 139, quoted by Armes in *A Critical History of British Cinema*, p. 51.

45 John Russell Taylor, *Hitch*, London, Faber, 1978, p. 50.

46 Truffaut, *Hitchcock*, p. 67. Cf. Rodney Ackland and Elspeth Grant, *The Celluloid Mistress*, London, Allan Wingate, 1954, pp. 36–7.

47 Daniel Snowman, *Britain and America*, New York, New York University Press, 1977, p. 130.

48 David Pirie, *A Heritage of Horror: the English Gothic Cinema*, London, Gordon Fraser, 1974.

49 Truffaut, *Hitchcock*, p. 172.

50 Joseph Gelmis, *The Film Director as Superstar*, New York, Doubleday, 1970, p. 221.

51 Raymond Durgnat, *Eros in the Cinema*, London, Calder and Boyars, 1966, p. 68.

52 Andy Medhurst, '1950s War Films', in *National Fictions*, ed. Geoff Hurd, London, BFI, 1984, p. 38.

53 Thomson, *A Biographical Dictionary of the Cinema*, p. 174, in the entry on Terence Fisher.

54 Sue Aspinall and Robert Murphy (eds.), *Gainsborough Melodrama*, BFI Dossier no. 18, London, British Film Institute, 1981; Jeffrey Richards, *The Age of the Dream Palace*, London, Routledge & Kegan Paul, 1984.

Julian Petley

CINEMA AND STATE

The relationship between the cinema and the state in Britain finds expression in two main areas. The first is economic, and mainly concerns attempts to protect the British film industry from the worst effects of American competition. The second is, broadly speaking, ideological, and has to do with censorship.

The state's interventions in the economic affairs of the British film industry have recently been expertly dissected by Margaret Dickinson, Sarah Street and Simon Hartog,[1] and the first part of this chapter is inevitably something of a gloss on their invaluable work.

A major problem for the British film industry from its very early days has been the extent of Hollywood's domination of British screens. Of course, this problem is hardly unique to Britain, but it has been greatly exacerbated in Britain by the fact of Britain and America sharing a common language, so that there is no need for costly dubbing or subtitling of the Hollywood product. However, the problem goes far deeper than the mere number of American films on British screens; it involves American penetration of the British film industry itself, a process experienced by numerous other British industries and encouraged by successive British governments. Indeed, such have been the levels of American capital invested in film production in Britain that at times the vast majority of films produced in Britain have only nominally been 'British'. In 1968, for instance, 90 per cent of all production capital was American. The industry's reliance on American capital, combined with the Americans' deep penetration of the British film industry itself through its network of British subsidiaries, makes for an extremely powerful lobby, on both sides of the Atlantic, against any moves to disengage the industry from this relationship of dependency.

Of course, not all the British industry's problems have stemmed from the fact of American competition or involvement. Bitter

31

internal divisions between and even within the various sectors of the industry have also played their part, as has the gradual growth of a monopoly situation. However, every attempt to set up some kind of independent, supervisory body such as a Films Commission or a Film Authority, a move advised by almost every independent report on the industry since 1936, has been furiously resisted by the trade and consequently dropped.

Even before the end of the First World War Britain's film industry was beginning to suffer from the adverse effects of American competition, thanks to a combination of shortage of capital, artistic paucity, rising costs and, of course, the considerable strength of the American rival. By 1922 the production sector was in a state of crisis. Various remedies were suggested, and when the Conservative government finally moved on the issue it was in the direction of commercial protection. Thus the Cinematograph Films Act of 1927 obliged distributors to acquire, and exhibitors to show, minimum quotas, or percentages, of British films: $7\frac{1}{2}$ per cent in the case of distributors and 5 per cent in the case of exhibitors. By 1936 both quotas were to have risen to 20 per cent. To qualify as 'British' the production company did not have to be British-controlled, only to have a majority of British company directors. The Act was to remain in force for ten years, administered by the Board of Trade and served by an Advisory Committee consisting of eight members of the trade and five independent ones – thereby ensuring a trade dominance.

Even within its own limited terms the Act was barely an adequate measure, and it did very little to help establish a healthy, indigenous British film industry which would be independent of America both economically and culturally. As the role allotted to the Board of Trade demonstrates, the Act, like all future films legislation, was conceived primarily within the framework of commercial policy. There may have been a certain rhetoric about the cultural significance of nationality, a certain vague notion of 'Britishness', but there was little real concern with the *kinds* of film which a properly British film industry might or should produce. Compared to, for instance, France or the USSR there was at this time little interest in the art of the film, or in the cinema as what might now be called a 'cultural industry'. More typical of the level of debate was Lord Newton's concern with the 'industrial, commercial, educational and Imperial interests involved'[2] (a concern nicely summed up in the phrase 'trade follows the film'), or the various worries expressed by moral and religious bodies over the supposed evil effects of cinema-going.

The Films Act came up for review in 1936, and Walter Runciman, President of the Board of Trade, set up a Committee under the chairmanship of Lord Moyne. Abuses of both the spirit and the letter of the law were rife: 'quota quickies' (cheap British films made or acquired by British distributors simply to comply with the quota law) flourished, American distributors were encouraging exhibitors into illegal blind- and block-booking practices, and American interests were increasingly penetrating not only the distribution sector but also production. And in general terms the British film industry suffered from a lack of stable, long-term financial support, and from the absence of any coherent overall films policy.

The Board of Trade, industry-dominated as it was, favoured leaving things as they were. The Moyne Committee, however, thought differently. Noting that 'lack of finance is a powerful factor in enabling foreign interest to obtain control', it recommended that the government should 'take such steps as may be practicable to encourage financial interests to constitute one or more organisations to finance British film production, in approved cases, on reasonable terms'.[3] In other words, something like the Filmkreditbank which had recently been set up in Germany. The quota system was to be tightened: 20 per cent for renters, 15 per cent for exhibitors, both to rise to 50 per cent within ten years. Most importantly, though, the Committee recommended the establishment of an independent Films Commission with considerable powers which 'should, in addition to exercising its normal administrative functions and acting as a tribunal to give impartial judgments on matters dividing the film industry, have powers of initiative and control. . . . Absolute independence from professional or any other pecuniary connection with any branch of the film industry is essential in all the members of the proposed Commission'.[4] Such a body would be able to examine such pressing problems as release reform, overbuilding, distribution of box-office receipts, financial instability, rising production costs and so on.

The industry may have been divided on the question of quotas (with the exhibitors and the American-dominated distributors obviously having a vested interest in keeping profitable American films in plentiful supply). However, it was united in its desire to ensure that the proposed Commission never became law.

Thanks to its powerful allies in the Board of Trade, the industry was able to ensure that the new Films Act of 1938 was but a minor modification of its predecessor. Instead of a Films Commission there was created a Cinematograph Films Council along the lines of the Advisory Committee of the 1927 Act, very much a trade-dominated body whose function was simply to 'keep under review the progress of the British film industry and report to the Board of Trade'. The quota for features was fixed at 15 per cent for distributors and 12½ per cent for exhibitors (with 'multiple quota' being introduced in the case of particularly expensive films, a move which accorded well with the Board of Trade policy of inducing American companies to invest in British film production). The Act also contained provisions to safeguard studio wages and labour conditions.

Thus the new Films Act followed very much in the footsteps of its predecessor, and demonstrated government's willingness to accept an increasing influx of American finance (and thus control) in place of any attempt to reorganise the industry. By 1939 the self-imposed limits of state intervention had already been clearly marked out, and the future structure of the industry was already evolving: a mixture of American domination and the steady growth of a home-based monopoly in the shape of Rank and ABPC. Ties between Rank/ABPC on the one hand, and the American companies on the other, meant that the issues of domestic monopoly and American domination were inextricably linked.

During and immediately after the Second World War these various issues were debated with renewed interest, however, thanks to the dramatically changed circumstances. Thus in 1940 the Cinematograph Films Council recommended that the government should set up a films bank to ensure the continuation of British production. In the course of the ensuing consultations between the Treasury, the Bank of England and the Board of Trade it was agreed that the industry's financial problems were partly the result of its own structures and practices, and that it was more in need of independent supervision or control than of new sources of finance. Accordingly, discussion of the bank was dropped and the President of the Board of Trade, Sir Hugh Dalton, returned to the notion of the Films Commission. However, in the face of renewed agitation from the trade the Board eventually decided that the growth of Rank would bring a degree of order to the fragmented and divided industry, and thus that there was now less need to impose controls from outside.

The problem of monopoly was then raised anew by Michael Balcon, one of the two producers' representatives, in the Cinematograph Films Council in 1943. The Council then appointed a committee of four independent members, under Albert Palache, which, in spite of obstruction from the industry, produced a report, 'Tendencies to Monopoly in the Cinematograph Industry'. Again, the idea of a films bank and the need for independent supervision was stressed, and this time concern about American penetration was linked to worry about increasing monopolisation at home, especially in the exhibition sector. Not surprisingly the industry reacted venomously and the report's recommendations were never taken up. However, the Palache findings did provide the basis for a vigorous campaign for state intervention (including, in some cases, national-isation) by the film trade unions and sections of the Labour Party.

By the end of the war the political climate had changed considerably in Britain, and very much in the Left's favour. In the cultural field this change manifested itself in support for the principle of subsidising the performing and visual arts. As Dickinson and Street point out: 'the creation of the Arts Council in 1946 provided a formal framework for the provision of state support for the arts. The development of sound broadcasting had also set new precedents for the management of a popular medium. . . . Both the Arts Council and the BBC were held up as offering useful models for the development of films policy.'[5] However, such models would not be followed: in spite of the election of a Labour government in 1945, the view prevailed, in both the Board of Trade and the most powerful sections of the industry, that the industry's interests were best served by American investment and large-scale home-based units of the Rank type.

After the war the new President of the Board of Trade, Sir Stafford Cripps, showed some interest in the problem of the film industry, but the new government was faced with such a welter of new legislation to put before Parliament that consideration of the industry was left until 1948 and the expiry of the Cinematograph Films Act. By this time the Council was dominated by the representatives of the combines, whose counsels also held sway at the Board of Trade, and so the new Act signalled very few changes. As a result of American pressure in the General Agreement on Trade and Tariffs negotiations, the distributor's quota was dropped altogether. The exhibitor's quota was made more flexible, with the Board of Trade being able to fix the percentage after consultations with the Films Council.

The end of the 1940s also saw an intensification of the industry's long-term state of crisis. This suggested that mere protectionism was not enough to ensure the industry's survival, and led to two important state interventions in the industry in the shape of the National Film Finance Corporation and the Eady Levy.

The aggravation of the crisis was caused, in the first instance, by factors outside the industry. With the post-war loan from America nearly exhausted, the date by which sterling had to be made convertible with the dollar (July 1947) approaching fast, and an increasing balance of payments deficit, the government was prepared to take fairly aggressive measures. One of these was the announcement by the Chancellor, Sir Hugh Dalton, in August 1947, of a duty on all imported film which would absorb 75 per cent of remittable revenue. The Motion Picture Export Association of America responded with a boycott. Taken by surprise, the Board of

35

Trade appealed to British producers to step up production and finally began to consider a films bank. When the duty was withdrawn in March 1948, it was agreed that blocked earnings could be invested in British production (thereby facilitating further American domination), and there was a glut of both British and American product. Small producers were now on the edge of bankruptcy, and even Rank was badly hit.

It was at this time that Harold Wilson was appointed President of the Board of Trade. Later to become Prime Minister, he was one of the very few political figures to take a major interest in the film industry. As Margaret Dickinson describes him: 'Up to a point he agreed with the case for intervention, accepting that there was a need to check monopolistic practices and to safeguard the production of British films with measures which might not meet with the approval of other sections of the industry. Unlike the left wing of his party, however, he thought this could be done without interfering fundamentally with the structure of ownership and control. He set out to develop techniques of co-operation and persuasion, hoping to persuade rather than compel the industry to introduce reforms.'[6]

One of his first measures was to attempt to stem the flood of American imports which followed in the wake of lifting the boycott, by using his powers under the 1948 Act to raise the quota to 45 per cent. After complaints from the exhibitors this was dropped to 40 per cent, and then in 1950 to 30 per cent where it remained until abolition in 1983. Wilson also set up the National Film Production Council, a body composed of employers and trade union representatives which was charged with devising ways of increasing efficiency; and he commissioned three inquiries into various aspects of the industry: the problem of mounting production costs, the possibility of a state studio, and possible ways of increasing the revenue reaching producers from the distribution and exhibition sectors. This last inquiry was the most thoroughgoing of the three, and the resulting Plant Report echoed many of the findings and recommendations of the Palache Report, including the establishment of a film authority. However, Wilson's inquiries were hampered by obstruction from the industry; having decided not to pursue a policy of coercion, he could do little to implement any of the inquiries' suggestions.

Wilson's two major achievements were the National Film Finance Corporation and the Eady Levy. With the formation of the NFFC a version of the much touted film bank idea finally came to fruition. It was intended to encourage independent production, and not to finance a state sector in competition with private enterprise. The Act setting up the NFFC, the Cinematograph Film Production (Special Loans) Act, was passed in March 1949, and the NFFC was constituted

State funding: *The Third Man* (1949), one of the first films supported by the National Film Finance Corporation

in April with a revolving fund of £5m, increased to £6m in 1950. As it developed, the NFFC kept very much within its original brief of supplementing, rather than supplanting, private capital. Normally, it spread its resources over a large number of films by providing much needed 'end money', i.e. that part (usually 30 per cent) of a film's budget not covered by the loan raised on the distributor's guarantee. The NFFC helped to make more than 750 films, including *The Third Man* (1949), *Saturday Night and Sunday Morning* (1960), *The Servant* (1963), *The Europeans* (1979), *Black Jack* (1979), *Babylon* (1980), *Gregory's Girl* (1980), and *Another Country* (1984).

The Eady Levy, so named after Sir Wilfred Eady, the Treasury official who devised the scheme along with Wilson, was another attempt to encourage ailing British production. It followed the model of schemes already developed in France and Italy. A voluntary arrangement was devised whereby, in return for a reduction in Entertainments Duty, exhibitors agreed to pay a levy on the price of each cinema ticket: this levy was paid into a fund which was subsequently shared out among producers of British films in proportion to their box-office earnings. The Levy was made statutory in 1957. Unlike in France and Italy, the Levy was not used to encourage certain *kinds* of production, and indeed it may well have contributed to further influxes of American capital by encouraging American companies to form British subsidiaries to produce 'British' films that could qualify for Eady money. By 1984, the Levy was raising about £4.5m per year.

By the mid-1950s, with the rapid expansion of television, cinema attendances were in sharp decline. On the whole, consecutive governments left film legislation as it was. During the 50s the Conservatives reduced Entertainments Duty, and they finally abolished it altogether in 1960. With Labour and Conservative governments alike pursuing laissez-faire policies towards the industry, it

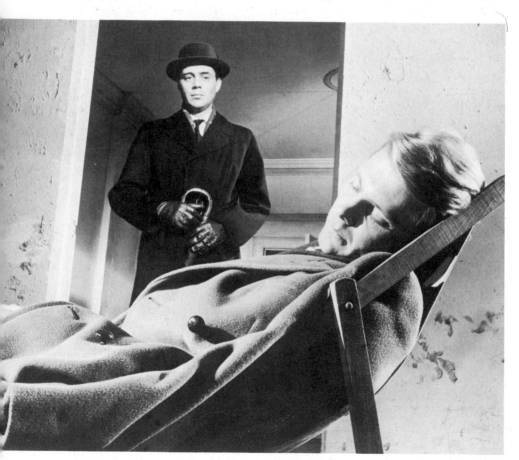

The Servant (1963), part-funded by the NFFC

evolved according to the logic of market forces. Both monopolisation and American penetration increased dramatically. The former was most noticeable in the exhibition sector with the growth of the Rank/ABC duopoly. This situation was the subject of a Report by the Monopolies Commission in 1966, which found that there was indeed a monopoly and that it did indeed operate against the public interest, but felt unable to recommend that the government should use compulsion to bring about any changes, even minor ones. The process continued apace, so that by 1978 the duopoly accounted for 37 per cent of all cinema screens.

The Cinematograph Films Act of 1960 made no major changes to its predecessor. The 1970 Act increased the lending power of the NFFC by a further £5m, but before the money could be made available the Conservatives returned to power and declined to advance the funds made available under the Act. Eventually a further £1m was provided from public funds, but the NFFC's scope of action was severely reduced.

The early 1970s also saw a withdrawal of American capital from the 'British' production sector. The consequent studio closures and loss of work revived the call within the technicians' union (ACTT) for nationalisation. This was subsequently modified to a call for increased state aid and a change in the cinema's relationship to television. The situation for the properly British film was indeed bleak. As Margaret Dickinson puts it: 'the remaining American investment tended to be concentrated into very expensive films, which were rarely particularly "British" in character. A good deal of work consisted in servicing films which had been conceived and shot in the United States.'[7] By the mid-70s Labour was back in power and Harold Wilson was again Prime Minister. In August 1975 he set up a Working Party to consider 'the requirements of a viable and prosperous British Film industry over the next decade'. Its report was published in January 1976 and recommended, *inter alia*, the establishment of a single body responsible for the film industry, the British Film Authority. Meanwhile an Interim Action Committee was set up to take over the Working Party's advisory role and to elaborate on some of its proposals – including that of a Film Authority. Some of the proposals were to be incorporated into the new Cinematograph Films Act of 1980.

By 1980, however, a new Conservative government was in power and had very different ideas. An Act was rushed through which postponed any major decisions by prolonging for five years most of the provisions of the existing legislation, although with some significant modifications. Government financing for the NFFC was wound up – in future the Corporation was to be financed out of the

Eady Levy. And the quota could be suspended at any time during the life of the Act. Subsequently, in summer 1982, the Secretary of State announced that the quota would indeed be suspended from January 1983. In 1984 the Chancellor announced the ending of a crucial tax-shelter device from which producers had benefited since 1979: recipients of this fiscal aid included *Chariots of Fire* and *A Passage to India*. In July of the same year the government's long-awaited White Paper on the industry was published: the Eady Levy, the NFFC and the Cinematograph Films Council were all to be abolished. The NFFC is replaced by the British Screen Finance Corporation, a consortium made up of Thorn-EMI, Rank, Channel 4 and the British Videogram Association. It is to have a budget of £3m per year, half of which will be provided by the government. Its aim is to provide up to a third of the finance for between eight and ten low-budget films a year. The government's proposals have been greeted with outrage from the independent production sector, but they are hardly very surprising. They are simply the application to the film industry of the Conservatives' avowed free market economic principles. The present government is hostile to the very notion of subsidy, and reserves a special contempt for arts subsidies. The government's various pronouncements on cable and the future of the BBC suggest that it has no interest in 'cultural policy', and that provided that a modicum of employment is secured it does not care where the finance comes from, nor if the result is 'wall to wall *Dallas*'.

As Dickinson and Street conclude: 'The withdrawal of state support will leave the industry exposed to market forces almost as much as it was sixty years ago. This will not make for a fundamental change in direction. Finance and profit have always been the main factors in deciding what films are made and shown in Britain. The system of state aid was not designed to replace or to compete with commercial finance, and it failed to reverse the long-standing trends towards monopoly and American control. Nevertheless, it represented a commitment to the maintenance of a production base in Britain.'[8] It was a production base which allowed for independent activity of various kinds, from the BFI Production Board to the larger-scale undertakings of those grouped together in the Association of Independent Producers – activity which would never have been undertaken by the dominant commercial interests. It is this activity which will suffer as a result of the state's latest interventions in the British film industry.

Censorship ·

To include the topic of censorship under the heading 'Cinema and State' may at first sight seem odd, since there is, strictly speaking, no state censorship of films in Britain. However, the links between the cinema and the state in the area of censorship are many and varied, even if they are not always immediately visible.

There is in fact no legal requirement in Britain that films should be subjected to examination, and if deemed necessary to cutting, before being shown to the public. The beginnings of the present system of censorship lie in the Cinematograph Act of 1909, which was intended 'to make better provision for securing safety at Cinematograph and other exhibitions'. The Act, however, also allowed councils to impose whatever conditions they wished, 'so long as those conditions are not unreasonable'. Quite against the spirit of the Act, the courts ruled that it was 'not unreasonable' to include specifications as to film content. The powers of censorship which local authorities had thus usurped were confirmed at law. (And even when this usurpation was threatened by the disappearance of inflammable film – its successor, safety film, not being covered by the 1909 Act – the authorities' powers were safeguarded by the passing of the Cinematograph Act of 1952.)

Local authority concern about film content was an expression of the moral panic that accompanied cinema's early years in many countries, except that in Britain these puritanical moralisings were accompanied by a peculiarly vehement 'not in front of the servants' attitude. Faced with increasing amounts of local censorship, the industry reacted by appointing in 1913 its own censorship body, the British Board of Film Censors. To begin with, this was widely ignored by local authorities, who doubted its supposed independence from the industry and regarded it as mainly cosmetic. Soon the Home Office began to take steps towards establishing a government-appointed censorship body. However, when Prime Minister Asquith resigned the scheme was dropped, and in 1920 the London and Middlesex County Councils adopted the BBFC's certificates as obligatory for their licences. Most local authorities soon followed suit.

Two points need to be made clear, however. Firstly, the local authorities do still possess statutory powers of censorship, and sometimes use them. Secondly, the BBFC's independence from government has frequently been more apparent than real.

Local authority activity remained fairly dormant until the late 60s/ early 70s, when the conjuncture of a more liberal regime at the BBFC and the growth of puritanical pressure groups such as the Festival of Light provoked numerous local bans on films such as *The Devils, A*

41

Protecting the public

Clockwork Orange, Straw Dogs, and *Last Tango in Paris.* More recently, controversy has been rarer, for several possible reasons. Firstly, the present BBFC under James Ferman is a rather more censorious body than it was in the liberal days of John Trevelyan. Secondly, a certain watershed may have been reached by films like the above, and viewers may well have become accustomed to levels of sex, violence and language that were once thought unacceptable. And thirdly, many local councils – and especially the generally liberal Association of Metropolitan Authorities – seem to have ceased to regard moral watchdoggery as a proper function for local government. However, it should be pointed out that when the tabloid press mounted a sensationalist campaign over the alleged blasphemy and bad taste of *Monty Python's Life of Brian,* various local councils became concerned. In the event, 101 asked to view the film. Of these 62 confirmed the BBFC's 'AA' certificate, 28 gave it a local 'X', and 11 banned it outright.

The question of the BBFC's independence from the government of the day is a more complex one. Relations between the Board and the government have generally been warm; apart from the abortive attempt to set up a system of state censorship in 1916, the Board has received continuous support from the Home Office and, eager to establish and maintain its credibility, has actively sought Home

Office guidance on controversial matters. More importantly, it is now generally accepted that the President of the BBFC is ultimately appointed by the Home Secretary: at the very least, it is extremely hard to imagine a President being appointed who is *not* acceptable to the Home Office, or one staying in office whose actions consistently run counter to Home Office thinking. The PEP report in 1952 stated that 'the practice is to elect a man [*sic*], usually prominent in public life, who is acceptable to a Trade Committee as well as to the Home Secretary and the licensing authorities'; while John Trevelyan in 1963 stated that the President 'is appointed by a joint committee representative of all branches of the film industry, after informal consultation with the Home Secretary and the principal local authority associations.'[9]

Certainly in the decades prior to World War II the relationship between the cinema and the state in the area of censorship was an extremely close one – for all the BBFC's *apparent* independence. So close was this relationship, in fact, that Nicholas Pronay and Jeremy Croft conclude that the cinema had been 'under extensive political censorship long before the Second World War'.[10] What this meant in

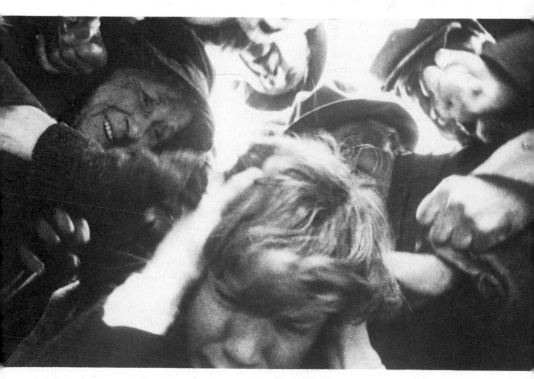

A Clockwork Orange, banned by some local authorities in 1971

terms of content is clearly summed up by John Trevelyan: 'Up to the last war the Board clearly considered itself the guardian of public morality, allowing no departure from the accepted code of conduct and behaviour, the protector of the establishment, the protector of the reputation and image of Britain in other countries, and the protector of cinema audiences from such dangerous themes as those involving controversial politics.'[11] This last phrase is crucial, for although the Board fussed and fumed greatly over questions of sex, nudity and personal morality, its main task, as Pronay and Croft say, 'was to control the power of the cinema to affect the political outlook of uneducated people, especially those who went to the cinema regularly in the 1930's: the urban working class'.[12]

The government did not have to tell the BBFC what to do — it knew perfectly well already. A look at the background of the Presidents in the 1930s is illuminating. Edward Shortt (1929–35) had been Chief Secretary for Ireland and subsequently Home Secretary, and Lord Tyrrell (1935–47) had been head of the Political Intelligence Department and Permanent Under-Secretary of State at the Foreign Office. Joseph Brooke-Wilkinson, Secretary of the Board from 1913–49, had been in charge of British film propaganda to neutral nations during the First World War and was also a member of the secret CID Subcommittee on Censorship. Of the four examiners at work in 1939, three had high-ranking military backgrounds.

Given the political backgrounds of those who ran the BBFC, the Board's *formal* position is largely irrelevant. As operated until the last war, the BBFC was one of those typically British institutions whose legitimacy depends on an artfully constructed mask of political neutrality but which are, in fact, forms of quasi-state apparatus helping ruling interests maintain their hegemony. With its bans on the great Russian classics, on American newsreels critical of Nazi Germany and Fascist Italy, on 'references to controversial politics', 'relations of capital and labour', 'subjects calculated or possibly intended to foment social unrest or discontent' and so on (by 1930 there were no less than ninety-eight rules!) it is perhaps hardly surprising that in 1937 Lord Tyrrell could say to the Exhibitors Association: 'We may take pride in observing that there is not a single film showing in London today which deals with any of the burning questions of the day.'[13]

Although relations between the cinema and the state are now rather less intimate in the arena of censorship, the BBFC still enters into a certain kind of relationship with the state in the legal domain. Indeed, one of its main functions today is to protect the cinema from the courts by ensuring that films shown do not break the laws of the land. These include the Cinematograph (Animals) Act of 1937, the

44

Obscene Publications Act (since 1977) and the Protection of Children Act of 1978. It does need to be stressed, however, that possession of a BBFC certificate is no cast-iron guarantee of freedom from prosecution. As Lord Denning said in Raymond Blackburn's case against the GLC over its decision to pass *More About the Language of Love*, 'the British Board of Film Censors is not a legal entity. It has no existence known to the law. It is but a name given to the activities of a few persons.' However, since the 1977 extension of the Obscene Publications Act to cover film, private prosecutions of the Blackburn variety have ceased: now prosecution of producers, exhibitors or distributors can take place only with the consent of the Director of Public Prosecutions. And quite clearly a 'gentleman's agreement' exists in this area, by which the DPP will not proceed against certificated films. Of course, what would happen if the BBFC became 'unacceptably' liberal, or the DPP decided to go on a 'moral' crusade, remains an intriguing question.

If one includes Post Office and Customs legislation too, it becomes clear that Britain is, in Western European terms, a comparatively heavily censored country. Foreigners often express surprise at just how heavily censored films in Britain are, especially as the BBFC is essentially a trade rather than a statutory body. The crucial point is, of course, that the BBFC is largely at the mercy of the laws of the land and the courts which interpret them. It also has, as we have seen, close links with the Home Office and with established opinion. The result is not a system of state censorship, but it is also not one which is as independent of the state as it is normally assumed to be.

Notes

1   Margaret Dickinson and Sarah Street, *Cinema and State,* London, British Film Institute, 1985. See also chapters by Simon Hartog and Margaret Dickinson in James Curran and Vincent Porter (eds.), *British Cinema History*, London, Weidenfeld & Nicolson, 1983.
2   Dickinson and Street, op. cit., p. 15.
3   Ibid., p. 62.
4   Ibid., p. 70.
5   Ibid., pp. 3–4.
6   Dickinson, op. cit., p. 87.
7   Ibid., pp. 93–4.
8   Dickinson and Street, op. cit., p. 248.
9   Both quoted in Neville March Hunnings, *Film Censors and the Law*, London, Allen & Unwin, 1967.
10   Nicholas Pronay and Jeremy Croft, 'British Film Censorship and Propaganda Policy during the Second World War', in Curran and Porter

(eds.), op cit.

11 Quoted in Guy Phelps, 'Out of Fear and Ignorance', in *Index on Censorship*, vol. 10, no. 4, August 1981, p. 6.

12 Pronay and Croft, op. cit., p. 145.

13 Quoted in Nicholas Pronay, 'The Political Censorship of Films in Britain Between the Wars', in Nicholas Pronay and D. W. Spring (eds.), *Propaganda, Politics and Film 1918–45*, London, Macmillan, 1982. For useful information on this subject see Jeffrey Richards, *The Age of the Dream Palace*, London, Routledge & Kegan Paul, 1984.

Robert Murphy

UNDER THE SHADOW OF HOLLYWOOD

The relative power of the British and American economies has changed so much over the past hundred years that it is easy to forget that the cinema was born into a world where Britain still had pretensions to being the foremost industrial nation. Though British businessmen were uncomfortably aware that markets were being stolen from them by their more dynamic American colleagues, in the Indian summer which lasted until 1914 world trade continued to expand and it hardly seemed to matter that Britain's share of it was shrinking and increasingly confined to its own colonies. But in the 20s Britain's economic stagnation became more visible. After a frantic post-war boom, Britain's staple industries – coal, textiles, shipbuilding – fell into decline, and by the middle of 1921 unemployment had soared to over two million. While the American economy enjoyed a whirlwind expansion, Britain seemed to be sinking into the doldrums.

By the mid-20s the cinema had become the major form of popular entertainment, crowding out the music halls and even the theatres from the city centres. And the films that filled the British cinemas were almost exclusively American. By 1926 thirty-seven British films competed with over five hundred American imports. With film, as with other industries, there was a feeling that the Americans had exploited wartime disruptions to establish an unfair advantage, but that if the proper measures were taken then Britain could regain its predominant position. It was less the well-being of British film producers than the interests of British industry generally that caused concern. As a spokesman for the Federation of British Industries put it:

We have interested ourselves in this matter because of its bearing on our national prestige and position. It is perhaps unfortunate for

47

the film trade that its normal activities do react in such an important manner on the national life and our international position, but the fact remains . . . The Federation first took the matter up because they felt that the prestige of the country as a whole, and thereby the prestige of British industry also, was being seriously affected through the gradual disappearance of British films from the screens of the Empire and the world.[1]

Three decades earlier the film industry in Britain had had bright beginnings. Manufacturers of projectors and cameras were able to hold their own against foreign competition, and the films of the British pioneers – Paul, Williamson, Smith, Mottershaw, Haggar, Hepworth – were innovative and internationally popular. Robert Paul invented, early in 1896, the first film projector to be placed on the open market, and received orders from all over the world; and in July 1897, when he attempted to float a £60,000 company, he was able to report profits of nearly £13,000 for the year 1896–7.[2] By contrast Edison's first projector, introduced into Britain in April 1896, was a dismal failure, and until 1898, when the Gaumont Chrono, the large-format American Biograph and the Charles Urban Bioscope began to appear on the market, Paul's main competition came from established British magic lantern manufacturers such as Riley Brothers of Bradford and Wrench and Sons of Holborn.

But before long it was American rather than British entrepreneurial talent which was taking the initiative. Frank Maguire and Joseph Baucus had come to Europe in 1895 to market Edison's Kinetoscope but found a more profitable occupation in sending back to America the films made by Paul, Lumière, Méliès and the other European pioneers. In May 1898 they reconstituted their interests into the £25,000 Warwick Trading Company. Another American, Charles Urban, who was enjoying considerable success with his lightweight, hand-cranked projector, the Urban Bioscope, was appointed Chairman. Warwick was involved in film production, the export of European films to America and the sale of equipment. Warwick rapidly became the most important film company operating in Britain, handling the films of the Brighton film-makers James Williamson and G. A. Smith and of enterprising provincial companies like Frank Mottershaw's Sheffield Photo Company. It also employed a large staff of mobile cameramen who specialised in filming wars and other dramatic news events. By 1903, when Urban left to form his own company, Warwick had an annual output of over 500 films a year, far more than any other company in Britain.[3]

Most British companies were small partnerships or one-man businesses operating with minimal resources. James Williamson, the

Suburban film-making: Cecil Hepworth's *Rescued by Rover* (1905)

prime mover in the so-called Brighton School, prided himself on performing all the technical jobs himself and using his family and friends as actors. Cecil Hepworth regarded it as rather daring in 1905 to employ actors in *Rescued by Rover*, though other parts were played by his family and himself.[4] These men, immensely ingenious and enterprising and often steeped in the traditions of optical entertainment, producing films in suburban back-garden studios, were within their limits very successful, but as technicians rather than businessmen they tended to be left behind as film production developed as a major industry.

Urban's departure from Warwick drained it of much of its best personnel: the Charles Urban Trading Company was the leading British film company and remained so until the outbreak of war. Its main rivals were subsidiaries of the French Gaumont and Pathé companies. Pathé Frères, founded in 1896 to manufacture cameras and projectors, had expanded into production, exhibition and the manufacture and processing of film stock by 1902. During the next five years, more than fifty branch offices were established throughout the world, and the original capital of 24,000 francs increased to five million. In 1911, Pathé opened British studios at Alexandra Palace in north London. A. C. Bromhead persuaded Léon Gaumont to let him open a British Gaumont company as early as 1898; with Gaumont's cameras, projectors and films as the mainstay of the business, he was able to branch out into handling the films of the small British producers and eventually to open his own Gaumont studio at Shepherd's Bush.

The American film industry had involved major financial interest from the start. J. Pierpont Morgan had backed Edison's electric lamp patents and helped form the massive General Electric Corporation to exploit them. It was with Morgan's financial backing that Edison was able to wage his twenty-year war on those who infringed his film patents. In the event, Edison's Motion Picture Patents Company crumbled under the entrepreneurial onslaught of his independent rivals. But if Carl Laemmle, William Fox, Marcus Loew and Adolph Zukor started off in a small way, their success attracted hefty financial support. After 1915, when Edison's trust was declared illegal, there was a rapid process of consolidation. Zukor merged his Famous Players production company with Paramount, the first of the national distribution concerns, and in 1919 raised ten million dollars in Wall Street to buy up large numbers of cinemas. First National, MGM and Fox followed suit in turning themselves into vertically integrated concerns able to reduce the speculative element in film production by making programmes of films which would be guaranteed effective international marketing and a regular outlet in tied chains of cinemas.

British film producers failed to take full advantage of the massive expansion in demand for film which occurred between 1909 and the outbreak of war in 1914. 1,842 films were issued on to the market in Britain in 1909, 7,554 in 1913; among these the proportion of British films remained steady at around 15 per cent.[5] By 1909 big capital had begun to penetrate the exhibition side of the industry in Britain with the formation of Provincial Cinematograph Theatres by the financier Sir William Bass. In 1913, PCT attempted to move toward vertical integration by establishing a production company, London Films, bringing over George Loane Tucker, Harold Shaw, Edna Flugrath and the screenwriter De Witt Bodeen from America to fill the leading positions. They returned to America when war broke out, and the company failed to prosper without their expertise. It looked increasingly as if British film production was stuck at a cottage industry stage of development.

The outbreak of war promised new hope. France and Italy had hitherto supplied over 50 per cent of Britain's films, but with the disruption caused by the war imports from Europe were severely restricted. For a time it seemed that British film production might expand to fill the vacuum, but the government showed little interest in encouraging film production and the industry's ranks were depleted by conscription. By 1918, at least 80 per cent of the films shown in Britain came from Hollywood.

Film, along with other industries, profited from the post-war boom. Hepworth Picture Plays was formed as a £100,000 private company in April 1919, and increased its debenture capital at the end of the year and several times throughout 1920 as plans went ahead for an ambitious studio complex.[6] Two British renting concerns branched out into production in 1920. Ideal Films Ltd. was floated in May with a capital of £115,000 and Stoll Picture Production in the same month with a capital of £400,000. The publishing magnate Sir Edward Hulton helped to establish a large distribution company, Film Booking Offices, incorporated with a capital of £100,000 in October 1919, and Lord Beaverbrook bought a controlling interest in PCT which increased its capital to £3 million in March 1920.[7] Another Fleet Street Baron, Lord Rothermere, bought out Pathé's British interests and in association with Stoll began a vigorous campaign to export British films to Europe, America and the Empire.[8]

Prosperity, however, was short-lived. Hepworth's flotation of a £250,000 public company in March 1922 had little appeal to a depressed and nervous stock market and was badly undersubscribed. By June 1924 he was bankrupt.[9] By this time Rothermere had pulled in his horns after the dismal failure of his export drive, and a severely contracted Pathé company was passed over to Beaverbrook. Ideal abandoned film production early in 1924; and though Stoll produced 37 per cent of the total British output of 1925, it too faced severe economic difficulties and was forced drastically to reduce its production programme.[10]

It was alleged that unfair tactics were being used by the Americans, particularly the practice of block booking whereby exhibitors were induced to accept mediocre films along with a handful of quality films. This left cinemas booked up well into the future and with little space to fit in more than the occasional British film. In 1926 the Imperial Conference endorsed the recommendations of the Federation of British Industries that this and other restrictive practices be legislated against and a compulsory quota of British films imposed on exhibitors. The industry was frightened into setting up its own Joint Committee which agreed on similar but milder measures.

A few British producers and directors – Michael Balcon, George Pearson, Herbert Wilcox – had achieved some success in the 20s: Pearson by exploiting a popular British star, Betty Balfour, Wilcox and Balcon by importing American stars like Mae Marsh, Dorothy Gish and Betty Compson. But most British films were of an even

American import: Mae Marsh, with Ivor Novello, in *The Rat* (1925)

poorer quality than the block-booked American programme pictures, and, being dependent for their returns solely on the British market, cost more to rent than their American equivalents. Though the renters and the bigger circuits realised the necessity of compromise, the independent exhibitors fiercely resisted any interference with their programming, and rejected the Joint Committee proposals. The government was left with no alternative but to impose its own solution. The first Cinematograph Films Bill was introduced in Parliament in January 1927 and passed into law by December. The Bill, which despite vigorous debate was passed virtually unamended, outlawed block booking and introduced a compulsory quota – $7\frac{1}{2}$ per cent for renters, 5 per cent for exhibitors – from 1928 onwards, which was to rise by $2\frac{1}{2}$ per cent a year to reach a maximum of 20 per cent by 1936.

The effect of the Quota Act was apparent even before it became law. In March 1927 a substantial production company – British International Pictures – was launched by John Maxwell, head of a leading British distribution company. In the same month the financier Isidore Ostrer organised the merger of a number of distribution, production and exhibition concerns into the £2½ million Gaumont-British Picture Corporation. Over the next year another eleven film companies were floated on the stock market.

There was some concern in the trade press that legislative protection would provide golden opportunities for already discredited directors and producers to worm their way back into the industry. As Herbert Wilcox unkindly put it: 'However the British film industry may be restored, it will not be by offering a subsidy to failure. It seems to me that the quota would in practice create an "awkward squad" of British films which would immediately become the laughing stock of the world.'[11] Wilcox's suspicions proved to be well-founded. 1928 saw a considerable increase in the number of films produced, but their quality left much to be desired. By the middle of 1929 some of the new production companies were already in deep financial trouble and one studio correspondent complained that 'a number of inexperienced and utterly incompetent bluffers . . . are sitting in fat jobs for which they have been proved utterly unqualified'.[12]

They were not to sit there much longer. The coming of sound devastated the 'quota companies'. By the end of 1931 seven of them had declined into bankruptcy, and the combined capital of the eleven companies floated between March 1927 and 1928 had shrunk in value from £2,322,000 to £254,295.[13] The only British production company to make a profit during this period was British International. Maxwell had been shrewd enough to equip his Elstree studio with RCA recording equipment at the first opportunity and to build up a circuit of cinemas (ABC) which would guarantee an outlet for his films.

The other major British film concern, Gaumont-British, survived too, but rather more precariously. Among its subsidiaries was a sound equipment company, British Acoustic, which had grown out of the collaboration between the old Gaumont company and the Danish inventors P. O. Pedersen and Valdemar Poulsen. A. C. Bromhead, Chairman of Gaumont-British, and his brother Reginald, who served as Managing Director, wished to bring their investment to fruition and install British Acoustic equipment in the two studios and 300 cinemas owned by the corporation. Isidore Ostrer had doubts about the viability of the cumbersome British Acoustic apparatus, but was aware that buying in the expensive equipment offered by the American companies, RCA and Western Electric, would put a severe strain on the corporation's already overstretched financial resources. He solved the problem by making a secret and extremely lucrative deal with William Fox. Ostrer bought up the remaining one and a quarter million pound share capital of Gaumont-British and offered Fox a deal which would give him control of the corporation. Either Fox – who within months had lost control of his own company – was tricked, or in some way he defaulted on some minor condition of the deal, for when the smoke finally cleared it was discovered that control of Gaumont-British was exercised through a holding company, the Metropolis and Bradford Trust company, and that Ostrer and the Fox Corporation had an equal number of shares.[14] The balance was held by an independent chairman, Lord Lee of Fareham. Lee, a British businessman who had made his fortune in America, was married to the daughter of the President of the Chase National Bank, a major shareholder in Fox. He was nevertheless deeply patriotic and determined not to let the company pass into American hands. He was assisted here by the Bromheads, who before agreeing to abandon British Acoustic and their high positions in Gaumont-British insisted that the Board pass a resolution removing the voting rights of non-British shareholders. It was not until 1944, after J. Arthur Rank had firmly taken the company in hand, that Fox representatives were allowed seats on the Gaumont-British Board.[15]

Between 1927 and 1932 it looked as if, despite protective legislation, the Americans had increased their domination over the British film industry. The lion's share of the market in sound equipment had been won by RCA and Western Electric, and the popularity of American talkies allowed the Hollywood majors to extend their control over exhibitors by instituting a percentage system of booking.[16] British producers had proved dilatory and ineffectual in the face of the technological revolution, and in some areas of the country – notably the East End of London and the cities of Scotland – the poor quality of English talkies aroused derision and contempt.

On the other hand, the requirements of the quota legislation ensured a steady demand for British films. In fact, cinemas tended to show more British films than they were legally required to. In 1932, for example, when the quota for exhibitors was 10 per cent, British films filled up 24.27 per cent of screen time.[17] The ABC and Gaumont-British cinemas provided an outlet for the films of their associated production companies, but independent cinemas were even more generous in according playing time to British films. Many of them were poor quality films foisted on exhibitors by American companies which fulfilled their quota obligations in the cheapest possible way. But the few remaining British companies found an enthusiastic market for their talkies. In 1930 Herbert Wilcox made *Rookery Nook*, the first of a string of Ben Travers farces, for £14,000 and grossed £150,000 with it. Basil Dean was equally successful in

1931 with the Gracie Fields vehicle *Sally in our Alley*, and starting in the same year Michael Balcon produced a regular supply of popular British pictures at the Gaumont-British studios.

The more far-sighted American executives attempted to cash in on this surprising popularity of British sound films. J. C. Graham, the long-established head of Paramount's London office, had experimented with British film production in the early 20s but the poor demand for British films led him to sell off his Islington studio to Balcon in 1924. In 1931 he struck a deal with Herbert Wilcox whereby Wilcox's British and Dominions company would make twelve films for Paramount at an average cost of £30,000. Graham was also responsible for starting Alexander Korda on his British career. Korda was a Hungarian exile who, after a lukewarm reception in Hollywood, had worked for Paramount in France. The modest success of his first British film, *Service for Ladies*, led to Korda's newly formed London Films company being commissioned to make a further six pictures for Paramount and three bigger-budget films for United Artists.

United Artists was different from the other Hollywood companies in that its films were supplied by affiliated independent producers. It had no studios of its own. With its original producing partners – Griffith, Fairbanks, Pickford, Chaplin – in one way or another quiescent, it was short of product and prepared to gamble on British producers making films acceptable to the American market. With Korda's first film the gamble paid off successfully. *The Private Life of Henry VIII* opened at the Radio City Music Hall in New York in October 1933 and drew large crowds. By the end of the year it had grossed $500,000, an unprecedented amount for a British film. Though the profits were real enough, *Henry VIII*'s success had a symbolic importance too. It fulfilled the long frustrated British ambition to prove they could produce films that were more than a match for Hollywood. The fact that the director was Hungarian hardly seemed to count in view of the film's quintessentially English subject matter.

Korda's success provoked a wave of big-budget production in Britain. Korda himself, with backing from the Prudential Assurance Company, was able to build large studios at Denham to provide a home for many of the new production companies set up to make prestige films. Over the next three years the industry polarised between extremely low-budget films produced or commissioned by the American companies to fulfil their quota obligations in Britain, and increasingly expensive British pictures made with an eye on the rich rewards of the American market.

A thriving undergrowth in cut-price film-making sprang up which made Hollywood's poverty row look luxurious by comparison. The 'quickies' made at Shepperton and Twickenham or at the American-owned studios at Teddington and Wembley were shot in a period of twelve days or less and made for a standard cost of around £1 a foot. Directors would often make six or eight films a year, and 'Uncle' Julius Hagen instituted a night-shift at his Twickenham studio in order to make the fullest use of time and space. In 1934 George Pearson directed eight films there, three of them at night. 'All vaulting ideas of film as an art had to be abandoned, only as a capable and speedy craftsman could one survive in that feverish and restless environment.'[18]

Those who have left accounts of their quota quickie experience (besides Pearson, they include Adrian Brunel, Michael Powell, and the actor Henry Kendall, who in a hectic two years starred in twenty-four quickies) seem to have adopted from the English stage and music hall the spirit that long hours and poor pay don't matter as long as the work is fun. As Brunel put it, 'Instead of being ashamed, I was rather pleased with myself, for I believed that we were evolving a technique that showed what could be done when facing fearful odds.'[19] Because of the mainstream industry's concern with aping Hollywood – borrowing foreign directors and importing 'ace' technicians – it was often the quickies which provided opportunities for talented, off-beat directors (for example, Brunel, Powell, John Baxter) and indeed for young British actors (Laurence Olivier, John Mills, Jack Hawkins, Wilfrid Hyde White, Vivien Leigh, Sally Gray, Rex Harrison, Donald Wolfit, James Mason, and many others).

Inevitably, on such ludicrously low budgets most of the films were extremely shoddy. Brunel, a cutter and scriptwriter as well as a director, expressed annoyance and frustration at the petty tyranny of the pound-a-foot regime. Of one of James Mason's early films, *The Prison Breaker*, he notes that 'to have cut the film, say five minutes, might have made it an acceptable little film of sixty-four minutes, instead of a rather terrible film lasting sixty-nine minutes – but such a cut would have eliminated most of the producer's profits.'[20]

In contrast to this sort of extreme parsimony was the extravagance of the new British companies making films for the world market. Korda's two H. G. Wells films, *Things to Come* and *The Man Who Could Work Miracles*, were reputed to have cost £350,000. But despite their cost, British films fared badly in America. United Artists complained that American audiences found the Elisabeth Bergner picture *Dreaming Lips* offensive, and that nearly all British films were either slow or incomprehensible. According to Tino Balio, of the ten films Korda delivered to UA after *Henry VIII* only *The Ghost Goes West* – a whimsical romance between a Scottish ghost and an American tourist directed by a Frenchman, René Clair – achieved anything like success.

Complaints of unfair practices were heard again, directed both at the way British films failed to find an audience in America and at the dismal quality of American quota pictures. There was an awareness that British production methods were profligate, and some annoyance at the prominence of Continental expatriates in the new Korda-style production companies. But large modern studios had been built, and important financial interests were now involved in the industry. British film production had become big business. In 1928 the total value of British films in production amounted to £500,000; in 1937 it was £7 million.

The Moyne Report, commissioned by the government in 1936 to consider the future of the Quota Act which was due to expire in 1938, reflected these concerns. The Americans were condemned for undermining the spirit of the Act. It was suggested that the quota be progressively increased until it reached 50 per cent, and that a Films Commission be appointed which would assess the quality of those films submitted for quota qualification. To ensure an adequate supply of British films, it was suggested that the government set up a special film bank to encourage reputable investors to put their money in the industry. Before legislation could be drafted, however, the boom collapsed. By the middle of 1938, most of the prestige independent production units operating from Denham had given up the ghost, and control of the studio itself passed from Korda to J. Arthur Rank. A survey carried out by *World Film News,* the organ of the documentary movement, and a secret investigation by Bank of England officials, both concluded that the boom had been highly speculative and that big-budget films had been made with little regard for their likely returns.[22]

Thus when the second Cinematograph Films Act was passed in June 1938, its provisions were much more conciliatory than those of the Moyne Report. Despite American pressure, the renter's quota was retained, but it was reduced from 20 to 15 per cent. There was to be no Films Commission and thus no quality control. Quota quickies were to be stamped out by instituting a minimum cost of £7,500 for any long film submitted for quota. This was hardly very onerous. In addition, there was an attempt to encourage the Americans to go for quality rather than quantity: films costing three times the minimum qualified for double quota assessment, and films costing five times the minimum qualified for triple assessment.[23]

During the boom, some of the American companies had been swept along by the general enthusiasm, and had declared themselves willing to begin prestige production in Britain. Warner Brothers announced its intention of bringing over Hollywood stars to act in the films made at its small Teddington studio – though none materialised; MGM enticed Michael Balcon from Gaumont-British to head a prestige production unit at Denham, where 20th Century-Fox had already set up New World Pictures to make *Wings of the Morning*, Britain's first Technicolor movie; and Columbia made plans to move in to the huge Amalgamated studios being built at Borehamwood. The 1938 Act was partially successful in sustaining these initiatives despite the slump. Columbia abandoned the Amalgamated studios but entered into a co-production deal with Korda. Fox took over Gracie Fields from Basil Dean and attempted to fashion her talents for the American market. MGM commissioned two films from Gaumont-British's production subsidiary Gainsborough, Carol Reed's *Climbing High* and Hitchcock's *The Lady Vanishes*, and went ahead with its own production programme: the three films it made, with Hollywood directors, before the outbreak of war – *A Yank at Oxford* (Jack Conway), *The Citadel* (King Vidor) and *Goodbye Mr Chips* (Sam Wood) – proved remarkably popular in America.

The war brought considerable disruption to the British film industry but it also fostered the spirit of co-operation between British and American companies. Columbia formed its own production unit to make a string of popular George Formby comedies. Fox closed down New World Productions and its own small studio at Wembley and followed MGM's example of letting Gainsborough supply its quota films. RKO, which had provided backing for Herbert Wilcox's *Victoria the Great*, continued to support his Imperator company during the war, and produced its own box-office hit with the wartime weepie *Dangerous Moonlight*. Warner Brothers kept open its Teddington studio until 1944, when it was destroyed by a flying bomb.

Because of the requisitioning of studios and the consequent restriction in the number of films that could be made (208 British features in 1937, 47 in 1941) the quota was suspended in October 1942. The agreement reached in the early days of the war whereby the American companies repatriated only a third of their British earnings also ended when America entered the war, but relations remained amicable. Sympathy for Britain's plight made British films more acceptable to American audiences, and government pressure helped to ensure adequate distribution. According to Sidney Bernstein, a special adviser to the Ministry of Information:

When I went to America for the Government I knew we could only get worthwhile commercial presentation of British features through the eight major American companies. I am glad to say that, after some negotiations, they agreed to give commercial

Over here: Michael Balcon flanked by Jack Conway and Robert Taylor, on location for *A Yank at Oxford* (1937)

distribution to eight British features and eight shorts a year even though they knew it meant that these films would displace their own.[23]

There was a marked improvement in the quality of British films, reflected in box-office takings. *In Which We Serve* grossed $1.8 million in America, and British films ranging from realist war dramas like *49th Parallel* (US title: *The Invaders*) and *Target for Tonight* to escapist melodramas such as *The Man in Grey* and *Madonna of the Seven Moons* rivalled the top Hollywood pictures in popularity with British audiences.

With a pride in the achievements of British film production there came a resentment that America was taking too little notice. As Gregory Dawson, J. B. Priestley's fictitious scriptwriter, pointed out:

Some of us here in the film business can't help feeling rather bitter. . . . Our people here were up to the neck in the war, and half the time they lived like rats in holes, with anything that would explode or burn raining down on 'em. And if they found their way through the black-out to spend a shilling or two at the pictures – what did they see all too often? The Sunset Boulevard notion of the war. The American Way of Life. Yanks winning the Battle for Democracy. The March of Time. And occasionally films about London Taking It, a London full of dukes and toothless costermongers, films produced or directed often by Englishmen who'd hared across the Atlantic in Thirty-Nine and seemed to have forgotten what England was like.[24]

This sort of impatient chauvinism was widespread among writers and critics who had rejoiced at the emergence of a realist British cinema in the war years. But it was a very different ethos which was to inspire Britain's most serious attempt to challenge Hollywood.

Since his first involvement in the industry in 1933, J. Arthur Rank had steadily built up his interests so that by 1944 he controlled two-thirds of the available studio space, two cinema circuits, each of approximately 300 halls, the largest British distribution company and total assets of over $200 million. Though his profits came mainly from his exhibition interests, Rank had become increasingly involved in big-budget film production and was convinced that he had a powerful enough organisation to break into the American market. Tentative approaches towards United Artists with a view to taking over Korda's partnership in the company failed to make headway, and Rank persuaded UA's chief negotiators, Theodor Carr and Arthur Kelly, to help him set up a new international distribution company, Eagle-Lion. UA agreed to handle Rank's films while the new organisation was being built up, but proved an unsatisfactory partner; and in 1945 Rank made alternative arrangements with Universal. Rank had acquired a major share in the company when it was reorganised in 1935, and could expect to exercise considerable influence on the way his films were handled.

In December 1945 it was announced that Rank and Universal would come together to create a $10 million distribution company, United World Pictures, which would handle sixteen films a year, eight from Rank, eight from International Pictures Inc., a highly successful independent production company set up by Leo Spitz (ex-President of RKO) and William Goetz (son-in-law of Louis B. Mayer). Exhibitor hostility towards British films would be overcome by insisting that Rank and International films were booked together as a package. It was a sound and practical strategy but it reckoned without the internecine conflict between Hollywood and the American Justice Department. In June 1946, before UWP had even started business, block booking was declared illegal.

Disappointed but undeterred, Rank worked out a more flexible arrangement with Universal and International, revived Eagle-Lion, and attempted to use his influence as the most important exhibitor of Hollywood films in Britain to ensure that the majors looked on his own films with reciprocal favour. By June 1947 he had managed to get the Big Five to provide him with $2 million worth of play-dates on their affiliated circuits.[26]

In terms of the British market the Americans were worried, but less about pressures from Rank (whose circuits needed American films as much as the American films needed his circuits) than about the threat of action by the British government, which was eager to save precious foreign currency by restricting the flow of imported 'luxuries'.

In August 1947 the axe fell. An *ad valorem* tax of 75 per cent was imposed on the import of foreign films. Hollywood angrily announced a total boycott of the British market and withdrew its support from Rank. Bookings of British films suffered badly; although Rank tried hard to dissociate himself from the government and maintain friendly relations with the Americans, the dispute dragged on and he was persuaded to change his tactics. The growing shortage of American films in Britain seemed to provide an opportunity for British films to capture a greater share of their own home market. Rank increased production accordingly. When the embargo was lifted in March 1948 and the backlog of Hollywood pictures flooded into Britain, Rank offered space on his two circuits for only a tiny proportion of them. With a programme of sixty new British feature films, ten re-issues, nine 'curtain-raisers' and the films of his American allies Universal and Eagle-Lion, he set out to prove that Britain could manage without Hollywood.

Unfortunately, this was not true. British films had proved increasingly popular in the war years, but they still constituted a small percentage of the total supply, and British audiences were not so patriotic as to stomach only a diet of British films. Attendance at Rank's Odeon and Gaumont cinemas fell dramatically throughout 1948. The following year Rank admitted losses of £4,646,000; studios were closed down at Denham, Shepherd's Bush, Islington and Highbury, and Hollywood films resumed their dominant position on the Rank circuits.[27]

Britain's challenge to Hollywood had failed, but, as had happened after the boom of the mid-30s, failure initiated another wave of Anglo-American co-operation. The Films Act of 1948 had dispensed with the renter's quota, and the extremely high exhibitor's quota introduced to protect Rank's production programme was necessarily reduced once production was cut back. From 1950 onwards it was maintained at a steady 30 per cent. By the agreement which had settled the import duty dispute, only a proportion of American earnings in Britain were to be remitted to America. It was hoped that frozen funds would be used to finance film production in Britain. In fact, as the Hollywood studio system crumbled under the impact of the divorcement decrees and the rapid spread of television, 'runaway production' became widespread, in France, Spain and Italy as well as in Britain. Encouraged by lower costs and by the subsidy for British films instituted as the Eady Levy from 1950, American involvement in British film production rose throughout the 50s. By 1956 one-third of all British films had American backing.[28]

In contrast to the quota quickie days of the 30s, the predominant trend in the 50s was to make big-budget pictures which would appeal to American as well as British audiences. Production was centred at the MGM studio at Borehamwood with its ten enormous sound stages, a vast back-lot of standing sets, and a tank larger than some lakes. It was used by Columbia and Fox as well as MGM for films such as *The Miniver Story, Invitation to the Dance, Mogambo, Island in the Sun, Anastasia, The Barretts of Wimpole Street, Cockleshell Heroes, Bhowani Junction,* and a series of historical epics – *Ivanhoe, The Knights of the Round Table* and *Quentin Durward.* Warner Brothers acquired a dominant share in the BIP/ABC company in the early 40s following the death of John Maxwell, and along with Disney and RKO made occasional use of BIP's Elstree studio for their big-budget pictures, including *Moby Dick, Rob Roy, King's Rhapsody, Captain Horatio Hornblower* and *Indiscreet.*

Though Rank had failed to carve out a substantial share of the American market in the 40s, films like *Henry V, Great Expectations* and *The Red Shoes* had established the reputation of British films as adult and sophisticated among a small but increasingly important middle-class audience which looked askance at the commercial vulgarity of Hollywood. Art house cinema exhibition expanded rapidly in the late 40s and throughout the 50s as mainstream cinema declined. British films – particularly those which were ostentatiously English like the Ealing comedies – attracted a strong cult following. However, since they were sold to American distribution companies for small flat fees, they brought only minor profits to their British producers.

In 1957, the Rank Organisation attempted once again to grab a more substantial share of the American market. By March 1958 a network of ten distribution exchanges had been established throughout the United States, and cinemas were leased in major cities as showcases for the Rank product. Michael Powell's *The Battle of the River Plate* (US title: *Pursuit of the Graf Spee*) attracted large

The Great White Whale in Wales: Gregory Peck in John Huston's *Moby Dick* (1956)

audiences, but many of the Rank films were too insular to appeal to American tastes and in September 1950 the venture was abandoned.

Enterprising independent producers, whether British (Romulus – the Woolf brothers), American (Warwick – Cubby Broccoli and Irving Allen) or cosmopolitan (Sam Spiegel), fared better, and a number of British-made films which combined British and American talent and money – *The African Queen* and *Bridge on the River Kwai*, for example – were extremely successful in America. And at the opposite extreme to the genteel, whimsical Ealing films, Hammer with its gory remakes of horror classics – given widespread distribution by Columbia – reached a different sort of cult audience.

In the 60s the flow of American money into the British film industry turned into a flood. According to the National Film Finance

Corporation, by 1966 75 per cent of production finance came from American sources. A year later it was 90 per cent.[29] Moreover, there was a tendency for the films backed by the Americans to be recognisably British subjects, rather than Hollywood pictures made for cost reasons in British studios. The popularity of English rock groups like the Beatles and the Rolling Stones and the development of a myth of 'swinging London' made British society suddenly exciting, charismatic and fashionable, an impression confirmed by the energy and panache of films like *Tom Jones*, the James Bond films and *A Hard Day's Night*. After decades in which Britain had followed American trends, it seemed that the process had been reversed. London was seen as the centre of a youth-oriented cultural revolution which young Americans found fascinating and appealing. By 1965 all the majors and two mini-majors – Filmways and Avco-Embassy – had set up British production subsidiaries. American and Continental directors were brought over (Otto Preminger for *Bunny Lake is Missing*, Truffaut for *Fahrenheit 451*, Antonioni for *Blow Up*), but generally it was British talent which was sought after. The consequent boom caused costs to rise. Tony Richardson had made *Tom Jones* for United Artists in 1962 for $1.3 million (it brought in over $16 million at the North American box-office). In 1968, he needed $6½ million to make the much less successful *Charge of the Light Brigade*.

Some of the films brought in considerable profits for their backers – *Blow Up* for MGM; the Beatles and Bond Films for UA; *Alfie* for Paramount; *To Sir With Love* and *Georgy Girl* for Columbia – and there were squawks of protest that British talent was being exploited for the benefit of foreigners. But to the Americans it was the losses which were more apparent. In three years in the late 60s Universal made thirteen films in Britain, including Chaplin's *Countess from Hong Kong*, Losey's *Boom* and *Secret Ceremony*, and a number of cheaper films by promising British directors (Peter Hall, Peter Watkins, Jack Gold, Karel Reisz, Albert Finney). None did more than break even and many of them flopped badly. UA's early successes were balanced out by expensive failures like *The Battle of Britain*; Fox virtually gave up its British programme after the disappointing reception afforded *Modesty Blaise* – though it was to be the most active American company in the 70s; Paramount ran into trouble with an expensive musical, *Half a Sixpence*, as did Columbia and MGM with their historical epics *Cromwell* and *Alfred the Great*.[30]

The 60s were years of deepening crisis for the Hollywood companies, many of which were taken over by non-film conglomerates (United Artists by Transamerica, Paramount by Gulf and Western, Warners by Kinney National). Money was poured into blockbusters in a desperate attempt to win back audiences, and losses incurred on British films were dwarfed by some of the Hollywood disasters. In 1969, MGM declared a loss of $35 million, Fox of $36.8 million, and Warners of $52 million. The other majors, with the exception of Disney, fared little better. But between 1968 and 1970 the success of a number of American films – *The Graduate, Easy Rider, Midnight Cowboy, Butch Cassidy and the Sundance Kid, Woodstock, Mash, Five Easy Pieces* – seemed to indicate that the focus of the youth revolution had switched from Britain to America.

The emergence of the new Hollywood was a painful process. The next few years saw an increasing contraction in the direct production activities of the majors as studios were developed for real estate or opened to tourists, and props were auctioned off to those nostalgic for Hollywood's golden age. Operations in Britain were naturally vulnerable once they ceased to be profitable. In February 1969, Universal terminated its British production programme. At the end of the year MGM announced the closure of its Borehamwood studio. The NFFC had warned of the danger of too heavy a reliance on

Hollywood England: Otto Preminger directing Laurence Olivier in *Bunny Lake is Missing* (1965)

American finance, and predictably there followed a weeping and wailing and gnashing of teeth as investment was withdrawn. But until the mid-70s the Americans provided at least 50 per cent of the finance for film production in Britain, and it was not until 1976 that there was a significant drop in the number of films made.

The two major British companies, Rank and ABC, had made no attempt to compete for talent with the American companies in the 60s, contenting themselves with support for well-tried British comedies and horror films. In 1969, ABC was taken over by the music and leisure conglomerate EMI, and the actor/writer/director Bryan Forbes was asked to begin a production programme at Elstree. The fourteen films backed by Forbes proved almost as unsuccessful as Universal's unlucky thirteen, and their failure spelt the end for Elstree as a fully serviced studio. Both Rank and ABC–EMI would now prefer to invest in the films of independent producers rather than to initiate their own projects.

With a few noticeable exceptions the 70s saw little of the exuberant experimentation of the previous decade; the British film industry concentrated on producing a steady diet of comedies, horror films and soft-core sex films, and became progressively less interesting to the Americans. The British theatrical market continued to shrink throughout the 70s, so that it became no longer economic for each of the majors to maintain substantial distribution offices. Columbia merged with Warners and was soon joined by EMI to form Columbia-EMI-Warner; Universal, now controlled by MCA, ended its long-standing distribution agreement with Rank, and formed Cinema International Corporation (CIC) with Paramount and MGM.

Towards the end of the decade the development of cable, video and pay-TV created valuable ancillary markets in America which came to seem more important than the shrinking European theatrical market. British talent and British investment was drawn increasingly to America. Directors like Peter Yates, Guy Hamilton, John Guillermin and J. Lee Thompson were already forging successful careers in Hollywood, and they were now followed by others such as Alan Parker and Ridley Scott. The alternative for younger or less orthodox directors like Ken Loach, Mike Leigh, Mike Hodges, Stephen Frears and Jack Gold was to work in television.

With Hollywood companies once again enjoying big profits, British companies were tempted to emulate their success by making big-budget international pictures. Lord Grade's Associated Communications Corporation, hitherto primarily concerned with television, turned to film production in 1976 and made around fourteen films a year until 1981, several of them Hollywood-scale blockbusters like *Green Ice*, *Escape to Athena* and the ill-fated *Raise the Titanic*.[31]

Grade had risen to prominence with his brothers Bernard Delfont and Leslie Grade by building up the most powerful talent agency in Britain. In 1967 it had been taken over by EMI, and after EMI's takeover of ABC Delfont was given charge of the film interests of the conglomerate. The attempt at a medium-budget production programme under Bryan Forbes (1969–71) had yielded disappointing results, whereas EMI's subsequent backing for John Brabourne's lavish Agatha Christie cycle, starting with *Murder on the Orient Express* in 1974, was at first very profitable. Seeing the initial success achieved by his brother at ACC, Delfont was easily persuaded that the 'international' film was where the money lay.

In 1978, with *The Deerhunter*, EMI began producing a programme of big-budget films in America. A year later a joint distribution company (AFD-EMI) was established to handle the films of ACC and EMI in America. To maintain a costly national distribution network throughout the USA it was essential that the new company had an abundant supply of top-class commercial films. This EMI and ACC failed to supply. The success of *The Deerhunter* and ACC's *The Muppet Movie* was disastrously counterbalanced by the failure of mega-buck flops such as *Can't Stop the Music, Honky Tonk Freeway* and *Raise the Titanic*. In 1981 the venture was abandoned. Grade was deposed from ACC after it was revealed that its films division had made a loss of £26.4 million, and the corporation withdrew from film production. EMI was taken over by the electrical giant Thorn. After a certain amount of internal wrangling, Delfont and his production chief Barry Spikings resigned, and Verity Lambert, a television executive responsible for a number of successful TV series, was brought in to head a more modest British-based production programme.

1981 was a bleak year for the British film industry. Cinema attendance fell to an all-time low of 63.8 million (compared to 1,635 million in 1946) and only twenty-six British feature films were given theatrical release. However, three of those films – *Time Bandits, The French Lieutenant's Woman* and *Chariots of Fire* – proved extremely popular in America. After years in the doldrums British films were once again fashionable. The success of *Time Bandits* was the most remarkable in that it had been marketed in the USA by its British producers, HandMade Films. HandMade's decision to distribute the film in America itself came from an exasperation at the arrogant indifference of the American majors. Its success and that of *The French Lieutenant's Woman* – made with American backing – made them change their attitude. The next big British film, *Gandhi*, was eagerly snapped up by Columbia, rightly sensing that like *Chariots of Fire* it was destined for Oscar-winning success.

Exhibition of films has become much more flexible over the past ten years, and the distinction between art-house and mainstream commercial distribution has narrowed considerably. *Chariots of Fire* was initially given a very limited release in both Britain and America, but its unexpected popularity was quickly picked up on and exploited to the full. The majors have now set up 'classics divisions' to deal with re-issues of their own films and with imports such as *Another Time, Another Place* and *Experience Preferred but not Essential*, British made-for-TV movies which have made healthy profits in America.

Video, cable and network television are becoming less parasitic on the film industry and now play an important role in the finance of films. In Britain the advent of Channel 4, a new television channel relying on independent film and TV companies for a large percentage of its product, has been a major factor in the current revival in film production. The two major new British film companies, Goldcrest and Virgin, both tested the water by investing in co-productions with Channel 4. Virgin has yet to prove that it can duplicate its success in the record industry, but Goldcrest, successful with *Gandhi* and *The Killing Fields* and lower-budget projects like *The Dresser, Cal* and *Another Country*, has provided an inspiring example to those hitherto reluctant to invest in film production. Though now a wholly-owned subsidiary of the publishing conglomerate Pearson-Longman, Goldcrest funded its expansion from a £250,000 film development company to a major production company with a capital of £26 million by attracting financial support from a range of institutional investors, from the National Union of Mineworkers Pension Fund to the Scottish merchant bankers Noble Grossart.[32] Prudential Assurance, which had kept clear of film production since its costly relationship with Korda in the 30s, has provided backing for Lewis Gilbert's Acorn Films and John Wolstenholme's United Media Finance Corporation; Victor Matthews' newspaper and publishing empire Fleet Holdings set up Britannic Films and Television in collaboration with the Industrial and Commercial Financial Corporation, an investment trust owned by the four major British banks; Thorn-EMI raised £18 million from City investors which it promised to back with £18 million from its own coffers for film production in Britain.

1985, the 'Year of the British Film', is likely to see the complete dismantling of government support for the industry. The quota was suspended at the end of 1982 and will not be reintroduced. The Eady Levy, from which British producers drew support, was abolished at the end of 1984, and the NFFC, which was given £1½ million a year from the fund, will henceforth be dependent on the major British companies for its finance. The government justifies its action by arguing that the film industry is now robust enough to stand on its own two feet – though ironically a year or two ago the argument would have been that the industry was such a sickly 'lame duck' that the kindest solution to its problems would have been some form of euthanasia.

The position of the industry has changed so much over the past sixty years that there is some excuse for abandoning protective legislation designed to ameliorate conditions which no longer exist. The cinema's place as the major mass medium has been taken over by television, which – through the restriction on the percentage of non-British material broadcast and the shelter of the franchise system for the commercial companies and the licence fee for the BBC – remains very much a protected industry. But the boom in the video industry in Britain, and in the pay-TV and cable industry in America, has done something to reassert the importance of film, if not of the cinema. Films like *Educating Rita, 1984, The Company of Wolves* and *A Private Function* indicate that the success of *Chariots of Fire* heralded a trend which is being followed up with some perspicacity by British film producers. But the Association of Independent Producers and the Association of Cinematograph and Television Technicians warn that the current revival could easily evaporate, with British investors withdrawing their money more ruthlessly than the Americans did at the end of the 60s.

The American government has always recognised the importance of the film industry, and in a variety of ways has tried to foster it. British governments have tended to confine their actions to maintaining the existence of a film production industry at the least possible cost and with a minimum of intervention in the way the industry has been run – the reports of the Monopolies Commission, for example, have been singularly ineffectual. Until the government fully grasps the importance of providing a framework and a climate in which film production can flourish, the British film industry is likely to remain under the shadow of Hollywood.

Notes

1   *The Times*, 12 January 1926. I am indebted to William Lafferty's unpublished doctoral thesis, "The first implementation of magnetic sound in the motion picture industry: Ludwig Blattner and the Blattnerphone', for this quotation and for data on the plight of the British film industry generally in the late 1920s.

2   PRO: BT 31 7366/52215. Nevertheless, 'Paul's Animatographe Ltd' failed to get beyond the prospectus stage.

3   Rachael Low and Roger Manvell, *The History of the British Film, 1896–1906*, London, Allen & Unwin, 1948, p. 25.

4   Cecil Hepworth, *Came the Dawn*, London, Phoenix House, 1951, p. 66.

5   Rachael Low, *The History of the British Film, 1906–1914*, London, Allen & Unwin, 1949, p. 134.

6   Rachael Low, *The History of the British Film, 1918–1929*, London, Allen & Unwin, 1971, pp. 109–12.

7   Ibid., p. 123.

8   Georges Sadoul, 'Napoleon of the Cinema' (obituary of Charles Pathé), *Sight and Sound*, vol. 27, no. 4, 1958, p. 183.

9   Hepworth, *Came the Dawn*, p. 191.

10   Low, 1918–1929, pp. 156–7.

11   *Daily Film Renter*, 18 March 1927, p. 8.

12   *Kinematograph Weekly*, 24 October 1929, p. 57.

13   See Robert Murphy, 'Coming of Sound to the Cinema in Britain', *Historical Journal of Film, Radio and Television*, vol. 4, no. 2, 1984, pp. 143–60.

14   See Upton Sinclair, *Upton Sinclair Presents William Fox*, Los Angeles, 1933; Metropolis and Bradford Trust Company, Special Resolutions, Companies House Records, CR 2330/32.

15   Lord Lee of Fareham, *A Good Innings*, London, John Murray, 1974.

16   Western Electric had made 1,500 installations by early 1932, 200 of them replacements of other systems. *Kinematograph Weekly*, 5 April 1932, p. 17.

17   *Minutes of Evidence taken before the Committee on Cinematograph Films*, 5 May 1936, Table 1, p. 9.

18   George Pearson, *Flashback*, London, Allen & Unwin, 1957, p. 193.

19   Adrian Brunel, *Nice Work*, London, Forbes Robertson, 1949, p. 171.

20   Ibid., p. 167.

21   Tino Balio, *United Artists*, Madison, University of Wisconsin Press, 1976, p. 144.

22   F. D. Klingender and Stuart Legg, 'Secrets of British Film Finance', *World Film News*, January 1937, reprinted as *Money Behind the Screen*, London, Lawrence and Wishart, 1937. See Margaret Dickinson and Sarah Street, *Cinema and State*, London, British Film Institute, 1985, for the Bank of England investigation.

23   Sarah Street's 'The Hays Office and the defence of the British market in the 1930s', *Historical Journal of Film, Radio and Television*, March 1985, deals in detail with the 1938 Act.

24 Sidney Bernstein, *Film and International Relations,* London, Jackson Press, 1945, p. 13.
25 J. B. Priestley, *Bright Day*, London, Heinemann, 1946, p. 246.
26 *Variety,* 11 June 1947, p. 1.
27 Political and Economic Planning, *The British Film Industry*, London, PEP, 1952, p. 109.
28 *Kinematograph Weekly,* 13 December 1956, p. 79.
29 NFFC Annual Report for year ending 31 March 1970, p. 5.
30 See Alexander Walker, *Hollywood England,* London, Michael Joseph, 1974. Walker's book is based on interviews with all the leading figures involved in the American invasion.
31 Linda Wood, *British Films 1971–1981*, London, British Film Institute, 1983, deals comprehensively with Grade's intervention in the film industry.
32 For the development of Goldcrest into a major company, see Robert Murphy, 'Three Companies: Boyd's Co., HandMade and Goldcrest' in Martyn Auty and Nick Roddick (eds.), *British Cinema Now*, London, British Film Institute, 1985.

Andrew Higson

'BRITAIN'S OUTSTANDING CONTRIBUTION TO THE FILM'
THE DOCUMENTARY-REALIST TRADITION

The opening sentence of the 1947 survey *The Factual Film* proposes that 'the documentary is Britain's outstanding contribution to the film'.[1] It is not an uncommon claim. Indeed, it has for some time been the view of the British film cultural orthodoxy. The purpose of this chapter is to investigate the nature of this contribution.

The documentary movement as such is rooted in the late 1920s and the 1930s: the forms of documentary and the wider culture which supports it are very much a product of that particular time. Of course, there continue to be documentary film units after the 1930s, but their relationship to, or place within, British film culture changes outside that specific context. In part, this chapter is an account of this changing relationship, and it is therefore by no means simply about documentary film-making. It is an attempt to tease out the implications of Alan Lovell's claim that 'the importance of the documentary movement lies not in the quality of individual films, but in the impact it had in general on the British cinema'.[2] Under the unique circumstances of World War II, the documentary idea came to inform both much commercial film-making practice and the dominant discourses of film criticism. This coming together of documentary and feature film-making is later, and influentially, renewed in the 'New Wave' cycle of films of the late 50s and early 60s, and again in the pervasiveness of documentary modes in television.

In a sense, there is no need for this chapter to be written – or rather, no need for it to be written again. There are already numerous accounts both of the documentary movement itself and of the subsequent feature films and television programmes which in one way or another draw upon, or depend upon, the rhetoric of documentary film-making of the 1930s. (Significantly, many of the accounts of the documentary movement have been written by the documentarists themselves.[3]) This superfluity of accounts of British

72

documentary-realist film-making is a consequence of the fact that British cinema as a whole has habitually been thought through (that is, constructed) in terms which derive from the documentary idea. As Peter Wyeth and Don Macpherson put it, 'this tradition . . . has set the very terms in which film-making is thought about in Britain'.[4] Thus, while other traditions of British cinema are either little known or largely ignored (the Gothic, the fantastic, the melodramatic), this tradition is known and celebrated; and this chapter does, after all, need to be written precisely in order to challenge the processes by which a particular history of British cinema is written as the history. What this chapter must do, then, in the limited space available, is both reconstruct a familiar map of British cinema, and at the same time de-familiarise that construction. The starting point must be the ideologies and practices of the documentary movement as it emerged in the late 20s and the 30s.

The documentary movement and the documentary idea

The documentary movement is overwhelmingly associated with the name of John Grierson, who effectively founded the movement in the late 20s and who did much as administrator, polemicist and creative influence to shape the form of British documentary. The first documentary film unit was set up by Grierson at the Empire Marketing Board in 1929. His qualifications were a long-standing interest in the question of communication in a mass democratic society, and a similarly developed interest in cinema both as a possible means of communication and as an aesthetic medium in its own right (he had already made a film, Drifters, which caused a considerable stir when it was shown at the Film Society in 1929, in the same programme as Eisenstein's Battleship Potemkin). The other key figure at this stage was Stephen Tallents (knighted in 1932), the secretary of the Empire Marketing Board, and a pioneer in the field of public relations. Thanks to Tallents and Grierson, the EMB unit managed to establish a crucial framework for film sponsorship which would be widely adopted by both public and private institutions. The EMB unit itself was a branch of the Civil Service; in 1933, with the dismantling of the Board, the unit moved to the General Post Office. In 1940, the GPO unit was taken over by the Ministry of Information and renamed the Crown Film Unit. In addition, the 30s and 40s saw the proliferation of numerous other documentary units (not to mention the workers film movement). But this documentary film movement is simply one strand in a much broader field of social practice. Social documentation as a mode of cultural-political intervention cuts right across radio, journalistic and literary writing (Orwell, Priestley, Greenwood, etc.), photojournalism and

73

photography (Brandt, Spender, *Picture Post*), social anthropology (Mass Observation), and so on. All these practices developed social documentation as a tool in the ideological enterprise of communicating, from a variety of standpoints, between the citizen and the state in the democratic society.

Within this context, cinema is appropriated as the ideal means of mass communication, documentation and education: it is appropriated, then, for a social-democratic project. This social-democratic interest in the cinema is at one level a radical challenge to the given form of cinema in the 1930s, the decade of the dream palaces. This cinema of spectacle encouraged cinema-going as a routine habit, an utterly familiar social practice, underpinned by the idea of going out to 'be entertained', uplifted from everyday reality into a world of wish fulfilment. The documentary idea constructs a quite different social function for cinema, one which posits cinema as a means of communication, not a medium of entertainment.

In order to make further sense of the documentary idea, it is necessary to relate its development to another ideological struggle taking place on the terrain of cinema: the struggle to establish an authentic, indigenous national cinema in response to the dominance of Hollywood, or rather to the idea of Hollywood as an irresponsible cinema of spectacle and 'escapism'. In part, this is bound up with the more generalised fear of an encroaching mass culture, against which must be erected, in this case, a responsible and artistically respectable cinema. Indeed, as Alan Lovell has pointed out, the documentary movement 'captured the interest in film as an art that was developing in Britain in the late 1920s'.[5] The documentary film units thus become the site of a self-conscious exploration of intellectual and artistic ideas. Perhaps paradoxically, documentary is at the same time articulated in terms of 'realism'; hence Grierson's influential definition of the purpose of the documentary film: 'the creative interpretation of actuality'.[6]

Thus at the heart of the documentary idea is a powerful differentiation between 'realism' and 'escapism': between a serious, committed, engaged cinema, and mass entertainment. Further, this logic posits the 'realist' cinema, with its foundations in the documentary film movement, as the key point of reference in the call for an indigenous 'British' cinema. What should be remembered is that within British film culture, ideas of realism, of aesthetic experimentation and of national cinema are bound to a particular social-democratic conception of the possible function of cinema, and thus come to structure and delimit the possibilities of cinema in general in Britain. In particular, the conceptualisation of the role which cinema might play in a cultural programme for political change has predominantly

74

remained bound to the realist aesthetic as formed in and around the documentary movement in the 1930s.

In this context, it is worth examining in more detail the particular way in which the documentary movement wins over, but at the same time contains, the developing interest in cinema as an art in the 20s and 30s. Certainly, the movement is valorised in film cultural memory as the site of intellectual, artistic and aesthetic experimentation in the cinema. But there is also clearly a tension within the movement, which will develop into a more overt conflict, between this concern for aesthetic principles and experimentation and a concern for education and propaganda. It is significant, then, that in order to 'remember' Alberto Cavalcanti and Humphrey Jennings, two key figures within the documentary movement, it is necessary to remember *against the grain*, as it were, of dominant film cultural history. And yet it was Cavalcanti who took over the direction of the GPO Unit after Grierson's departure in 1937. Significantly, both he and Jennings took idiosyncratic routes into British documentary film-making. Cavalcanti had been very much involved with the French avant-garde cinema of the 1920s (his early films, such as *Rien que les heures*, had themselves been an early influence on British documentarists); and he was brought into the GPO Unit by Grierson expressly to develop the Unit's work on sound. Similarly, Jennings' career before he joined the GPO Unit had much more to do with the concerns of British modernism than with a belief in the importance of mass communication.[7]

The tension between aesthetic concerns and social concerns is by no means clear-cut: there is little sense of being able to say that this film is aesthetic, while that one is social. It is a much more complex series of shifting emphases, not simply within the films themselves, in terms of the strategies and devices of representation which they employ, but also in the writings, reviews, books, etc., which stress one particular way of making sense of a film rather than another. Although Grierson in retrospect talks of the 'quite unaesthetic purpose' of documentary,[8] it is clear that his earlier and highly influential definition of documentary as 'the creative interpretation of actuality' depends upon a strong aesthetic sense and purpose: this is no naive 'window-on-the-world' conception of documentary realism as mere record. On the contrary, it is an acknowledgment that it is aesthetic principles which determine the particular combination of sounds and images that make up a film, and which produce one desired view of the social world rather than another.

The subsequent separation of propagandist concerns and aesthetic concerns really needs to be understood in terms of the institutional context within which the documentarists were working, a context in which it became necessary to define themselves not as 'dabbling aesthetes', but as responsible politicians (for the purposes of their credibility within government and related circles) and responsible film-makers (for the purposes of their credibility with the rest of the film industry).

In fact, it is not so much that propaganda and aesthetics are separated – as if that were really possible anyway – as that one particular set of aesthetic strategies become synonymous with good propagandist film-making, as already suggested. What this means is that, as part of the process by which documentary realism comes to dominate thinking about cinema in Britain, films tend to be thought of only in terms of theme, character and subject matter: the manifest content of the film, as it were. This has produced a film culture which has been profoundly mistrustful of anything other than a particular de-dramatised naturalistic form: 'style' becomes something which gets in the way of the message of the film.[9] Thus documentary cinema is at the same time one of the key places where the idea of cinema as an art is taken up and explored, and the place in which, owing to a certain political necessity, such aesthetic experimentation is closed off. Hence the ossification of one particular aesthetic as the appropriate form for the development of a 'responsible, engaged

The idea of work: *Industrial Britain* (1933)

cinema', while exploration of other aesthetic forms is looked down upon as an *irresponsible* project.

How does this complex and often contradictory interweaving of social and aesthetic concerns work itself out in the films of the documentary movement? The social-democratic impulse proposes that the documentary film – and social documentation in general – fills an information gap in establishing communication between the state and the citizen of the new democracy, thereby constructing a 'public sphere'. The documentary film institutes a public gaze at public processes, where 'public' implies a sense of common, uncontested social activity and social knowledge. Rather than dealing with the desires of an individual hero-protagonist, which might, crudely, be seen as the work of the narrative film, the 30s documentary tends to deal with the work of a particular 'public' institution, or activity, that can be broadly perceived as *social*. Thus *Night Mail* (Basil Wright and Harry Watt, 1936, made for the GPO Film Unit) deals with one aspect of the work of the General Post Office (the night mail train from London to Scotland), clearly a *public* institution; while *Industrial Britain* (Robert Flaherty and John Grierson, 1933, made for the Empire Marketing Board) deals with the idea of work (industrial labour as continuing the age-old traditions of craftsmanship). In order to construct this idea of a common public sphere, labour must be taken out of the context of economic class relations: the interests of the capitalist class are transformed into the public interest. Thus *Housing Problems* (Edgar Anstey and Arthur Elton, 1935) is made to publicise the British Commercial Gas Association, who sponsored it. At this level, its focus is on the role of the gas companies in aiding slum clearances and the construction of new housing. Similarly, the party political government becomes subsumed into the idea of the benevolent state, above divisive politics (the GPO is simply a *public* institution). In the same movement, the documentary film addresses the spectator as a citizen of the nation, not as a subject of one or another antagonistic class, race or sex. The citizen is addressed as someone to whom this unitary reality is immediately explicable (a particular ideological position is rendered familiar, natural, common sense).

Many of the documentaries focus on a particular aspect of social life as a social problem – and, in particular, the idea of poverty as a social problem. Thus *Housing Problems* deals with slum housing, while *Enough to Eat* (Edgar Anstey, 1936, for the Gas Light and Coke Company) deals with poor nutrition. Again, the citizen is addressed as someone who has a role to play in solving the social problems presented in the films. *Enough to Eat* addresses a citizen whose duty it is to eat better, and to encourage others to eat better, as much

77

as someone who recognises it as the duty of the state to provide the material means for better nutrition. These social problems are removed from the arena of antagonistic power relations and depoliti-cised, and the films effectively construct the working class as victims deserving of 'our' (i.e., the public's) sympathy. At the same time, films like *Industrial Britain* draw on the undoubted influence of the poetic realism of Robert Flaherty's earlier 'anthropological' films, to construct the working class as heroes: such films gaze at the socially useful labour of Britain's artisans and craftsmen. Other films continue this tradition: *Coalface* (Alberto Cavalcanti, 1936, for Empo) looks at coal miners in this way, while *North Sea* (Harry Watt, 1938, for the GPO) does the same for fishermen. It is of course the smooth and benevolent functioning of the public institutions which can alleviate social problems and thus transform the victims into heroes in their assigned role in the democratic society.

One of the principal aesthetic strategies mobilised by the documentarists in this bid to articulate a public sphere is montage editing, as opposed to the continuity editing of the classic narrative realist film. This is itself indicative of the huge interest in Soviet montage cinema in British film cultural circles in the 1920s and 1930s. Indeed, montage becomes the defining characteristic of cinema as art, in Russia (at least in the late 20s), in Britain, and internationally, while the documentary units are the prime site for the exploration of montage in Britain. In fact, montage as it develops in the documentary movement is influenced as much by the rhythmic potential of the editing in *Turksib* (Viktor Turin, USSR, 1929) and *Berlin – Symphony of a City* (Walter Ruttmann, Germany, 1927) as it is by the work of the more well known Russian film-makers of the 1920s. Thus while the documentarists develop some of the editing and film construction ideas of Eisenstein, it is to produce a sense of unity and harmony rather than of conflict and contradiction. What is maintained is something common to almost all editing strategies – the emphatic effect of rhythm, tempo and momentum (some of the key terms in the film reviewing discourse of Grierson). At an intellectual level, the function of montage construction for the documentary movement is the ability to hold in play several different scenes of action (and indeed different times) at the same moment: in other words, to construct a much broader, more extended diegetic world. Thus, *Industrial Britain* does not concentrate on just one worker, but on many workers throughout Britain. This montage principle is mobilised right across the spectrum of documentary film-making in the 1930s.

To generalise, we might suggest that there are three dominant forms of the documentary as it develops in this period. There is the poetic documentary, in which montage is most foregrounded: *Industrial Britain, Song of Ceylon* (Basil Wright, 1934–5, made for the Ceylon Tea Propaganda Board), and *Coalface,* which was specifically conceived as an exploration of the possibilities of sound and image montage. It should be noted, however, that the poetic ambiguity of these films – the metaphorical and associative possibilities of the montage juxtapositions – are often contained by the imposition of a voice-over, which, as in the case of *Industrial Britain*, institutes a particular reading of the images. Second, there is the story-documentary, the forerunner of the television documentary-drama. This is particularly associated with the films worked on by Harry Watt, in which we can see an increasing use of certain narrative strategies and devices alongside montage constructions. Thus *Night Mail* is partly in the loose narrative form of 'a day (or night) in the life of . . . ', while there are stronger moments of narrative gathered around the figure of the new postal worker being initiated into his job. This work of narrativisation is extended in *North Sea*, where there is again a juxtaposition of continuity editing and montage editing techniques. This story-documentary strand will be picked up later in the chapter. Third, there is the instructional documentary, which finds its early embodiment in *Housing Problems*, a mixture of voice-over, interviews and a montage of illustrative images (there are few signs of shot matching, or reverse-field strategies, perhaps the key elements in narrative continuity editing).

In *Housing Problems*, the relation of the spectator of the film to the social problem of poor housing, and its solution in the slum clearance programmes and the rebuilding of new homes with gas appliances, is clearly regulated by the (upper middle-class) voice of authority in the voice-over which introduces and takes us through the film. That voice intervenes between the spectator and the diegesis, keeping us at a distance from the working-class victims of the film. In so doing, it sanctions a public gaze at these victims, rather than addressing the spectator as involved in and identifying with their emotional states. The voice-over thus situates the other, less authoritative voice-over (the voice of the councillor) and the various other discourses of the film – notably the discourses of the interviewees – and regulates their meanings in relation to each other. It also situates the spectator at a point from which all these varyingly private discourses are intelligible. In other words, as in the story documentary, the means by which one idea or activity is related to another, and the means by which one sector of society communicates with another, are constructed as natural, as being above the particular power relations which structure a social formation, and outside the control or jurisdiction of any individual citizen. But *Housing Problems* cannot simply be written off

The public gaze: *Housing Problems* (1935)

for the way in which it places the spectator in relation to the working-class protagonists in the film through this hierarchy of discourses. There is a remarkable freshness in the direct-to-camera interviews with working-class people. At the same time, there can be no unproblematic celebration of this film simply because it does extend its social discourse to the representation of working-class figures.

The range of documentary modes indicates the extent to which a certain aesthetic innovativeness is evident, albeit to differing degrees throughout the movement; but it also indicates the tensions and divergences which characterise the movement, and which become increasingly sharp towards the late 30s.

The documentary-realist tradition

The documentary idea, then, is built on a complex and often contradictory ideological terrain. A set of ideas and practices emerge which come to structure the possibilities and limitations of British cinema and British film culture: the attempt to articulate a public sphere; the attempt to construct a responsible, engaged cinema, which is also a *national* cinema; the working through of an idea of art cinema, and so on. At the heart of this cinematic-political discourse is a powerful differentiation, as we have seen, between 'realism' and 'escapism'. This is not, however, reducible to a distinction between 'fact' and 'fiction'. The aesthetic implications of Grierson's maxim, 'the creative interpretation of actuality', refuse such a reductionism, which is further complicated by the development of the story documentary form, which employs some of the devices and strategies of the narrative film – that is, the *fiction* film.

Within these terms, a familiar map of British cinema emerges, as a particular tradition of film-making is constructed, a tradition which thereby fulfils the 'realist vocation' of cinema. The tradition produces a particular reading of the period prior to the screening of *Drifters* in 1929: a reading which 'notes' Lumière as a potentially realist film-maker, which celebrates the work of Percy Smith and his *Secrets of Nature* series, and which picks up certain silent feature films for their 'realistic' qualities – that is to say, for their similarities to certain features of the documentary films of the 30s. The 30s are of course the period of the documentaries, and of certain feature films which again seem 'realistic' – some of Asquith's and Hitchcock's films for their attention to the surface details of English provincial life; films which construct as their object social problems such as poverty and unemployment (for example, *South Riding*, 1938, and *The Stars Look Down*, 1939).

The war years of the 40s are not the years of the Gainsborough melodrama, but that Golden Age when the documentary and the feature film momentarily come together and a truly national cinema seems to have been found (the wartime films of Ealing are perhaps the most widely known from this period). Most of the 50s are skipped over as a 'dead' period, except for one or two late offerings from Ealing, some of Grierson and Baxter's work at Group 3, and the Free Cinema films (and related polemical literature) of the mid-50s; until the tradition is once more fully renewed not in Hammer's monstrous eroticism, but in Britain's 'New Wave' – the Woodfall films, the social problem pictures, the 'kitchen sink' films (*Room at the Top*, 1958; *Sapphire*, 1959; *Saturday Night and Sunday Morning*, 1960; *A Taste of Honey*, 1961 – all of them British Film Academy Best Films for their year of release). Finally the documentary-realist tradition

81

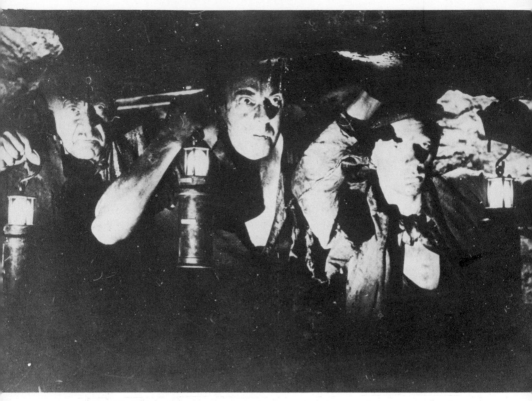

The realist vocation: Carol Reed's *The Stars Look Down* (1939)

finds its home in British television, in the early drama work of
Sydney Newman at ATV, series such as *Z Cars*, the documentary-
drama tradition and particularly the work of Ken Loach and Tony
Garnett, even the 'soap opera' tradition of *Coronation Street* and
Brookside, and indeed in the forms of television news, current affairs,
and straight documentary. This television work will in its turn have
an influence upon British cinema.

   To detail this tradition is not simply to list a series of films. It is to
draw attention to the ideological work involved in constructing this
tradition, the work of defining as synonymous a cinematic realism
and an indigenous cinema, and the work of repressing the traditions
of the gothic, the expressionist, the melodramatic, the 'magic' realist.
This work smoothes out the tensions which threaten to destroy the
appearance of a coherent and continuous evolutionary development
of 'British cinema'. Clearly, continuities do exist within the tradition,
but it is necessary to conceptualise the development of the tradition
in terms of a series of breaks and renewals within the discourse of

social and moral 'responsibility', and, correspondingly, within the documentary-realist aesthetic.

There is a constant attempt within the documentary-realist form to articulate a common, public sphere of responsible social activity, as distinct from the spectacular cinema of 'escapism', which apparently foregrounds individual desire and wish fulfilment. But the conjunction of a liberal humanist morality and a social-democratic politics insists also that a space be marked out within the public sphere for the expression of the private, the personal, the emotional, the individual. The history of British realism then becomes the history of the changing conceptualisation of the relation between the public and the private, between the political and the personal – thus between the state and the citizen (the 'man in the street', TV's 'viewer at home').

This developing relation involves different mobilisations of the devices and strategies of documentary and narrative fiction – of, respectively, the documentary's distanced public gaze at 'universalised' social processes and people, and the individuated private looks of the fictional protagonists in narrative cinema. That is to say, the documentary and the narrative fiction construct two relatively distinct systems of looking, which bind the spectator into the text in different ways. The narrative film tends to draw the spectator into the organisation of looks within the diegesis, within the world of the fiction played out for us 'up there' on the screen, by means of the devices of point of view, shot/reverse shot, and eyeline matching. In the documentary there is a quite different system of looks, which create a different relationship for the spectator to the figures on the screen: to put it crudely, the camera no longer looks from the position of diegetic figures. As John Caughie suggests, 'the figures of the drama exchange and reverse looks, the figures of the documentary are looked at and look on'.[10] The developing form of British documentary realism as an articulation of the public and the private is, then, dependent on the different ways in which these two systems of looking are combined in the films. This is never simply an aesthetic matter, since it also depends on the changing valorisation of the institutions of documentary and narrative film-making within the mainstream of British film culture.

In order to understand these shifts, it is necessary to return once more to the documentary movement in the 1930s. The period up to around 1937 is characterised by an uneasy separation between the two institutions of the documentary movement and the film industry's mode of highly dramatised spectacular narrative fiction. Around 1937, however, the form of this separation alters as a break develops within the documentary movement itself. Thus one section of the movement (associated with Grierson) argues in effect for a final severance of all links with the dominant institution of cinema: it argues for documentary as an instructional, educative mode of exposition, a mode which subordinates all other considerations to the clarity of the propagandist point. From 1937, this strand of the movement argues also for the creation or exploitation of a market – and thus a condition of spectating, or communicating – outside of and separate from that established by the exhibition practices of dominant cinema. The other strand or emphasis within the documentary movement, associated most clearly with the work of Cavalcanti and Watt, works not for the severance of documentary and narrative cinema, but for their convergence in the story documentary, which becomes perhaps the key representational form in wartime British cinema.

World War II and the Golden Age of British Cinema

The movement into the war years of the 40s is a movement into an ideological climate which requires the articulation of the public sphere as the sphere of a national interest immediately recognisable as transcending sectional interests; but there is also the requirement that the individual citizen should be in no doubt as to the importance of the assigned role which he or she must play. The 'national interest' must be able to accommodate the private and the domestic; it must be able to accommodate the emotional capacity of the individual, if necessary by demonstrating the irresponsibility of holding private, and particularly romantic, interests above the national interest. This complex balance is only achieved, in cinema, by the interweaving of the various documentary modes of address with the mode of 'realistic', studio-centred narrative fiction. In so far as these different modes can be distinguished, it is clear that the story documentary and the narrative fiction film are converging, both in terms of the aesthetic devices and strategies used, and in terms of the personnel involved (thus both Watt and Cavalcanti join Ealing Studios during the war).

Harry Watt's films for the GPO and Crown Film Units are perhaps the key examples of the story documentary tendency. The progressive narrativisation of the action in these films is finally sealed in his move to Ealing Studios, and the making of narrative features such as *Nine Men* (1943). *North Sea* (GPO, 1938) and *Target for Tonight* (Crown, 1941) can both be seen in terms of this move between documentary and narrative modes. *North Sea* deals with the difficulties faced by the men on a fishing boat caught in a storm on the North Sea, in order, finally, to demonstrate the work of the land-sea radio network run by the GPO in securing the safety of these men. *Target for Tonight* deals with the planning and execution of a

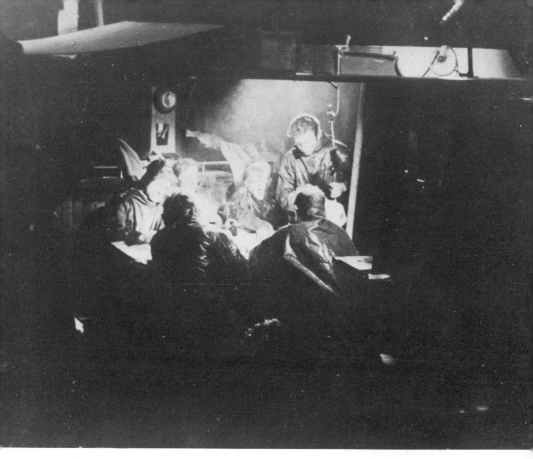

The national interest: *North Sea* (1938)

bombing raid on an enemy target, and the worry over the safety of
one missing aeroplane, which does finally limp home to base. To say
that these films narrativise their action is to indicate that there is
temporal development, and a structural movement from the definition of a goal to be achieved (the return home of the fishermen in
North Sea, the bombing of the target and the safety of those involved
in *Target for Tonight*), through various blockages to that goal, to the
successful fulfilment of the goal and textual closure. These films also
try to hold together two different forms of characterisation: on the
one hand, the stereotyping, or *typage* (another Soviet influence) of
the documentary film – that is, the casting of non-professional actors
who bear a physical resemblance to the social type to be represented;
and on the other hand, the psychological realism of the narrative
fiction film – that is, the progressive inscription of character with the
marks of a unique individuality. What remains from the early 30s
conception of documentary is an emphasis on the narrativisation not
of individual desire but of public (social) process. In many of the
story documentaries of the late 30s and early 40s, the power of the

state is visible only as the power to set in motion a chain of communication which has a double function: it prepares for the successful completion of an act in the national interest (the securing of a haul of fish in *North Sea*, the bombing of an enemy target in *Target for Tonight*) and, at the same time, it protects the private, sectional interests of a relatively individuated but tight-knit community (ensuring the safety of the fishing boat in *North Sea* by the actions of the land-sea radio network; investigating the missing aeroplane T for Tommy in *Target for Tonight*). The chain of command and the communications network established in *Fires Were Started* (Humphrey Jennings, 1943, Crown) and *Western Approaches* (Pat Jackson, 1944, Crown) can similarly be seen as instituting an image of the state as a benevolent entity, mapping and sustaining a set of relations between different sectors of society, and ensuring the smooth running of the public process.

As suggested, the form of the documentary is retained to the extent that the narrative is not organised around a single main protagonist, but employs a form of montage construction in order to map out a fuller world constituted in terms of the relations between a variety of groups within an extensive but delimited social system (in *North Sea*, the women and the domestic sphere, the 'lost' trawlermen at sea, their 'safe' colleagues and employers, and the staff of the radio station; in *Target for Tonight*, the full staff of the RAF, from messenger boy through pilot to top brass).

This contained multiplicity of interests demands a combination of montage and continuity editing; a combination of the distance of the establishing shot and the group shot (the public gaze) and the psychologisation of the point of view shot (the private gaze); and, overall, a combination of episodic montage construction and tightly causal narrative flow.

The parallel development of the studio-centred narrative film can be seen in a film like *Millions Like Us* (Launder and Gilliat, Gainsborough, 1943), which moves into the documentary-fiction mélange from the other end, so to speak. The film is a sort of popular history of the home front from the outbreak of the war; it concentrates initially on the members of one lower middle-class family, and in particular Celia, one of the two daughters, who eventually leaves home to live in a hostel and work at an aircraft engineering factory, along with many other such 'mobile women'. The narrative now concentrates on this new community, where Celia marries a young man from the RAF, who is later killed in action. It is only, in the end, the communal bonds of the hostel – and by implication the nation – which can hold Celia together. But the tight causal development of a goal-directed narrative and the psychological development of a

86

Nation as community: *Millions Like Us* (1943)

central hero-protagonist are constantly deflected and marginalised in
their inevitable progression towards textual closure, by a series of
devices and strategies derived from the documentary form. Thus
there is a dispersal of narrative attention on to a multiplicity of
narrative lines. The ideological effect of this is an articulation of
nation as responsible community *and* individual desire, an articulation which finds a place for both the public and the private, by
inserting the vulnerable individual within the protective communal
interest. It should be noted, however, that at the same time as this
holding together of public and private, there is a parallel but
contradictory movement of holding them apart. Again, this is the
product of an ambiguous tension between documentary and
narrative modes, modes which tend to engage the spectator in
different ways. Thus certain sequences depend entirely upon a
montage construction, such as the sequence showing the production
process of assembling a complete aeroplane (or the arrival of the

'mobile women' at the factory where they are to engage in the production of just one small part of the aeroplane engine). On the other hand, there are scenes which depend on the classical narrative editing strategies of moving from establishing shot to point of view shot, particularly through shot/reverse shot structures and eyeline matching.[11]

Obviously, the story-documentary is not the only mode employed during the war years. In addition, we can see in this period perhaps the fullest achievement of the poetic documentary mode in British film-making, in the work of Humphrey Jennings from *Spare Time* (1939) onwards, and particularly in his collaborations with the editor Stewart McAllister (for instance, *Listen to Britain,* 1942, Crown). With the partial exception of *Fires Were Started* (1943, Crown), his story documentary about an auxiliary fire-fighting unit in the Blitz, Jennings' films were resolutely organised on the principle of montage editing; both the more popular reviewers and the 'instructional' documentarists overlook or criticise the films, the former for lack of psychological engagement, the latter for ambiguity of propagandist message.

The third documentary mode feeding into the articulation of a national cinema in the war years is the form of the instructional documentary, the province of numerous shorts, 'Food Flashes', scientific and instructional films for the Armed Forces, etc. Significantly, this mode of documentary production is least written into the histories of cinema in this period. It is clear that the critical discourse developed by contemporary film reviewers, and reproduced in key surveys such as Roger Manvell's *Film*, favoured the mode of the studio-centred narrative film which drew on the realist aesthetic as developed around the documentary idea. These reviewers acknowledged the worthiness of the story documentary (while almost ignoring the instructional documentary) but complained of their lack of involvement in the action of such films – in effect, they were worried by the distancing effect of the public gaze. Their discourse expressed a need to interweave the emotionally engaging psychological realism of the strong narrative film with the social responsibility of the documentary's articulation of a public sphere.

Post-war developments
The ideological conditions of World War II had thus established the possibility of a remarkable convergence of documentary and narrative fiction modes but had also paradoxically set the terms for the consequent marginalisation of British documentary. Post-war documentary film-making, if one is to accept the dissatisfactions of

the *Sequence* generation of film critics, is overwhelmingly involved in the refinement of the public gaze in the form of the instructional and scientific documentary.[12] Further, the story documentary form had become more fully narrativised in the film-making practice of, notably, Ealing Studios, in the form of the 'realist' (as opposed to 'escapist') narrative feature film. (Interestingly, when Grierson returns to British film production in the early 50s, it is not in documentary but in feature film-making in the government-sponsored Group 3, which was seen as a training ground for new film-makers.)

The mainstream of documentary-realist film-making in the period between the end of the war and the mid-1960s is therefore narrative feature film-making. While these films continue to explore contemporary cultural and political discourses to some extent, and while they have clearly taken on board the morality of the realist aesthetic as articulated in the documentary idea, they must also now be seen as working within an established genre of British narrative cinema. There is an exploration of conventions of representation established in the conjunction of the documentary idea and a feature film industry working within the terms laid down by the Ministry of Information during World War II.

The immediate post-war period is crossed by two contradictory strands, which value differently the iconographic and thematic patterns of the wartime films, and, in particular, the moral strength of the idea of community. Ealing provides clear examples of both. On the one hand, there are those films which struggle to reproduce the wartime conditions of siege and insularity: once more, they assert and explore the idea of community, represented by a proliferation of narrative protagonists and a multiplication of incidental narrative lines (for example, *Whisky Galore!* and *Passport to Pimlico*, both 1949). On the other hand, there are those films which to some degree *assume* that community, that network of inter-relations, as already constructed, and go on to explore the possibility – or danger – of its deconstruction by the intrusion of violent and erotic forms of individual desire (*It Always Rains on Sunday*, 1947, and *The Blue Lamp*, 1950).[13] The threat of this deconstruction or dismantling of the assumed community seems to represent an anxiety over the post-war reassertion of private, sectional interests, an anxiety over the difficulty of producing a common sphere of public agreement. The public-private political relation embodied in the documentary idea seems to have been generically reworked into an emphasis on the community, and its most 'domestic' form, the family. Or, to be more specific, it has been reworked into the narrative convention of community, or family, versus individual: social responsibility

89

versus individual desire. This is of course a narrative structure utterly familiar from the genre of the domestic melodrama. Hence the possibility of seeing that key British film of the 40s, *Brief Encounter*, as both domestic melodrama and British realist film.

Narrative has also entirely subsumed the public gaze of the documentary. In these Ealing films specifically documentary *devices* are absent, although the strategies of a broad diegetic focus and montage construction are reworked in the narrative form of multiple plot lines and characterisations and episodic story construction. It is precisely the ossification of aesthetic conventions into a 'too familiar' generic pattern which seems to characterise the period of the early 50s. Ealing's project seems repetitive, nostalgic, even stagnant. By now, the interest of British film critics has turned to European cinema and in particular Italian neo-realism,[14] while straight documentary film-making seems to fail to engage with either 'popular' or intellectual concerns.

Two movements in the late 50s and early 60s, however, bring attention back on to the British realist tradition. Firstly Free Cinema, a series of film programmes at the National Film Theatre which included several documentaries made by young British film-makers, accompanied by various manifestos and polemics by the Free Cinema group; and secondly, the 'New Wave' cycle of feature films, from *Room at the Top* to *This Sporting Life*, and in particular the films of the Woodfall company. Once again, these movements constitute at the same time a break with and a renewal of the British realist tradition, or genre. They both conform to the expectations of the genre, and transgress them in limited ways, thus producing a new sense of freshness, vitality, reality. Free Cinema is perceived as, firstly, a radical challenge to the existing forms of documentary film-making, which the group saw as now part of the Establishment rather than as critical of it (which was how the 30s documentary movement was understood by its apologists); but also, secondly, as a challenge to the existing form of the feature film industry. Two of the leading voices and film-makers behind Free Cinema, Lindsay Anderson and Karel Reisz, had been centrally involved with the journal *Sequence*. Together, *Sequence* and Free Cinema constituted a reassertion of the concern with aesthetic questions which had initially contributed to the documentary project. Significantly, the one documentarist they did admire was Humphrey Jennings, always the most 'poetic' and least instructional of the earlier documentary film-makers.[15]

The Free Cinema films made by Anderson (*Wakefield Express*, 1952, *O Dreamland*, 1953, *Every Day Except Christmas*, 1957) and Reisz (*We are the Lambeth Boys*, 1959, and, with Tony Richardson, *Momma Don't Allow*, 1955) are all clearly distinct from conventional instructional documentaries. The exposition is much looser and more ambiguous, but there is still a clear reliance on montage construction and an interplay of the public gaze and private points of view. *Every Day Except Christmas,* about the workers at the Covent Garden market, also operates within the liberal humanist tradition of representing working people as dignified and heroic. But while this film looks at work, several of the others take as their object leisure: they worry over and ambiguously celebrate specific cultural forms. This is very much a renewal of the mass culture discourses of the 20s and 30s film culture, with a familiar anxiety over the erosion of traditional, organic culture by mass culture (for example, *O Dreamland's* vision of the working-class seaside resort, Margate). They seem also to pose the question of whether the newly emergent perception of 'spontaneous youth culture' (the jazz club in *Momma Don't Allow*) has come to replace the traditional forms of working-class culture as the site of 'real', 'authentic' cultural values. These

Public gaze and private view: Lindsay Anderson's *Every Day Except Christmas* (1957)

films emerge in, and articulate the concerns of, a new political-cultural climate, a new ideological formation: specifically, the culture of commitment and the founding of the new Left in the mid-50s. It is a climate in which cultural questions are clearly perceived by liberal and left intellectuals as political questions, and in which people from a broadly radical political position – and notably, for our purposes, Lindsay Anderson's liberal humanism – argue for the necessity and the duty of the artist to be clearly committed to the communication of a politically responsible set of values. Once again, the chosen form across the arts is conceptualised in terms of realism.[16]

For cinema, this engagement with the culture of commitment and the form of realism is worked out in terms of the possibilities of an established genre. In the 'New Wave' feature films (*Saturday Night and Sunday Morning, A Kind of Loving*, etc.), the political relation between the public and the private is once more explored in the generic form of the relation between the domestic community and the individual. The 'national community' of the war years has now become the 'traditional working-class community', which on the one hand is nostalgically valorised as the site of authentic cultural values and a responsible morality, but on the other hand is constructed as tainted by the encroaching mass culture, the culture of consumerism, affluence, social mobility – the culture of television. The community now constitutes the backdrop, the setting for the exploration of the psychological complexity of the (usually) young working-class male protagonist of these films. Both the community of the neighbour-hood, and its most domestic form within the genre, the family, have become intrusions on the private (sexual) life of the individual – now the hero of the film.[17]

The relations between the elements of the genre have almost, it seems, been turned upside down, in the period from the 40s to the 60s. An example: in 1943, in the Ealing film *The Bells Go Down*, a petty criminal eventually saves the life of his old enemy, the local policeman, and both individuals are fully inserted within the folds of the community. In 1950, in a later Ealing film, *The Blue Lamp*, the police force itself is the centre of the community, while a new form of criminality is identified: a delinquent and recklessly individualist criminality with no sense of moral responsibility, and a dangerous threat to the fabric and well-being of the community. By 1962, and *The Loneliness of the Long Distance Runner*, the petty criminal has become the hero, while the police and borstal staff, as the official representatives or at least managers of the community, are construc-ted as threats to the integrity of the individual.

The 'New Wave' films now *acknowledge* the separation of the individual from key political decision-making processes, and use the generic form to explore this social gulf as much in psychological terms (alienation as a state of mind) as in sociological terms. In the end, it does seem that social relations are marginalised in favour of personal relations, and the formal strategies of the genre are newly inflected towards this exploration of – if not fulfilment of – individual desires. The narratives are resolutely organised around a single central protagonist, a single psychology and subjectivity, and no longer require a multiplicity of plot lines. Vestiges of montage construction remain, both in the relatively episodic structures of the narratives, and in, for instance, the numerous montage sequences in Tony Richardson's films (especially *A Taste of Honey* and *The Loneliness of the Long Distance Runner*). Significantly, however, montage no longer constructs a common public sphere of social existence, but is directed towards the articulation of a private personal experience. Thus *Saturday Night and Sunday Morning* has a relatively episodic narrative structure not because it tries to hold together a variety of interlocking elements, but because it deals with loosely connected moments in the development of a character. Similarly, the montage constructions in Richardson's films produce a poetic experience of a state of mind – for instance, the montage of shots of the canal which a melancholy Jo walks beside in *A Taste of Honey*, or the montage of shots of the countryside as an 'ecstatically free' Colin goes running in *The Loneliness of the Long Distance Runner*. In other words, the function of montage construction has shifted from an articulation of the look of the documentary, the public gaze, to the privatised look of the narrative protagonist – that is, from an 'objective' statement of commonality and universality, to a 'subjective' impression of experience. It is this establishment of an intensified psychological realism which seems as remarkable in these films as their attempts to foreground working-class protagonists.

Running alongside this post-war development of documentary-realist film-making as a genre of narrative cinema in Britain is the incorporation of the documentary idea into the institutional form of television. A few points on television therefore seem in order. Firstly, realism as a specific aesthetic emerging from the documentary idea of the 1930s is one of the most pervasive forms in British television, cutting right across drama, documentary-drama, news and current affairs, and documentary itself, as well as numerous popular series and serials. Indeed, the very segmental form of television's flow reproduces the montage construction of the 30s documentary and the multiple plotting of the 40s realist feature films. This thorough domestication of the documentary idea allows television as an institution to take over the form of the public gaze: the ubiquitous TV eye casts its gaze round the world, and brings this world of public

Running free: Tom Courtenay in *The Loneliness of the Long Distance Runner* (1962)

affairs into the home, the private, domestic sphere of the viewer.[18] This gathering together of the documentary idea and the Reithian ethos of public service broadcasting (itself initially voiced in the same political-cultural climate as the documentary movement) continues the processes of post-war documentary-realist cinema: constructing a world of public affairs, while at the same time addressing the citizen – now the viewer at home – as separate from but influenced by that sphere. Television proposes itself as mediating between these two spheres of the public and the private. Hence the ideology of impartiality which determines the television schedules; and which allows the BBC in particular to represent itself as relatively autonomous of the state, and as above sectional interests – but able to communicate between those different interests.

Perhaps the most celebrated radical form of the documentary-realist tradition in television is the documentary-drama as developed by Loach and Garnett, among others. As John Caughie has noted, their aesthetic project is not dissimilar to the development of the story documentary and the marriage of documentary and narrative modes during World War II.[19] But of course the conditions are different: a national interest can no longer be so easily assumed or constructed. And, crucially, many of the documentary-dramas have been radically critical of those institutions which manage and regulate the public sphere (the police and the legal system in *Law and Order*; party political and trade union leadership in *Days of Hope*, the general provision of housing in *Cathy Come Home*). As such, the new marriage of documentary and drama forms has met considerable conservative resistance, something quite unknown in the 1940s.

Conclusion

One question that clearly stands out is whether the term 'realism' can have any consistency in relation to such a wide range of cinematic and televisual practices. In part, the term suggests a set of aesthetic principles common to almost all claims to realism, to do with questions of verisimilitude and motivation. At that level, this British tradition is not dissimilar to classic Hollywood cinema. But at another level, the 'realism'/'escapism' distinction suggests a certain nuancing or even transgression of the strategies used by Hollywood to achieve verisimilitude and motivation. This nuancing has been most noticeable in relation to theme and iconography: each successive realist movement in British cinema and television has been celebrated both for its commitment to the exploration of contemporary social problems, and for its working out of those problems in relation to 'realistic' landscapes and characters. In particular, since the 1930s, these films and television programmes have consistently been proclaimed as politically progressive because they extend the conventional social discourse, because they deal with working people. While the force of such representations cannot be denied, it should also be noted that the particular conventions of representation adopted tend to foreground not so much the issue of class as the issue of citizenship, and the idea of a universal humanity.[20]

Finally, in this history of, not exactly a genre, but a particular

95

conception of cinema and its social function, some note should be made of the new independent cinema which has developed in Britain in the last two decades. In a return to one strand in the documentary movement of the 30s, but perhaps in closer alignment with the workers film movement of the same decade, film-makers outside the film industry and the traditional institutions of the sponsored documentary have again proposed and struggled to construct a cinema which is independent of the ideological and economic frameworks of the dominant cinema, and which conceptualises cinema in terms of the possibility of a radical cultural-political function. For some this has involved working in ways which recall some of the strategies of the British realist genre (for example, Cinema Action, Amber, and, in a different way, Richard Woolley's social problem film *Brothers and Sisters*); for others it has meant radically breaking with the documentary-realist aesthetic and ideology, and rethinking the possibilities of (Soviet) montage through the ideas of, among others, Brecht and Godard.[21]

Notes

1 The Arts Enquiry, *The Factual Film*, London, PEP/Oxford University Press, 1947.

2 Alan Lovell and Jim Hillier, *Studies in Documentary*, London, Secker & Warburg/BFI, 1972, p. 35.

3 See, on documentary: Forsyth Hardy (ed.), *Grierson on Documentary*, new edition, London, Faber & Faber, 1979; Elizabeth Sussex, *The Rise and Fall of British Documentary*, Berkeley/London, University of California Press, 1975; Paul Rotha, *Documentary Film*, rev. ed., London, Faber & Faber, 1952; Eva Orbanz (ed.), *Journey to a Legend and Back: the British realistic film*, Berlin, Volker Spiess, 1977. For more critical analyses, see: Lovell and Hillier, op. cit.; Stuart Hood, 'John Grierson and the Documentary Film Movement' in James Curran and Vincent Porter (eds.), *British Cinema History*, London, Weidenfeld and Nicolson, 1983. On later British documentary-realist film-making, see: Roger Manvell, *Film*, rev. ed., Harmondsworth, Penguin, 1946; Basil Wright, *The Long View*, London, Secker & Warburg, 1974; Michael Balcon et al., *Twenty Years of British Film 1925–45*, London, Falcon Press, 1947; Roy Armes, *A Critical History of British Cinema*, London, Secker & Warburg, 1978; Lovell and Hillier, op. cit.; Orbanz, op. cit.; Sussex, op. cit.

4 Peter Wyeth and Don Macpherson, 'The Third Front', *Sight and Sound*, vol. 47, no. 3, Summer 1978, p. 143.

5 Lovell and Hillier, *Studies in Documentary*, p. 35.

6 John Grierson, 'The Documentary Producer', *Cinema Quarterly*, vol. 2, no. 1, Autumn 1933, p.8.

7   See Mary-Lou Jennings (ed.), *Humphrey Jennings: Film-maker, Painter, Poet,* London, BFI/Riverside Studios, 1982.

8   Hardy (ed.), *Grierson on Documentary*, p. 112.

9   I have developed this argument at greater length in 'Space, place, spectacle', *Screen*, vol. 25, nos. 4–5, July-October 1984.

10   John Caughie, 'Progressive Television and Documentary Drama', *Screen*, vol. 21, no. 3, 1980, p. 30.

11   For comparative analyses of similar wartime films, see Andrew Higson, 'Addressing the Nation: Five Films', in Geoff Hurd (ed.), *National Fictions: World War II in British Films and Television,* London, BFI, 1984; and Charles Barr, *Ealing Studios,* London, Cameron and Tayleur/David and Charles. 1977.

12   The film magazine *Sequence* was published between 1947 and 1953.

13   For analyses of these post-war Ealing films, see Barr, *Ealing Studios,* and John Ellis, 'Made in Ealing', *Screen*, vol. 16, no. 1, Spring 1975.

14   For an analysis of British film criticism in the 1940s, see John Ellis, 'Art, Culture and Quality: Terms for a Cinema in the '40s and '70s', *Screen*, vol. 19, no. 3, Autumn 1978.

15   For a more detailed analysis of Free Cinema, see Lovell and Hillier, *Studies in Documentary.*

16   See Robert Hewison, *In Anger: culture and the cold war,* London, Weidenfeld and Nicolson, 1981; and Jenny Taylor, 'Introduction: situated reading', in J. Taylor (ed.), *Notebooks/Memoirs/Archives: Reading and Rereading Doris Lessing,* London, Routledge & Kegan Paul, 1982.

17   For more detailed analyses of these 'New Wave' films, see John Hill, 'Working-class Realism and Sexual Reaction: Some Theses on the British "New Wave" ', in Curran and Porter (eds.), *British Cinema History.*

18   See John Ellis, *Visible Fictions,* London, Routledge & Kegan Paul, 1982.

19   Caughie, 'Progressive television and Documentary Drama', pp. 23–4.

20   For more detailed analyses of realism which have a bearing on the arguments developed here, see Ellis, *Visible Fictions,* pp. 6–10; Raymond Williams, 'A Lecture on Realism', *Screen,* vol. 18, no. 1, Spring 1977; Caughie, 'Progressive Television and Documentary Drama'; and Higson, 'Space, place, spectacle'.

21   For discussions of independent cinema, see Ellis, *Visible Fictions*; Simon Blanchard and Sylvia Harvey, 'The Post-war Independent Cinema – Structure and Organization', in Curran and Porter (eds.), *British Cinema History*; Rod Stoneman and Hilary Thompson (eds.), *The New Social Function of Cinema,* BFI Production Board Catalogue, 1979–80, London, BFI, 1981.

Julian Petley

THE LOST CONTINENT

Although things have improved somewhat since Peter Wollen's remark that 'the English cinema . . . is still utterly amorphous, unclassified, unperceived',[1] a major problem with much subsequent writing about the subject is its failure to maintain any critical distance from the still dominant realist aesthetic. The result is that words such as 'realism', 'realist' and 'realistic' still tend to be used in untheorised 'common-sense' fashion as if their meaning were quite unproblematic, their connotations *necessarily* and *essentially* positive and laudatory. Increasingly, however, this aesthetic has been submitted to scrutiny and criticism. Thus Andrew Higson: 'the central problem with so much writing on British cinema is precisely its allegiance to a particular realist aesthetic. The terms of that discourse must be unravelled in order to understand why *certain* British films have been vaunted and valorised, if the same seemingly trenchant conception of "British cinema" is not to be repeatedly reproduced . . . The institution of British cinema as an object for historical investigation needs to be re-conceptualised.'[2]

Of course, the vaunting and valorising of certain British films on account of their 'realism' entails, as its corollary, as the other side of the coin, the dismissal and denigration of those films deemed un- or non-realist. As Charles Barr has pointed out, 'the preference for a certain kind of realistic surface, for an "everyday" verisimilitude, has been a recurrent factor in English film criticism and has inhibited response to a wider range of films with an allegorical or poetic dimension'.[3] These form an other, repressed side of British cinema, a dark, disdained thread weaving the length and breadth of that cinema, crossing authorial and generic boundaries, sometimes almost entirely invisible, sometimes erupting explosively, always received critically with fear and disapproval. Like repressed libidinal forces these films 'form a current running underground, surfacing

98

only intermittently, for instance in the line of lusty Gainsborough Productions of the 40s (Margaret Lockwood as *The Wicked Lady*) and in the films of Michael Powell. Such work finds itself commonly written off as being in bad taste . . . . Increasingly, in a kind of reversal of Gresham's Law, "good taste" drives out bad, and rules absolutely in the early 50s, leaving sex and violence – the very phrase still retains its scandalous overtones – so repressed and deplored, so unintegrated, that they deviously force their way up again like the *Dead of Night* visions – most spectacularly in the explosion of British horror films, a cycle to which Powell contributes with the most execrated film of his career, *Peeping Tom*.'[4]

The problem, however, is not simply the lack of certain signifieds (summed up in the phrase 'sex and violence'); it is also a question of the British cinema's *apparent* signifying paucity, formal invisibility, and concomitant stress on 'content'. Thus, for instance, Raymond Durgnat remarks that 'if a clearly marked personal style is one's criterion of interest, then few British films reward the concern given to such directors as Dreyer, Buñuel, Franju and Renoir';[5] while Thomas Elsaesser notes the lack of directors with 'a specifically cinematic eye . . . an awareness of form and style'[6] and bemoans the fact that the majority 'appear neither to have mastered the subtler techniques of the "liberal" dramaturgy which formed the distinction of Hollywood – the mixing or balancing of audience sympathies, the visual and dynamic definition of a moral or psychological conflict, the symbolic use of detail and particular to indicate universals, the thematic use of colour and 'scope, the transformation of descriptive information and dialogue into action, "genre" stylisation through strong plots – nor did they develop a "reflective" style in the manner of the European film-makers with their highly intellectualised use of cinematic space, camera positioning and montage, or the free handling of narrative fictions. . . . What is so rare in the British cinema, in other words, is a film where the subject is undercut by the style, and the story subverted by the point of view from which it is narrated.'[7]

It could be argued, of course, that 'auteurism' is not a particularly useful or fruitful approach to the British cinema, and that Elsaesser is simply confusing his own critical preference for one particular mode of signification with cinematic specificity itself. None the less, both these writers are pointing towards a set of commonly perceived tendencies in British cinema which could be summed up as follows: a hostility towards stylisation, the hegemony of the 'documentary spirit', the elevation of 'contents' over 'forms', isolation from wider European artistic trends (and especially from modernism in its various forms) from the 1920s onwards, the conflation of moral prescriptions with aesthetic criteria, or the elevation of the former over the latter, so that, in Andrew Tudor's words, 'aesthetics is reduced to morally prescribed social theory . . . the measures of aesthetic taste are limited to two: the social responsibility of the film, and its effectiveness in achieving this socially responsible aim'.[8]

It could also be the case, however, that the absences and lacks bemoaned by Durgnat and Elsaesser are, to an extent, more apparent than real; that they may be partly a function of a certain way of conceptualising the British cinema. The realist aesthetic is so deeply ingrained in British film culture that it not only renders 'deviant' movies either marginal or completely invisible (Roger Manvell's survey in 1969 of 'New Cinema in Britain' dismisses the horror cycle in a single footnote), but also imposes a 'realist' framework of interpretation like a stifling blanket over the entire area of British cinema. The result is that films come to be perceived 'naturally' and 'commonsensically' within this realist framework, and that the realist pantheon dominates most writing about British cinema and thence goes on to determine what is thought 'worth' circulating in distribution on 16mm and video, what films are preserved in the National Film Archive, and so on. (According to Charles Barr, *Witchfinder General* [Michael Reeves, 1969], vilified at the time of its release but in fact one of the towering achievements not simply of British horror but of British cinema *tout court*, was explicitly turned down by the National Film Archive selection committee.[9])

It is impossible to discuss British cinema, and especially its 'deviant', non-realist strands, without reference to dominant critical discourse of one kind or another, be it weighty works of film history or the film criticism in the daily and Sunday press. Indeed, it's impossible to talk about cinema *as a whole* without reference to discourse of this type. As Christian Metz argues, the institution of cinema consists of three machines: the industrial machinery of production, distribution and exhibition; 'the mental machinery – another industry – which spectators "accustomed to the cinema" have internalised historically and which has adapted them to the consumption of films';[10] and finally the 'writing machine' which valorises certain films and, in the same moment, the same action, downgrades and devalues others. As Metz so aptly states, 'it is often to exalt a certain cinema that another has been violently attacked'.[11] The relevance of Metz's formulations to the study of the British cinema has been clearly signalled by Andrew Higson: 'the dominant discourse of British film criticism "writes" British cinema into film cultural memory as a realist cinema, thus effectively blocking off other ways of conceptualising the institution and working through the question of national cinema. It is now necessary to treat this writing machine as an integral part of British cinema as a national institution, in order to see how "British cinema" becomes constituted as such."[12] This is why, here, I shall concentrate as much on the 'writing machine' as on the objects which fuel it and which it, in turn, helps to produce.

In Britain, as elsewhere, the cinema's birth and early years were attended by a whole range of influences (developments in photography, painting, theatre, music hall, etc.) not all of which pushed it in the direction of the 'realistic'.[13] It is necessary at this point, however, to distinguish between two rather different uses of the term 'realism'. The first is wide-ranging: here a work is considered realist simply if it is a lifelike representation or a faithful copying of reality. Since most films ask us to believe that their diegetic world is 'real', these films can all be considered, in Colin MacCabe's phrase, as 'classic realist texts'.[14] The second use is narrower and more or less synonymous with the term 'naturalist', indicating a searching out and detailed observation of elements of the social environment frequently excluded from systems of representation. In cinematic terms this normally means an emphasis on working-class or 'problem' subjects, films like *Saturday Night and Sunday Morning* (Karel Reisz, 1960) or *Poor Cow* (Ken Loach, 1967).[15]

All the films discussed in this chapter can be described as more or less 'realist' in the first sense. However, this is obviously an extremely broad category. To quote Higson: 'Clearly, different films, and particularly different genres, mark themselves as *more* realistic, or *more* fantastic. . . . All dominant cinema, all "classic realist texts" work as fantasy for the spectator, but at the same time they make greater or lesser claims on our rapture and credibility, continually playing on this thrilling tension between believing that the diegetic world is real, and recognising that it is fantasy, between seeing the fiction as present and recognising it as absent.'[16] It is with films in which the 'fantasy' element is at its most obvious that this chapter is primarily concerned, films which, in generic terms, resolve themselves into horror, science-fiction, melodrama and 'film noir'. In authorial terms the situation is obviously more complicated – Hitchcock, Powell and Pressburger, and Losey are obvious candidates for consideration. Alberto Cavalcanti, Thorold Dickinson and Michael Reeves certainly rate a great deal more attention than is usually paid to them; and subjects for further research, even if only as 'metteurs en scène' in some cases, might include Arthur Crabtree, John Gilling, Sidney Hayers, Seth Holt, Freddie Francis, Don Sharp, Vernon Sewell, Brian Clemens and Gordon Hessler, to name but a few.

As Rachael Low has observed of British cinema, 'the germs of all types of films were present from the beginning',[17] and no one reading the first three volumes of *The History of the British Film* could fail to be struck by the sheer heterogeneity of the early British cinema's output: fantasy films *à la* Méliès, melodramas of all kinds, detective stories, crime dramas and even the occasional horror film all flourished alongside the more literary and 'respectable' fare for which British cinema has become (in)famous. Undoubtedly this latter aspect had become predominant by the coming of sound and was not infrequently noted at the time; but undoubtedly too the sheer *extent* of its domination has been exaggerated by the exclusions, elisions and distortions of the 'writing machine', already fully in operation by this time and already fuelled by the realist aesthetic.

Not everything, however, can be blamed on a certain mode of conceptualising British cinema history. Certain factors have indeed militated against the full development of the subjects, genres, styles and directors under consideration in this chapter, and these factors are much the same as those which have hindered the development of cinema *as a whole* in Britain. Firstly, the British cinema, even in its early days, became increasingly dominated by literary and theatrical conceptions. The writer, though badly paid by Hollywood standards, tended to be regarded as the major creative force in film-making, and most screenplay writers were primarily men of the theatre or literature. Thus adaptations and original screenplays alike tended not to be conceived in specifically cinematic terms. Similarly, most film actors came from the stage, and there was very little attempt to build up a star system on the Hollywood model. Many producers and directors also had a theatrical background, and the overall result of this theatrical dominance was that 'many films were nothing more nor less than celluloid records, of very varying adequacy, of whole stage productions, with stage directions very little changed by the director'.[18] Even the popular melodrama which, in America, furnished Griffith and others with such cinematically fruitful material, seems to have had a less productive relationship with cinema in Britain. Secondly, the activities of censorship apparatuses and various 'moral' lobbies cannot be underestimated, and their effectiveness acted only as an unfortunate spur to the increasingly 'respectable' aspirations of sections of the British film industry. Orwell's remark that 'the genuinely popular culture of England is something that goes on beneath the surface, unofficially and more or less frowned upon by the authorities'[19] is nowhere more applicable than in the case of the British cinema. Thirdly, there is the perennial question of foreign, and especially American, penetration of the home market. Even before the First World War, this was well under way; and there was a general recognition among audiences and

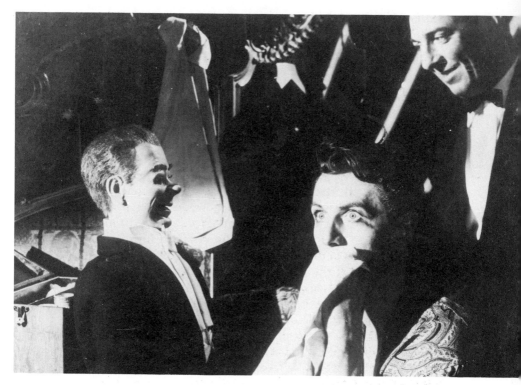

The fantasy element: Michael Redgrave in one of the Cavalcanti episodes of *Dead of Night* (1945)

producers alike of the inferiority of much British product. Whether in the development of the star system, the feature-length narrative, the popular genres, or the 'art film', British films all too often seemed tame and unexciting compared to American or Continental imports.

Clearly there lies at the root of these factors a mélange of economic and ideological determinants. Much of the industry's plight in these early years can of course be put down to a simple lack of capital, which meant that it failed to develop an adequate production base, failed to compete effectively either abroad or on the home market, and had to rely to a large extent on talent whose primary source of remuneration lay elsewhere (i.e. in literature and theatre). However, as Rachael Low suggests: 'It is legitimate to wonder whether there was not a certain innate snobbery, which hampered the British film's development as an industry. . . . Creative energy does not always require high pay to sting it into action. If films had been socially accepted as an outlet for imaginative impulses as readily as they were, for example, in America, more talent might well have been attracted by the new medium of expression for its own sake. One is left with the impression that in Britain the film had to overcome the resistance of a particularly inelastic social and intellectual pattern. In France and Italy the film might be a younger sister of the arts, in America art itself. In England it was a poor relation, and, moreover, not a very respectable one.'[20]

In this respect the case of Alfred Hitchcock is particularly instructive. By the early 20s (the beginnings of Hitchcock's film career) modernism in all the arts was already well established on the Continent, but British cultural life was barely touched by it. Abroad, film was already widely accepted as an art form in its own right, and in France, Germany and Russia film theory was already beginning to be developed. In Britain, however, to quote Rachael Low: 'Far from valuing the film, the cultural and academic elite was either hostile or indifferent to it and, being ignorant of its nature, quite unaware of its potential as an art.'[21] Gradually, however, a number of critics and film-makers did begin to take an interest, if not in film theory then at least in 'the art of the film', and to consider film as at least a *potential* art form. Hardly surprisingly, their attentions focused primarily on Russia and Germany, the former for its development of montage and the idea of cinema as socially useful (this attracted the burgeoning documentarists), the latter for its *mise en scène* ('Expressionism'), in which cinema's quality as 'art' was seen to reside. Significantly, in the mid-20s both Herbert Wilcox and Michael Balcon were involved in a number of Anglo-German co-productions, though admittedly for primarily financial rather than aesthetic reasons, and these and other German links produced such 'Germanic' works as *Moulin Rouge* (E. A. Dupont, 1928), *Shooting Stars* (Anthony Asquith, 1928), *Underground* (Asquith, 1928), *Piccadilly* (Dupont, 1929), *The Informer* (Arthur Robison, 1929) and *After the Verdict* (Henrik Galeen, 1929).

It was in Germany, as part of a W & F/Emelka deal initiated by Balcon, that Hitchcock made his first complete features as a director, *The Pleasure Garden* (1926) and *The Mountain Eagle* (1926). Though Hitchcock's most famous British films – *Blackmail* (1929), *Murder* (1930), *The Man Who Knew Too Much* (1934), *The 39 Steps* (1935) and *The Lady Vanishes* (1938) – all belong to various areas of the crime genre, his British work actually spans a number of genres, from the romantic (*The Pleasure Garden*) and the musical (*Waltzes from Vienna*, 1933) to the comic (*The Farmer's Wife*, 1928). What unites all his work, however, is his individual style, his personal vision, and his penetrating explorations of the film as a means of expression. Critical reactions to his work were distinctly schizophrenic. Rachael Low is particularly perceptive on this point. Noting the common class background of the new cinephiles, she remarks that 'because of their background and upbringing they tended to have a certain veneration for abroad as the natural home of taste and culture, and an attitude of condescension to the predominantly lower and middle-class British film industry. . . Had Hitchcock been German, Russian or French, had he even presented himself as a more conventionally bohemian figure, he would almost certainly have been taken more seriously. As it was, the rather ordinary man, working first in humdrum Islington and later at Elstree . . . was tagged with a grudging label "very clever entertainer, but not an artist",[22] a tag that later evolved into the bathetic label 'the master of suspense'.

Hitchcock's imaginative and inventive handling of narrative structure was regarded merely as ingenious continuity, and the consensus was that he was a clever-clever technician with nothing to say and a rather dubious and 'inartistic' interest in manipulating audiences' emotional reactions. Moreover, the workings of the realist aesthetic meant that Hitchcock's films tended to be valued for what today seem bizarre and even perverse reasons. Thus *The Ring* (1927) is greeted by the trade paper *The Bioscope* (6 October 1927) as 'a truthful and unglamorised picture of hard-working fairground folk, and also of the boxing ring, presented with a richness of incidental detail', while the same paper (8 March 1928) calls *The Farmer's Wife* 'an excellent picture of rural life thirty or forty years ago'. The concomitant of this attitude is, of course, the dismissal and denigration of those Hitchcock films which do not lend themselves to such an essentially sociological approach: the charge here is of trivial content decked out with self-consciously 'tricky' form. John Grierson furnishes a particularly extreme, but not entirely unrepresentative, example of this approach in his review of *Murder* (in the *Clarion*, October 1930) in which patronising and denigrating references to 'Hitchcock's cleverness' and 'talkie novelties' add up to a dismissal of Hitchcock as 'no more than the world's best director of unimportant pictures'. He does, however, find things to admire in the director: 'Hitchcock is the only English director who can put the English poor on the screen with any verisimilitude. . . . He is the one director who is familiar with them to the point of genuine observation.' There then follows what must be the most off-beam prescription in the history of film criticism: 'Will Hitchcock, for a change, take counsel of Arnold Bennett and give us a film of the Potteries or of Manchester or of Middlesbrough – with the personals in their proper place and the life of a community instead of a benighted lady at stake?'

Hitchcock was fortunate. He left Britain and was able to work successfully in a more congenial cinematic climate. His work, including his British period, has received the attention it so richly deserves, from a number of different perspectives,[23] so that truly bizarre films such as *Rich and Strange* (1932) and *Number Seventeen*

(1932), both maligned at the time of their original release, can now be viewed without the distorting lenses of the realist aesthetic. By the 30s, however, this aesthetic was well established and crossed a number of divisions in the critical community, as witness the following review of *Jew Süss*: 'With all the sympathy in the world for the suppressed Jew, I fancy that there are other problems worthy of being tackled at some expense by our native film industry. At the cost of being repetitious, I suggest that there is still unemployment, there is still shipbuilding, and there is still farming. We have an industrial North that is bigger than Gracie Fields running round a Blackpool funfair. We have a fishing fleet or two and a railway system, and some fairly acute problems of education.' Grierson again? No, C. A. Lejeune in the *Observer* in 1934.[24] Of course, it was the 30s which saw the birth of the British documentary movement, although this, it should be remembered, had its distinctly formalist side in Len Lye, Alberto Cavalcanti and Humphrey Jennings, whose relations with the 'realists' were often less than comfortable.

Undoubtedly one of the major victims of the realist aesthetic is Michael Powell, one of the British cinema's few indisputable 'auteurs' in the full sense of the term. To say that his work has been seriously compared with that of Minnelli, Godard, Welles, Gance and Vidor should be indication enough of the problems which his cinema raises for the native writing machine. For Powell explores a very different dimension of 'Englishness' that is almost diametrically opposed to the cold, hard empiricism which lies at the cultural root of the realist aesthetic: Powell's ancestors are not Mill, Locke and Hume but Romanticism and the Gothic. His work takes in almost mystical conjurations of the English countryside (*A Canterbury Tale*, 1944); Ossian-esque evocations of the wild Celtic spirit (*The Edge of the World*, 1937; *I Know Where I'm Going*, 1945; *Gone to Earth*, 1950); and above all, weird delvings into sexual pathology, as in *Black Narcissus* (1947), surely one of the most truly *hysterical* films ever made, and his masterpiece *Peeping Tom* (1960) whose appalling treatment at the hands of the British critics virtually ended Powell's directorial career in Britain, furnishing an excellent example of the very real *power* of the writing machine in Britain.[25]

Powell's best known early work, *The Edge of the World*, about the depopulation of the Scottish islands, was well received, being praised by Grierson and compared by C. A. Lejeune to Flaherty's *Man of Aran*. However, both the subject-matter and the style of Powell's films soon began to cause consternation, and he, like Hitchcock, rapidly acquired the label of 'mere technician'. The dominant view is best summed up by Raymond Durgnat, Powell's earliest and most perceptive British champion: 'Michael Powell has been fashionably

'Surely one of the most truly *hysterical* films ever made': Michael Powell's
Black Narcissus (1947)

dismissed by critics as a "technicians' director", a virtuoso of the
special effect, with a joltingly uneven story sense, for whom, indeed,
a narrative was only an invisible thread permitting the startling
juxtaposition of visual beads. To observers of the simplistic distinction between "style" and "content", he seemed a stylist and a
rhetorician, camouflaging an absence of idea by a weakness for
grandiose, out-of-context effect.'[26] But it was not just the supposed
formal 'excesses' that proved too much for the British critics; more
disturbing still were Powell's excavations of the frequently seamy,
steamy underside of English stiff-upper-lippery, excavations that
took him into the distinctly unfashionable, infra dig but, of course,
highly productive, realm of melodrama. As Durgnat notes, 'Powell
lived in a class and a country which suspects, undermines, is
embarrassed by, emotion',[27] and so it is hardly surprising that his
films, which fairly overflow with emotion, mysticism even, should
raise such a storm. The irony is, of course, that had Powell been
anything other than English he would not have made the films that he
did: like English horror films they are simply the recto to the verso of

the empirical tradition and its attendant realist aesthetic. Perhaps the last word here should go to Durgnat: 'He remains the upholder, through its lean years, of the Méliès tradition. His films shed not a little light on English thought and the English soul, in its restraints, its pusillanimity, its nostalgia for a German Expressionism, its coy amorality. . . . They relate to . . . a spectacular cinema which asks the audience to relish the spectacle *as such*, to a school of "Cinema" which is always exquisitely conscious of not only its cinematic effects but its cinematic *nature*.'[28]

Of course, it is precisely this kind of formal self-consciousness, this self-reflexive spectacularity, working to mark the fictional world as a world of fantasy, allied to an uneasy working over of normally repressed or elided ideological tensions within the text, that has attracted the attention of various theorists to the hitherto critically despised genre of the melodrama; in the wake of productive work on Hollywood melodrama,[29] attention has recently been turned to the indigenous product in the shape of Gainsborough melodrama.

Extremely popular during the latter days of the war and throughout the second half of the 40s, Gainsborough's output was prolific. It included 'problem' films such as *Good Time Girl* (David MacDonald, 1948), *When the Bough Breaks* (Lawrence Huntington, 1947) and *The Boys in Brown* (Montgomery Tully, 1949), 'films noirs' like *The Upturned Glass* (Lawrence Huntington, 1947) and *Daybreak* (Compton Bennett, 1948), costume melodramas in the shape of *The Man in Grey* (Leslie Arliss, 1943), *The Wicked Lady* (Leslie Arliss, 1945), *Caravan* (Arthur Crabtree, 1946), *Jassy* (Bernard Knowles, 1947), and contemporary melodramas like *Love Story* (Leslie Arliss, 1944), *Madonna of the Seven Moons* (Arthur Crabtree, 1944), *The Seventh Veil* (Compton Bennett, 1945). Hardly surprisingly, most of these films were desperately disliked by the critics, and *Daybreak* and *Good Time Girl* fell foul of the censor too. Sue Aspinall and Robert Murphy argue that the contemporary critics regarded Gainsborough's 'energetic, florid and often determinedly un-realistic films as an unhealthy aberration'[30] and cite overwhelming evidence to back up this claim. Thus Dilys Powell found them 'inferior films on trivial conventional themes, trivially handled – undeserving of the popular success they have won',[31] while William Whitebait complained that 'with *Madonna of the Seven Moons* we slip back almost as far as it is possible to slip. It is notably bad. . . . Everything in *Madonna of the Seven Moons* is treacly: characters, dialogue, situation'.[32] Meanwhile Simon Harcourt Smith in *Tribune* states that 'perhaps because I am, by inclination at least, an historian, *The Wicked Lady* arouses in me a nausea out of proportion to the subject',[33] while after the making of *Good Time Girl* Herbert Wilcox called on producers to make 'what one might call open pictures, happy, unclouded pictures. We do not want sadism, abnormality and psychoanalysis. That sort of thing is no good for the average audience – they do not understand it and in most cases do not want to understand it'[34] (Gainsborough's box-office receipts suggest precisely the reverse).

As in the case of Powell, the critics' complaints centre on two factors: the films' lack of 'realism', and their alleged 'unhealthy' quality. However, from a different critical perspective, one not hinged on the realist aesthetic, Gainsborough's visceral vitality, its lack of concern with historical accuracy and verisimilitude, its flouting of conventional notions of good taste, its overt working away at ideological problems specifically related to sexual desire, all appear as positive, productive factors. As Sue Aspinall states, 'costume melodrama did not ask to be taken for reality. It was unashamed fantasy, drawing attention to its own lack of realism precisely through its use of cliché-ridden dialogue and extreme characterisation'.[35] Phoney accents, artificial, studio-bound sets, repetitive forms, the general avoidance of naturalist technique and historical 'documentation', all work to produce a certain detachment in the spectator. Furthermore, to quote Sue Harper, 'the effective, spectacular aspects of *mise en scène* are foregrounded to produce a vision of "history" as a country where only feelings reside',[36] and it is the very vagueness of the settings, their precisely 'fantastic' quality, that makes all sorts of 'extreme' behaviour possible, behaviour that would never have got past the censor if presented in a more 'realistic' framework or genre.

During the 40s there was a strong movement among certain sections of the film industry and the critical fraternity to create a distinctively British 'quality film', the nature of which has been perceptively analysed by John Ellis.[37] Discussion of the 'quality film' is beyond our scope here; however, reference to Ellis' citation of C. A. Lejeune's remark that 'the test of all good technique is unobtrusive service', and to his capsule distillation of the 'quality film' as 'a unified and purposeful whole; it has the poetry and logic of a smooth flowing pattern; it controls the seduction of the photographic in the interests of a visual narrative; it adopts a restrained yet adult tone'[38] should amply demonstrate that the films with which we are concerned here define themselves precisely *against* this particular notion of 'quality'. Such films, especially melodramas and 'films noirs', were produced in quantity throughout the late 40s and early 50s, and their current 'invisibility' can only be put down to the malign workings of the 'writing machine'.

It is not simply a question of rediscovery (or rather, in many cases, discovery) but, more to the point, one of redefinition. Take, for example, the output of Ealing, often regarded as expressing a rather cosy, conventional, petit-bourgeois vision of England. This may be true enough of some of the studio's output but it is hardly an adequate description of its entire range. Even a cursory glance will reveal discordant elements, such as the work of Robert Hamer, or Cavalcanti's story of Nazi invasion *Went the Day Well?* (1943) which, as Charles Barr remarks, 'continuously undermines the seductiveness of cosy English façades',[39] a process in which Cavalcanti's highly formalised style plays a key role. Similarly it was Ealing which produced one of the British cinema's most stylish and disturbing supernatural thrillers, *Dead of Night* (1945), notable particularly for the formal expressivity of the Hamer and Cavalcanti episodes. The underrated *Pool of London* (Basil Dearden, 1951) and *Nowhere to Go* (Seth Holt, 1958) are both excellent examples of 'film noir', while *Saraband for Dead Lovers* (Basil Dearden, 1948) is a costume melodrama *à la* Gainsborough. Perhaps most fascinating of all is *Frieda* (Basil Dearden, 1947), ostensibly a film about post-war

Gainsborough melodrama: *Jassy* (1947)

Anglo-German reconciliation, but in fact a searing, full-blooded and often extraordinarily violent domestic melodrama. As Barr notes, 'all kinds of conflict seem to be seething just below the rational humanist surface',[40] and occasionally the masked, suppressed emotions burst through in a most startling fashion, notably in a brutally relentless fight scene and in the film's darkly delirious climax in which Frieda is rescued from drowning (just) in a bizarre sequence whose Gothic/Romantic overtones evoke nothing less than the horror genre.

During the late 40s and early 50s Britain produced a fine crop of 'films noirs' (sometimes with the aid of exiles from the Hollywood blacklist) which match many of their Hollywood counterparts in terms of formal stylisation, sheer physical brutality, urban sleaze and underlying existential pessimism. Examples such as *Odd Man Out* (Carol Reed, 1947) and *The Third Man* (Reed, 1949) are well known but merely the tip of the iceberg. We can add, from a long and potentially fascinating list, *Mine Own Executioner* (Anthony Kimmins, 1947), *They Made Me a Fugitive* (Alberto Cavalcanti, 1947), *For Them That Trespass* (Cavalcanti, 1948), *Noose* (Edmond T. Greville, 1948), *No Orchids for Miss Blandish* (St. John L. Clowes, 1948), *Brighton Rock* (John Boulting, 1949), and the various spiv movies discussed elsewhere in this book; also *Obsession* (Edward Dmytryk, 1950), *Night and the City* (Jules Dassin, 1950), *The Woman in Question* (Anthony Asquith, 1950), *Give Us This Day* (Dmytryk, 1950), *Secret People* (Thorold Dickinson, 1951), *The Long Memory* (Robert Hamer, 1952), *The Man Between* (Carol Reed, 1953). As in the United States, this sub-genre extends sporadically into the late 50s and early 60s to take in such exotic late blooms as *Hell Drivers* (Cy Endfield, 1958), most of Losey's work up to and including *The Criminal* (1960), and interesting stragglers such as *Yield to the Night* (J. Lee Thompson, 1956), *Hell is a City* (Val Guest, 1960), *Payroll* (Sidney Hayers, 1961) and *Four in the Morning* (Anthony Simmons, 1965).

Like so many 'noir' directors in Hollywood, Losey in England was an alien in an often inclement environment, on which he turned a particularly searing and unflattering eye. In turn his early work was generally either ignored or reviled as baroque, hysterical or melodramatic. To state that his work has been compared to Aldrich, Fuller and Brecht should in itself give some indication of his reception by the British critical establishment, whose dislike of the visceral, sheerly *physical* quality of much American genre cinema was matched only by their horror of artists who mix art and politics (and left-wing politics at that!). Significantly, Losey's least typical and most literary British film, *The Go-Between* (1971), was also the most unreservedly popular with the critics. Losey's early British work also

Losey's *The Damned* (1962), made for Hammer

includes an extraordinary melodrama in the Gainsborough mould,
The Gypsy and the Gentleman (1957), and a strikingly bleak and
sombre horror film for Hammer, *The Damned* (1962), which carries a
powerful anti-nuclear charge. Not for nothing does Durgnat call
Losey a 'philosophical stylist':[41] even his most minor films express
his own particular vision of the world, and do so in a style which owes
a good deal to the strengths of Hollywood syntax, as well as to other
more personal influences. Certainly they come across as peculiarly
'un-English'. Whereas native English cinema tends to tone down
emotional 'excess' and to regard melodrama as a pejorative term,
Losey tends to play *up* the passion and play *down* the touches of
'realistic' detail so beloved by the critical consensus. Thus Losey's
early films tend to resolve themselves into a series of high-pressure
temps forts, in which stylistic elaboration is notable by its obvious
presence as opposed to its discreet absence, as witness in particular
Blind Date (1959) and *Time Without Pity* (1956), the latter existing at
screaming point for its entire length.

For the country which produced Mary Shelley, Lord Byron, Bram Stoker, Anne Radcliffe, Charles Maturin, Matthew Lewis, M. R. James, Algernon Blackwood, William Hope Hodgson and William Beckford, Britain was peculiarly slow in developing the horror film and the whole area of fantasy cinema. (Undoubtedly, factors mentioned earlier such as American penetration, censorship, and dominant notions of taste and quality, played a key role here.) Nevertheless, even from its earliest days the British cinema showed a certain predilection for the fantastic, many early examples being inspired by a desire to exploit the seemingly magical potentialities of moving film *à la* Méliès. Thus, for example, *Photographing a Ghost* (George Albert Smith, 1897), *The Big Swallow* (James Williamson, 1901), *The Clown Barber* (Williamson, 1899), *Voyage of the 'Arctic'* (R. W. Paul, 1903), *Alice's Adventures in Wonderland* (Cecil Hepworth, 1903), *D.T.'s or the Effects of Drink* (William Haggar, 1905), to name but a very few. Meanwhile the numerous films about fire, on one level at least, bear witness to the beginnings of cinema's long love affair with scenes of destruction, which reaches its climax in the disaster movie: witness *Sensational Fire Engine Collision* (1898), *Plucked from the Burning* (R. W. Paul, 1898), *Fire!* (Williamson, 1902), *Firemen to the Rescue* (Hepworth, 1903) and so on. Similarly,

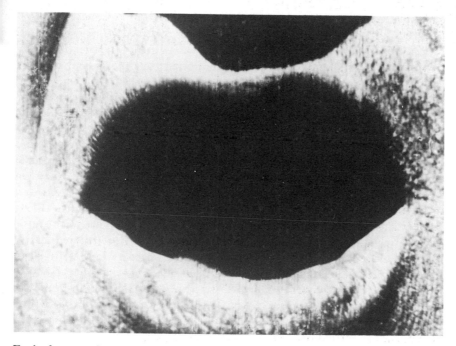

Early fantasy: James Williamson's *The Big Swallow* (1901)

various films about speed demonstrate cinema's early involvement in the business of providing visceral thrills, for instance *Views from an Engine Front* (Hepworth, c. 1900), *Down Exeter Incline* (Warwick Trading Company, 1898) and *Monorail* (R. W. Paul, 1898).

Early examples of horror proper, as opposed to fantasy or 'trick films', would include *The Mistletoe Bough* (Clarendon, 1904), *The Haunted Curiosity Shop* (R. W. Paul, 1906), *The Basilisk* (Cecil Hepworth, 1914), *The Man Without a Soul* (George Loane Tucker, 1916), and *The Sorrows of Satan* (Alexander Butler, 1916). One of fantasy cinema's recurrent favourites, *She*, was filmed for the first time by Will Barker in 1916 and again by Leander de Cordova in 1925, while the first British Sherlock Holmes film, *A Study in Scarlet* (George Pearson) appeared in 1914. Strictly speaking, the Holmes stories are tales of ratiocination and detection but their articulation, both literary and cinematic, often veers towards the Gothic: witness *The Hound of the Baskervilles*. Also of interest from the point of view of the fantastic is the 1915–1917 *Ultus* series, the British cinema's answer to the Fantômas and Judex films in France. Two versions of *The Ghost Train* (Geza von Bolvary, 1927, and Walter Forde, 1931) deserve mention as early examples of comic spookiness, while *High Treason* (Maurice Elvey, 1929), *The Tunnel* (Elvey, 1934) and *Things to Come* (William Cameron Menzies, 1936) represent relatively rare British ventures into science-fiction.

During the late 40s and early 50s the faltering vein of indigenous cinematic horror and fantasy had almost completely dried up and many American examples were banned outright by rigid censorship. Isolated works appear here and there, however, such as the fascinating first episode, *In the Picture* (Wendy Toye), of the portmanteau film *Three Cases of Murder* (1955), *Queen of Spades* (Thorold Dickinson, 1949), *Corridor of Mirrors* (Terence Young, 1947), *The Monkey's Paw* (Norman Lee, 1948), *Pandora and the Flying Dutchman* (Albert Lewin, 1950), *Miranda* (Ken Annakin, 1948) and the first British vampire movie of the 50s, *Mother Riley Meets the Vampire* (John Gilling, 1952).

As is now well known, the beginnings of the meteoric rise of the British horror film, aptly described by David Pirie as 'the only staple cinematic myth which Britain can properly claim as its own',[42] are marked by Hammer Films' adaptations, both directed by Val Guest, of Nigel Kneale's immensely successful television serials *The Quatermass Xperiment* and *Quatermass II*, and by *The Curse of Frankenstein* (Terence Fisher, 1957) and *Dracula* (Fisher, 1958). The sheer volume of material that followed, the remarkable quality of much of it, and the tremendous public response, all demonstrate that a peculiarly British lode of considerable richness was being mined, one which censorship had for years almost completely sealed off. As Jean-Paul Török notes in the second of his seminal articles on 'H-Pictures': 'Horror has become in Britain a new and clearly defined cinematic genre with its own rules and styles. There is much talk now of Free Cinema. However, by its power of suggestion, its frenzy, its invitation to voyage towards the land of dark marvels and erotic fantasy, isn't the English horror film the real Free Cinema?'[43] The shrieks of the critics were almost as loud as those of Dracula's victims,[44] but fortunately, and for once, their protestations were in vain (except, of course, for their 'success' in virtually ending Michael Powell's British career), and there can be little doubt that the increasingly liberal moral climate of the 60s played a key role in finally allowing this long repressed area of British cinema to flourish as never before. Thanks to David Pirie and Raymond Durgnat, British horror cinema has actually managed to achieve in its own native culture some of the critical attention it so richly deserves, so I shall confine myself here to a few general observations.

First, the existence of a flourishing popular genre provided, along the lines of the Hollywood model, a framework of regular opportunity, a productive space, in which to work. Thomas Elsaesser's description of the horror genre as 'a temporary refuge for aesthetes, idealists and visionaries'[45] is clearly borne out by the filmographies of Powell, Losey, Holt and Reeves, the last situating his entire small but impressive *oeuvre* within this particular field. As Pirie observes: 'The case of Reeves clearly indicates that by the middle of the 1960s the horror genre was just about the only part of the British film industry vital enough to really have a chance of sustaining new directorial talent at grass-roots level . . . it did represent an established cinematic field in Britain, where almost for the first time the aspiring film-maker could work within a tentative cultural tradition. What was more, it was a tradition that by about 1966 had lost some of its original rigidity and was beginning to hunt for new talent and new ideas.'[46] Just how far presumed audience familiarity with generic conventions allows the determined and inventive director or script-writer to go is illustrated by the extraordinarily complex narrative structures of *Scream and Scream Again* (Gordon Hessler, 1969) and *Demons of the Mind* (Peter Sykes, 1971), while the opportunities for sophisticated parody are excitingly exploited by *Captain Kronos, Vampire Hunter* (Brian Clemens, 1972). It should also be remembered that it was in the horror genre that Polanski first found work in Britain, with *Repulsion* (1965) and *Dance of the Vampires* (1967).

Secondly, British horror of the 50s and 60s is a great deal more than the output of Hammer. Companies such as Amicus, Tigon, Tyburn and Anglo-Amalgamated also produced a notable body of work.

More or less concurrently with Hammer's (re-)discovery of Dracula and Frankenstein, we find fascinating specimens from elsewhere such as *Corridors of Blood* (Robert Day, 1957), *Grip of the Strangler* (Robert Day, 1958), *Blood of the Vampire* (Henry Cass, 1957), *Fiend Without a Face* (Arthur Crabtree, 1958), *Jack the Ripper* (Robert Baker/Monty Berman, 1959), *Circus of Horrors* (Sidney Hayers, 1959), *Horrors of the Black Museum* (Arthur Crabtree, 1958) and, of course, *Peeping Tom*. Of these films, several ran into censorship problems, and several were shot in two versions – a hot one for less censorious countries and a cool one for the natives. Even by modern standards there is something peculiarly disturbing (and peculiarly English) about these films, a sensation of powerfully negative, barely suppressed desires, in which sexuality, violence and death are inextricably linked, almost dripping off the screen. Török remarks that 'here we arrive at horror degree zero . . . a morbid complaisance with the macabre, with the corruption of the flesh, and with the sadistic pleasure of transgressing the final interdict of death', concluding that the importance of films such as *The Flesh and the Fiends* is that they 'lay bare the mechanisms of the pleasure which we take in them'.[47] These are the films which Pirie calls Sadian, but which could perhaps more accurately be termed Selwynian, after the eighteenth-century aristocrat George Augustus Selwyn whose fascination with sights of suffering was legendary. (It should also be noted that 'le vice anglais' refers as much to *watching* flagellation and other violence for sexual pleasure, as to having it inflicted upon one.[48])

Thirdly, Hammer is a great deal more than the various Gothic cycles. Its output includes a 'Hitchcockian' pathology cycle, featuring films such as *Taste of Fear* (Seth Holt, 1960), *Paranoiac* (Freddie Francis, 1962), *Hysteria* (Francis, 1964), and *The Nanny* (Holt, 1965), and a cycle of exotic fantasy which takes in films such as *She* (Robert Day, 1964), *Slave Girls* (Michael Carreras, 1966), *When Dinosaurs Ruled the Earth* (Val Guest, 1969, based on a treatment by J. G. Ballard), and one of Hammer's most bizarre and underrated works, *The Lost Continent* (Michael Carreras, 1968). There are also such fascinating excursions into history as *The Stranglers of Bombay* (Terence Fisher, 1959) and *Rasputin – the Mad Monk* (Don Sharp, 1965).

With the passing of the horror cycle, the British cinema lost the last sustained body of work of the kind which this chapter has attempted to explore. The reasons for this are economic rather than ideological and are obviously intimately related to the decline of the British cinema as a whole. It also needs to be pointed out, however, that the so-called New British Cinema, with its orientation towards naturalism, the small screen and the literary script, is hardly a fertile seed-

The romantic agony: *The Company of Wolves* (1984)

bed for the kind of cinema discussed here. Worse still, the new climate of censoriousness whipped up by the 'video nasty' moral panic has spilled over into film censorship, making this a particularly inopportune time for any British film-maker to venture into horror. It is hard to imagine a masterpiece like *Death Line* (Gary Sherman, 1972) being made today, for instance. Similarly, many of the horror films discussed above would not be passed uncut, if at all, on video in Britain today.

On the other hand, the signs are not all hopeless. Films such as *Xtro* (Harry Bromley Davenport, 1983) and *The Company of Wolves* (Neil Jordan, 1984) show that the British cinema's repressed underlife still flares from time to time, while John Boorman has produced a consistent body of work which does not fit in easily with any conventional notions of 'realism'. And, of course, there are *other* ways of attacking the realist aesthetic than those discussed here; these are the province of sections of the independent sector (discussed elsewhere) and also, to some extent, of television (and especially

Channel 4) where the anti-realist battle is now being carried on in ways very different from those discussed above. Finally, and perhaps most importantly, there is the growing assault on the 'writing machine', a task barely begun as yet but decidedly on the agenda. One suspects that if the institution of the British cinema could be radically reconceptualised and wrested from the grasp of the still tenacious realist aesthetic, then the films discussed in this chapter would look less like isolated islands revealing themselves, and more like the peaks of a long submerged lost continent.

Notes

1   Peter Wollen, *Signs and Meaning in the Cinema,* London, Secker & Warburg/BFI; Bloomington, Indiana University Press, 1969, p. 115.
2   Andrew Higson, 'Critical Theory and "British Cinema"', *Screen,* vol. 24, no. 4–5, July-October 1983, pp. 91–3.
3   Charles Barr, 'Straw Dogs, A Clockwork Orange and the Critics', *Screen,* vol. 13, no. 2, Summer 1972, p. 21.
4   Charles Barr, *Ealing Studios,* London, Cameron and Tayleur/David and Charles, 1977, pp. 57–8.
5   Raymond Durgnat, *A Mirror for England,* London, Faber & Faber, 1970, p. 4.
6   Thomas Elsaesser, 'Between Style and Ideology', *Monogram,* no. 3, 1972, p. 5.
7   Ibid., pp. 9–10.
8   Andrew Tudor, *Theories of Film,* London, Secker & Warburg/BFI; New York, Viking Press, 1973, p. 75.
9   Barr, 'Straw Dogs, A Clockwork Orange and the Critics', p. 30.
10   Christian Metz, 'The Imaginary Signifier', *Screen,* vol. 16, no. 2, Summer 1975, p. 19.
11   Ibid., p. 21.
12   Higson, 'Critical Theory and "British Cinema"', p. 81.
13   Cf. Michael Chanan, *The Dream That Kicks,* London, Routledge & Kegan Paul, 1980.
14   Cf. Colin MacCabe, 'Realism and the Cinema', *Screen,* vol. 15, no. 2, Summer 1974, and 'Principles of Realism and Pleasure', *Screen,* vol. 17, no. 3, Autumn 1976.
15   For a more detailed discussion on this point, see Raymond Williams, *Keywords,* London, Fontana, 1976; 'A Lecture on Realism', *Screen,* vol. 18, no. 1, Spring 1977; 'Realism, Naturalism and Their Alternatives', *Cine-Tracts,* Autumn 1977–Winter 1978.
16   Higson, 'Critical Theory and "British Cinema"', p. 91.
17   Rachael Low, *The History of the British Film, 1896–1906,* London, Allen and Unwin, 1948, p. 46.
18   Rachael Low, *The History of the British Film, 1906–1914,* London,

Allen and Unwin, 1949, p. 130.

19   George Orwell, 'The Lion and the Unicorn', in *Collected Essays, Journalism and Letters*, Vol. 2, London, Secker & Warburg, 1968, p. 78.

20   Low (1906–1914), pp. 137–8.

21   Rachael Low, *The History of the British Film, 1918–1929*, London, Allen and Unwin, 1971, p. 305.

22   Ibid., pp. 305–7.

23   Eric Rohmer and Claude Chabrol, *Hitchcock*, Paris, Editions Universitaires, 1957; Raymond Durgnat, *The Strange Case of Alfred Hitchcock*, London, Faber & Faber, 1974; Donald Spoto, *The Art of Alfred Hitchcock*, New York, Hopkinson and Blake, 1976; Maurice Yacowar, *Hitchcock's British Films*, Hamden, Connecticut, Archon Books, 1977.

24   Quoted in Paul Rotha and Richard Griffith, *The Film Till Now*, rev. ed., London, Vision Press, 1949, p. 549.

25   Cf. 'The Scandal of Peeping Tom', in Ian Christie (ed.), *Powell, Pressburger and Others*, London, British Film Institute, 1978.

26   Ibid., p. 65.

27   Ibid., p. 73.

28   Ibid., pp. 73–4.

29   Cf. *Monogram*, no. 4, 1972; *Movie*, no. 29–30, 1982; *Screen*, vol. 18, no. 2, Summer 1977; *Wide Angle*, vol. 4, no. 2, 1980.

30   Sue Aspinall and Robert Murphy (eds.), *Gainsborough Melodrama*, BFI Dossier no. 18, London, British Film Institute, 1983, p. 1.

31   Ibid., quoted p. 6.

32   Ibid., quoted p. 71.

33   Ibid., quoted p. 74.

34   Ibid., quoted p. 10.

35   Ibid., p. 29.

36   Ibid., p. 40.

37   John Ellis, 'Art, Culture and Quality – Terms for a Cinema in the Forties and Seventies', *Screen*, vol. 19, no. 3, Autumn 1978.

38   Ibid., pp. 27–8.

39   Barr, *Ealing Studios*, p. 31.

40   Ibid., p. 75.

41   Durgnat, *A Mirror for England*, p. 234.

42   David Pirie, *A Heritage of Horror*, London, Gordon Fraser, 1973, p. 9.

43   Jean-Paul Török, 'H-Pictures', *Positif*, no. 40, July 1961, p. 49.

44   For the most sustained example of the dominant Anglo-Saxon approach to horror cinema see Derek Hill, 'The Face of Horror', *Sight and Sound*, vol. 28, no. 1, Winter 1958–9.

45   Elsaesser, 'Between Style and Ideology', p. 9.

46   Pirie, *A Heritage of Horror*, pp. 155–6.

47   Török, 'H-Pictures', pp. 46–7.

48   For further discussion of this fascinating topic see Mario Praz, *The Romantic Agony*, London, Oxford University Press, 1970.

Brian McFarlane

A LITERARY CINEMA?
BRITISH FILMS AND BRITISH NOVELS

A literary title acquired by a Hollywood studio was habitually referred to as a 'property'. These days, the term 'property developer' has taken on sinister connotations, suggesting one who engages in the brutal transformation of a fondly regarded site into something rich and strange – and inferior. Those serious-minded persons who lamented the cutting in half of *Wuthering Heights* in William Wyler's 1939 film, or who berated MGM for updating the costumes of *Pride and Prejudice* (1940) by thirty years to suit Greer Garson's figure, would no doubt regard 'property developer' as just the term for those vulgarians engaged in Hollywood adaptation of the classics. The British cinema, however, has drawn as frequently on the novel as the American cinema, without rousing so much wrath on the grounds of violating the spirit or letter of the original.

If British cinema has been markedly literary, as the American cinema – similarly indebted to the novel – has generally not been, this is due as much to the *kind* of adaptation as to the number. There has not often been a radical approach to the original material but, rather, a characteristic tendency to be awed by or to trade on the prestige and popularity of the source novels, and the result has often been to contribute another unadventurous element to the British cinema at large. There is no reason why an adaptation should, *per se*, be any more or less exciting than a film based on an original screenplay, but in fact the bold treatment of a novel (for instance, Tony Richardson's *Tom Jones* or Ken Russell's *Women in Love*) has been the exception. More often, British adaptations have exhibited a decorous, dogged fidelity to their sources, content to render through careful attention to their *mise en scène* the social values and emotional insight of those sources rather than subjecting them to critical scrutiny or, indeed, to robust exploitation. To think of MGM in its heyday, the Hollywood studio most consistently associated with the prestige adaptation, is to recall at least as vividly that studio's 'house style' (opulent decor, lustrous camerawork, the generating of star vehicles) as the fact that so many of its major films were derived from novels. In contrast, the standard British film version of the novel has been a prime example of those pervasive qualities of 'good taste, characterised by restraint, understatement and sophistication' which Alan Lovell identified as the British cinema's 'negative reactions' to the more dangerously flamboyant and vigorous aspects of Hollywood.[1]

In its record of the first fifteen years of British cinema, Denis Gifford's *British Film Catalogue* rarely attributes a screenplay or source credit of any kind, but significant changes start to occur around 1910. If cinema grew out of less sophisticated entertainments, its mainstream has, from this time onward, seemed headed towards the representational richness of the nineteenth-century novel, and it is certainly the case that, once having established itself as a primarily narrative form, British cinema started to use the native novel tradition as a vast resource. This pattern has been sustained. In the early years of sound there would be a sudden but short-lived falling-off in the number of novels adapted and – predictably – a corresponding upsurge of film versions of plays. In 1922, 70 films (23 per cent of the total output) had been novel adaptations; in 1930 there were only 9 (5 per cent of the total), none of them of any consequence as films, with A. E. W. Mason as the only source name of the slightest literary eminence.[2] By 1935, however, the number of literary adaptations had risen to 36 (26 per cent of the total of feature films for that year). There would be a similar sharp decline in the war years, with no more than nine adaptations in any of the years from 1940 to 1946, a period in which British cinema was in important ways more directly in touch with the national life than at any other time; but this decline was again short-lived, and the established proportion of novel adaptations was quickly restored. With the exception of the war years themselves, those periods in which such adaptations have most strongly dominated coincide with what are commonly seen as the most fruitful periods in the history of British cinema generally: they include the post-war 1940s, and the 'realist' period from roughly 1959 to 1963.

The Silent Period

The British silent film adaptations I have seen suggest several tentative generalisations and, in their range, a foreshadowing of the decades ahead. There was, at first, a stripping down of the plot of the original to its bare bones. The difficulties imposed by this process – ensuring narrative clarity, retaining some sense of character in figures reduced to a few fleeting appearances – varied from author to author. Given that many early adaptations ran for an hour or less, it is

The Passionate Friends (Maurice Elvey, 1922), adapted from H. G. Wells

surprising that film-makers were not more daunted in their dealings
with Dickens. What makes for absorbing reading in an 800-page
novel may not easily adjust to the exigencies of an hour-long film.
That the Cecil Hepworth-Thomas Bentley film of *David Copperfield*
(1913) appears to move at a cracking speed is not due to fluent
camerawork or editing but to its dispensing with character elaboration and its reducing of narrative to a skeleton framework, sometimes
at the expense of motivation and logical development. Eight years
later Maurice Elvey's *Bleak House* begins with a disclaimer that
suggests he was alert to the problem: this film, we are warned, will
focus on only one of the many stories to be found in the novel (Lady
Dedlock's). In fact, Elvey is still not ruthless enough in view of the
film's running time of 68 minutes. There are still too many
characters, many of them inadequately developed and their connections with each other obscure, suggesting perhaps that the film-
makers were counting on some degree of audience familiarity with
the text. However, in his 1922 adaptation of H. G. Wells' *The
Passionate Friends,* Elvey very successfully reduces the original to

essentials of plot and character, cutting himself adrift from the exegetic *longueurs* and awkward narrative mode of one of Wells' most sterile, didactic novels. In this case, the stripping down, perhaps inevitable in adaptations, particularly silent ones, works in favour of dramatic tension, since what is lost often bore only tangentially on the central situation.

If the cinema's future was to lie with narrative, then there was clearly value in a tried and trusted plot. Plot and rudimentary character drawing were the aspects of novels which were most readily amenable to film treatment and these were what silent film-makers seized on. As well as prestige and popularity, it seems likely that early film-makers saw the value of established plots before screenwriting developed as a sub-branch of the art of the cinema. This was, of course, not peculiar to British cinema at this or any other time. By the end of the silent period, the adaptation had become a staple of British cinema; and by the end of this period, the main sub-genres of adaptation were established, and would persist. They include: the classics (above all, Dickens), the thrillers (Conan Doyle, Edgar Wallace, later joined by Christie, Fleming and Deighton); the empire-boosters (A. E. W. Mason, John Buchan, etc., whose influence in cinema persists long after one would have supposed their ideological positions no longer fashionable); the upper-middle-brow novel (Wells, and, later, Maugham and Graham Greene, among many others); the regional story (Arnold Bennett, Hall Caine, followed by Winifred Holtby, Stan Barstow *et al*); and the popular best-seller (ranging through various levels of respectability to include the likes of Baroness Orczy and Ethel M. Dell, doyenne of 'the kind of fiction classed as day-dreaming'[3]).

It had become quite clear in the silent cinema that there was little correlation between the quality of a novel and that of a film derived from it – and little reason why there should be. Few would argue the superiority of Wells, let alone Mrs Belloc Lowndes, over Dickens; the fact remains that *The Passionate Friends* and *The Lodger* (1926) are infinitely more accomplished films than the Dickens adaptations referred to. Perhaps the length and narrative complexity of Dickens works against his fluent adaptation; perhaps the films suffer from the too reverent approach to major 'classics'; but, perhaps most important, the pleasures of Dickens' characters and episodes are rhetorically encoded so that they are less susceptible without serious loss to transference to the screen. Less stylistically distinctive authors may transfer better because there is less that is intransigently verbal to be lost. The silent cinema's passion for the classics seems, at least with hindsight, a doomed venture. It seems not to have realised that much of their pleasure lay in the authorial voice which largely eluded

Point of view: *Tom Brown's Schooldays* (Rex Wilson, 1916)

– and continues to elude – film adaptation, and in the dialogue given
to the characters which, obviously, silent cinema could not make
much of. It has become a cliché that films derived from second-rate
fiction are more likely to be successful *as films* than those derived
from classics. The silent screen was already offering some evidence of
this, as it staked out the literary territory and dug with results that
reflected, not the prestige of its sources, but the varying degrees of
film-makers' command of the screen's representational mode.

In fact, the history of British film adaptations from 1910 to the end
of the silent period is really the history of the development of what
Noël Burch has called the 'Institutional Mode of Representation'.[4]
That is, many of the points of narrative technique one might note
about these films would apply equally to contemporary British films
which were not adaptations. *David Copperfield* is a good example of
primitive film – little camera movement, no scene dissection, no use
of close-up – whereas *Tom Brown's Schooldays* (1916) reveals some
neat continuity cutting (from faces peering into a shop to their
owners entering), a clear use of a point-of-view shot as a girl watches
boys fighting, a move away from the tableau-like frontality of
Copperfield, and some vestigial scene dissection. We are, that is,
getting *into* the picture. *Bleak House,* though still plot-heavy, has one
tensely dramatic scene (in which the lawyer Tulkinghorn confronts

Lady Dedlock with news of a former lover's death) which gains its power from fluid editing involving changes of camera angle and a discreet use of close-up. On the evidence of *Bleak House, The Hound of the Baskervilles* (1921), and *The Passionate Friends,* Elvey appears to have had at this stage more instinctive 'feel' for cinema's narrative capacity than Hepworth. *Comin' thro' the Rye* (Hepworth's 1923 adaptation of Helen Mather's novel) is full of long, slow fades instead of, for example, seamless reverse-field cutting, and suggests that though Hepworth had been around longer, and not to diminish his pioneer's contribution, he had learnt less than Elvey. In their transferring and adapting of novels to the screen in the 20s, there can be little question as to who had the superior grasp of the new medium as a purveyor of an old story.

My reference to the way the novelistic pleasures of dialogue and the authorial voice necessarily eluded the silent film-maker (the latter, of course, largely eludes *any* film-maker) leads me to note how much use is made of the *written* word in the silent adaptation. Even more than most silent films, those adapted from literary sources were likely to feel the need for verbal assistance in narrative clarification. I refer to the use of both inter-titles and diegetic writing. The way the former are used suggests uncertainty about what their best function might be. In *David Copperfield,* each sequence is introduced by a summarising and linking title. There are no dialogue titles at all, and the effect of the inter-titles is that the film resembles a series of tableaux – David Runs Away to Dover, The Routing of Uriah Heep, etc. Without the explanatory titles, a good deal of the speedy, over-populated narrative would be largely incomprehensible. *Tom Brown's Schooldays*, directed by Rex Wilson from his own screenplay, uses its inter-titles for dialogue as well as exposition, and in one unusual instance a conversation between Tom and his friend East is conveyed by means of their inset faces at the upper corners of the title frame mouthing the words recorded in the frame. This device, though artificial, does maintain a continuity sometimes vitiated by the use of long dialogue titles. By 1922, Elvey minimises the potential disruptiveness of long dialogue titles in *The Passionate Friends* by his visual representation of the dialogue sequences, which rely a good deal on alternation within and between segments. And Hitchcock's *The Lodger*, from Mrs Belloc Lowndes' thriller, the latest and much the most distinguished of the British silent adaptations I have seen, uses comparatively few dialogue titles, its narrative control being effected in other ways.

As for diegetic writing: letters, newspapers, and notices of various kinds frequently act as bearers of crucial narrative information. Sometimes these are presented in eye-straining medium close-up

125

(like the 'CAREFUL – HE BITES' placard round David Copperfield's neck); sometimes the camera closes in on an insert without any diegetic motivation; sometimes, as film-makers acquired an ampler sense of the cinema's narrative capabilities, such writing would be the subject of 'proper' scene dissection. Elvey's *The Hound of the Baskervilles* makes much use of the written word: a death notice in a newspaper, a marriage certificate, and Watson forever writing letters to Holmes. These are sometimes shown as 'vignettes' (a masking and highlighting effect common in the period), but generally presented as part of the narrative rather than merely inserted. In *The Passionate Friends* such writing is presented in fully naturalistic close-up, and, by the time Hitchcock is adapting *The Lodger*, the close-ups of typewriters tapping out the story of the seventh victim, and of the newspaper placards announcing this, are subsumed into a fluently edited sequence which is a model of narrative clarity achieved wholly in visual terms.

The Late 30s

In the prolific film-making years from 1935 to 1939, the percentages of feature films derived from novels were 25, 27, 25, 41, and 54 respectively.[5] The adaptations were mainly from popular novelists like James Hilton and A. J. Cronin, from celebrants of Empire like Mason, Rider Haggard and Kipling himself, from thrillers by Edgar Wallace, Conan Doyle and others, rather than from the classics. The only film versions of certifiable classics were *The Mill on the Floss* (1937, directed by Tim Whelan, with a fine vivid Maggie Tulliver from Geraldine Fitzgerald) and *Scrooge* (1935, directed by Henry Edwards, from Dickens' *A Christmas Carol*). As one looks at the film adaptations of the period – imperial adventures, thrillers, a batch of socially conscious films – they seem to reflect, in this genre breakdown, the rise of the British studio system rather than the realities of British life or a particular state of literary culture.

Roy Armes claims that 'the key factor in the film-making of the period was the studio, which determined the economic structure of the industry, the organisation of work within it, and the essential stylistic features of the films produced'.[6] The adaptations in the categories noted are essentially products of the major studios – Gainsborough, London Films, Gaumont-British and MGM (Denham) – and, if the aim of studio production was, as Armes claims, 'to present significant action and star performance with the utmost clarity to a spectator who must never be disturbed in his willing suspension of belief',[7] this may account for what, in their miscellaneous way, these films have in common. At first glance less coherent than the 'literary cinema' of the post-war years or the 'realist' period

'An unquestioning attitude to existing values': imperial authority in *Sanders of the River* (1935)

of 1959–63, the films of the latter half of the 30s share a *reassuring* quality. The decade may have been beset by economic crises and growing political anxiety; class division may have been cruelly apparent in the nation at large; but whenever a hint of disturbance appears in the films it is settled in ways which reinforce a comfortable image of Britain (no doubt a commercially wise strategy too). Anthony Aldgate believes that 'the British cinema had a positive and purposeful part to play in shaping the "national life" because it helped . . . to achieve that high degree of consensus which seemingly characterised British society during the 1930s'.[8] Whether film-makers were consciously working towards this end or whether, as Armes sees it, the kind of escapism produced created an effect of harmony at odds with the reality, the films themselves in the main reflect an unquestioning attitude to existing values. A thriving studio system was not a likely source of subversive art and, unlike in the products of some of the Hollywood studios, subversion seemed scarcely to seep in at the edges.

The two major film-makers in Britain at this time – Alexander Korda and Alfred Hitchcock – were both associated with adaptations that bear out a comforting view of Britain. Korda, the founder and head of London Films, and the nearest approach to a Hollywood-style producer, was responsible during this period for four famous films of Empire: *Sanders of the River* (1935), from Edgar Wallace's novel; *Elephant Boy* (1937, from Kipling's 'Toomai of the Elephants'); *The Drum* (1938) and *The Four Feathers* (1939), both from novels by A. E. W. Mason (whose *Fire Over England* of 1936 was filmed the following year by the American director William K. Howard with a cast headed by Flora Robson, Laurence Olivier and Vivien Leigh). The combination of Korda's avowed Anglophilia and the source authors chosen ensures that these are not films which offer any criticism of the workings of Britain's far-flung Empire. The four films (all directed by Korda's brother Zoltan, joined by Robert Flaherty on *Elephant Boy*) may have owed their contemporary popularity largely to the adventure and spectacle of their stories, but as far as their producer was concerned they are hymns of praise to the spirit of Empire. In this respect they may well have been old-fashioned even in the 1930s, as Jeffrey Richards has suggested: 'In films, the Empire is unchanged and unchanging. Its doctrine is the doctrine that had emerged by the last decade of the nineteenth century.'[9] They were not, however, so old-fashioned or antithetical to public taste as to prevent them achieving Hollywood-style success. The notion of the British colonial service, civil and military, keeping its end up in remote and difficult places underlies these novels and the films adapted from them.

The thrillers of these years, though unpretentious by comparison with the Korda extravaganzas, characteristically present the routing of vaguely sinister foreign powers which have designs on British life and values. This is true of Walter Forde's *The Four Just Men* (1939), from Edgar Wallace's novel, and of Hitchcock's four notable thrillers – all adaptations – of this period. They are *The 39 Steps* (1935), from John Buchan's novel, *The Secret Agent* and *Sabotage* (both 1936, from Somerset Maugham and Joseph Conrad respectively) and *The Lady Vanishes* (1938), from Ethel Lina White's novel. While not chauvinistic or imperial flagwavers like the Korda films (Hitchcock was merely the son of a Leytonstone tradesman, not a Hungarian *émigré*), these films nevertheless present plucky Britishers outwitting devilish foreigners. The latter are not usually from specified countries but represent forms of political threat. Foreign agents have employed a music hall performer, 'Mr Memory', to memorise a secret formula in *The 39 Steps*; a British secret service agent (John Gielgud) is sent to Geneva to uncover a foreign plot

Plucky British and sinister foreigners: Hitchcock's *The Lady Vanishes,*
released in the month of Munich

in *The Secret Agent*; in *Sabotage,* an anarchist (Oscar Homolka) is
involved in terrorist activities in London (Conrad's novel is in fact
called *The Secret Agent*); and, in the year of Munich, an improbable
English counter-espionage agent (Dame May Whitty) falls victim to
a spy ring on her way home to London from somewhere vaguely
Balkan in *The Lady Vanishes*. Though dissimilar in tone – the first
and fourth are much more bracing and light-hearted entertainments
than the other two – these films do have elements in common, as
suggested above. Further, all but *Sabotage* show nice young Hitchcockian couples thwarting foreign plotters; without lapsing into
xenophobia, they evince a preference for Englishness over otherness;
and Hitchcock's oft-professed valuing of suspense over surprise is
clearly evident in narratives more smoothly executed and invigorat-
ing than any hitherto found in British films.

All four films are of course adaptations; however, none of them is
famous as an adaptation as, say, David Lean's Dickens films are.
Though Hitchcock has often drawn on novelistic sources, and his
other two late 30s films (*Young and Innocent*, 1937, from Josephine
Tey's *A Shilling for Candles*, and *Jamaica Inn*, 1939, from Daphne
Du Maurier's novel) are also adaptations, he has shied clear of
filming the major classics. In his interviews with François Truffaut,
he said: 'What I do is to read a story once, and, if I like the basic idea, I
just forget all about the book and start to create cinema.'[10] Conrad's

The Secret Agent is the nearest to a literary classic that Hitchcock ever filmed, and *Sabotage* is very far from the sort of fidelity Lean seems to have aimed at. There is no sense of his looking for 'visual equivalents', and, though the four films under discussion here are all comparatively modest in the Hitchcock canon, they are, for British films, unusually bold adaptations. Hitchcock's views on adaptations are not likely to lead to the creation of a literary cinema. By avoiding novels for which he has a high regard, he grants himself the freedom simply to take what he wants from source material and 'to create cinema'. The kind of respect for the source one more usually finds in British adaptations of novels may win praise from middle-class critics with a strongly literary bias, but leads often to a decorous literalness – and to the BBC—TV classic serial.

The Hitchcock adaptations are interesting partly for their cavalier approach to their source material and partly for the way they seem to belong, thematically, to the period. The second half of that sentence is true also of the third major figure of the period in British films, the first half distinctly not. Victor Saville, producer and/or director of some of the most popular British films of the 30s, became production head of MGM's British studios in 1938. In this role, he was responsible for two very successful adaptations of middle-brow English novels, both directed by Americans. They were King Vidor's *The Citadel* (1938), from A. J. Cronin's novel, making mildly critical gestures at the lure of easy rewards in the medical profession and at class divisions; and Sam Wood's *Goodbye Mr Chips* (1939), from James Hilton's gentle celebration of the English public school (and, by implication, the class system it derives from and perpetuates). Whatever criticisms of English life are hinted at in these films, they both end in claiming full moral approbation for their professional heroes, played in both cases by Robert Donat at the peak of his popularity. Saville's interest in English institutions is again apparent in the film he directed for London Films in 1938: *South Riding*, adapted from Winifred Holtby's cross-sectional account of life in a between-wars Yorkshire town and surrounding community. In the kind of consensus his film arrives at, it is very much of its time; in its attitude to the business of adaptation it is at a considerable remove from Hitchcock's views.

South Riding has a prefatory word for the author to whom 'this pictorial impression of her book is respectfully dedicated'. This suggests a modest approach to the process of adaptation; in fact, Saville's film is considerably more than a 'pictorial impression' of Holtby's sympathetic account of six people working for the country, trying to balance the claims of their private lives against those of the community. The film, without that rushing through a series of episodes which disfigures some of the Dickens adaptations, maintains a lively and often enlightened sense of crucial oppositions (private and public allegiances, the rural and the urban), these rendered through Saville's sure grasp of the power of *mise en scène*. A series of alternations dramatises the clashes between gentleman-landowner Carne (Ralph Richardson) and the business interests of fellow-councillors Snaith (Milton Rosmer) and Huggins (Edmund Gwenn): the conflicting claims of horses and cars, of the hunt and roadworks, are established in compositions which highlight their incompatibilities and their inevitable clashes.

The film opens and closes in the Council chambers, emphasising its fidelity to Winifred Holtby's belief in local government as 'the front-line defence thrown up by humanity against its common enemies of sickness, poverty and ignorance' (opening caption). In the final scene, members of opposing political persuasions, including Carne and pro-Labour headmistress Sarah Burton (Edna Best), combine to rout Huggins for misuse of Council knowledge in land deals. The 'villains' are not conceived of as belonging to a class or to a political party but rather as self-seeking *individuals*. 'I never attacked the establishment in any way,' Saville said in 1972,[11] relegating to the level of a subconscious appeal 'the elements of social commitment' he found in books and plays like this. John Clements' performance, as Joe Astell, is a serious, sympathetic Socialist hero rare in British films of the 30s (or since), but the film is considerably. less pro-Left than the novel. I am sorry that the National Film Archive print omits the original final scene in which the Coronation is used as a device for showing a cross-class consensus at work: it sounds a very apt image for summarising Saville's benevolent, essentially conservative liberalism.

It is not just that Korda, Hitchcock and Saville are arguably the three most successful film-makers working in Britain at this time that leads one to concentrate on their work here. As a group they reveal certain approaches and strategies at work in British adaptations in the later 1930s. Without having much in common superficially, each in his own way draws on the English novel as a source for films which reinforce certain images of Britain. If Korda is frankly uncritical of these, Saville tempers his criticism by a belief in a (British) spirit of compromise and co-existence; Hitchcock's attitudes are more problematic, but the chief outcomes of his narratives would not disturb a comfortable feeling of British superiority. Their choice of novels, apart from the absence of the 'classics', covers a range characteristic of the British adaptation (i.e. more or less safely middle-class and middle-brow). Their approaches to the process of adaptation may seem widely divergent. Korda and Saville both seem to aim at fidelity to the original: Korda in the interests of perpetuating its imperial sentiments with all the screen's potential for extravagant spectacle, Saville anticipating Lean and, two decades later, the British realists in a respectful approach to his material. Hitchcock's cavalier approach, however, led him to Hollywood, where respect for the literary precursor was less daunting. However, their contribution to late 30s British cinema is more coherent ideologically than either their range of literary borrowings or their strategies for dealing with them might have suggested.

The Post-war 40s

For whatever reason, the literary adaptation was at its lowest ebb in British cinema in the war years. Only 45 of the 350 films released in the years 1940–45 were derived from novels, of which the most popular were four Gainsborough costume melodramas: *The Man in Grey* (1943, directed by Leslie Arliss), *Fanny by Gaslight* (1944, directed by Anthony Asquith), *Madonna of the Seven Moons* (1944, directed by Arthur Crabtree), and *The Wicked Lady* (1945, directed by Arliss). They are important films in British cinema history, not because they are adaptations, but because they proved that home-grown escapism could be as compelling at the box-office as the Hollywood brand; and later commentators have found them a phenomenon worthy of further study.

The post-war literary cinema boom really got under way with David Lean's *Great Expectations* at the end of 1946. In the four years 1947–50, 115 of the 314 feature films released were derived from novels; that is, over a third. When 56 adaptations from plays are added, it will be seen that well over one-half of the total output derives from (more or less) literary sources. In fact, there is in each year of this period scarcely a handful of either critically or commercially significant films based on original screenplays, the most notable being the T.E.B. Clarke-scripted Ealing films *Hue and Cry* (1946) and *Passport to Pimlico* (1949). Even the Powell-Pressburger team, perhaps the most cinematically venturesome in the British cinema, based four of its five films of this period on novels, and the fifth (*The Red Shoes*) is indebted to Hans Andersen.

The Powell-Pressburger films of the period remain obdurately cinematic and non-literary. At the time they were frequently criticised for their visual and emotional excesses which set them apart from the discretion and taste of Carol Reed and David Lean, the two most highly valued directors of the time. *Sequence* found them pretentious, putting down *The Red Shoes* (1948) very briskly; *Punch* found *Gone to Earth* (1950) 'intrinsically artificial and pretentious'; *Picture Show* felt that *Black Narcissus* (1947) lost power by 'wandering into side-tracks'; while virtually no one had a good word for *The Elusive Pimpernel* (1950). *The Small Back Room* (1949), a tense thriller based on Nigel Balchin's novel, fared better, though twenty years later Raymond Durgnat still carped about 'an (ill-advised) expressionist sequence.'[12] Their films, though based on respectable novels, were too visually exhilarating to be trusted. Unlike Lean and Reed, and apart from *The Small Back Room*, they habitually worked in colour throughout the years of post-war austerity. Further, they were liable to confront sexual passion in a very un-British way: Kathleen Byron's nun lusting after David Farrar in *Black Narcissus* has no parallel in 40s cinema. They did not respect their sources as Lean and Reed seemed to; if they had done so, if they had been more 'literary', they might have had a better press at the time – and fewer admirers since. The characteristic adaptations of this period are the films of Lean and Reed: nothing exotic or flagrantly sexual here, but a respectful approach to respectable literary sources which has always found favour with the British critical establishment.

Then, almost everyone thought well of Lean and Reed, unaware of course that this was the best of times for them. Reed had won some acclaim for his 'realism' in *Bank Holiday* (1938) and his adaptations of A. J. Cronin's sombre best-selling novel of mining strife *The Stars Look Down* (1939) and of H. G. Wells' *Kipps* (1941). But his main contribution to Britain's 'literary' cinema derives from his three films of the late 40s: *Odd Man Out* (1947), from F. L. Green's novel about the last hours of an IRA gunman, and his two collaborations with Graham Greene, *The Fallen Idol* (1948) and *The Third Man* (1949). In all three, he worked closely with the authors: F. L. Green and R. C. Sheriff (playwright and screenwriter) wrote the script for *Odd Man Out*; Graham Greene radically reworked his 1935 story 'The Basement Room' for *The Fallen Idol*, and wrote the screenplay for *The Third Man*, his only other successful screenwriting venture being that for Reed's *Our Man in Havana* (1960), also, arguably, Reed's happiest return to form after the 40s. Reed's and Greene's creative personalities chimed perfectly in their two 40s films: both films are studies in disillusionment and the melancholy of innocence brought face to face with corruption. *The Fallen Idol,* smaller in scope than *Odd Man Out* or *The Third Man,* is dominated by a small boy's point of view, as he peers from under tables or through banisters at the shabby adult world around him, and allows Reed's predilection for the unusual camera angle plenty of play. Not as much, however, as *The Third Man*, where the restless, ornate camera style works, with perhaps curious versatility, to accommodate both Greene's vision of post-war pessimism and Orson Welles' bravura appearance as Harry Lime.

The literary culture: David Lean's *Great Expectations* (1946)

Like Lean, Reed seems to see his task as the visualising of a respected verbal source rather than, as with Powell and Pressburger, the creation of a wholly new work in relation to which the original author stands as a resource and a starting point. The Lean and Reed films can be more easily assimilated by and into the literary culture of their time, offering no major affront to the texts adapted, exhibiting a British restraint in presenting relationships, and exploiting a realism that is more in line with the great tradition of the English novel. Their later careers suggest that neither had enough personal vision or visual flair to galvanise inferior material. In this sense, they are good examples of what Charles Thomas Samuels called 'novelistic cinema' in which 'the greatness is based on a prior narrative invention'. But, he continues, 'Something lies beyond: cinema in which story, characters and theme are not so much captured through the resources of film-making as they are created by them'.[13] He was writing about Reed, but it might just as well have been Lean.

Nevertheless, the achievement of Lean's Dickens films is not negligible. If they do not feel particularly Lean-like (and one is not sure what that might mean), they frequently do feel notably Dickensian, *one* of the qualities one might welcome in films based on Dickens. They are in most ways superior to the other British Dickens adaptations, and *Great Expectations*, especially, is a very interesting film of its period. There have been over thirty British films derived from Dickens, of which Lean's two films for Cineguild are the most famous. *Great Expectations* and *Oliver Twist* (1948) are essentially 'faithful' adaptations, but Lean has not been afraid to excise characters or plot strands in the interests of narrative clarity. These films understand the way in which *mise en scène* in its fullest sense offers the prime cinematic equivalent of the linguistic density of Dickens' prose style. By comparison, Cavalcanti's *Nicholas Nickleby* (1947), for Ealing, suffers from a dull hero (Derek Bond) and from John Dighton's shapeless screenplay which clings resolutely – and fatally – to the novel's picaresque procedures; Brian Desmond Hurst's *Scrooge* (1951) is a charming but socially less ambitious piece of work than the Lean films; and Noel Langley's good-humoured *Pickwick Papers* (1952) has nothing like Lean's stylish control of camera and *mise en scène*. None of the musicals adapted from Dickens – Carol Reed's *Oliver!* (1968), Ronald Neame's *Scrooge* (1970) and Michael Tuchner's *Mister Quilp* (1974), based, precariously, on *The Old Curiosity Shop* – takes intelligent advantage of the opportunity the genre might have offered for a radical reworking of the texts. And worst of all is the Delbert Mann School of Classical Adaptation usually made with an eye to US television screenings: his own *David Copperfield* (1969), as well as his *Jane Eyre* (1971) and *Kidnapped* (1972); Joseph Hardy's Technicolored, Christmas card-pretty *Great Expectations* (1975); and Clive Donner's *Oliver Twist* (1983), which completes the laundering process of Dickens on film. No doubt these films, on reaching their transatlantic destinies on the small screen, are presented as being 'educational' and 'prestigious' occasions, but the Lean films worked the 'cultural heritage' angle much more potently, both in publicity and in the goods actually delivered. Against the assorted insipidities of Mann and company, one remains grateful to Lean.

Lean has not sought to make critiques of the novels or to deconstruct their instabilities; rather, he has found a visual style that achieves an intelligent fidelity to the texts. *Great Expectations* and *Oliver Twist* share certain key Dickensian attributes: heroes who provide blank sheets on which experience will write the lines, both of them orphans who will succeed to more prosperous futures (apt heroes for the late 1940s), though the greater maturity of *Great Expectations* subjects this 'progress' to a closer scrutiny; each hero is surrounded by a cast of grotesques (just lying in wait for, say, Francis L. Sullivan or Martita Hunt), comic and villainous, though again the later novel is less black-and-white in its discriminations; and each novel is fascinated and repelled by the dangers and corruptions of post-Industrial Revolution London. If *Great Expectations* is the more powerful film, it may well be because it offers Lean a sturdier, more single-minded approach to narrative. Both are remarkably handsome films, *Oliver Twist* perhaps a little self-consciously so in its romantic approach to city squalor. There is nothing in it quite so memorable as the opening sequence of *Great Expectations,* with the young Pip (Anthony Wager) running along the edge of the marshes under a lowering sky, the gibbet silhouetted against it, and the churchyard scene with its famous moment of shock as the convict Magwitch (Finlay Currie) erupts into it. It is a classic of visual storytelling (a 1950s television version virtually repeats it), and a triumph of *mise en scène.* So is a much later scene which has Estella (Valerie Hobson) seated in what was once Miss Havisham's chair, her prayer-book beside her, as she tells Pip (John Mills) that she enjoys being 'away from the world and its complications'. The position, the posture, the prayer-book: through these details Lean established how far Estella has come towards filling the role for which her guardian has prepared her, by visual recall of the earlier scene.

This very satisfying touch is an invention of the film's; so is the whole final sequence in which Pip tears down the heavy, rotten drapes to let the light into the gloom of Satis House. With hindsight, it does not seem too fanciful to see this (adaptor's) gesture as a letting in of light not merely on the British film industry but on British life at large after the rigours of the war years. Valerie Hobson herself said recently: 'In this immediate post-war period there was a feeling of an end and a new beginning – a tremendous feeling of a Renaissance, of a burgeoning of all the talent that had been squashed in by money restraint during the war.'[14] The publicity surrounding the film's production stresses the no-expense-spared attitude towards re-creation of sets and costumes, as though there was indeed a sense of luxurious release, of seeking to do full justice to rendering on film a prime example of Britain's cultural heritage. And in its scrutiny of class structure, in the significance of Satis House as symbol of an ossified attitude to wealth and class, *Great Expectations* may be seen as very much a product of its time and place.

The Last Wave 1959–1963
After the Lean-Dickens and Reed-Greene films, the next important burst of adaptations (and, indeed, of British films) is the 'realist' series that began with Jack Clayton's *Room at the Top* (1959), from John Braine's novel, and ended with Lindsay Anderson's *This Sporting Life* (1963), from David Storey's novel. Anderson, writing in *Declaration* in 1957, asked:

What sort of cinema have we got in Britain? First of all it is necessary to point out that it is an English cinemà (and Southern English at that), metropolitan in attitude, and entirely middle-class. This combination gives it, to be fair, a few quite amiable qualities: a tolerance, a kind of benignity, a lack of pomposity, an easy-going good nature. But a resolution never to be discovered taking things too seriously can soon become a vice rather than a virtue, particularly when the ship is in danger of going down. To counterbalance the rather tepid humanism of our cinema, it must also be said that it is snobbish, anti-intelligent, emotionally inhibited, wilfully blind to the conditions and problems of the present, dedicated to an out-of-date, exhausted national ideal.[15]

He might have been anticipating these films, which directed their attention firmly towards regional (mainly northern) and working-class life. Though some of them are adapted from plays (Tony Richardson's *Look Back in Anger, The Entertainer* and *A Taste of Honey*), they were plays whose lives had begun, significantly, not in the West End but, more venturesomely, at the Royal Court or Stratford, East London. Whether derived from plays or novels, these films had little in common with the rural/small town ambience of *South Riding*, and located their emotional energies in the working classes, hitherto – in British films – predominantly a source of comic relief from the affairs of their social betters, not in fact regarded seriously. Characteristically, the films were derived from modern post-*Look Back in Anger* novels, their protagonists dimly, usually inarticulately, aware of the inadequacies of their lives and kicking against the constraints of class. In *Room at the Top*, Joe Lampton (Laurence Harvey), a clerk in local government, aspires to marrying out of his working-class background and achieves his goal at the cost of suppressing the real feeling he has been surprised into by his affair with a married woman, Alice Aisgill (Simone Signoret). The film no longer shocks with its unexpected reality, but it was important at the time for taking its hero's self-interested aspirations seriously, for its unglamorised picture of life in a charmless northern town, and for its emotional and sexual candour. Jack Clayton's subsequent career has included several adaptations, from *The Innocents* (1961), a stylish version of Henry James' *The Turn of the Screw*, to his elephantine *The Great Gatsby* (1974); he is, in fact, a 'literary' director, in general so respectful of his sources in rendering their surfaces that the films sometimes seemed overwhelmed by their art direction. In *Room at the Top*, however, with a coarse-grained best-seller on his hands, he seems less inhibited, and the screen incarnation of Joe Lampton's rise and rise is at least as forceful as its source novel.

137

Like its successors in this sub-genre of working-class, regional adaptations, *Room at the Top* is sociologically much more vivid than the original novel. Karel Reisz's *Saturday Night and Sunday Morning* (1960), from Alan Sillitoe's novel, John Schlesinger's versions of Stan Barstow's *A Kind of Loving* (1962) and Keith Waterhouse's *Billy Liar!* (1963), Tony Richardson's film of the Sillitoe novella *The Loneliness of the Long-Distance Runner* (1962), and Anderson's *This Sporting Life,* from David Storey's novel, are all more interesting than the novels they are derived from, largely because of the way ideological information seeps into every frame. As a result of the unobtrusive but insistent evocation of time and place, the protagonists' lives are seen played out against the backgrounds that shape and confine them: streets of drab council houses, the threadbare popular culture of fairground, dance hall, and TV quiz programmes, and the routine, mindless work.

These are not films which push towards the consensus of *South Riding* (or of the Gracie Fields film *Sing as We Go* [1934]). Joe Lampton may marry the magnate's daughter but he forfeits his potential for manhood in the process; he will knuckle under. Borstal boy Colin Smith (Tom Courtenay) purposely loses the long-distance race to spite the prison governor (Michael Redgrave) and thus to thumb his nose at the Establishment, even when it looks benign. Vic Brown (Alan Bates) in *A Kind of Loving* settles for the eponymous compromise with the dim Ingrid (June Ritchie) whom he has fecklessly made pregnant, but he knows that he is shutting himself into a world of telly-watching inanity. *Billy Liar* (Courtenay again) is so rooted in the safety of his northern life, with the daily jabs at authority, that he turns down the challenge of London, Liz (Julie Christie), and the chance to realise his aspirations. Frank Machin (Richard Harris), the footballer hero of *This Sporting Life*, exploited by the business interests which control the club, remains locked in emotional inarticulateness. Of the protagonists in these films, it is Arthur Seaton (Albert Finney) of *Saturday Night and Sunday Morning* who stays most powerfully in the mind: he is aggressive, crudely heroic in the face of a system bent on grinding him down; and there is the gloss of adventure and danger on him despite the oppressiveness of the system. At the film's end, his affair with married Brenda (Rachel Roberts) messily concluded, he seems set for the working-class marriage trap with Doreen (Shirley Ann Field). 'You shouldn't throw stones like that,' she chides him. 'It won't be the last one I'll throw,' is his answer, and the remark epitomises the note of real resilience Karel Reisz has found in Arthur's proletarian assertiveness. As with Joe Lampton and Vic Brown, Arthur's sexuality leads to unwanted pregnancy: all three want more from life

Kicking the system: Albert Finney in *Saturday Night and Sunday Morning*
(1960)

than their circumstances seem to allow. At the end, only Arthur,
about to enter the marriage that has ensnared the other two, suggests
a strong enough addiction to life to survive intact.

For a few years, these films, with their roots in Free Cinema, the
Royal Court Theatre, and a generation of 'angry' young novelists,
seemed to promise new hope for British cinema. Though the new
realism they offered, and their outspokenness about the social
constrictiveness of British life and institutions, have now lost their
power to startle, there is no denying how influential they were at the
time. The 'Swinging 60s' led the cinema in different directions, away
from the kinds of realism these directors had espoused. (Not that I
want to make them sound too alike: Anderson has always aimed at a
poetic rather than a literal realism, and Richardson was fatally lured
by a New Wave flashiness which persists to this day.) It is true,
nevertheless, to say that at no other period in British film-making has
there been so close a congruence between contemporary film and
literature, and it is a congruence rooted in the representation of a

particular class and region. The films that grew out of these novels adhered closely to the narrative lines of the originals; however, they are stamped with a distinctively cinematic look and feel that allow for individual emphases but confer a collective identity on them as a sub-genre. They brought new and valuable names (actors as well as directors) into British cinema when they were needed, and they held up to serious scrutiny a whole stratum of society that British cinema had traditionally overlooked or patronised.

These films marked a distinct break with the discreet, 'tasteful' tradition of British film adaptation. (So, too, in their notably different way, did the Hammer versions of the Dracula and Frankenstein novels, films which drew on aspects of British life normally repressed in mainstream British culture.) For a time the realist films seem to offer a new direction for British cinema. There were other significant adaptations during this period – appropriately enough, *Sons and Lovers* (1960) directed by Jack Cardiff from D. H. Lawrence's earlier masterpiece of working-class regional life, Clayton's *The Innocents* (1961), Richardson's jokey, flashy *Tom Jones* (1963), from Henry Fielding's 18th-century picaresque romance, and Joseph Losey's *The Servant* (1963), from Robin Maugham's novella – but the *flavour* of the period remains essentially that of social realism.

Since then the British cinema has been in a state of continuing crisis. So far as adaptations go, it is not possible to locate much sign of coherence or recurring patterns. At the end of the 60s, there were two notable films by Joseph Losey, both derived from novels, and offering sharply critical views of English life from an outsider's point of view. They were *Accident* (1967), from Nicholas Mosley's novel, and *The Go-Between* (1970), from L. P. Hartley's novel, both of which may be seen as continuing the critique of English society begun with *The Servant*. All three films had screenplays by Harold Pinter. There were two further films based on novels by D. H. Lawrence: Ken Russell's wayward, sometimes brilliant *Women in Love* (1969), audacious not only for Alan Bates and Oliver Reed's nude wrestling match but also for how much of Lawrence's talk it dared to retain; and Christopher Miles' more careful but less memorable *The Virgin and the Gypsy* (1970).

The 70s and the early 80s, in their floundering search for audiences, have dabbled in most of the literary sub-genres established in the silent period. The most ambitious attempt at adaptation, Karel Reisz's *The French Lieutenant's Woman* (1981), from John Fowles' clever-clever novel and Pinter's screenplay, was caught between faithfulness to the book's procedures (they tried to do more than tell a 19th-century story of sexual repression and obsession) and adventurousness (they tried, and failed, to find an appropriate way to offer a contemporary gloss on this story to replace Fowles' authorial intervention). Its failure is the more depressing in view of the main trends in adaptations in recent years: Agatha Christie's cardboard thrillers (*Murder on the Orient Express*, 1974, *Death on the Nile*, 1978, etc.), vivified by all-star casts of ageing legends, amusing, if scarcely taxing the screen's resources; the inevitable forays into Ian Fleming; and Delbert Mann's pedestrian 'picturisations' of the classics.

One wants something more daring than these approaches: 'fidelity' is a pointless criterion. Perhaps screenwriting is still too unadventurous an art, despite exponents distinguished in other fields (Greene, Eric Ambler, Nigel Balchin, Pinter and today's Ian McEwan). Or perhaps Frederic Raphael (author of screenplays for *Darling* and *Far from the Madding Crowd*) is right in his analysis of what ails much screenwriting: 'The obsession with story, with telling, gets in the way constantly of the film-maker's proper art, which is showing.'[16] A cinema which draws heavily on adaptations is not necessarily 'novelistic', but is likely to be if it does not know how to display its narratives in visually effective terms. Further, the film-maker using a novel as a source needs to be aware of what can and cannot be adapted; or, rather, what can be *transferred* (those elements of narrative not tied to language) and what properly requires *adaptation,* and, this distinction made, some intelligent, imaginatively daring choices about how the cinema's resources may be used to effect this process. A film-maker may or may not choose 'faithfully' to transpose the original; he may, for his own purposes, wish to extrapolate from it or make a critical commentary on it. Whatever approach he chooses, if the film is to have its own inherent value, he will need to have his own clear point of view on the material at hand. It will be indisputably David Lean's – *not* Charles Dickens' – *Great Expectations* we shall go to see. In the long history and pervasive influence of the novelistic adaptation in British cinema, this has not often happened. With certain honourable exceptions (Hitchcock, Powell, a few others), film-makers have applied their skills externally to a pre-existent reality, instead of reworking it from within, 'to create cinema', in Hitchcock's phrase.

Notes

1   Alan Lovell, 'The British Cinema: The Unknown Cinema', a discussion paper for a BFI Education Department seminar, London, 13 March 1969, p. 7; reprinted as 'The Unknown Cinema of Britain', *Cinema Journal*, Spring 1972.

2   All figures based on Denis Gifford, *The British Film Catalogue 1895–1970*, Newton Abbot, David & Charles, 1973.

3   Q. D. Leavis, *Fiction and the Reading Public*, London, Chatto and Windus, 1932 (reprinted 1978), p. 54.

4   Noël Burch, *Correction Please, or How We Got Into Pictures*, London, Arts Council of Great Britain, 1979, p. 3 (booklet produced to accompany Burch's film of the same title).

5   I am defining feature films, rather arbitrarily, as films lasting more than 60 minutes (all figures from Gifford).

6   Roy Armes, *A Critical History of the British Cinema*, London, Secker & Warburg, 1978, p. 113.

7.   Ibid., p. 114.

8   Jeffrey Richards and Anthony Aldgate, *The Best of British*, Oxford, Blackwell, 1983, p. 31.

9   Jeffrey Richards, *Visions of Yesterday*, London, Routledge & Kegan Paul, 1973, p. 7.

10   François Truffaut, *Hitchcock,* New York, Simon and Schuster, 1966, p. 49.

11   Interview with Victor Saville in *Victor Saville*, London, British Film Institute, 1972, p. 12.

12   In *Movie*, no. 14, 1965 (reprinted in Ian Christie, ed., *Powell, Pressburger and Others*, London, British Film Institute, 1978, p. 67).

13   Charles Thomas Samuels, *Mastering the Film and Other Essays,* Knoxville, University of Tennessee Press, 1977, p. 39.

14   In an interview with the author, June 1984.

15   Lindsay Anderson, 'Get Out and Push' in Tom Maschler (ed.), *Declaration*, London, MacGibbon, 1957, p. 137.

16   Frederic Raphael, Introduction to *Two for the Road*, London, Jonathan Cape, 1967, p. 30.

Geoff Brown

'SISTER OF THE STAGE'
BRITISH FILM AND BRITISH THEATRE

To begin with, a potted production history. Early on 26 January 1917, the distinguished stage actress Irene Vanbrugh stood on the platform at St Pancras railway station, wrapped up against the cold and snow, mustering strength for the rigours ahead. In time she was joined – grudgingly – by almost all the surviving actor-managers and important playwrights of the Victorian and Edwardian years: among them Sir Squire Bancroft, president of the Royal Academy of Dramatic Art, who had helped to popularise the three-walled boxed set and the kind of drawing-room dramas housed within; Sir John Hare, first manager of the Garrick Theatre; Sir Arthur Wing Pinero; Sir James Barrie; Sir George Alexander, not yet recovered from the previous night's opening of *The Aristocrat* at his own St James's Theatre; Sir Johnston Forbes-Robertson, the greatest Hamlet of the age; and Bernard Shaw. Clearly, these were not train-spotters. They were preparing to travel to Elstree for a day's work on the prologue of *Masks and Faces* – an Ideal film, made to boost RADA's sagging finances; and Irene Vanbrugh was their shepherdess.

Once out of the snow in the film studios, the knights and luminaries strenuously refused to wear any make-up, and moved into a set representing the RADA council room, replete with round table, paper, and quill pens. One by one, they stood before the director Fred Paul and acted out a minuscule version of the real-life meetings that had inspired the entire bizarre venture. In the completed film Barrie, playing nervously with his hands, suggests as a solution to the Academy's debt problem an all-star production of Charles Reade and Tom Taylor's *Masks and Faces,* a 19th-century comedy set in the theatrical world of 1740. Others weigh in with supportive comments. 'The "Pictures" owe much to the Stage. It shall repay . . . ' declares Pinero in a dialogue title; he spoke from experience, having seen three of his own plays filmed the previous year. Sir John Hare's title card piquantly puts the film/stage relationship in a nutshell: 'There should be no caste-prejudice. The Film is the Sister of the Stage.' With a few more vignettes successfully in the can, Vanbrugh led her troupe back to St Pancras and the London theatres.

The filming of the prologue completed almost a year's work on this illustrious slice of the British cinema's theatrical tradition. On the surface, *Masks and Faces* might show Film and Stage in an embrace of brotherly love, but the production was marked and marred by sibling rivalry. Stage actors who pledged support became trapped in other assignments. Sir George Alexander, for all his noble words in the prologue about the film's value as 'a worthy memory of the English stage of today', caused notable havoc by refusing Dennis Neilson-Terry, one of its leading players, any further time off from his own stage rehearsals. The film world, too, kicked the theatre's shins. The Samuelson company, Ideal's rival (and a previous employer of the director Fred Paul), loaned the services of their contract artiste Gladys Cooper on the understanding that the film was being made for charity; on learning that it wasn't, they insisted all her scenes be removed. The impasse was resolved by judicious blackmail: if Cooper's existing scenes were retained, said H. B. Irving (another stage luminary corralled into the cast), Samuelson could secure his own services. Samuelson happily bit the carrot.

The interest and value of *Masks and Faces* extended beyond the prologue's personnel and the production history: the film is competently mounted by the standards of the time, with expressive performances from Vanbrugh herself, Winifred Emery and Forbes-Robertson. Yet it is the prologue that haunts the mind. There is something so eloquent, so ironic, about these late Victorian notables giving a friendly handshake to an industry – and indeed a century – in which most would take little part; an industry, moreover, that would bite hard into their own cherished professions. Bancroft, Hare and Alexander would be dead by the time talkies arrived to poach directly on theatre's territory; among the dramatists, Pinero's creative force was mostly spent – only Shaw would grapple decisively with the practical problems of merging theatre and cinema.

Yet though most of these personages come from a distant age, the arguments and attitudes prompted by *Masks and Faces* prove pertinent to the entire history of British theatrical cinema – a history stretching from Esmé Collins' 1896 film of a scene from the play *The Broken Melody* to the latest adaptations of *Steaming* (Joseph Losey, 1984), *Plenty* (Fred Schepisi, 1985) and *Insignificance* (Nicolas Roeg, 1985). Films offered stage talent tempting possibilities for wider audiences and greater income (RADA came out of *Masks and Faces* with £2,000 for their building fund). The stage, in turn, offered the cinema pre-sold publicity, cultural prestige, and a magic gateway to ecstatic, patriotic reviews. 'It is a play that no other country in the world could have produced,' declared the *Bioscope* reviewer of *Masks and Faces,* 'and with native talent on native soil it can safely challenge the whole world as an English masterpiece of unexampled merit.'[1]

But before the theatrical tradition in British cinema is surveyed more closely, these underlying factors should be drawn out further. One obvious factor is geographical. The film studios scattered at various times around London's outskirts – at Elstree, at Ealing, at Walton-on-Thames, at Denham, at Shepperton – have all been a short train ride from the railway termini and the West End. Actors could film during the day and be back in their stage dressing-rooms by early evening, though this regime often meant bewildering changes in mood (Michael Redgrave, in 1938, switched from Launder and Gilliat's *The Lady Vanishes* to Chekhov's *Three Sisters*). Such dual lives were difficult to lead in America, where the film and theatre centres were always on opposite sides of the continent.

Theatre's grip on British cinema started very early. Early cinema looked to the London stage for expertise in acting; it took until 1927 for a separate professional acting association, the Film Artistes' Guild, to be formed. The stage could also supply ready-made characters and plots, bred from 19th-century realism, even though the lengths of most plays far exceeded the available footage of silent cinema. There was little incentive or opportunity to write original cinema scripts; the number of stage and literary adaptations rose steadily during the production boom of the early 1910s (*The Bioscope* estimated the total amount of adapted material in May 1916 at 95 per cent). Salaries for screenwriters were notoriously low, and those who persevered in their trade – such as the prolific Eliot Stannard and Kenelm Foss – had little authority over the way their work was handled.

The stage also allowed early cinema to bask in the reflected glory of respected cultural traditions. *Masks and Faces,* with its gaggle of Sirs and ostentatious star cast, provides one example; but the landmark film is Will Barker's *Henry VIII* (1911), derived from Beerbohm Tree's stage production, mounted at His Majesty's in 1910. Barker's film treatment adheres to the norm of most early Shakespeare adaptations: the actors were simply shoved before a static camera with their stage costumes and sets to perform selected abbreviated scenes. But Barker distinguished himself from the pack by the unprecedented ballyhoo generated through the film's prestige cast, material, high rental price, and abnormal length (2,000 feet). He also titillated public interest by restricting the availability of prints; after

145

six weeks, he said, all copies would be destroyed, and he kept his word, staging a public burning at his Ealing studio on 13 April 1911. The film itself duly prompted critical reverence and considerable public interest, though the dumb show seems to have left some perplexed: *Kinematograph Weekly* reported how one stalls spectator rose to complain to the actors on screen that audiences couldn't hear a word they were saying.[2]

Perhaps the numerous title cards should have alerted the gentleman to the presence of a new medium; yet one can still understand part of his confusion. The static camera of early cinema viewed actors and settings with the unchanging gaze of a stiff-necked spectator staring into a proscenium arch and a three-walled, realistic set. In several instances the theatrical accoutrements were not merely implied – they were physically present. Spectators enjoying the Co-operative Cinematograph Company's potpourri of scenes from Frank Benson's *Richard III* (1911) could feast their eyes on the boards and floor-cloth of the Stratford Memorial Theatre, on the painted stage backdrops of London streets and Bosworth Field. Early cameramen sought out serious stage productions just as they sought out sporting events, Tiller Girls, Dan Leno pantomimes and other notable sights. Topicality played an important part. *English Nell*, in which Marie Tempest scored an early success as Nell Gwyn, opened in the West End in late August 1900; by September, the Mutoscope and Biograph company already had a scene from Act Two ready for public exhibition.

In the earliest years, the stage treated film more as a mother than a sister, for theatre buildings – mostly music-halls – gave the new technological wonder its first commercial home (the Lumière cinematograph and R. W. Paul's home-grown apparatus appeared from March 1896 at two Leicester Square theatres, the Alhambra and the Empire). But when Irene Vanbrugh led her august gentlemen to Elstree, moving pictures had long passed the status of music-hall novelties: there was an industry behind them, with new audiences and fortunes to be won. Theatrical personalities from all parts of the spectrum acknowledged the cinema's possibilities and appeal. William Haggar, a regional showman who toured with melodramas and Shakespeare, added films to his repertoire in 1898, and soon began shooting brief versions of his own stage shows, such as *The Maid of Cefn Ydfa* (1902); films, after all, could be 'toured' more easily than the live article. The actor-manager Beerbohm Tree, who laid great stress on audience appeal in his grandiose Shakespeare productions, was another early adventurer, and descended on to the Thames embankment in 1896 to film a snatch of his *King John* – a spurious tableau representing the signing of Magna Carta. One detects a related evangelical urge in the Shakespeare films of Laurence Olivier, flamboyantly launched half a century later with *Henry V* (1944) – prestige packages designed to impress, to spread the theatrical gospel. 'Cor look,' Raymond Durgnat quotes two Cockney lads as saying, standing before a poster for the 1955 *Richard III*, 'four Sirs in one picture!'[3] Olivier, Gielgud, Richardson, and Cedric Hardwicke (knighted, like the others, purely for his theatre work): the perfect team for missionary work in the Odeon jungles.

Mercenary ambitions played their part too, and helped take the edge off the snobbish disdain – the 'caste-prejudice' – that many actors at first felt toward the upstart medium. Michael Redgrave once recalled Ralph Richardson's blunt words when Redgrave was dickering with Gainsborough's proffered contract: 'Films are where you sell what you have learnt on the stage.'[4] At first, these stage skills were bodily transported with scant acknowledgment of the cinema's need for intimacy, restrained gestures, and the thought behind the action. Matheson Lang rampaged through 20s films in the same thick character make-up he used on stage; others fretted over the cinema's demand for shooting out of continuity, for duplicating the same gesture in repeated takes, for placing the feet on the appointed chalk marks. 'I always feel the camera should come to *me*, instead of me go to the *camera*,' Edith Evans reportedly declared to Asquith during a hiccough in the shooting of *The Importance of Being Earnest*.[5] Her theatrical instinct in this case was right: one comes before Evans' Lady Bracknell on bended knees, or one comes not at all. But whatever the actor's attitude, by mid-century the cinema was firmly established as a regular part of the stage performer's life; so much so that the *Oxford Companion to the Theatre* could consider Sir Barry Jackson's post-war plans for a permanent company at Stratford as 'still imperilled by the remoteness of Stratford from film studios'.[6]

Stage playwrights also found the cinema a fruitful market-place, though few in the silent era were ever asked to write original material. Barrie's work on *The Real Thing At Last* (1916) – a spoof about British and American ways of filming *Macbeth* – was an exceptional instance. Those eminent authors who attempted direct participation generally found their presence unwelcome. The novelist E. Temple Thurston pinpointed the position, for both dramatists and novelists, at the Cinematograph Exhibitors' Association conference in 1921: 'Your work stopped at the studio floor,' Thurston recalled Cecil Hepworth telling him. Thurston concluded that such rebuffs encouraged a dubious attitude of 'lucrative indifference'.[7] The attitude continued once talkies theoretically strengthened the playwright's arm. Terence Rattigan contributed to over twenty film scripts – seven based on his own plays – yet he regarded cinema only as a financial safety-net. Some writers eventually found the means to step beyond the studio floor barrier, blending and expanding their established style with the methods of the cinema, but they were few: Noël Coward, briefly, in the 40s; Harold Pinter, working with Joseph Losey; Charles Wood, working mainly with Richard Lester.

In the silent era, the reliance on title cards inevitably restricted the expressive range of theatrical adaptations. As in other matters, the film of Benson's *Richard III* – only survivor from a series of Stratford productions filmed *in situ* in 1911 – provides an extreme example. Title cards absorb almost half the running time of the extant print, offering both an explanatory line of prose ('Lord Mayor of London offers crown to Richard, which he reluctantly accepts') and a quotation ('Then I salute you with the Royal title,/Long live King Richard, England's worthy king'). Once the title has been navigated, the situation is acted out in hectic style, with leading players and spear-carriers indiscriminately bunched together. We then move, with a jerk, to another title card, another reading session.

In many ways *Richard III* is a freak antique: other contemporary films made great strides towards bending Shakespeare to the cinema's developing demands. Two years later, Hepworth and the Gaumont company joined forces to present Sir Johnston Forbes-Robertson's famous interpretation of Hamlet, first seen in 1897 and maintained in the actor's repertoire ever since. The film was mounted shortly after Forbes-Robertson had given his farewell performances in England (he was then 60), yet it is in no way a simple transcription of a stage production. Hepworth took his cast and crew to Lulworth Cove, his favourite location spot, where Elsinore was constructed in canvas and plaster and the Ghost was let loose on the stones and boulders of the Dorset shore. Other locations included the Hertfordshire garden of Forbes-Robertson's sister-in-law – site of the graveyard and Ophelia's wanderings.

Yet it is in the studio interiors, shot at Walton with settings inspired by Hawes Craven's Art Nouveau stage scenery, that the film's virtues – and vices – can best be seen. At worst, the director E. Hay Plumb fails to keep track of the actors (and forlornly twists the camera in an attempt to keep pace with Hamlet, busily exiting stage left). But at best, scenes are neatly shaped for the camera's eye (the players scene, for instance, with the King and Queen in the right foreground, Hamlet sprawled mid-field on the ground between two lines of spectators leading the eye back to the players at the rear). The film also draws on the camera's ability to isolate details: Polonius, dead behind the arras, is rewarded with his own cut-away shot, while Hamlet receives the sole close-up, applying poison to a goblet and sword-tip.

Sir J. Forbes-Robertson Acts "Hamlet" for the Cinematograph.

The real thing at last: part of the *Daily Mirror*'s picture report (28 June 1913) of the Hepworth–Forbes-Robertson *Hamlet* by the sea

The film's main strength, however, derives from Forbes-Robertson himself. 'I've got a mouth like a cavern!' he is supposed to have said on inspecting his celluloid self, though there is little extravagance about his interpretation, renowned at the time for its intelligence and restraint. The cinema's camera spotlights his mature age in a way a stage performance would not, but as the film proceeds the power of his performance holds sway; only a few semaphoric gestures suggesting anguish, hands clutching head, disturb the dignified style. Critics showered the film with superlatives: 'This great work, expounded by the foremost artistes in the dramatic profession, cannot fail to receive public approval,' noted the *Kinematograph Weekly*.[8] There is no concrete evidence, however, that the ecstatic reviews captured the feelings of the ordinary spectator, suddenly dosed with culture.

Shakespeare films, by their nature, were isolated events, never part of the staple cinema diet; one can better inspect the theatrical influence at work by considering the use of contemporary dramatists.

At the time of *Masks and Faces*, the most favoured playwright for adaptation seems to have been Sir Arthur Wing Pinero, elegant purveyor of fashionable entertainments from an earlier age: seven of his biggest Victorian successes were filmed between 1915 and 1921, including *The Second Mrs Tanqueray, Trelawny of the Wells, The Gay Lord Quex*, and *The Magistrate*. But ten years later, the man of the hour was of the hour itself – Noël Coward, the 20s' brightest dramatist, who had three versions of recent plays released within twelve months in 1927–8. In announcing his studio's new acquisition, Gainsborough production chief Michael Balcon pointed to Coward's material as a means of countering undue American influence on the content of British films: '*Easy Virtue* is the answer; a country house play with county people.'[9] It wasn't, of course; there is rather more to British life than can be contained in a country house play. Yet Balcon was right to sense the importance of Coward's cinema debut; and the material and style of *Easy Virtue* (directed by Hitchcock) and *The Vortex* (directed by Adrian Brunel) offer particular food for thought.

Once again, lack of speech proves a distinct handicap, and the facetious titles sprinkled throughout *The Vortex* are poor compensation for Coward's special brand of repartee and lancing wit. But Coward's material survives – material far more sophisticated, provocative and pertinent than the cinema at this point could generally find for itself. *The Vortex* presents a savage portrait of a frivolous society hooked on appearances, fashion and youth – a 'vortex of beastliness,' in Coward's words – though the characters are all somewhat laundered to meet the demands of film censorship. Florence (Willette Kershaw, an American import) is still the vain, middle-aged woman doting unreservedly on the young boy Tom, though she never openly admits his lover status, as she does in the play. The bohemian life of her son Nicky (Coward's stage role, winningly played by Ivor Novello, with his pretty profile well to the fore) is also rendered more innocuous; here, he trembles on the brink of drug addiction rather than drowning in the vice from the curtain's rise. The film also concludes with far more optimism and forgiveness than Coward offered on stage. Where Florence and Nicky ushered in the final applause with desperate promises to improve their lifestyles, they now stand in close-up with Nicky's long-suffering fiancée, locked in a mutual, unconvincing embrace.

Brunel's written account of the production stresses the absurdities of filming a censored text. In fact, much of the vortex's beastliness survives, despite the script's soft-pedalling. Brunel also mentions livening the proceedings with camera tricks and other bits of business.[10] The most noticeable of these is the zig-zag subjective shot of Nicky casting his eyes at the 'futurist decoration' in Florence's town house. 'This room is a bit strenuous,' he declaims, via a title; so, indeed, is the effect, for Brunel's tricks are never integrated into a consistently expressive style. Characters and props are stiffly deployed, emphasising the four-square, cavernous nature of Clifford Pember's sets; despite the bursts of camera virtuosity, we still sniff the West End stage.

Hitchcock's version of *Easy Virtue* affords the perfect complement. The play itself is less interesting. The drama of Larita, the woman with a past, her wimpish husband John, and his hidebound family was consciously designed as a modern equivalent of Pinero's drawing-room dramas; even at the time, it struck critics as old-fashioned. But Hitchcock's treatment consistently breathes fresh life into the material. The script adaptation is radical. Larita's past – the subject of vague allusions on stage – takes up almost half the running time, and two divorce hearings in a courtroom provide a neat framing device for the remodelled story. But it is Hitchcock's early mastery of visual story-telling that impresses most: the use of symbolic objects and leitmotifs (the judge's eyeglass; the lenses of the journalists' cameras, hounding the heroine); the advancement of character and plot through natural, wordless human behaviour (the husband's clumsiness with the cocktail shaker; the way the engagement is

Still stage-bound: *The Vortex* (1927)

relayed solely through the telephone operator's changing expressions). The film is also marked by subtle character groupings, eloquently conveying conflicting emotional viewpoints (the mother, for instance, looks from the background with withering disdain as John introduces Larita to his old flame). In the late 20s and 30s, Hitchcock was heavily engaged in theatrical adaptations: Galsworthy's *The Skin Game* (1931), O'Casey's *Juno and the Paycock* (1930), the slim rural comedy of Eden Phillpott's *The Farmer's Wife* (1928). It is customary to treat such films as assignments, dutifully undertaken; but one must not underestimate the lure of the theatre in Hitchcock's creative personality, nor its possible influence on his striking sense of spatial manipulation. Only a theatre aficionado would have toyed with the continuous-take experiments of *Rope*, or would have bothered embalming Frederick Knott's mystery thriller *Dial M for Murder* with such graceful 3-D imagery. One recalls, too, Hitchcock's late obsession with filming Barrie's play *Mary Rose*, which he first saw in his twenties.

Hitchcock's *Easy Virtue* shows what an imaginative silent director could do with a theatrical text; but the absence of sound still circumscribed the relationship of film and stage. When Balcon commissioned Coward to write an original subject for his leading male star Ivor Novello (himself a vital stage acquisition), Coward responded with a costume piece, *Concerto*; Balcon then realised that it demanded music, and the project collapsed. With the onset of talkies, renewed efforts were made to involve dramatists and stage actors in film production. In August 1928, the theatrical producer Basil Dean wrote to his friend John Galsworthy with a film version of *Escape* in mind: 'By timely action the theatre might regain a great deal of influence over the screen and at the same time make certain that an author's work was not shamelessly misrepresented.'[11] Galsworthy, replying, stuck out for textual fidelity, and tried to insist on financial compensation if any of his words were altered; though when *Escape* finally emerged on film in 1930, much had been changed, with benefit. There was even an exclamation mark after the title. Bernard Shaw, typically, stuck out even further, and secured a British International Productions contract in 1930, condemning his adapters to provide nothing more than 'faithful reproductions of the play as written and designed for ordinary theatrical representation;'[12] any deviation would need Shaw's consent. The short-term result was *How He Lied to her Husband* (1930) and *Arms and the Man* (1932) – tedious films bogged down with talk.

Galsworthy and Shaw's strictures reflect, in part, the natural protective instincts of the self-respecting author. But they also mirror the anxious, combative spirit of the British theatre as the 30s dawned, under joint attack from the cold economic climate and new technological developments. Theatre managements had already fought prickly battles with the newly formed BBC over radio broadcasts, and secured strict agreements in 1925 over the limited use of stage excerpts on the air. Now another brand of canned goods loomed, with a far greater potential audience.

Some theatrical luminaries responded with direct attack. Sir Nigel Playfair, renowned manager of the Lyric Theatre, Hammersmith, had been happy enough in 1917 to appear in the cast of *Masks and Faces*, but in a 1931 article he took pains to pour scorn on current British films – 'the majority of which are directed by people without taste, with no sense of language, and with nothing to express but the crudest sentimentality or worse. Against such attacks the theatre, the human theatre, should stand as a bulwark.'[13] To many observers the bulwark required a concrete form and organisation and it is surely no coincidence that 1930 saw a renewed propaganda effort for the establishment of a National Theatre: William Archer and Harley Granville-Barker's classic book of 1907, *A National Theatre: Scheme and Estimates,* was revised and updated; the project's Committee also made a direct, and discouraging, appeal to Parliament.

In such a context, Basil Dean seems almost a renegade – actively pursuing cinema production with the Associated Talking Picture company (formed in 1929 with Dean as managing director) and a newly built Ealing studio. But Dean is a paradoxical figure. In some ways he perfectly fits the pigeon-hole description of Thorold Dickinson, who worked at ATP as an editor: 'Basil Dean was a theatre man, he made canned plays.'[14] For Dean regularly filmed the plays and dramatists he had showcased on the stage (Galsworthy, Margaret Kennedy's *The Constant Nymph,* C. L. Anthony's *Autumn Crocus*). He also endeavoured, in 1934, to establish a joint working company for film and stage work (a failed venture, though some of Dean's theatre staff – Carol Reed and Basil Dearden among them – found profitable work at Ealing).

Yet the best of Dean's films were far from canned plays. He was obsessed, sometimes to dottiness, with open-air shooting; and unlike some other contemporaries he had the knack of making his locations work in the material's favour. When Shaw's *Arms and the Man* ventured before the cameras on a pretty riverside location in North Wales, the film plummeted to the level of a stiff open-air pageant. But Galsworthy's *Escape* emerged bedecked and enlivened with its hunting scenes, Hyde Park Corner traffic, and assorted views of Dartmoor. Dean was determined to bend sound effects to his purposes, too: the early scenes are endearingly over-orchestrated with yelping hounds, traffic hoots, and a performing Hyde Park band. The distinguished stage star Gerald du Maurier caught Dean's adventurous spirit and threw caution – plus his drawing-room clothes – to the winds, clambering over walls and rugged terrain as the unjustly convicted prisoner making a grand dash for freedom.

On *Loyalties*, Thorold Dickinson served as editor, and is responsible for the film's visual highlight: Basil Rathbone's suicide fall subjectively caught by a spinning camera (suspended on a rope from a Park Lane roof). But the entire film is impressive, with its subtle script adaptation (by W. P. Lipscomb) and frank depiction of anti-semitic feeling in a class-conscious society. As with Coward in the 20s, Galsworthy's plays brought a heightened moral consciousness into British films; one looks in vain for another release of 1933 that focused so sharply on social injustice, on class and race warfare.

Loyalties, however, was just one of forty-nine British feature films with stage antecedents that emerged in 1933; one cannot impute similarly serious purposes to *She Was Only a Village Maiden, Waltz Time, A Cuckoo in the Nest, Britannia of Billingsgate*, or others from the horde of theatrical adaptations. Some – like the Ben Travers farces, simply transferred by their stage producer Tom Walls – relied wholly on the proven popularity of the material and cast. Others went through the scenario department mill to emerge as vehicles for studio stars; still others merely proved handy in keeping the quota quickies coming. By the end of the 30s, when the British cinema's latest production bubble had burst, the favoured candidates for adaptation were solid, middle-brow West End successes by Rattigan, Priestley, Dodie Smith, Esther McCracken, treated by directors confidently pursuing an unambitious style. This is the British cinema's middle ground: the cinema of establishing long-shots followed by mechanical mid-shots seen from the alternate shoulders of familiar character actors; the cinema of directors without a personal viewpoint. Many of those who worked in this territory – among them Basil Dearden, Henry Cass, Harold French – had extensive theatrical experience, and were trained by the theatre to be illustrators rather than interpreters. Carol Reed's films extend beyond this territory, yet his active denial of the director's own personality hints at his own conventional theatre background: 'I don't think that a director who knows how to put a film together need impose his ideas on the world,' he said in interview with Charles Thomas Samuels; 'You must always take the author's side.'[15]

Such a passive attitude might work if the author in question were in fact Rattigan, or Priestley, or Dodie Smith, or other contemporary playwrights who created self-contained, self-sufficient worlds easily recognised by contemporary audiences. But what if the author were Shakespeare? Gone were the days of Benson's *Richard III*, when the director could plonk down his camera before Stratford's floorboards; yet British cinema had been ducking the bard for years – indeed, there had been no direct confrontation with a Shakespeare text since *The Merchant of Venice* in 1916, choked with the gestures and scenery of Matheson Lang's current production at St James's Theatre. By the mid-30s, with Reinhardt's *Midsummer Night's Dream* as a stimulus, Shakespeare films reared their head again. At the start of 1936, Korda had hopes of a *Hamlet* with Robert Donat, to be co-directed by William Cameron Menzies and Miles Malleson; but by September his thunder had been stolen by Paul Czinner's *As You Like It*, with the director's wife Elisabeth Bergner as a Germanic Rosalind, and Laurence Olivier, fresh from his success in Gielgud's stage production of *Romeo and Juliet*, as an all-leaping, all-ardent Orlando.

At one fell swoop, *As You Like It* re-established the dormant tradition of the theatrical film as a prestige cultural package. Korda himself couldn't have filled the film with more international expertise. William Walton wrote the music; the great Lazare Meerson designed the stylised sets; while the role of Rosalind had been one of Bergner's successes in Germany. The press coverage was considerable (Bergner's accent exerted particular fascination), and respectful. All these classy trimmings were achieved, however, at the expense of any coherent cinematic style. The treatment was suggested initially by the *Masks and Faces* veteran J. M. Barrie, a great admirer of Bergner's fey style; but neither Bergner nor Olivier could convey much grace while struggling with a gnarled Arden forest straight from a German fairytale or the extraordinary menagerie of geese, peacocks and garlanded sheep with tinkling bells.

British cinema waited eight years before tackling Shakespeare again, in *Henry V*. This was another prestige package, and generated intense public interest both at home and abroad; an ecstatic cover article in *Time* magazine told all America how to pronounce the actor-director's name ('O'lívvy yay').[16] The film's origins lay in a television adaptation proposed by the pioneer producer Dallas Bower, and shelved with the onset of war. Bower had also produced Louis MacNeice's radio adaptation of *Alexander Nevsky*, incorporating Prokofiev's music – which might provide a source for the film's visual treatment of Agincourt. Building on Bower's framework, Olivier propelled the heavily cut text through a shifting range of styles and settings. At first we watch a performance of *Henry V* at the Globe playhouse; the camera then penetrates a stage veil to reach artificial sets partly copied from medieval illustrations. For Agincourt, we climb further up the reality ladder, to open-air locations (in Eire) and massed extras from the Irish Home Guard. We then

'The blast of war': Olivier's *Henry V*, a contemporary call to arms

descend, ending as we started with the Elizabethan stage and audience.

There is no space here to examine all the intricacies of this bold conception, or indeed the practical problems of mounting a Technicolor epic requiring entire armies, horses, bright period costumes and quantities of chain mail (the latter came mostly from the Old Vic). But the purpose and effect of *Henry V* is of paramount importance. For this is not only a starry slab of culture; *Henry V* is, explicitly, a British war film, with the bard and the British theatrical tradition joining forces to boost the nation's morale. There is nothing token about the opening dedication 'to the commandos and airborne troops of Great Britain': the patriotism and bravery of Britain's current war effort is constantly evoked with the help of cosmetic surgery on the text, the elaboration of Agincourt (the play's only on-stage battle concerns the braggart Pistol and a cowardly Frenchman), and many specific lines. 'Now all the youth of England are on fire,' proclaims Leslie Banks' Chorus; some of the current wounded youth of England, indeed, were among the extras. The visual style plays its propaganda part, too: the artificial sets and vivid colours help root Henry's conquest – or 'D-Day of 1415' as one newspaper report on the film put it – in the realm of glorious British legend.

Olivier's acting is impassioned but precise; he really seems like O'lívvy yay. During the war his fevered tones could also be heard declaiming literary texts in Humphrey Jennings' *Words for Battle* (1941) and Basil Dean's propaganda pageant 'Salute to the Red Army', staged at the Royal Albert Hall in 1943. The participation of Olivier – and Ralph Richardson – in such projects carried a special cachet in wartime. For these were not only leading exponents of Britain's theatrical tradition, part of the country's heritage currently under attack; they were also officers of the Fleet Air Arm, and permission had to be obtained for their services. Scripts and subjects were rigorously vetted. Olivier's overlords found Asquith's *The Demi-Paradise* (1943) acceptable, for it promoted Anglo-Soviet relations; Powell and Pressburger's *Life and Death of Colonel Blimp* (1943), however, failed the test. But the Archers at least bagged Richardson for *The Volunteer* (1944), an imaginative and engaging treatment of a standard propaganda device: following the progress of a recruit. The volunteer in question is Richardson's stage dresser, introduced handing his master an Othello costume inside-out in the summer of 1939; at the end, the dresser has become a nimble, trained mechanic. Richardson himself progresses through the film from stage actor to propaganda film actor (dressed in beefeater gear at Denham), to Fleet Air Arm pilot, hopping round the world in gold braid. For all the differences in scope and treatment, *The Volunteer* reflects the same impulse that prompted Olivier's *Henry V* – the impulse to put the British theatrical tradition in battle dress.

But the war did more than cast the classical stage actor in a new propaganda role; the war also opened up the kind of opportunities that Basil Dean and others looked for in the wake of the talking picture, particularly the greater involvement of stage authors. Within the years of World War Two, Terence Rattigan's scripts developed from simple adaptations of polished stage comedies (his own *French Without Tears*, 1939, Esther McCracken's *Quiet Wedding*, 1941), to the vivid depiction of wartime camaraderie in the RAF Film Unit's *Journey Together* (1945) and *The Way to the Stars* (1945, partly based on his play *Flare Path*). Noël Coward spread his wings further still, and moved directly into film production with Filippo Del Giudice's Two Cities Films. As Alan Wood relates in his book *Mr Rank*, Coward was the second choice of prestige writer for the reactivated company, after Bernard Shaw. Coward proved a fortunate replacement. Shaw's wartime films with Gabriel Pascal – *Major Barbara* (1941) and the expensive folly *Caesar and Cleopatra* (1945) –

avoided the literalness of the first Shaw films made by BIP, but they remained glued to the contours and talk of their sources. Coward, however, struck out with fresh material, writing, co-directing and taking the lead part in *In Which We Serve* (1942), a salute to the Navy and a veiled tribute to Mountbatten, and building a body of work that C. A. Lejeune appraised in 1947 as 'probably the nearest thing we have to a valid modern school in British cinema'.[17]

Coward's opening appearance in *In Which We Serve* seems deliberately calculated to blow away his former aura of dressing-gowned languor. As Captain E. V. Kinross, RN, the Mountbatten surrogate, he stands on the HMS 'Torrin', peering through binoculars at the battle of Crete, and quietly accepts a hearty cup of cocoa. Yet despite the odd surroundings – and the odd drink – he is still very much Noël Coward the stage personality, and he addresses his shipmates rather as Olivier addresses the soldiers at Harfleur, with an authority and resonance that derives primarily from the performer, not the screen character. Coward's theatrical instincts also emerge in the neat separation of characters into classes, and the crisp dialogue exchanges; the structure and style can be traced back specifically to the social kaleidoscope and warm patriotism of *Cavalcade*. This theatrical residue never clogs up the film, for which thanks are partly due to the co-director, David Lean; in between the set pieces, the business of naval warfare is sharply conveyed, while Coward the writer hits on effective phrases blending his own style with common feelings. One of the men rescued from Dunkirk asks Captain Kinross what life in England is currently like; 'Gentle, you know,' comes the resonant reply, 'not exactly smug, not exactly warlike, either.'

Given the original achievement of *In Which We Serve*, one regrets that Coward's subsequent films drew more directly on pre-existing stage material, though the eloquent romance of *Brief Encounter* (1945) was skilfully expanded from his one-act play *Still Life*. Had *This Happy Breed* and *Blithe Spirit* been pre-war plays, they would doubtless have been modestly adapted in black-and-white; but the British cinema's new confidence and prestige now demanded Technicolor luxury. So Frank Gibbons' happy middle-class breed came to the screen in 1944 in bright but dainty decor, while the Condomines of *Blithe Spirit* (1945) lived among the most vivid curtains, flowers and furniture (pink and blue predominating). In such films, Coward's part in a 'valid modern school' of British cinema appears somewhat suspect: the films are not exactly warlike, either, but they *are* smug.

Yet for a time, during the war, Lejeune's 'valid modern school' existed, born of the necessity to define and showcase the nation's

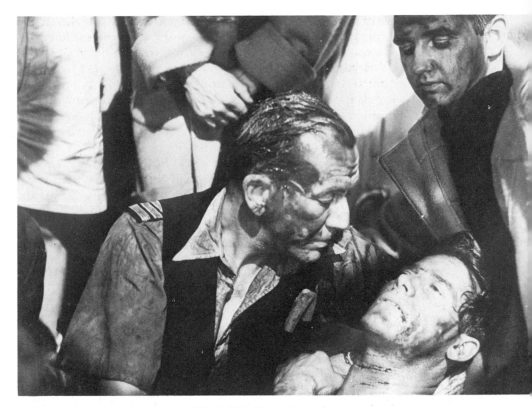

Off stage: Noël Coward in *In Which We Serve* (1942)

fighting spirit by every available means – from a Shakespeare text to the documentary skills of the Crown Film Unit. Once the wartime spur was removed, old habits crept back: theatrical material became something to lean on, not something to mould for a specific cinematic purpose. Frederick Lonsdale's drawing-room classic *On Approval* had arrived in the cinemas in 1944, directed by Clive Brook with engaging stylistic tricks. Opening shots showed combat footage; 'Oh dear, is this another war picture?' the commentator E. V. H. Emmett asked. It was not, but the war had somehow to be acknowledged, before Lonsdale's trivialities could be reached. But when Asquith filmed an earlier drawing-room classic, *The Importance of Being Earnest*, some eight years later, there was no need to 'apologise' so inventively for the material. The film is presented as an actual stage performance in the late Victorian era. The opening credits appear on the pages of the theatre programme clutched by a well-dressed couple, and we first see Michael Redgrave's Jack Worthing as an image in the lady's opera glasses; the final credits are duly unfurled on the theatre's plush red curtain, just descended. One recalls Edith Evans' words, quoted earlier: 'I always feel the camera should come to *me*, instead of me go to the *camera*.' Throughout his career, Asquith displayed a similar attitude to Rattigan, Shaw, and his other dramatic subjects: the camera always came to the play.

Four years after the release of *The Importance of Being Earnest*, John Osborne's *Look Back in Anger* appeared at the Royal Court Theatre and opened new doors in British cultural life. Instead of late-Victorian drawing-rooms with ormolu clocks and writing desks, audiences saw a dingy attic flat in the Midlands with gas stove, ironing board and posh Sunday papers in disarray; instead of absurd repartee oiling the wheels of conventional society, they heard furious speeches exposing the sores and rifts of current British life. British cinema took time to adjust to Osborne, Kingsley Amis, John Braine, Colin Wilson and other misnamed 'angry young men' (some more ironic than angry, a few almost middle-aged). Jimmy Porter might have been railing at the Royal Court, but the plays on view at the country's Odeon and ABC cinemas in 1956 were mostly traditional farces – John Chapman's *Dry Rot* (directed, appropriately, by Maurice Elvey, nearing the end of his epic career), or *Sailor Beware*, with Peggy Mount railing as Ma Hornett (one-woman personification of the mother-in-law joke).

Two years later, the Romulus company responsible for both those farces extracted a film from John Braine's novel *Room at the Top*, notable for its comparative sexual candour and open acceptance of the go-getting hero's greedy aspirations. Then in 1959 *Look Back in Anger* emerged on screen – the first production of Woodfall Films, formed by Osborne, Tony Richardson (director of both stage and film versions) and the future Bond producer Harry Saltzman. Though Osborne and Richardson were prime movers in Woodfall, they did curiously little to preserve the exact spirit and personnel of the original. Writer and television dramatist Nigel Kneale was brought in to adapt the play, while Richard Burton returned from Hollywood to star (only Mary Ure repeated her stage performance). Even amidst the initial euphoria, some observers pointed out the screen's muffled representation of Britain's raw, regional, 'angry' voices: Stuart Hall, writing in the magazine *Definition*, detected the 'Old Vic burr' in Laurence Harvey's Joe Lampton (*Room at the Top*), while Burton's Jimmy Porter was deemed 'too Shakespearean'.[18] And the passing years have only emphasised the tentative nature of the British cinema's 'revolution'.

The excitement of the moment, for instance, caused some critics to trumpet Tony Richardson as a young brave artist, striving to break the fossilised habits of British cinema: but if one takes the long view,

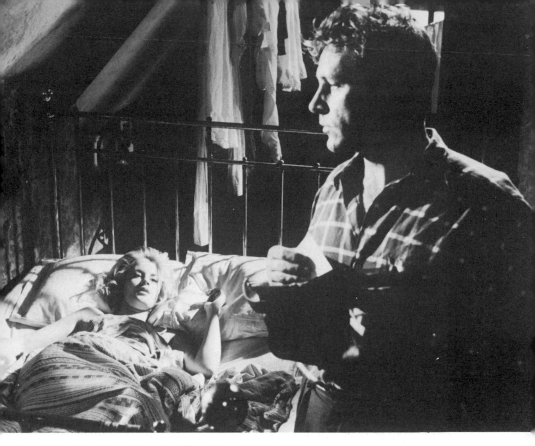

Look Back in Anger (1959): Mary Ure, Richard Burton

he appears as nothing more, or less, than the post-war Basil Dean. Like Dean, he maintained dual directing careers in both cinema and theatre, and regularly transferred some of his most successful stage productions (*Look Back in Anger* and *The Entertainer*, 1960, from the Royal Court; *Hamlet*, in 1969, from the Roundhouse, where the film was shot). Like Dean, he also displayed a childlike faith in location shooting as a means of obscuring the material's theatrical origins – a trick that works well in *A Taste of Honey*, 1961, though the open-air scenes of *The Entertainer* only point up the overbearing theatricality of Olivier's Archie Rice. There is a further, minor parallel in the directors' relationships with editors. Just as Thorold Dickinson played a pivotal part in adding pace and panache to *Loyalties* (1933) and *Sing As We Go!* (1934), so Seth Holt, working uncredited, gave *The Entertainer* its own shape and edge. (Holt's flair for cutting was demonstrated officially in Reisz's *Saturday Night and Sunday Morning*, another Woodfall offering from 1960.)

Richardson was not alone among the new talents of British cinema in displaying abiding theatrical connections. Throughout the years,

Lindsay Anderson, another Royal Court alumnus, has worked far more consistently in the theatre than in the cinema; while among the regional actors thrown up in the late 50s, only Richard Harris has cut loose from his British theatrical moorings and permanently ascended into Hollywood. A few of his old colleagues, indeed, have abandoned cinema for years on end: twelve years separate Tom Courtenay's appearances in *One Day in the Life of Ivan Denisovich* (1971) and *The Dresser* (1983). Such matters partly reflect personal taste and ambition; but they also reflect the fluctuating economic and artistic health of the British film industry in the 60s and 70s, subject to the vagaries of American finance and uncertain public taste.

These were comparatively good decades for the British theatre, particularly the 60s. The National Theatre finally established a track record and an identity at the Old Vic; the Royal Shakespeare Company broke new ground at Stratford and the Aldwych; new voices appeared in the West End, notably Joe Orton. The cinema duly took note. 1968 alone saw the emergence of film versions of Peter Brook's experimental RSC production *US* (retitled *Tell Me Lies*), Osborne's *Inadmissible Evidence* (directed for Woodfall by another peripatetic talent, Anthony Page), Frank Dunlop's Pop Theatre production of *The Winter's Tale* (featured at the 1966 Edinburgh Festival), and *A Midsummer Night's Dream,* directed by Peter Hall with the Royal Shakespeare Company. Zeffirelli's youthfully romantic *Romeo and Juliet* appeared; Jack Gold made his cinema debut with a powerful treatment of John McGrath's play *Events While Guarding the Bofors Gun*, starring the new actor of the moment, Nicol Williamson (also featured in *Inadmissible Evidence* and Tony Richardson's *Hamlet*). Fodder, suddenly, is almost banished: among the year's tally of releases, only Ray Milland's *Hostile Witness*, based on a conventional West End courtroom drama, recalls the old, unambitious days.

Yet it is hard to divine any imaginative forward thrust in this late-60s upsurge of theatrical cinema. One senses, instead, signs of retreat, to the cinema as a transcription system for significant stage productions; to theatrical films as prestige cultural packages, precisely aimed at the British art house and selected foreign markets (particularly in America). Laurence Olivier's *Three Sisters*, released in 1970, provides a particularly doleful example. This is Olivier's first film treatment of a classic stage property since *Richard III* in 1955, but the style and intentions are far different. In all his Shakespeare films Olivier attempted, with varied success, to find ways of balancing the demands of the established text with the imaginative possibilities of cinema: *Henry V* drew on the cinema's aptitude for spectacle, and its wartime role as the nation's comforter; *Hamlet* gloried in deep-focus travelling shots and the exploration of barren castle interiors. In *Richard III*, the theatre won back some ground, though the use of a composite set aided fluidity, and the battle of Bosworth Field (shot in Spain) echoed, even if it never capped, the Agincourt scenes of *Henry V*. But in *Three Sisters* Olivier follows the unambitious example of the 1965 *Othello*, directed by Stuart Burge. Two interpolated sequences aside (one a fantasy, the other a flash-forward), the camera is content to record, not interpret. In such circumstances, 'The National Theatre of Great Britain and Alan Bates' (as the billing in the opening credits phrases it) can only recreate the letter of their 1967 production. The spirit has evaporated, somewhere in the empty spaces of Josef Svoboda's stylised sets or in the too respectful distance between camera and performer.

British cinema experienced better results approaching the dramatists of the 60s, rather than the theatrical companies. Harold Pinter began a fruitful association with Joseph Losey, stretching from *The Servant* (1963), *Accident* (1967) and *The Go-Between* (1970), to their unfilmed treatment of *A la recherche du temps perdu*. In one way the partnership conforms to the traditional rules of quality cinema, applicable on both sides of the Atlantic: when you hire a famous writer, always tether him to the work of *another* famous writer. So, in another age, Hugh Walpole buckles down to *David Copperfield* and *Little Lord Fauntleroy*; Pinter hones and transmutes Robin Maugham, L. P. Hartley, Proust. Once we take the films as a group, however, common themes and stylistic traits soon emerge: the workings of memory, the conflict of past and present, the multiplicity of emotional responses to a single set of circumstances. These are matters that cinema is well equipped to handle; Losey's training, temperament and 'foreign' status also made him an ideal interpreter of Pinter's anguished internal landscapes and clinical fascination with the class structure of British society.

Charles Wood's collaborations with Richard Lester have received less critical attention and respect, yet they provide another valuable instance of the writer's hand uniquely fitting the director's glove. Wood's plays show continuing obsessions with the business and trappings of war (particularly the Imperial kind) and the vanities, madness and delusions of show business; they also, at best, display flamboyant verbal dexterity. Lester found a welcoming home for Wood's talents in *The Knack* (1965, from Ann Jellicoe's play), the frenzied satire of *Help!* (1965), the crazy black comedy of *How I Won the War* (1967) and, more recently, the bitter-sweet *Cuba* (1979). Wood also proved an ideal writer for Tony Richardson's unfairly maligned *The Charge of the Light Brigade* (1968), which placed the

Crimean war in a three-ringed circus of buffoonery, spectacle and social satire. Wood's subsequent stage play *Veterans* (1972) – an amusing account of life on a Turkish film location – made specific use of his *Light Brigade* experience, not least in the personality and vocal cadences of John Gielgud (the film's Lord Raglan), cast as the brick-dropping actor Sir Geoffrey Kendle.

Kendle spends most of *Veterans* sitting in a chair fussing with sun-tan lotion, his costume, letters from home and an airline bag with assorted comforts. Gielgud himself, in *An Actor and his Time*, provides a parallel picture of life on the film set or location: hours spent quietly over a crossword puzzle, a magazine or novel; hours spent happily gossiping. He also pinpoints *The Charge of the Light Brigade* as the first film that gave him room to manoeuvre in a character part.[19] In the years since 1968, the character parts have multiplied, though only one – in Resnais' *Providence*, written by David Mercer – offered a role of substance (as the dying writer Clive Langham). In the 70s, bizarre and wasteful cameo appearances seemed the only place possible for esteemed stage actors in British cinema; for the number of theatrical adaptations shrunk in line with the film industry, and only Derek Jarman's punk-tinged *Tempest* of 1979 attacked its material with imagination.

The Knack (1965)

164

Once a measure of confidence, success and finance returned to the industry, so did the theatrical adaptation: *Privates on Parade* (1983), *Educating Rita* (1983), *The Dresser* (1983), *Another Country* (1984), all based on solid commercial successes, and all guaranteed to sharpen the sense of *déjà vu* in this latest cautious revival of British cinema. The personnel and material of *The Dresser*, for instance, eerily conflate two prime periods of British theatrical endeavour: the Royal Court/Woodfall era, and the wartime days of the actual play – set backstage during a provincial performance of *King Lear,* subject to the ravages of Hitler's bombs and the actor-manager's crumbling memory. The director, Peter Yates, may now be indelibly associated with *Bullitt, The Deep* and other Hollywood genre pieces; but he began in Britain as a repertory actor and spent some years at the Royal Court (he also directed Woodfall's film version of N. F. Simpson's *One Way Pendulum* in 1964). The stars provide stronger links, through Albert Finney and Tom Courtenay, leading lights of the 60s new wave. But now they are fixed in character roles: Finney, as the grandiloquently decrepit 'Sir', swathed in padding and ageing make-up; Courtenay, swamped by the stage mannerisms of the homosexual dresser Norman, who cajoles and cossets his master. 'It's much nicer than having to whack it to the audience every night in theatre,' Courtenay told one interviewer; though he 'whacks it' just as hard to the camera, with tiresome results.

Privates on Parade provides another instance of the theatrical film looking backwards to old habits, and some old mistakes. The stage director Michael Blakemore had earlier scored a critical hit with his hour-long *Personal History of the Australian Surf* (1981), a quirky portrait of his childhood years in Australia, inventively blending staged re-creations, newsreels and on-the-spot observations with a nicely judged ironic tone. For his feature debut, however, Blakemore returned to the theatre's womb and directed one of his recent successes, Peter Nichols' musical play about an entertainment troupe in Malaya, *circa* 1950. The material obstinately refuses to adapt itself to cinema. While the actors at the Aldwych Theatre could slip into the musical numbers via a simple lighting change, Blakemore struggles to kit out the sequences with fidgety alternations between colour and black-and-white, between the troops on the parade ground and the troupe performing on stage. The cast's ensemble playing is also thrown out of kilter by the importation of a 'name' actor, John Cleese, who belongs in a different film.

It is now almost seventy years since Irene Vanbrugh nervously led her theatrical knights up to Elstree for the prologue to *Masks and Faces*. Stage actors still make the train journey, though they do so now more for television productions. In the intervening years, the relationship between film and theatre has advanced, retreated, and now, to some extent, dispersed. In which tradition of British cinema, for example, can one place a new, fashionable director like Richard Eyre? His roots are assuredly in the theatre – at the Nottingham Playhouse and the National Theatre (where he directed *The Beggar's Opera*). His roots are also in video and television, where he directed *The Cherry Orchard* and an Ian McEwan script, *The Imitation Game*, for the BBC. His roots are also in contemporary British literature (McEwan again, who wrote the original script of *The Ploughman's Lunch*). The only place his roots are not, it seems, is in the cinema itself, despite the attempts in *Laughterhouse* (1984) to evoke Howard Hawks' *Red River*. 'The Film is the Sister of the Stage,' Sir John Hare had said. This particular sibling relationship may not be so apparent today, but British film seems destined always to be *somebody's* sister.

Notes

1   *The Bioscope*, 8 March 1917, p. 993. Production details of *Masks and Faces* are drawn from *To Tell My Story* by Irene Vanbrugh, London, Hutchinson, 1948, pp. 112–17.
2   *Kinematograph Weekly*, 2 March 1911; quoted in *Shakespeare on Silent Film: A Strange Eventful History* by Robert Hamilton Ball, London, Allen and Unwin, 1968, p. 82.
3   *A Mirror for England*, London, Faber & Faber, 1970, p. 111.
4   *Mask or Face: Reflections in an Actor's Mirror*, London, Heinemann, 1958, p. 123.
5   *'Puffin' Asquith* by R. J. Minney, London, Leslie Frewin, 1973, pp. 141–2.
6   *The Oxford Companion to the Theatre*, second edition, ed. Phyllis Hartnoll, Oxford, Oxford University Press, 1957, p. 774.
7   *The Bioscope*, 28 July 1921, p. 33.
8   *Kinematograph Weekly*, 24 July 1913; quoted in *Shakespeare on Silent Film*, p. 191.
9   Quoted in *A Talent to Amuse* by Sheridan Morley, Harmondsworth, Penguin, 1974, p. 128.
10   *Nice Work*, London, Forbes Robertson, 1949, pp. 130–4.
11   *Mind's Eye: An Autobiography 1927–1972*, London, Hutchinson, 1973, p. 86.
12   Quoted in L'Estrange Fawcett, *Writing for the Films*, London, Pitman and Sons, 1932; for more details of BIP's Shaw films, see Geoff Brown, *Launder and Gilliat*, London, British Film Institute, 1977, pp. 36–7, 46–7.
13   'The Theatre and the Film', in *The English Review*, March 1931, p. 338.
14   *Film Dope*, no. 11, January 1977, p. 5.

15 *Encountering Directors*, New York, Putnam, 1972, p. 166.
16 *Time*, 8 April 1946, p. 26.
17 *Chestnuts in her Lap*, London, Phoenix House, 1947, p. 163.
18 'Jimmy Porter and the Two-and-Nines', *Definition,* no. 1, February 1960, p. 11.
19 *An Actor and his Time*, Harmondsworth, Penguin, 1981, pp. 157–8, 178.

Andy Medhurst

MUSIC HALL AND BRITISH CINEMA

Literature, theatre, television, music hall – of the four cultural practices and institutions discussed in this group of essays, music hall is clearly the odd one out. Not because it is in any way less worthy of attention (unless one subscribes to an insupportable elitism), but because, quite simply, it no longer exists. Indeed, it has not existed as a discrete cultural entity for around seventy years. So while literature, theatre and television enjoy a continuing and contemporary relationship with cinema, the relationship between cinema and music hall is of necessity retrospective.

There was, of course, a brief period of co-existence between music hall and cinema, which is usually seen in terms of the overlapping and interlinked decline of the former and rise of the latter. The issues involved in this notable cultural shift (which are far more complex than the usual glibly dovetailed accounts allow) are examined below.

But what of the subsequent decades? Here the key phrase is the 'music hall tradition', and the key problem it raises is one of definition. Which films, which genres, which performers should be allotted a place in this tradition? More fundamentally, what do we mean when we speak of such a tradition? In order to restore some precision to what has become a label of lazy convenience, any consideration of the 'music hall tradition' must be prefaced by a look at the nature of the music hall institution itself.

The Nineteenth-century Music Hall

The dominant popular image of the music hall, as fostered by the long-running BBC TV series *The Good Old Days*, remains one of a regrettably lost world of Edwardian plushness. This image has, as the BBC series' title suggests, become a talisman for nostalgia, but its vision of chandeliers and sentiment masks the true history of the music hall institution.

The nostalgic image chooses the Edwardian era as its preferred moment, but a number of historians have convincingly argued that by this time the music hall was in its period of final decline.[1] In fact, the very success of the institution at this time in commercial terms can be seen as clear proof that what had once been the cultural mode best capable of expressing the social and political outlook of the working classes had become just another way of making large amounts of money for the entrepreneurial few. The development of the music hall institution is especially instructive in that it demonstrates the growth of the first entertainment *industry*. The music hall marks the first instance of the transformation of hitherto unregulated patterns of recreation into the profitable commodity of leisure. It is a model example of Victorian capitalism in full flow.

The roots of the music hall, the raw material out of which those dazzling Edwardian theatres were later constructed, lay in the established traditions of musical entertainment in public houses. Such entertainment existed on a mostly impromptu and amateur basis, but the increase in profits it brought to those pubs where it took place was soon capitalised on by a number of entrepreneurs in London and the cities of the industrial north. Musical entertainment began to be offered on a much more systematic and professional basis. Stages were built inside the larger pubs; then, as demand grew and profits rose, extensions were built on to pubs, and finally entire new buildings were needed to cater for the sizeable audiences. Thus the music halls, as these buildings were known, originated as offshoots of the sale of alcohol.

As already indicated, songs formed the content of these entertainments. Not only the famous comic and sentimental songs that still figure strongly in nostalgic images of music hall, but also, in the early days, songs of topical comment and political protest. These latter, however, stood little chance of surviving as the hall owners, ever in search of greater profit, attempted to move upmarket. Halls became increasingly elaborate, culminating in the Empire Leicester Square, and ticket prices were adjusted to restrict working-class access. An Act of Parliament in 1878 closed down most of the remaining small halls on the pretext of inadequate safety regulations, thus concentrating even more power in the owners of the large city-centre venues. These began to operate a circuit system, so that the more popular performers could tour the country – a final blow to the politicised songs, which tended to be purely regional in character, referring to local events such as strikes. Directly political material more or less disappeared from the halls (with the odd reactionary exception in favour of the Conservative party), leaving the blend of comedy and sentiment as dominant.

The halls by this time featured far more than only singers. Circus acts such as contortionists, jugglers and performing animals filled the lower half of the bills, and comic or dramatic sketches were popular. Songs remained at the heart of the halls, however, and even though these were no longer explicitly political, they still at their best spoke directly to working-class audiences by dealing with what one historian has evocatively described as 'the occupations, food, drink, holidays, romances, marriages and misfortunes of the back streets'.[2]

There did remain, though, a space at what could be called the very bottom end of the market, now that the smaller and cheaper halls had been closed down. There was no very cheap, immediately available street-corner entertainment any longer. It was into this historical milieu that film emerged.

Music Hall and Silent Cinema

The initial relationship between music hall and film was one of straightforward commercial exploitation. In March 1896 the Cinematographe Lumière became one of the 'acts' at the Empire Leicester Square. Marketed as a new scientific wonder, it rapidly established its popularity, and soon all the major variety theatres (a more accurate name by now than music halls) featured a cinematographic display.

The capitalist entrepreneurs of the West End were not, though, the only people to realise the potential of film, and many travelling fairs took the new sensation to parts of the country that had no lavish variety theatres. And in the back streets of the larger cities appeared cramped one-room venues in which films were shown. These became known as penny gaffs, named after the analogous back-street theatres of the mid-nineteenth century. Besides sharing the name, the film penny gaffs also received the same kind of condemnation from the guardians of bourgeois morality. This can be taken as virtual proof that film had become a genuine popular cultural experience, a working-class leisure activity out of the hands of the major theatre capitalists. This state of affairs could not last, however, and the building of cinemas began to follow the same pattern as had the construction of the halls. But in the earliest years film can be seen as occupying a similar social and cultural space as the precursors of the music hall.

As for the more interesting question of similarities in subject matter between the halls and film, the major problem was obviously the lack of sound. Yet since the main attraction of film in its earliest days was its 'magical' ability to capture and reproduce movement, there were acts from the variety theatres who were admirably suited. Hence a spate of films of physical variety acts, jugglers and the like, captured in titles like *Irene Latour – Contortionist* (1901) or *The Everhardts' Clever Hoop Manipulation* (1902).

Attempts were made to remedy the lack of sound, with several series of films designed to be screened in synchronisation with either live or gramophone-recorded sound. The first set of the latter came as early as 1900, the Phono-Bio-Tableau Films, which were clearly aiming at the variety audience by including Vesta Tilley's *Algy, the Piccadilly Johnny* and G. H. Chirgwin's *The Blind Boy*. Not only were these two among the very best variety stars of the time, but these two songs perfectly demonstrate the favoured comic and sentimental modes. The largest number of synchronised-film series came between 1906 and 1910, when competing companies such as Gaumont's Chronophone and Walturdaw's Cinematophone featured variety stars like Vesta Tilley and Harry Lauder. (These series were not confined to variety material – they also offered opera and hymns.)

The most important link between cultural modes forged in the halls and the new possibilities of film was, of course, silent comedy. In the early days of the halls, comedy had been confined to comic songs, but with the expanding range of performers and the influx from circus and fair traditions, comic sketches had found immense popularity. Slapstick film comedy evolved out of these sketches, but unlike other variety acts it could make a virtue out of silence by reverting to older traditions of mime. Michael Chanan has made an eloquent case for seeing silent film comedy as a return to the glories of comic mime which had been all but lost in the transition to commodity leisure: 'When you look at the growth . . . of silent film comedy, you can't help feeling that here you have the most successful revival of the great period of the art a century earlier, before its commercial decline – an art capable not only of popular intelligibility but also of possessing a degree of subtlety, of tenderness and of critical insight we do not normally recognise in any commercial form.'[3] This does suggest a convincing reason for the immense popularity of silent film comedy: that it evoked a half-forgotten tradition of clowning and by doing so found a way to bypass and subvert the later encrustations of the commodity forms of music hall humour in favour of a return to untainted folk roots.

Discussion of silent film comedy always tends to focus on the great Hollywood exponents, though it should not be forgotten how many of these had learned their trade in the British halls. Tracing the development of British silent comedy is tricky, with little to go on except titles and synopses, but even from these some significant patterns emerge. The chase film, with its supreme demonstration of the kinetic thrill of filmed movement, was extremely popular. There

Fred Evans as Pimple in *Pimple's Wonderful Gramophone* (1913)

were a number of specific comic stereotypes, featured in hundreds of films, all recognisable by their uniforms – policemen, convicts, tramps, boy scouts, 'anarchists' (long beards and black hats), and, in an intriguing response to social and political events, suffragettes. The immediate recognisability of these types could be seen as film's answer to the variety stage's fondness for dialect humour; that is, a tramp looked 'naturally funny' in the same way that an Irish accent sounded 'naturally funny' (the ideological structures implicated in such stereotype-based humour are complex, but space precludes examining them in further detail).

Another trend was parody. The great music hall comedian Dan Leno made only a few films before his death in 1904, but these included parodies of the overwrought melodramatic films of the time, such as his *Burlesque Attack on a Settler's Cabin*, in which he appeared with two other music hall stars, George Robey and Joe Elvin. The most remarkable parodies were those featuring the character Pimple, as portrayed by Fred Evans. Between 1912 and 1922 there were over one hundred and eighty Pimple films. Many of these satirised contemporary events or fashions either directly (*Pimple Does the Turkey Trot* burlesqued 1912's dance craze, while 1915's *The Kaiser Catches Pimple* speaks for itself) or indirectly (in

Pimple's Inferno he falls asleep reading Dante and dreams that Hell is full of film comedians and suffragettes). It is no surprise, given the huge popularity that must have sustained Pimple through so many metamorphoses, that attempts were made to initiate similar series; hence the lists of films centred on the likes of Bumbles, Nobby, Biffy, Winky and Ponky, to name but a few.

As silent film drama became increasingly sure of its own codes and potentialities, fewer comedies were made, the only recurring example of comedy in the early 1920s being the rash of Pimples. Other kinds of variety act had long since disappeared from films, which is hardly surprising when one considers the drive towards lengthy dramatic narrative in the late silent era. There was little chance of accommodating the Everhardts' hoop manipulation, however clever, within the dictates of the classic realist text. The audiences for film and variety remained substantially similar, however, and a new generation of variety stars had emerged whose chance to make films would come with the introduction of sound. Now, at last, the true centre of the music hall experience, the comic and sentimental song, could be incorporated into cinema, and the early days of sound saw a flood of short films of variety acts.

As in the first days of film in the 1890s, so in the early sound period the main attraction was the 'magic' of the new technology itself; the pure signifier was enough, whatever the signified. The earliest sound films of variety acts were simple recordings of performances, with artists like George Robey, Robb Wilton, Nervo and Knox (later of the Crazy Gang), and Harry Lauder. The latter demonstrated the impressive longevity of his career by singing in a series of eight short films, two of which were the same songs he had sung for Gaumont's Chronophone in 1907. With the establishment of sound film, then, the great variety stars of the period could attain film stardom too. The British cinema of the 1930s was the decade of George Formby, Gracie Fields, Will Hay and the Crazy Gang.

The 1930s: Tradition versus Genre

1930 saw a flurry of musicals, most of them hurried and clumsy attempts to capitalise on the potential of sound. The most interesting of these was *Elstree Calling,* which dispensed with any attempt at plot (apart from some mercifully brief linking comedy scenes) and offered a self-proclaimed 'all-star vaudeville and revue entertainment'. The choice of words is significant, since the acts presented are a curious mixture of revue artists from the reasonably sophisticated West End musical comedies (such as Jack Hulbert) and variety stars. The two strands remain very separate, and one interesting difference is that while the revue performers make some attempt at maintaining the codes of mainstream cinema, the variety acts break those codes, with Will Fyffe playing quite deliberately to some putative off-screen music hall audience and Lily Morris playing direct to camera. Morris' two songs, 'Always the Bridesmaid' and 'Only a Working Man', are also performed in front of blatant stage backdrops presumably intended to connote 'music hall'. Her songs might strike the modern viewer as the most impressive and vital moments of an otherwise plodding film, but there is a sense in which she is being positioned by the text as some kind of curio, a hangover from more 'earthy' days set against the numb glamour of the lines of chorus girls. Music hall is thus referred to as something historical; something, by implication, superseded.

This may not be unconnected with the fact that *Elstree Calling,* as its name suggests, sets itself up as representing the best in London entertainment, and the marked feature of most of the variety stars of the 1930s (and indeed of subsequent decades) is their regional character. Formby and Fields would be classic examples here. Those two also raise what I would claim to be the central problematic of the 1930s variety star film – how to accommodate such performers within existing cinematic genres.

After the initial novelty of sound cinema, the plotless likes of *Elstree Calling* were no longer enough (except in certain Hollywood examples, where the allure of high production values compensated for the lack of narrative). But how could the variety stars, whose popularity was founded on short comedy or musical routines, be fitted into the demands of the ninety-minute narrative film? There were a number of options. Firstly, confine variety acts to short films only, where their established acts could be presented in unadorned form. Sandy Powell and Jimmy James, for example, featured in many shorts in the early 30s. Secondly, imitate Hollywood musicals. *Radio Parade of 1935* is an instructive example here. Basically a narrativised revue, featuring performers popular on radio but simultaneously satirising the pretensions and stuffiness of the BBC, its finale (after some pleasant low-key performances by popular British acts) is a ghastly attempt to copy Busby Berkeley. Even at this early stage, it was assumed that the musical was a purely American genre; so slavish imitation was mistakenly thought to be the way to success. Without Berkeley's visionary voyeurism, however, the finale of *Radio Parade of 1935* becomes a hamfisted mess.

A third alternative was to construct a comedy romance around an established variety star, leaving suitable spaces in the narrative for that star's musical performances. Hence the immensely popular films of George Formby and Gracie Fields. None of their films (with the possible exception of Fields' *Sing As We Go*) seems wholly successful today, appearing too fragmented and episodic – but to use that type of criticism against them is to approach their work with the wrong set of assumptions. These films were never particularly trying to be seamless narrative texts; they were unashamed vehicles for the talents of their stars. It is a significant index of the respective standings of Hollywood and British cinema that while nobody criticises, say, *Dames* for being 'unrealistic' or 'episodic', there are always complaints when George Formby produces his trusty ukelele. Formby's films, it is true, never bothered with the use of show business plots to excuse the sudden eruption of music into narrative, but they remain musicals of a sort.

Formby's (in)famous reliance on innuendo remained the core of all his songs, but the films' coating of light romantic comedy seemed to save them from the censors (although some of his songs were banned by the BBC). A variety star who did not have such good fortune was Max Miller. His popularity was such that he made many films, but that same popularity was based primarily on telling jokes so 'blue'

Radio Parade of 1935: Will Hay (centre) as radio's big chief

that they could never be allowed on screen. Thus Miller, visibly ill-at-ease, was put into various unsuitable genres (1934's *Princess Charming* was a self-proclaimed Ruritanian romantic musical) or made to sleepwalk through the tamest of farces. The decade's other great comedian was Will Hay, but he was more of a comic actor than a stand-up comic and his films were considerably more fully realised than Miller's. His most popular comedies featured him as a uniformed incompetent. His schoolteacher in particular (*Boys Will Be Boys, Good Morning Boys*, and others) has become one of the classic icons of British film comedy.

The films of Gracie Fields most clearly show the problems of finding an adequate generic vehicle for performers trained in the traditions of the variety stage. These films retain a certain power, largely through the humour and magnetism of their star, but most of them contain uneasy shifts between broad comedy, romantic comedy, gestures towards the Hollywood musical (especially in the late 1930s as Fields attempted to achieve success in the American market), and the kind of pathos common to most performers in the variety tradition. With Fields this is usually confined to sentimental songs, but later comics like Norman Wisdom tried to extend this aspect of their work into a charmless aspiration towards Chaplin-esque status. Of Fields' later films, *The Show Goes On* (1937) is the most instructive. With clear autobiographical references, it follows the career of a singer who achieves success only by making cutting parodies of the maudlin Victorian ballads she had previously sung (Fields' own singing style is curiously pitched between comedy and sentiment), but who then, having achieved stardom, appears in the film's finale in a bizarre sub-Astaire and Rogers cocktail lounge setting. The spectacle of Gracie Fields gamely shaking her way through a supposedly Latin American dance routine is a sad example of the lack of confidence on the part of the film's producers. The rest of the film, based on an exploration of the tensions between her career and the demands of her fiancé, and on an evocative account of the variety halls of the North, is here surrendered to an almost embarrassing aping of Hollywood norms. At least George Formby, whatever his faults, remained contentedly British in performance and appeal.

The other two important variety acts to begin successful film careers in the 1930s were the Crazy Gang and Old Mother Riley. The former, often compared to the Marx Brothers, but with a distinctly British line in innuendo, were three double acts who came together to perform in hugely popular West End shows. One of these became their first film, *O-Kay for Sound* (1937), where the use of a film studio plot allows the second half of the film to be simply a series of sketches (supposedly being 'filmed' for the studio). Despite their violent clowning, the Gang also prominently featured the sentiment so typical of the variety tradition in the songs sung by the most famous Gang members, Flanagan and Allen.

Old Mother Riley was a character played by Arthur Lucan, who featured in a large number of simple knockabout farces from the late 1930s to the early 1950s. Old Mother Riley was supposedly an Irish washerwoman, perpetually ready to fight off intruders or authority with her fists, and in the process displaying a crude vigour that led one critic to champion her as 'a comic heroine of titanic dimensions . . . the inextinguishable life force of the slums, a veritable Brunhilde of the backstreets'.[4] The Riley films offered perhaps the most honest solution to the problem of reconciling variety tradition and generic credibility: don't bother. The public that liked the act on stage would pay to come and see it on film, and it was the mass paying public that these films were made for. Fretting over their narrative flaws and absence of psychological credibility is, in the final analysis, a waste of time.

World War Two: the Mobilisation of Variety

The Second World War can now be seen as a pivotal moment in British film history. Films featuring variety performers are – like so many other genres – at their richest, most complex, and most significant during the war. The way in which variety performers were mobilised into the wider effort of propaganda is indicated by the fact that one of the successes of late 1939 was *Old Mother Riley Joins Up*. Whether one sees this process in the official terms of boosting morale or in the more analytic sense of securing hegemony, the films made by variety artists during the war played a significant part in shaping audience attitudes. This applies to different stages of the war and to a wide range of subject matter.

In the early period of the 'phoney war', the dominant plot is the catching of spies, as in the straightforward comedy vehicles for performers like Sandy Powell (*All at Sea*, 1939), Arthur Askey (*Band Waggon*, 1940 – a wartime variant on a popular radio series), George Formby (*Spare a Copper*, 1940), Will Hay (*The Ghost of St Michael's*, 1941), and inevitably Old Mother Riley (*Old Mother Riley's Ghosts*, 1941). Perhaps the most surreal image in any wartime film is found in the dream sequence of Formby's other 1940 success, *Let George Do It*: Formby attracts Hitler's attention with the line 'Oi, windbag', and punches him on the nose.

The comic potential of army life, away from actual combat, was treated by the Lancashire comedian Frank Randle in a series of films beginning with *Somewhere in England* (1940). For many years the top

The Crazy Gang in *O-Kay for Sound* (1937)

box-office attraction in the North, Randle remained virtually unknown in the South, and his films (made by the tiny Manchester
company Mancunian Films) fared accordingly – massively successful
in the North, often not even shown in Southern cinemas. Randle's
films were, like the Mother Riley series, farce sketches with an
offhand layer of plot.

Problems on the home front were the subject of comedies featuring
the Cockney double act Elsie and Doris Waters, in their roles as Gert
and Daisy. The issue of assimilating urban evacuees into rural society
was dealt with in *Gert and Daisy's Weekend* (1941), whereas in *Gert
and Daisy Clean Up* (1942) the two sisters prevent a black marketeer
from stealing a cargo of canned fruit – a narrative artfully designed to
secure audience identification among working-class women struggling to feed their families on wartime rations.

The Home Guard was the vehicle for another of Formby's
comedies, *Get Cracking* (1943), and later in the same year he changed
uniforms for *Bell-Bottom George*. Variety stars were used in the short
propaganda films made by the National Screen Service: in 1942 Will
Hay showed how to deal with incendiary bombs (*Go to Blazes*), while
Arthur Askey warned against the spreading of influenza germs (*The
Nose Has It*). Flanagan and Allen's most moving appearance came

not in a Crazy Gang film, but in the Workers' Playtime sequence of Humphrey Jennings' *Listen to Britain,* where they are structured as representatives of popular culture to complement the classical music recital in the National Gallery.

Whether directly referring to the war (Will Hay parodying the Nazis in *The Goose Steps Out*, for example) or acting in deliberately light fantasy comedies (Askey being washed ashore on a lost Pacific island in *Bees in Paradise*), clearly variety artists were fulfilling a particular ideological role during the war: offering a sense of continuity with pre-war times, attempting to defuse threats with humour, and most importantly reaffirming a notion of community.

The notion of community is crucial to popular culture as a whole. Popular culture offers the sense of belonging, of solidarity, of togetherness in the face of hardship. Perhaps that makes it a reactionary palliative, a deflection from change and struggle, but it also fulfils some basic emotional and cultural needs that cannot be

Arthur Askey, with Richard Murdoch, in *Band Waggon* (1940), based on a radio variety show

lightly dismissed. The music hall offered a sense of community to an urban proletariat involved in repetitive labour; it restored a feeling (illusory and transitory perhaps, but perceptible and felt) of belonging, after the alienation of the workplace. And it did so primarily through song, and later comedy. Singing together and laughing together – this was what bound the individuals in the music hall audience into a whole. Popular comedy thus has no time for the superior attitudes that make up witty, subtle, competitive types of comedy:

> Play on words is simple. There is no name-dropping, no juggling with esoteric information. There is no impulse to trick the other into a pessimistic attitude. . . . The implications are different, for a witty man is always in some way demonstrating his superiority. He has the skill to bend words. He has the special knowledge to make the right obscure reference that only you or I, of course, will understand. . . . But the humour of necessity isn't 'me' humour, it is 'us' humour, and instead of gambling with unique isolating qualities for its laughs, it rests heavily on the perpetual celebration of common factors.[5]

This helps to explain why the audience depicted within *The Show Goes On* responds to Gracie Fields only when she starts cracking jokes in her Lancashire accent, why Old Mother Riley can undermine modern technology with a pun on 'intercom' and 'winter coms' [winter combinations], and why the ending of an otherwise unexceptional wartime comedy called *I Thank You* (1941) provides one of the most astonishing images of community to be found in British cinema.

I Thank You stars Arthur Askey (the title being his catchphrase) as a variety artist trying to raise money to put on a show. After a series of farcical episodes based on the comic staple of mistaken identity, he finds himself working for an aristocratic lady who used to be a music hall star before marrying a Lord. The rest of the plot is too uninteresting to relate, but the climax of the film comes in one of the underground stations used as air-raid shelters. The ex-singer (played by the veteran music hall star, the great Lily Morris) is lured there by Askey. He reveals her identity to the crowd, demanding that she sing her most famous song. This she does, after some persuasion, and the whole crowd in the shelter joins in. The song is 'Waiting at the Church', a music hall standard from the 1890s, and so the overriding image is of the wartime shelter transformed into a Victorian music hall, with all the attendant notions of nationhood and community exerting their powerful emotional/ideological pull. This same song is used with similarly moving effect at the climax of *Millions Like Us*

Tommy Trinder as *Champagne Charlie* (1944)

(1943), as a means of bringing the isolated and suffering individual (the recently widowed Celia) back into the collective warmth and strength of the community.

It is significant that the best-known film biography of a music hall star was made during the war – *Champagne Charlie* (1944). The concentration in that film of shots of happy audience participation reveals its attempt to exploit the resonances of community noted above, but the narrative is not able to sustain the same level of intensity, or provide single images of breathtakingly iconographic power, such as can be found in *Millions Like Us* or even *I Thank You*. The leading actor in *Champagne Charlie*, the variety and radio comedian Tommy Trinder, is more interesting for other film roles, where in a number of wartime dramas he represented, in the unashamedly schematic range of characters such films offered, some spirit of cheery working-class decency. His reluctantly heroic fireman in *The Bells Go Down* (1943) is particularly notable.

The central, crucial ideology of community which fuelled these films was the variety tradition's major contribution to wartime cinema, and not surprisingly it also proved to be its downfall in the post-war period. Being so closely identified with one particular set of social circumstances, the variety tradition found it almost impossible to adjust when those circumstances suffered a dramatic shift. Indicative of this were both the dismal failure of Formby's 1946 film, *George in Civvy Street* (a flop of such proportions that he never made another film), and the release of a compilation of footage of old variety acts titled, with ominous reverence, *Those Were the Days*.

Since 1945: the Impact of Television

It should not, of course, be assumed that variety stars no longer made films after the war. The more regionally popular stars, in particular, continued to produce their usual low-budget features. Many of these, however, begin to smack of desperation, of a search for increasingly unsuitable novelties to bolster a tradition rapidly running out of steam. Hence the release of epics like *Old Mother Riley Meets the Vampire* (1952), complete with a visibly decaying Bela Lugosi. Frank Randle's last film was *It's a Grand Life* (1953), in which his co-star was that apex of British 50s glamour, Diana Dors. Their somewhat uncomfortable teaming is a graphic demonstration of the end of one era slamming uncomprehendingly into the beginning of another. Released in the same year, more significantly, was *Genevieve*, the massive success of which captured the centre of British film comedy for a whole squadron of bright young middle-class couples, thereby rendering the likes of Randle and Riley little more than Victorian grotesques.

One comedy star did emerge in the 1950s, though, who can be firmly placed in the variety tradition – Norman Wisdom. By shrewdly seizing on the two fundamentals of popular comedy, slapstick and sentiment, Wisdom brought about something of a renaissance for uncomplicated humour. He was never the most original performer (his striving after pathos reminds one of the excesses of Chaplin, and his unlikely winning of the pretty girl recalls Formby's equally improbable liaisons), but he was a master of slapstick chaos, as best displayed in his first success, *Trouble in Store* (1953). He later attempted a number of comedies in uniform (including that of a milkman, which is one that Hay or Formby never got round to doing), but the later films rely too heavily on the 'lovable idiot' persona, and topple over into sheer sentiment.

Sentimentality was not a charge that could be levelled against the *Carry On* films, which became Wisdom's successors as top box-office comedies. These began life as a one-off uniform comedy, *Carry On Sergeant* (1958), before growing into a once or twice per year institution that drove sensitive bourgeois critics to distraction and kept many Odeon cinemas in business. Staying in uniform at first

Slapstick and sentiment: Norman Wisdom, with Margaret Rutherford, in
Trouble in Store (1953)

(*Nurse, Constable, Teacher*), in the 1960s they found their richest vein
in generic parody (*Spying, Screaming, Cleo, Cowboy, Up the Khyber*).
Carry On films can be seen as slightly distant relatives of the variety
tradition, principally through their tireless fixation on sexual innuendo. They lack any warmth or evocation of community, and rely
on ensemble playing rather than the driving force of individual comic
talents (their stars were, importantly, comic actors rather than
comedians), but they remain the last major cinematic flourish of 'us'
humour. By their increasing sexual directness, however, they put an
end to the very traditions of innuendo that sustained them for so long.
After Barbara Windsor's brassiere had at last burst (in *Carry On
Camping*, 1969), where was the humour in teasing about the
possibility of such an occurrence? The innuendo of the variety
tradition depended, as Orwell perceived in his essay on Donald
McGill's comic postcards, on a certain fundamental sexual con-
servatism. Hence the relaxed censorship laws of the 1960s tended to
make the suggestiveness of the variety sex joke archaic in its coyness.

Censorship remained far more rigid, however, in the medium that
has increasingly become the last refuge of the variety tradition –

television. The growth of television, more than any other social or cultural change, caused the demise of the variety-tradition feature film. It did this by offering the opportunity to variety artists to escape the straitjacketing into genres that characterised the 1930s. TV variety shows, like their stage predecessors, offered the variety act ten minutes or so to perform its usual routine, rather than deflecting it, burying it, or spreading it too thinly with the addition of unconvincing narratives. Hence the great variety comedians of today, Ken Dodd or Les Dawson for example, have been spared the indignities of Max Miller's film career. Some TV variety acts have occasionally attempted to make films, but the example of Morecambe and Wise's cinematic disasters should serve to deter most attempts.

The other link between TV, variety, and cinema, is the trend to make film spin-offs from popular TV situation comedies. These are often thought of as products of the 70s, when sitcoms like *Steptoe and Son* and *On the Buses* were transmuted into films derided by critics but popular enough to generate sequels. Yet the late 1950s had seen a number of quick, cheap film versions of the leading sitcoms of the period, with *The Larkins* becoming *Inn for Trouble*, and *Whacko!* (the world's only flagellomaniac sitcom) becoming *Bottoms Up*. TV sitcom is perhaps the last vestigial link we have with the variety tradition (outside of the dwindling variety theatre shows). The use of a laugh-track could be seen as an electronic attempt to resurrect the security of communal laughter. The fondness for virtually prehistoric innuendo gestures towards the simpler delights of a 'pre-permissive' age. TV comedy is still not 'respectable', in the way that early music hall and popular comedy films were not respectable, so there is a link at the level of social function as well as that of content and style.

One final connection between variety and film in the post-war period is the way in which some variety stars became character actors. Most notable among these were Stanley Holloway and Jack Warner. Holloway's performance in *Passport to Pimlico* (1949) provides a tenuous but intriguing link between the working-class variety tradition and the petit-bourgeois comedies of social interaction perfected by Ealing Studios. *The Blue Lamp,* another seminal Ealing text, furnished an entire career for Jack Warner, as his character of P.C. Dixon was to emerge as the centre of the long-running TV series *Dixon of Dock Green*. This enshrining of a former variety comedian as the mythic image of the decent policeman is a nice irony, or a sad reflection, given the music hall's popularity among radical and even semi-criminal sections of the proletariat of nineteenth-century Britain. Warner's other key role, before Dixon, was as the head of the Huggett family, an endearing set of Cockney stereotypes who appeared in a sequence of post-war comedies beginning with *Holiday Camp* (1947).

Conclusion: Placing 'Music Hall'

One final question remains: how can we best place 'music hall traditions' within wider cultural history, or, for the purposes of this book, within film history? Clearly, the likes of Pimple or Old Mother Riley are less than central to film histories with commitments to privileging stylistic forms or directorial authorship. Yet any history of British cinema that realises the need to situate the cinematic institution within its shifting webs of social relations needs to pay great attention to the legacies of music hall. British popular culture would be unrecognisable without the diffused influences of music hall modes. Film comedy, and radio and television light entertainment, can only be thoroughly understood in relation to those influences.

Furthermore, since the development of the music hall institution represents the precise and crucial transition from folk culture to mass culture, the pivotal point when entertainment underwent its own industrial revolution, it should hold a special interest for historians committed to a materialist analysis of cultural production.

Such histories, however, have yet to be written, and all I can do here is to indicate and lament their absence. But there is one particular way in which music hall has been inscribed into cultural history, one particular reading of what music hall stands for, and by way of a conclusion I should like briefly to give examples of this reading, since it has direct implications for our understanding of the relationship between music hall and cinema.

The key term in this cultural-historical reading of music hall, just as in popular memory notions of music hall, is nostalgia. Music hall is identified as something lost but not replaced, something better than anything currently available in the sphere of popular culture. It becomes a repository of lost values. Writing a wartime review, George Orwell claimed that 'So long as comedians like Max Miller are on the stage . . . one knows that the popular culture of England is surviving',[6] a remark which obviously begs the question of what would happen when Miller or his equivalents were not on the stage, or at least on the centre of the stage.

This change had undeniably occurred by 1957, when Richard Hoggart published *The Uses of Literacy*. Music hall and variety traditions were reeling from the onslaught of largely Americanised youth cultures. Those traditions had, it could be argued, found a new location in television, but for Hoggart that only served as a symbol of their devaluation. Hoggart's book (a text of incontestable richness, despite its major conceptual and political limitations) sets out to be an examination of changes in popular culture, but his loyalty is always to what has gone rather than to what is current. It is no surprise that music hall occupies a central position in the history of popular culture which he constructs, that it stands as a key example of the organic, participatory working-class cultural experience which he sees as betrayed and replaced by modern mass culture. The problem with Hoggart is not his preferences, which are his own affair, but the way in which his overriding thesis of cultural deterioration leads him to mangle history. Hence he writes of 'a note which has never been silent in English working-class life since the Wife of Bath, which sounds in Shakespeare's clowns, Mistress Quickly and Juliet's nurse, in Moll Flanders, and in the nineteenth-century music-hall'.[7] Here a series of entirely different historical conjunctures are elided, and specificity is sacrificed in favour of tradition-building.

Tradition is a term crucial to the cultural writing of T. S. Eliot, whose essay written on the death of Marie Lloyd makes an intriguing companion to Hoggart's book.[8] The essay is seemingly an honest tribute to Lloyd's achievement and the affection felt for her by the public, but, with typical slyness, Eliot uses this as a cover for an attack on modern (in the context of 1923) mass culture. Eliot notes that Marie Lloyd never made films (this is in fact not true), applauding the fact that 'she never descended to this form of money-making', which almost implies she was in the music hall business for the love of it. She was, on the contrary, one of its highest-paid stars. The real substance of the essay, however, lies in the contrast Eliot makes between the audience experience of music hall (shared, communal, reciprocal) and the position of the cinema audience, 'lulled by continuous senseless music and continuous action too rapid for the brain to act upon', whose only possible response can be to 'receive, without giving, in . . . listless apathy'.

Both Eliot and Hoggart, then, from their very different ideological standpoints, seize upon music hall in order to attack subsequent popular cultural forms. The aspect of audiences' communal participation that they both identify is, of course, crucial to the music hall institution, but the use they put it to is, in the final analysis, reactionary. For Hoggart, this is an unconscious product of his nostalgia for vanished certainties, although with Eliot one can detect a less excusable motive – music hall, being more or less dead at the time he was writing, no longer posed any threat to established cultural values, while cinema, at that time the indisputably central mass cultural form, certainly did. Music hall was safe, it had become (again that key Eliot term) tradition. Hoggart's collusion in this construction of cultural history is especially regrettable, since it made

186

such a construction part of left cultural orthodoxy. The precise nature of the music hall institution became irrelevant to the general positioning of it as one of the glories of the proletarian past. The exact shape of its history was forgotten in the cosier contours of nostalgia.

Finally, what of the more recent attempts to reach a more distinct history? Michael Chanan's work on early cinema in Britain rightly stresses the centrality of the music hall as a cultural force, but always underpinning that work is the implied denigration of mainstream narrative cinema. Chanan, like Noël Burch, uses early cinema as a way of valorising the contemporary avant-garde, so that behind his fine and wholly appropriate eloquence in defence of the cultural validity of music hall traditions one can always detect the faint hum of the grinding of axes. Equally, historians who, like Gareth Stedman Jones, have criticised the music hall's slide into Toryism and jingoism seem to hold to a rather limited belief that the culture enjoyed by the working classes should always be in some way progressive. That this is not the case is proved, for example, by the current popularity of the television comedian Jim Davidson, whose work is as racist yet as popular as any warmongering song of the 1880s (with the Falklands replacing the Eastern Question). Terry Lovell's remarks on ideology and popular culture are pertinent here: ' . . . it is necessary to insist that because popular culture does not belong to the masses, feminism and revolution, it is not captured for reaction, patriarchy and domination either. Rather it is situated ambivalently and in contradictory ways, in relation to both.'[9]

While the impulse to see music hall through the frame of nostalgia is tempting and understandable, it also has its dangers. Primary among these, as revealed by Hoggart's work, is the way in which nostalgia seizes on selective aspects of the past and builds them up until they obscure any clear and fair view of the present and future. Thus the most 'Hoggartian' scene in British cinema comes in *A Kind of Loving* (1962), where the old popular culture values of a brass band concert are set against the new popular culture worthlessness (in the film's terms) of a TV quiz show. Similarly, it would be misrepresentative to keep clinging on to the past glories of music hall, since popular culture is a field that is constantly reshaping, always in a state of productive flux. Yet at the same time we need to remember and to celebrate the pleasures offered by music hall traditions, which proved socially central and consistently nourishing for so many decades (the immense and deserved affection felt for Morecambe and Wise's TV series could serve as an example of this). The achievements of these traditions have never been adequately recognised by most accounts of British film history. I hope this essay has begun to redress the balance.

Notes

1   Music hall still lacks a thorough history, to counteract the wealth of anecdotal and nostalgic books on the subject. Among the few serious studies, my account is particularly indebted to Gareth Stedman Jones, 'Working-Class Culture and Working-Class Politics in London 1870–1900: Notes on the Remaking of a Working Class' in Bernard Waites, Tony Bennett, Graham Martin (eds.), *Popular Culture Past and Present*, London, Croom Helm, 1982; Bernard Waites, 'The Music Hall', Open University Popular Culture Course Unit 5, Milton Keynes, Open University, 1981; Michael Chanan, *The Dream That Kicks*, London, Routledge & Kegan Paul, 1980.

2   Stedman Jones, op. cit., p. 115.

3   Chanan, op. cit., p. 135.

4   Jeffrey Richards, *The Age of the Dream Palace*, London, Routledge & Kegan Paul, 1984, p. 298.

5   Jeff Nuttall and Rodick Carmichael, *Common Factors/Vulgar Factions*, London, Routledge & Kegan Paul, 1977, p. 24.

6   George Orwell, *Collected Essays, Journalism and Letters*, vol. 2, London, Secker & Warburg, 1968.

7   Richard Hoggart, *The Uses of Literacy*, Penguin edition, Harmondsworth, Penguin, 1958, p. 141.

8   T. S. Eliot, 'Marie Lloyd' in *Selected Essays*, London, Faber & Faber, 1951.

9   Terry Lovell, 'Ideology and *Coronation Street*' in Richard Dyer (ed.), *Coronation Street*, London, British Film Institute, 1981, p. 49.

John Caughie
BROADCASTING AND CINEMA
1: CONVERGING HISTORIES

Histories of British cinema and of British broadcasting serve to establish their separate chronicles and developments. What they often miss are the terms by which these separate developments and the ideological impulses behind them can be seen to belong to the same culture. What I want to do here, from within the confusions, contradictions and uncertainties of the mid-1980s, is to unravel some threads, beginning with a small knot of historical coincidences.

1927. On 1 January, the British Broadcasting Company, incorporated as a private monopoly in 1922 to protect the interests of radio manufacturers, became the British Broadcasting Corporation. The change in title signified, albeit obliquely, a shift from private to public monopoly, from protection in the private, commercial interest to protection in the public interest. The new Corporation received its Royal Charter, its funding (a licence fee on receiving sets determined by government and administered by the Post Office), and its somewhat provisional independence from state control, on the condition that it used the public airwaves to provide a public service. John Reith, subsequently (and consequently) Sir John and later Lord Reith, had been General Manager of the Company since 1922; having manoeuvred effectively against the commercial interest of his private paymasters, he became in 1927 the first Director-General of the new Corporation. Monopoly, for Reith, was a moral imperative. Without monopoly, he later wrote,

> many things might not have been done so easily that were done. The Christian religion and the Sabbath might not have had the place and the protection which it was right to give them. . . . The Christian religion, not just as a sectional activity but as a

fundamental. And as to the Sabbath, one day in the week clear of jazz and variety and such like. . . . Almost everything might have been different. The BBC might have had to play for safety, prosecute the obviously popular lines, count its clients, study and meet their reactions, curry favour, subordinate itself to the vote.[1]

Public monopoly could only be justified by public service; but in order to serve the public, broadcasting had to be free both from the commercial pressures of mass entertainment and from the political pressures of mass persuasion. The name which was given to the various forms of negotiated relationship with the state and the market-place (with the state as the lesser evil by a long way) was independence.

1927. On 31 January, John Grierson returned to Britain from the United States, where he had spent two years on a scholarship studying mass communications (in 1927, for a student just out of a Scottish university, that in itself seems interesting) and writing about cinema. On his return, he went to see Stephen Tallents (later Sir Stephen Tallents), Secretary of the recently established Empire Marketing Board, a government agency charged with the promotion of Britain and British trade in the Empire and at home. The story is well known: Grierson persuaded Tallents and Tallents persuaded the Treasury that cinema, and specifically documentary cinema, should receive government funding to 'bring the Empire alive'. On the basis of government funding and sponsorship, Grierson recruited the film-makers of the EMB Film Unit, later to become the GPO Film Unit, and later still to become the basis of the Crown Film Unit to meet the more specific demands of wartime propaganda. This is the familiar narrative of the British Documentary Movement. In its various institutional forms during the 30s and 40s, the Movement was supported by a system of state sponsorship, creating a protected cinema outside the commercial sphere, operating as a service to a public whose interests were identified with the Imperial state: like Reith's BBC, a service independent from commerce, dependent on the state. For Grierson,

Cinema is neither an art nor an entertainment: it is a form of publication, and may publish in a hundred different ways for a hundred different audiences. . . . The facts are simple enough. In a world too complex for the educational methods of public speech and public writing, there is a growing need for more imaginative and widespread media of public address. Cinema has begun to serve propaganda and will increasingly do so. It will be in demand.

It will be asked to create appreciation of public services and public purposes. It will be asked from a hundred quarters to create a more imaginative and considered citizenship. It will be asked too, inevitably, to serve the narrower viewpoints of political or other party propaganda . . . [2]

This, for Grierson, is the future for the 'art of the cinema', a future which may lie not in cinemas, but in YMCAS, church halls 'and other citadels of suburban improvement'; it may even lie (in 1935) in television. (The way in which Grierson's notion of cinema as a form of publication anticipates by over forty years the Annan Committee's recommendations, published in 1977, on what the fourth television channel should be, suggests something of the continuity of the Griersonian institutional form.) What is certain is that 'in the commercial cinema there is no future worth serving'. As for Reith with broadcasting, so for Grierson with cinema, commerce is the enemy of any serious social or moral purpose. For both, the necessary refuge is provided by the state and by the service of the public interest which can give broadcasting and cinema their necessary independence from the market-place of public taste. It can make them 'serious' and lift them out of the realm of mere entertainment. The serious job of broadcasting and cinema is to create an audience rather than simply to pander to it; the public interest which is defined by Reith in terms of religion and morality is defined by Grierson in terms of civic education and an informed citizenry.

1927, then, marks the formal opening for both cinema and broadcasting of a relationship with the state and the public which has as its common terms public service and independence. This relationship is also the institutional form of an ideological hostility to commerce (or, more accurately, to Mammon) and a cultural hostility to the frivolities of 'mass entertainment' and the Dream Factory. The coincidence of 1927 is, of course, partly fortuitous. What I want to suggest, though, is that in 1927 a certain attitude to entertainment became institutionalised within British broadcasting and cinema, and that the solidity which the attitude gained from its institutionalisation has been a defining factor in the development of British film and television, and in the formation of an idea of 'serious' film and television which critics still promulgate and people carry in their heads. Reith left the BBC in 1938 and Grierson left the GPO Film Unit in 1937, but their influence would endure both within and beyond those particular institutions. 'Independence' and 'public service' occupy a position of such conscious or unconscious centrality in thinking about British film and television culture that it is only now, in the mid-8os, when both terms are seriously under threat, that we begin to discover, with a touch of panic, that they are not the natural condition.

To remain for a moment longer with coincidence, the neatness of the fit between Reith and Grierson does not stop with the accident of dates. The fact that both men were Scottish may be seen as more than a biographical curiosity. Reith was the son of a Church of Scotland minister, a son of the manse; Grierson was a dominie's son, brought up in a rural Scottish schoolhouse, his father the local headmaster, his mother the daughter of a family of Ayrshire radicals. Within Scotland, this kind of background, to which both men refer with respect, is more than a question of parentage; rather, it places both men in their formation within the institutions, church and school, which form the backbone of a very particular and peculiar form of popular democracy: the Scottish presbyterian community. The Church of Scotland, repressive and authoritarian in its moral and spiritual precepts, was democratic in its forms, operating for most of the nineteenth century, through General Assembly, Presbytery and local Kirk Session, a system of local government, free from aristocratic patronage or state charity, which undertook not only the moral but also the physical and social welfare of its parishioners. Education, poverty, disability, as well as correction, were under the supervision of Church government. The school was the secular arm of the Church welfare system. Within the community, the dominie was second in authority only to the minister and the elders of the Kirk: education was a thing to be treated with ponderous respect as the agency of a social and geographical mobility which transformed the 'local lad' into the 'lad of parts'. Many of the attitudes associated with all this, including masculinism and patriarchy, are still apparent in Scottish educational institutions today.

It isn't necessary, then, to go to the mystical excess of Reith's biographer ('the dark and simple superstitions of Calvinism had been bred in his bones like a hereditary disease'[3]) to see that there might have been something in Reith's institutional patrimony which would make it easy for him to find nothing particularly strange or contradictory in an institutional arrangement which attempted to hold together authoritarianism, paternalism, moral guidance and public service. Nor is it difficult to find in Grierson's writing ('I look on cinema as a pulpit and use it as a propagandist'[4]) the often biblical tones of a Scottish secular radicalism informed by a passionate respect for universal education and community service. Significantly, by the beginning of the twentieth century the Scottish presbytery was a system of local democracies quite at ease with the state, distinct from the tradition of English popular democracies which had been formed in organised conflict with the state for much of the nineteenth century. Reith and Grierson, quite different in most respects, shared a tradition which saw no contradiction between serving the people and serving the state.

Again, the coincidences, if only at a symbolic level, serve to tie a series of knots within the development of British film and television culture and its institutional forms. The coincidences can be extended into a kind of institutional Scottish country dance, with Reith and Grierson exchanging partners. After the war and his retirement from the BBC, Lord Reith became the first chairman of the National Film Finance Corporation, with Group Three, a short-lived independent feature film company run jointly by Grierson and John Baxter (1951–55), as one of its first major clients. In the 1950s, when Scottish Television was given the commercial franchise for Central Scotland (under the chairmanship of the Canadian, Roy Thomson, who endeared himself to all enemies of commerce by declaring that a commercial television franchise was 'a licence to print money'), John Grierson was given a very popular weekly slot, *This Wonderful World*. This programme, for which Grierson selected and presented extracts from international documentary, ran from 1957 to 1966, and brought something of the prestige of public service and the documentary movement to commercial television. In the 30s, Grierson had urged the artist to 'organise his independence' by 'going direct to public service for his material and his economy'. In the 40s, Reith urged on the National Film Finance Corporation a recognition of the influence which the film industry 'can exercise over so considerable a proportion of the population – interests, outlook and behaviour; in the projection of England and the English way of life to the Dominions and foreign countries; in the enhancement of the prestige and worth of England'.[6] The same terms reverberate backwards and forwards between Reithian broadcasting and Griersonian cinema, forming an ideological and cultural nexus which comes to define the serious purpose of film and television. This seriousness of purpose helps to explain the ferocity of the debate over commercial television in the early 50s, when public service seemed threatened by the debased Americanised values of commercial television. The interiorised values of public service and independence also help to explain something of the difficulty which 'serious' British critics and 'serious' British producers seem to have with the idea of entertainment.

Moving out from the cluster of institutional, biographical and ideological knots, it is clear that, though they may be founded on the same terms, the histories of cinema and television are far from identical. The line of development of public service broadcasting is more or less continuous. The Reithian tradition became a fact, confirmed by wartime and by post-war cultural reconstruction. Even commercial television, whose arrival was predicted as the end of broadcasting as we knew it, was quite quickly institutionalised as a kind of quasi-public service, until it is now, with Channel Four, the main hope of a recycled and regenerated public service. The line of development of a 'public service cinema', if such a term is even appropriate, is far less clear, existing only intermittently as a fact, though consistently important as an idea whose time is always about to come and as an ideal whose failure to materialise has provided British critics with an always available reproach with which to berate the British film industry.

For broadcasting, it was in the immediate post-war period that the 'cultural mission' of elevating national standards was most explicitly undertaken. This was a time when the BBC had ceased to be at the service either of direct national propaganda, or of Reith's own narrower moral and religious imperatives, and was beginning to plan a service, including a television service, which would interweave more fully with the fabric of national life. Director-General William Haley had stated in 1943:

> The BBC must provide for all classes of listener equally. This does not mean it shall remain passive regarding the distribution of these classes. It cannot abandon the educative task it has carried on for twenty-one years to improve cultural and ethical standards.[7]

And he restated the policy in 1949:

> The aim of the BBC must be to conserve and strengthen serious listening. . . . While satisfying the legitimate public demand for recreation and entertainment, the BBC must never lose sight of its cultural mission. . . . The BBC is a single instrument and must see that the nation derives the best advantage from this fact.[8]

As a part of the fabric of national life, broadcasting was charged through the charter of the BBC with entertainment, information and education, but its self-adopted 'educative task' in the period immediately after the war was a redistribution of classes by raising cultural standards towards an approved level, leading listeners from light entertainment on the Light Programme, through talks on the Home Service, to 'serious listening' on the Third Programme. This was not, as it might be now, an invisible, unconscious ideology at work, surrounding broadcasters like the air they breathed; it was a conscious, agreed policy, referred to unashamedly by Haley as the

The single play: *The Shadow of the Ruthless*, directed by Philip Saville in 1959 for ABC TV's 'Armchair Theatre'

'slow but rewarding process of raising public taste',[9] and endorsed by the Labour Education Minister of the day as the laudable project of turning Britain into a 'Third Programme nation'. This was the climate in which television had to fight within the BBC for committed attention: even in the early 50s, its growing popularity was as much an embarrassment to the tradition of BBC thinking as it was a sign of success.

The discourse of public improvement seems only possible within the myth of consensus which reigned in the immediate post-war period, assuming as it did a society at peace with the world and with itself. After 1956, with a shift in the political and cultural climate and with the arrival of commercial television, such a clear and confident statement of the 'cultural mission' would be hard to find. But, at the same time, it would be hard to understand the disposition of post-war British television without a recognition of the determining influence of this concept of public service. In information and education, it guarantees the status of news and current affairs; in entertainment, it underwrites the tradition of the single play. 'Serious drama' is always expensive, always awkward within the schedules, and frequently controversial. It would be difficult to account for the survival of the single play (whether on videotape or on film) in Britain, long after it had disappeared or transformed itself beyond recognition almost everywhere else, without the concept of a cultural public service. In a post-war society celebrating the myth of classlessness, broadcasting, like the recently formed Arts Council, took on the traditional aristocratic role of cultural patronage, supporting the artist in return for the privilege of a state-protected monopoly. While radio supported the musician and the poet, television supported the single play as the mark of its cultural seriousness in the area of entertainment. Drama, in fact, with its prestige derived from the high national and international standing of British theatre, resolved that apparent dichotomy between entertainment and serious public service which always threatened to disturb the BBC's sense of its own mission.

It has to be stressed, though, that it was commercial television, anticipated and feared as giving a 'foot in the door' to pulp Americanism, which first developed the single play as a specific and vigorous televisual form with its 'Armchair Theatre', a regular Sunday night series, networked from 1956, which captured a large popular audience. Public service as an ideology was not the monopoly of the BBC, and commercial television, formed under licence to the state, could use the single play to show that, despite its advertisements and its game shows, it too was culturally serious. At the same time, as in America, the single play slot had a restricted life on commercial television, and the tradition of 'serious drama' shifted back to the BBC. Throughout the 60s and 70s, the schedules were peppered with single plays which were socially realist, often critically so, seeking out the 'nitty-gritty' of ordinary and under-privileged life, proclaiming themselves to be controversial, challenging, even shocking, asserting insistently that the public was best served by showing the harsh realities.

By the 1970s, after the success in particular of the BBC's 26-part dramatisation of Galsworthy's *The Forsyte Saga* (1967), the single play tradition had acquired two partners, or rivals, in the field of high-prestige drama: the classic serial, and the serialised historical costume drama. Both had the advantage of appealing to areas of cultural prestige – English Literature, and the history of the nation – within forms which were more cost-effective than the one-off play. Just as the single play derives its prestige from Britain's theatrical tradition, so literary adaptation fits comfortably into the needs of a public service system by recycling for a wide popular audience the classic literature of Britain's Great Tradition.

Social realism and literary/historical adaptation: throughout the

Prestige productions for the international TV market: Anthony Andrews and friend in Granada's *Brideshead Revisited* (1981)

70s the two co-existed, setting a standard, and securing for television a distinctive place within the national culture. Public service was its own justification. In the 80s, it is becoming clearer that a number of shifts were and are happening.

On the one hand, television, and particularly the BBC, was locked into a notion of prestige and seriousness which cost a great deal of money, more than could comfortably be raised by the licence fee system. On the other hand, that very prestige of Britain's literary tradition and historical pageant was discovered to be a highly saleable commodity on the growing international television market. The economic solution is fairly obvious: a movement of resources towards internationally prestigious adaptations which will recoup their costs in sales and pre-sales, and an exploitation of Britain's reputation as 'the least worst television in the world' to secure co-production and co-financing. This option is more readily available to commercial television, uninhibited as it is by any tradition of unease about commerce; its most striking results are *Jewel in the Crown* and *Brideshead Revisited*, both produced by Granada. The fact that the BBC's adventures in the international market have been less spectacular both in investment and in success may be commercial inaptitude, or it may be, as the privatisers would argue, that the BBC is inhibited by its reliance on 'public' money. But it may also be, more charitably, a lingering and uncertain memory of public service. It is fairly clear that the rush to foreign markets leaves a large gap in the BBC's inherited policy of public service and the national cultural mission. Hence the BBC's current ungainliness: neither one thing nor the other, depending on a notion of public service for its public funding, but insufficiently funded to provide the increasingly expensive service which it has persuaded itself that the public wants: a national service increasingly dependent on the international market. One of the things which drops off the bottom of the international economic ladder is that very single play which had secured television's cultural seriousness by reflecting the nation to itself, and which, as a developing tradition, had depended on the kind of gestation and nurture which is no longer available in a market-led cultural economy. Increasingly, the space which the single play had occupied is being evacuated by in-house production, to be colonised by the independent film industry which can do the job more economically. As Grierson predicted in 1935, the independents are indeed seeking their independence through television, and it is increasingly the heirs of Grierson rather than of Reith who are fulfilling and transforming the role of public service in the area of television entertainment.

The concept of a public service cinema has neither currency, continuity, nor an institutional stability to compare with that of the BBC. The idea of such a cinema appears in Grierson as part of a vision of a British art cinema which would be protected from commercial imperatives in order that it might serve the public by reflecting it to itself: educating it, informing it and entertaining it, without having to face what Grierson saw as the inevitable commercial pressure of pandering to it. Without the institutional base of a public corporation, such a cinema clearly could not exist as a coherent thing, and it disappeared on the one hand into sponsored cinema, supported by government or by industry for public relations more than public service, and on the other hand into an art cinema which became increasingly socially exclusive. But it continued to exist as an idea, fuelling the case, in the 1940s and the 1970s particularly, for subsidy and forms of state cultural patronage, and marking out a crestline of British film which would be traced from the Documentary Movement and the Crown Film Unit, through bits of Balcon's Ealing, surfacing briefly in Free Cinema and rising in Woodfall in the early 60s, disappearing in the late 60s into television and the drama documentaries of Loach and Garnett, and reappearing in a very contradictory form in the arguments in the 70s around the British Film Institute Production Board and the Independent Film-makers' Association. Importantly, this crestline implies an idea of what a

British film is, and of what a British film industry would look like.

More positively, without the base of a single acknowledged public service corporation, the notion of a public service cinema is distinct from the autocratic paternalism of the Reithian moral mission, and fits in contradictory ways into the post-Reithian notion of a cultural mission. Public service here had more to do with creating a national cinema which had the same kind of cultural edge as the single play gave to television. Such a cinema would be distinct from the epic gloss of the later Lean, and from what was often seen as the rather too slick professionalism of Hitchcock: Grierson's remark that Hitchcock was 'the world's best director of unimportant pictures' is quite typical. Crucially, it was to be distinct from anything that smacked of the Hollywood 'dream factory'. In the post-war period the model that was frequently invoked was the Italian neo-realist cinema.

The British art cinema was to be socially responsible rather than arty, and its aesthetic was to be realist, embodying what has been referred to as a 'documentary attitude'. With a striking irony, it is precisely the kind of modest, naturalistic realism which people thought of as the mark of a British art cinema, a realism committed not simply to the narration of action but also to the description of the

Public service and the 'documentary attitude': the Ken Loach/Tony Garnett drama documentary *Cathy Come Home*, shown on BBC TV in 1966

199

social world, which became in the 60s the mark of the prestige of British television drama. The aesthetic of British art cinema prepared the way for its co-option into British public service television. The desire for a socially responsible art cinema was satisfied, at least for a time, in scale, commitment and immediacy, by the social realism of the television single play.

Institutionally, the British art cinema was to be defined by its independence, a term which is more meaningful as a polemic than as a description, masking in its claim of independence from something its dependence on something else. Essentially, the insistence on independence signifies a desire for a space outside institutional control. For cinema, the dominating force was Hollywood, and the independence which is so recurrently sought is an independence from the need to compete with Hollywood in the market-place.

The desire for independence seems to have been formative for British cinema in the same way that public service has been for television. Grierson's insistence that if the art of cinema is to survive 'it will be wise for the artist to organise his independence' points to a relationship between art and organisation which may be one of the characteristics of British film production. The need for the artist to organise an independence which was never given to him or her as a stable institutional norm may explain why, if we were to follow Andrew Sarris and claim that the history of American cinema is the history of its directors, we would also have to say that the history of the British cinema is the history of producers. Grierson himself, Balcon, Dean, Korda, Powell and Pressburger, Lean, Richardson, Reisz, Anderson, Attenborough, Puttnam: none of them are purely directors, many of them are not directors at all. Outside of a studio system or a national corporation, art is too precarious a business to be left to artists: it needs organisers. The importance of the producer-artist seems to be a specific feature of British cinema, an effect of the need continually to start again in the organisation of independence.

The organisation of independence has certain requirements, of which two are worth mentioning here. First, it needs mechanisms of financial support for pre-production and production; second, it needs exhibition outlets. To satisfy the first requirement, a public service cinema in its purest, Griersonian form would go directly to the state for sponsorship, offering a specific service to a specific department, and working, with as much latitude as could be justified, within the framework of a commission. For such a system to think of itself as a public service, it had to accept a close identity between the interests of the state and the public interest, and, almost by its very nature, it was restricted, outside wartime, to the documentary or semi-documentary which provided information and education rather than to the feature film which provided entertainment. For an art cinema aspiring to the feature film, the appeal for state subvention had to be made to a broader sense of public service, one which depended on the recognition of cinema as an art form and a component of the national culture. Institutionally, the argument sought to escape the direct client relationship between cinema and state department. Between the late 1940s and the mid-1980s, the low-budget feature-film art cinema did indeed receive a small measure of financial support from the state, and, with it, some measure of recognition as a supportable public service. This came through the Eady Levy on cinema admissions, the National Film Finance Corporation, and certain quite important tax concessions and capital allowances. It was never a very stable system of support, and was in any case dismantled by the end of 1985, leaving television as an increasingly important source of production funding for the independent cinema.

Again, as has been noted, Grierson recognised that the future of the art of the cinema might not lie in the cinema at all, but in 'citadels of suburban improvement'. It was indeed one of the achievements of the Documentary Movement and the more politically radical working-class Kinos in the 1930s to develop a non-theatrical audience; and the importance of the Film Society movement for the development of British film culture should never be underestimated. Grierson also speculated on a 'controlled cinema', a municipal or state-controlled public service exhibition system which has never, in fact, materialised. What materialised in its place was the system of Regional Film Theatres administered (from 1967) by the British Film Institute, and, in Scotland, by the Scottish Film Council, alongside, in some cities, a circuit of independent commercial 'art house' cinemas. But, with the possible exception of London and Newcastle (no one, to my knowledge, has yet successfully explained Newcastle), these cinemas do little else than satisfy the demands of middle-class taste which the Rank/EMI exhibition duopoly fails to satisfy. They have little spare capacity to develop the kind of mass popular audience which the idea of a public service cinema in its Griersonian sense would seem to require. That audience seems to be watching television, and on television it is not always watching the bits that are conceived as public service.

What is becoming characteristic of the 1980s in the development of film and television culture is the increasing integration of independent cinema and public service television, not simply as common formative discourses but as a system of institutional dependencies. Serving the public implies finding an audience, and the audience has gone to television. To quote David Puttnam :'I make films for people

Experience Preferred But Not Essential (1982), produced by David Puttnam for Channel Four and subsequently released theatrically

to see. If I have a message to convey, I should convey it in whatever way the audience prefers to see it. In Britain the audience has an expressed preference to see my work on television.''[10] As the present government cuts off other sources of funding, Channel Four, the true heir of public service television, becomes an increasingly important source of pre-production funding. As television moves its resources in dramatic entertainment towards product for the international market, a space is left open in the public service area of television cultural programming for independent film-makers to occupy. This is not at all to suggest that the situation is a stable one in which public service television and independent cinema join forces to defend the public interest. It is rather that film and television are equally vulnerable to the current economic, political and ideological pressures against public service which come from domestic government, and to the pressures against national cultures which come from the growing power of the international market. The discourses of public service and independence, as they have traditionally been elaborated, may not be an adequate protection against these pressures.

The experience of Goldcrest Films and Television suggests some of the complexities of the current climate. Goldcrest is owned by the Pearson-Longman Group which also owns the *Financial Times* and Penguin Books. It was established to produce British films for cinema (*Gandhi, Local Hero, The Killing Fields*) and television. In 1981, its affiliated company Enigma (with David Puttnam as producer) made eight films for the first year of Channel Four's 'Film on Four' slot under the collective title of 'First Love'. Channel Four provided between £200,000 and £275,000 per film, and the rest of the budget and profit was to come from pre-sales to American cable TV which was then booming, and from limited American and British theatrical release. Each of the films was distinctly, if somewhat sentimentally, British, with something of the style of a single play on television but with an added visual sophistication derived from film production values.

In 1982, American cable companies were prepared to pay around £400,000 for the kind of television films which Goldcrest was producing. By 1984, with the beginnings of a collapse of cable in the face of video, which was just beginning to make real inroads into American domestic entertainment, the going rate had dropped to around £50,000. Since the Channel Four budget had remained level, this meant that the key to financial success was theatrical release, which might ensure a good price on the video market. But to gain a theatrical release, and, more importantly, distribution through an American major, without which films have to be sold territory by territory, low-budget films have to look like cinema films, not films for television. In 1984–5, therefore, Goldcrest's television plans were for ten films and a mini-series: six of the films budgeted at £1 million, and four at £500,000. Funding for the six major releases was to come from overseas sales and pre-sales.[11]

The coming together of the cinematic style and production values of the independent film-makers with the social reach of television, which seems at first sight to reinvigorate and transform the idea of public service with some of the values of entertainment, may be seen at second glance to be simply the first step towards the internationalisation of a national cinema and a national television system. Within its many contradictions, public service did provide a certain safeguard to notions of national culture.

The fragmentation into a utopia of local workshops and cable stations has a lot of economically based arguments to contend with. As in the manufacturing industries, so in the cultural industries: in a weak economy privatisation is the first step to either internationalisation or marginalisation. It is possible to be quite sanguine about the prospects of British film and television on the international market (the case of Goldcrest is encouraging); and it is equally possible to be positively enthusiastic about locally based film workshops. It is the area between that seems most under threat, and we do have to contend with the fact that historically it has been the medium-budget feature film and the indigenous drama (the area which public service might have claimed as its own) which has often seemed to represent the best chance of a genuinely diverse national popular film and television culture.

The significance of 1985, then, British Film Year, is that it may end a cycle for cinema and broadcasting which began in 1927. The Films Bill, which cuts off the unlamented Eady Fund and shuts down the National Film Finance Corporation, begins the process which will lead to a massive dependence on private, and hence ultimately Hollywood, funding: the same funding from which Grierson sought refuge in the EMB Film Unit. For broadcasting, it seems possible that in 1986 the BBC will be instructed to begin some limited experiment with advertising or with subscription as a means of raising revenue,

Film for the BBC: Alan Bates in *An Englishman Abroad* (1983, directed by John Schlesinger)

placing the Corporation into a dependence on commerce or public taste from which Reith had tried to rescue it in 1927. The point is not to mourn public service, but to organise, again, independence. It seems clear that the particular discourses of public service and independence under which the debates and defences were conducted in the past were always weak, and are now perhaps redundant. The quite difficult job now will be to find the new terms which will provide some sense of what a national film and television culture, or national film and television cultures, will look like after 1985.

Notes

1 J. C. W. Reith, *Into the Wind*, London, Hodder & Stoughton, 1949, pp. 90–1.
2 Forsyth Hardy (ed.), *Grierson on Documentary*, London, Faber, 1946, pp. 118–19.
3 Andrew Boyle, *Only the Wind Will Listen: Reith of the BBC*, London, Hutchinson, 1972, p. 34.
4 Quoted in *Grierson on Documentary*, p. 12.
5 Ibid., p. 120.
6 Memo to Harold Wilson, quoted by Margaret Dickinson and Sarah Street, *Cinema and State*, London, British Film Institute, 1985, p. 216.
7 Asa Briggs, *Sound and Vision: History of Broadcasting in the United Kingdom*, vol. IV, Oxford, Oxford University Press, 1979, p. 28.
8 Ibid., pp. 80–1.
9 Ibid., p. 76.
10 Quoted in *Independent Production Handbook: Film & Video*, London, Association of Independent Producers, 1982, p. 11.
11 Since this was written, Goldcrest has run into problems and these plans have been amended.

Charles Barr

BROADCASTING AND CINEMA
2: SCREENS WITHIN SCREENS

Near the beginning of *Simon and Laura*, a British film of 1955, two characters are asked to take part in a television programme. The man of the couple, played by Maurice Denham, used to be an actor; the woman (Thora Hird) is nervous, and asks if he will advise her – after all, she says, 'you've been in the entertainment business'. To which he replies, quick as a flash, timing it as a punch-line: 'This isn't entertainment, this is television.'

The gag is a neat illustration of an intense TV-consciousness that keeps surfacing within British cinema around this time. Visually, too, the screen within the screen is a frequent image in the films of this period – of, centrally, the decade from 1953 to 1963.

In *television* terms, the beginning of this decade is marked by the Queen's Coronation in June 1953, the BBC's live coverage of which gave an enormous boost both to the medium's status and to its audience figures, and by the debate over the proposal to introduce commercial television (otherwise known as Independent Television: ITV). In July 1954, the Conservative government's Television Act reached the statute book, ending the BBC's monopoly: the first of the regional ITV companies began broadcasting in September 1955. The other end of that decade is marked by the Report to Parliament of the Pilkington Committee on Broadcasting (1962) and by the ensuing legislation, which led to the opening of a second television channel by the BBC in 1964. Technologically, the feature of the decade is the introduction and progressive refinement of videotape recording, as crucial a landmark in TV history as the conversion to sound in the late 1920s is in film history. The number of TV licences issued in the United Kingdom rose, in round figures, from 2 million in 1953 to 12 million in 1963.[1]

In *cinema* terms, the decade 1953–63 was a period of severe decline in audiences and, partly in response to this, of changes in the structure of the industry. It saw the acceptance of X-certificate films by the major exhibition circuits; the decline of the vertically integrated combines of Rank and ABC as major production forces; the closing of Ealing studios, and the rise of a company of similar fame, scale and organisation but of very different subject matter in Hammer Films; the start of the *Carry On* series; and the emergence of Woodfall Films, and of similar independent production companies committed to broadening the range of British cinema in various ways. In retrospect, 1963 stands out as, above all, the year of Woodfall's *Tom Jones*. Initially, this was to be financed by Bryanston Films, the British consortium to which Woodfall belonged and of which Michael Balcon was chairman: before shooting began, the budget rose, Bryanston hesitated, and the American company United Artists stepped in to take over the funding. The film's startlingly large worldwide profits thus went mainly to them, and stimulated, for a few short years, an intensive American investment in British films. It was, in Tony Garnett's phrase, a form of 'colonisation', and had the ambivalent results that the word suggests.[2] In effect, 1963 marks at least the beginning of the end of a certain kind of coherent and autonomous domestic British cinema.

Clearly these developments in TV and in cinema are interrelated, in all kinds of ways. The film industry, with good reason, saw television as a major cause of the decline in its own audiences.[3] Its TV-consciousness can be charted through explicit pronouncements and policies (including its heavy restrictions on the sale of movie rights to TV); through changing strategies of production and marketing; and through a striking cluster of direct representations of TV within the film product itself. It is these I want to concentrate on here. There is something peculiarly interesting about TV scenes within movies. For a start, there is the sheer aesthetic kick of viewing the screen within the screen, the medium within the medium; moreover, the films acquire, as time goes by, increasing value as 'time capsules', fixing a certain stage both in TV's evolving technology and in available current perceptions of the medium and how it operates: 'available' perceptions rather than universal ones, since film-makers offering representations of TV are not disinterested parties, least of all in this 1953–1963 decade when tensions and polemics about the new medium were at their height. ('This isn't entertainment, this is television.') To sum up: TV was in these years young enough to be still an object of fascination, but mature enough to be recognised as a popular force and as a commercial threat; but a threat, not yet a conqueror. There still survived, through this decade, the coherent British domestic cinema I have referred to: largely (pre-*Tom Jones*) British-financed, concerned centrally with British audiences and

British culture, and concerned, therefore, with what TV was doing to that culture, that audience, and that cinema.

First, a flashback is necessary. The image of the screen within the screen echoes, in a sense takes the place of, that regular and eloquent image found in British films of the 1930s and 1940s, but above all of the Second World War years: the image of listening to another domestic medium, the radio. In two of the very first films of the war, complex and emotive audio-visual sequences are built up around the radio broadcast made on Sunday 3 September 1939 by the Prime Minister, Neville Chamberlain, in which he announced to the nation that 'we are now at war with Germany'. In *The Lion has Wings*, the feature film rushed out as instant propaganda by Alexander Korda, the wife and fiancée of two RAF officers listen respectfully to the broadcast in elegant surroundings; the men then enter and are told the news; 'No man could have done more' [than Chamberlain had done], is the response of the senior officer, Ralph Richardson. In *The First Days*, a collaborative short documentary production by the GPO Film Unit, we see the same broadcast received in a different spirit and in different surroundings, in workmen's cafés, and a modest suburban street; passers-by gather to listen at an open window and around a car radio, absorbing the news stoically, refraining from tributes. In itself this juxtaposition fixes a contrast between two attitudes, 'two nations', of 1939, and, correspondingly, between two forces within the film industry which were to draw closer together in a form of wartime 'consensus'. What they have in common already, before that celebrated rapprochement between fiction and documentary begins, is a celebration of radio as a technological marvel and a benevolent social force. Both sequences grow out of an initial montage of transmitters, aerials, wireless sets and listeners. It is a form of montage already familiar from a mass of 1930s documentaries which celebrate the state-run technologies of the GPO itself and of comparable institutions.

There are, plainly, very close affinities between public service documentary and public service radio, as John Caughie establishes in the companion chapter to this one. Both of them 'come into their own' during the war, and complement each other triumphantly. The wartime films of Humphrey Jennings are probably the ones that exemplify these affinities most powerfully, both through their repeated scenes of characters listening to the radio (the factory girls of *Listen to Britain*, the bereaved wife in *Fires Were Started*, the family of *A Diary for Timothy*), and in their whole tone and structure, in that they depict people from different regions, jobs, and cultural levels bound together emotionally by a national loyalty, and practically by a national administration, for both of which the spoken word, and also music, are of great importance. But film-makers from the non-documentary end of British cinema also adopt this model, and incorporate the image and sound of radio positively. The clearest examples of this are, for structure and tone, Launder and Gilliat's *Millions Like Us*, and, for the image of radio itself, Anthony Asquith's *The Demi-Paradise,* where the Soviet visitor is drawn into his host family (and by extension into the Allied cause) through listening to a Churchill broadcast in their company.

An important aspect of radio is that it does not constitute a threat to the cinema: it doesn't stop people going out to see films. Television was obviously destined to be more of a problem. It was a problem and embarrassment for Reith himself and for his immediate BBC successors, who had the responsibility for developing the new medium but found it hard to assimilate to their notions of cultural responsibility. It was technically inflexible, seeming to lend itself to the straight relay and to the lightweight magazine programme, and for a long time there could be no authentically national structure. An experimental service had been run from 1936, but it served only the London region, and closed down at the start of the war. Only slowly, after the war, did it extend its national coverage and its aspirations, and start to become more than a very junior partner within the BBC.

Cinema had from time to time depicted television for its novelty value, in films going back as far as the futuristic *High Treason* (1929) and the comedy revue *Elstree Calling* (1930), and TV sets are shown as part of the furniture in such post-war films as *Passport to Pimlico* (1949). But it was not until well into the 1950s that cinema addressed itself in a sustained way to a rival medium: through, among other things, two films that take television as their central subject.

These two films, *Meet Mr Lucifer* and *Simon and Laura*, are comedies with a clear 'group authorship'. Both are based on recent stage plays, adapted for the screen by writers other than the original playwright, and then realised by directors who have no strong authorial status and who, it appears, had no special personal involvement in these projects: they are modestly produced as part of an ongoing production programme. Thus, the films as we have them can be taken to 'speak for' (areas of) the mainstream commercial industry rather than for individual creators. *Meet Mr Lucifer* is an Ealing film released late in 1953: playwright Arnold Ridley, adapter Monja Danischewsky, director Anthony Pelissier. *Simon and Laura* is a Rank Organisation film released in the autumn of 1955: playwright Alan Melville, adapter Peter Blackmore, director Muriel Box.

Meet Mr Lucifer is centred on a veteran stage actor (Stanley Holloway) performing in an unsuccessful show: the audience has

Things to come: *High Treason*, directed by Maurice Elvey in 1929

deserted to television. The actor gets drunk, bangs his head, and during his time of unconsciousness has a fantasy in which he visits Hell and meets the Devil (hence the title). Here he learns that television is 'an *instrument* of the Devil, a mechanical device to make the human race utterly miserable'; he resolves to make people realise this and find their way back to the live theatre (and by implication to the cinema, an implication that will be confirmed in the film's ending).

The film sets up structures of opposition that are typically Ealing. The first person we see being made miserable by possession of a TV set is an old clerk (Joseph Tomelty) who is on the point of retirement. On his last day at the office we watch him operating an abacus while others use calculating machines. They are all given a complicated sum to do by a visiting dignitary, and the abacus man does it quickest. But he leaves, the abacus is phased out, and he is presented with a TV set, characterised at once as being soulless and anti-human like the calculators.

The TV set is shown creating fake community, fake togetherness, in two ways. First, it brings people together into the house of the set owner, but they are parasites rather than true friends. The viewers all look at the TV screen and not at each other, and when the set breaks down the guests desert its owner; later, they ignore him in the street. Television produces, then, a parody of that *community* which is so important to Ealing, and indeed to British cinema more widely, while at the same time, in a sub-plot, it is shown splitting up a family: the wife, in her obsession with TV, neglects the housework and cooking and so drives her man out of the house. The second kind of fake togetherness is the communion between the viewer and the screen. A lot of the film's comedy is based on the convention of direct address from screen to viewer: the naive viewer is shown responding directly to this address, believing he is being addressed personally – he obeys all instructions, speaks back to the screen, and so on. This may seem a rather obvious ploy, but there are some striking things about the way it is handled:

1. It is interesting for a start that the film should get such an enormous amount of mileage out of this aspect of television and treat it with such evident bitterness beneath the comedy surface. This is particularly strong in another plot strand about a lonely young man who watches TV in his solitary room and becomes obsessed with a seductive singer, Miss Lonely Hearts. The pay-off to this is his disillusion when he finds that her intimate close-up messages are not after all addressed personally to him, but that she is simply a paid performer in a mass medium; one, moreover, who is ready to sell her services to the highest bidder, a TV advertising agency in the United States, home of the commercialised horrors that may soon be inflicted upon British audiences.

2. The film shows direct address of this kind as being absolutely the dominant mode of television. It has fourteen separate segments of television material, shown on screens within the screen. Two of the fourteen are Interludes (goldfish in bowl; printed caption), three are Outside Broadcast relays (football, horse racing, dancing). The other nine are based on direct address to the camera by lecturer, singer, comedian, continuity announcer, cook, and others. From the perspective of today, it seems remarkable that there is no category of the fictional, but there is a logic in what the film is presenting as typical of TV output in this 'primitive' period. It's not that there was no drama on BBC TV in the early 1950s – there were several hours of it a week – but there was no tradition as yet either of popular drama or of original drama. Instead, there was the relaying, from theatre or TV studio, of pre-existing dramatic texts: classics or West End plays. It was only at

this precise period that the BBC was beginning, tentatively, to put money into original TV drama, and Situation Comedy had not yet evolved. Thus, the *fictional* was simply not a category that would have been perceived as basic to television in the way that both the Outside Broadcast relay, and the show based upon direct address, were perceived.

3. It is very noticeable that the direct look is represented by the film as being more widespread, in television practice, than it has become since: the codes governing access to the camera, as summarised for instance by Stuart Hood in his book *On Television*, operate less strictly.[4] Panel-game members and interviewees, for instance, look at the camera directly instead of routing their look through chairman or interviewer, and the same thing can be observed in *Simon and Laura* and in *Left Right and Centre*, the latter dating from as late as 1959. Three possible reasons for this discrepancy suggest themselves: (a) people did look at the television camera more liberally in those days, the codes being still in a state of relative fluidity, as in 'primitive' cinema; (b) the film-makers got it wrong accidentally; (c) the film-makers got it wrong maliciously, to create a sense of unease in the viewer. My sense is that the answer is a combination of (a) and (c), that the film-makers picked out and exaggerated that non-cinematic direct look as being characteristic of television, and as being uncomfortable both physically (disorienting and embarrassing the viewer, and conflicting with the kind of secure spectator-positioning that the cinema had long since mastered) and also morally (creating a fake intimacy).

Meet Mr Lucifer ends not with a return to live theatre, but with a happy cinema audience watching a 3D film – a form of cinematic direct address, but held within a secure framework. The audience are fully aware of themselves as being part of a mass, as well as individuals, but they don't pretend to be a community; and they are involved in a fictional diegesis which is clearly recognised to be fiction and illusion.

Where *Meet Mr Lucifer* is audience-centred, *Simon and Laura*, made two years later, is production-centred. Simon and Laura are a husband and wife team both in real life and on the television screen, in a pioneering BBC serial which becomes a fantastic success. The programme, inevitably for 1955, goes out live. In it, they keep their own names and act out an inventively scripted version of their own daily life, in a studio replica of their own house, attended by their own servants. And they have a very odd relationship with the camera.

At one point we see them acting out, for the TV serial, an important scene with a boy whom they are adopting. At the end of the scene, all

'An instrument of the Devil': *Meet Mr Lucifer* (1953)

three of them turn from facing each other to smile direct at the camera, and thus at the live TV audience. Likewise, when Laura is interviewed for the TV magazine programme *In Town Tonight*, the interviewer, after introducing her, moves smartly to a position as close as possible to the TV camera in order that her responses to his subsequent questions will automatically be addressed in its direction. This is in line with the conventions depicted in *Meet Mr Lucifer*; here, an extra tension is set up, within the shot, between TV codes and film codes. When Simon and Laura look into the TV camera, the film camera, *our* camera, remains at the 'correct' angle, observing invisibly. This corresponds to the different status of the two diegetic worlds being shown to us. *Simon and Laura*, the film, is fictional: it stars Peter Finch and Kay Kendall but is not entitled *Peter and Kay*. *Simon and Laura*, the TV series, is at most semi-fictional, though it is the type of drama we would now expect to be made *as* fiction, with actors playing roles and a strict observance of the Don't Look at the Camera rule. Looking at the time capsule of *Simon and Laura*, we are, surely, witnessing a stage in the evolution of Situation Comedy, a genre which did, historically, develop in radio and TV to a large extent out of the representation of notional events in the lives of known people: the Lyons, the Bradens, Hancock, Lucy.

Simon and Laura, the film, is resolved by a triumphant reassertion of the essential nature of the TV medium. First, the couple drop the pretence of marital harmony and fight on set during transmission, destroying the illusion on which the programme depends. Second, in the film's last scene, Laura and the (female) scriptwriter eavesdrop together, via the TV studio cameras and monitors which happen to be running, upon the man-to-man talk of their respective partners, Simon and the show's producer, as they reveal their true, loyally loving emotions. The two couples are thus restored, and TV is restored to its role, rooted in the ontology of the medium, as relay device, live relay being something which, by its nature, film can never achieve.

TV triumphs, then, but has been put firmly in its place. It cannot do, it mustn't be allowed to be able to do, what cinema can do. Cinema, by strong implication, presents a more autonomous and full-blooded experience. In *Simon and Laura,* the film uses the words which the TV show is compelled to censor. The film shows

Looking in: *Simon and Laura* (1953)

the plunging neckline which the TV show is compelled to raise. Repeatedly, films will show drama and emotion breaking up the decorously controlled environment of the TV studio: *Simon and Laura, Man of the Moment* (1955, with Norman Wisdom), *I'm All Right Jack* (1959). In *The Quatermass Xperiment* (1955: US title, *The Creeping Unknown*), the BBC is doing an Outside Broadcast from Westminster Abbey when the extra-terrestrial slime creeps into shot; the producer, confronted with this cosmic scoop, switches back instantly to the studio to avoid offending viewers. But the film, X-rated, early Hammer, confronts its audience with the full horror. Something comparable happens in the 1959 Anthony Asquith film *Libel*. The BBC is again transmitting a live OB, this time from a stately home, with its number one prestige front man Richard Dimbleby as the unctuous compere. Again, the presence of TV cameras and TV audience is foregrounded: the hostess (Olivia de Havilland), ushering Dimbleby around the dining room, tells him that 'We've laid it out specially for you – and the viewers'. By chance this programme is viewed by a visiting Canadian who knows her husband (Dirk Bogarde) and knows some dark secrets about his past. Soon, he tracks him down and confronts him, and the film then plays out the kind of intense melodrama, in this case a classic and powerful form of (in Freudian terms) the Return of the Repressed, that is the BBC programme's antithesis.

Both *The Quatermass Xperiment* and *Libel* are intelligently conceived and very strong examples of genre cinema, horror and melodrama respectively, which step outside the limits of respectable mid-1950s British cinema to offer experiences that go beyond, also, the standard range of television's output. Ironically, *Quatermass* itself had its source in television, in Nigel Kneale's six-part original series broadcast by the BBC in 1953: this was a landmark both in BBC policy, as a commissioned original TV drama, and in intensity of audience response. Kneale's own dramatisation of *1984* the following year had a comparable intensity; indeed, it made a much stronger impact than MGM's British-made film of the same novel released in 1956. Just at the time, in fact, when cinema was disparaging its grasp of the fictional, TV was rapidly developing its own forms of strong popular fiction: not only the Nigel Kneale dramas, but embryonic soap opera in *The Grove Family* (1953–6 – glimpsed in the TV studio scenes of *Man of the Moment*), and police series such as *Fabian of the Yard* (1955, on film) and, more importantly, *Dixon of Dock Green* (1955–76, studio). All of these were BBC productions, and the new commercial network would accelerate this move into popular fictional forms. P. C. George Dixon was, of course, a character created for Ealing's *The Blue Lamp* (1950). Thus, not long after Ealing made

215

Meet Mr Lucifer, a quintessentially Ealing-type dramatic product became regularly available on TV, a development with far-reaching implications.[5]

A slightly different angle on television from Lucifer's is found in the early films of the British 'New Wave' a few years later, but these too concentrate on non-fictional elements, as if reluctant to admit, or take seriously, TV as a dramatic rival. There are, anyway, other aspects of the medium which they view with stronger concern. Three of these films, involving three different directors working with three different new male stars, depict television in a particularly vitriolic way.

Directly after the credits of *Saturday Night and Sunday Morning* (Karel Reisz, 1960), the Albert Finney character, who still lives with his parents, returns home from work on Friday evening. His father is watching television, and stares fixedly at the advertisements, not looking away from the screen as his wife plies him with tea and his son attempts conversation.

The Loneliness of the Long Distance Runner (Tony Richardson, 1962) comes from the same company (Woodfall) and the same writer (Alan Sillitoe, again adapting his own recently published story). Tom Courtenay plays the runner, who is in juvenile prison after a conviction for theft. A series of flashbacks traces the background to this sentence. His father has died in an accident at work; in the weightiest of the flashbacks, the widowed mother uses up the compensation money in a shopping spree. Both in visuals and in music this sequence insistently mimics the style of a TV commercial. Arriving home, the family settles down to enjoy its new TV set. Mother's seedy boyfriend fiddles with the knobs, and the set comes to life with, predictably enough, a jingly commercial. Adults and children gaze fixedly at the set, and the looks which Courtenay directs at them, not it, go unreturned.

A third film to place its hero in front of the family TV set is *A Kind of Loving* (directed by John Schlesinger for Vic Films, also 1962). Alan Bates is forced to sit with his newly acquired wife and mother-in-law, in whose home the couple are living, as they watch a quiz programme.

In all three films, a violent animus against television is conveyed at various levels: choice of material shown, response to it by the characters, and, not least, the place of the TV scene within the narrative structure. All three virile heroes turn their back on set and viewers in disgust and go upstairs, in a liberating escape towards a space of individual desire. In *Saturday Night* and *A Kind of Loving* they dress to go out, to drink and socialise; in *Loneliness,* Courtenay goes to his room to commune with a photograph of

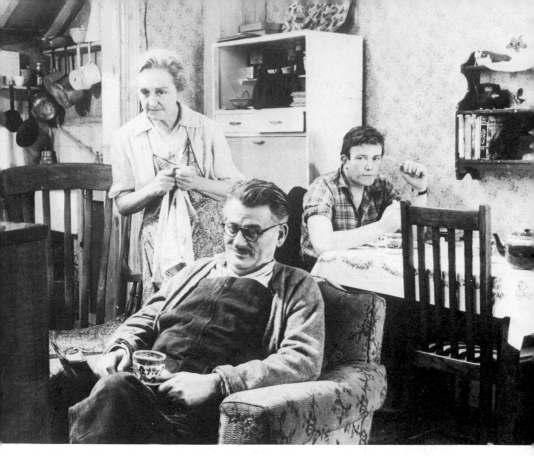

Fixed to the small screen: Albert Finney watches his parents watching in *Saturday Night and Sunday Morning* (1960)

his dead father whom the widow's behaviour is betraying. TV is associated with the domestic, the feminine; the father in *Saturday Night* has been feminised; the other two fathers are absent, but very important.

The scene in *A Kind of Loving* repays further scrutiny. While Bates watches the quiz show, his father is playing in a local brass band concert. He was keen to take his bride to it, but she and her mother insisted on a nice evening at home instead. The film cuts between concert and living-room. The rest of Bates' own family sit proudly in the concert hall, ruefully aware of the two empty seats adjacent to them. Father's big moment comes, and he plays his solo, the final note of which merges into the hollow brassiness of the chord heralding the quiz-master, in synchronism with the visual cut back into the living-room, where the reactionary gossipy conversation contrasts with the other family's solid good sense.

Andy Medhurst rightly describes this juxtaposition as 'Hoggartian' (page 187 of this book). Both the spirit and the actual terms of the opposition create a strong echo of Richard Hoggart's 1957 book *The Uses of Literacy*, which centres on the opposition, within a North of England context, between authentic, rooted cultural forms (including brass band music) and shallower mass media-related ones.[6] Hoggart became an extremely influential figure in this period, through the book and through two subsequent cultural interventions: first, an eloquent defence of D. H. Lawrence and his values at the 1960 trial of Penguin Books for publishing an unexpurgated text of *Lady Chatterley's Lover*,[7] and, second, his membership of the Pilkington Committee on Broadcasting which reported to Parliament in 1962. There are insistent connections in language, tone and opinion between this report and *The Uses of Literacy*: both, for instance, use the metaphor of 'candy floss' (a blown-up confection on a stick, characterised by sugariness without substance) as a key term in describing mass media triviality.[8] For Pilkington, triviality is 'a natural vice of television', one that is 'more dangerous to the soul than wickedness'.[9] All three of the 'New Wave' films referred to are a product of the period between the setting up of that Committee and the publication of its report, and they share its perspective on television and, more widely, on popular culture. Both Reisz and Richardson did their initial modest film work within Free Cinema, a movement which was robustly hostile to commercialised popular culture and whose personnel shared a broadly New Left outlook with Hoggart and, indeed, Alan Sillitoe. Schlesinger's background was different but also significant: he had served a film-making apprenticeship with British Transport Films, last real outpost in British cinema of the Griersonian documentary tradition (*Terminus*, 1960), and with the BBC's high-prestige cultural TV programme *Monitor*, the kind of television you didn't have to feel ashamed of staying at home to watch.

If the cut back in *A Kind of Loving* from concert hall to living room, from brass band to quiz show, is Hoggartian, it also carries a strong and poignant echo, whether conscious or not, of Humphrey Jennings, the one British film-maker whom the Free Cinema group admired wholeheartedly. The climax of *Listen to Britain*, the 1942 short film credited jointly to Jennings and his editor Stewart McAllister, is the cross-cutting between workers' canteen and National Gallery as two lunchtime audiences listen to two musical performances. In the canteen, Flanagan and Allen, members of the Crazy Gang variety act, sing their well-loved signature tune 'Underneath the Arches'. In the National Gallery, Dame Myra Hess plays a Mozart concerto to an audience of office workers, the Queen, servicemen, Sir Kenneth Clark of the Ministry of Information, and anyone else who has chosen to walk in off the street and pay the modest entrance fee. The final note of a Flanagan and Allen verse segues into the piano music, which is then detached from its diegetic source to function as accompaniment to a montage of London images. The effect of the elaborate audio-visual montage of which this sequence is a small but intense part is to create a seamless unity. Like the other elements of national life in wartime that McAllister and Jennings stitch together, the respective musicians and audiences are distinct from one another but on the same side; their particular locations, classes, jobs, tastes, differentiate them but do not divide them.[10]

Here as in other wartime films, the medium of radio is, as noted earlier, fully compatible with this vision of a united society, and is depicted as a strong constituent part of it. The triumphant transitional note, merging Flanagan and Allen with Mozart, expresses, in fact, a very 'BBC' ideology, as set out in the stated BBC policy of sustaining complementary or gradated programme channels that cater, responsibly, for different levels of 'brow'; it is a cut from, in wartime terms, Forces Programme to National Programme, or in post-war terms from Light Programme to Home Service. The analogous cut in *A Kind of Loving* is, manifestly, not triumphant but bitter, expressing not unity but division. TV can't be assimilated within a healthy culture – at least this kind of TV can't be.

After Pilkington
Not surprisingly, these early 1960s attacks on commercial television now have as dated a look as those other film representations of the medium from the 1950s. This is not to discount their sincerity and eloquence, and they may even have had a minor contributory effect on the medium's evolution through the definitive way in which they expressed, within another popular medium, that moral panic about the dangers of 'Americanised' commercialism which had been built up over a decade, ever since the notion of breaking up the BBC's television monopoly began to be seriously discussed. The Pilkington Report, which delivered a magisterial rebuke to ITV, and a pat on the back and a second channel to the BBC, in fact marks a crucial turning point. Fifteen years later, its successor, the Annan Report, could characterise ITV's output as, on balance, more dynamic and responsible than the BBC's; in 1981, H. V. Kershaw could write that 'The truth is, of course, that nowadays the BBC is much more of a commercial channel than is ITV', and it would seem hardly a paradox at all.[11]

In Annan's words, 'The Pilkington Report transformed the face of ITV', by ushering in stricter controls over its elements of excess.[12] At the same time, there had been significant shifts since the early 1960s in dominant attitudes to TV and to popular culture generally. The Annan Committee pointed out that certain ITV programmes had

> discovered the secret of making ITV more popular with the very political groups in society which 15 years ago would have been ideologically opposed to commercial television and for whom the BBC has now become suspect because they identify the BBC with authority. Granada and Thames make distinguished contributions to the network and Yorkshire has justified its place in the big five by the originality of some of its programmes. During the last 12 years, ITV has been fortunate in having such figures at its command as Lord Bernstein and Sir Denis Forman at Granada, Mr John Freeman who came to the rescue of London Weekend, and at ATV, Lord Grade, an impresario in the heroic mould.[13]

This is not the place to try to unravel the full background and full implications of such an analysis, and of the shifts that it both describes and embodies. But it has important significance for British cinema.

Essentially, the ITV network, limited and comforted by an elaborate system of controls over its autonomy, has taken its place within the established British framework of public service broadcasting. The reference in the Annan Report to Granada (based in Manchester) and to Yorkshire Television, as well as to London Weekend, stresses the 'national' spread of its programme-making. It has become a commonplace to see David Puttnam as having inherited the mantle of Michael Balcon as a determinedly and responsibly 'British' film producer, which is plausible up to a point, in so far as anyone can claim that role in today's changed film industry; but the true heirs of Balcon are, it can be argued, men like Denis Forman, Managing Director of Granada Television (and incidentally a former Director of the British Film Institute). Forman has, as Balcon had, a long-term institutional base and a commitment to a regular output of product, and operates a policy, like Balcon, of protecting the autonomy of a production team once a project has been initiated. This has been the framework for a substantial and diverse range of productions, including the documentaries of the Free Cinema graduate Michael Grigsby, ambitious and exportable film series like *The Jewel in the Crown*, and the everlasting twice-weekly series *Coronation Street*.[14]

Coronation Street began in December 1960: at precisely the time, that is, of the early deliberations of the Pilkington Committee and of the release of *Saturday Night and Sunday Morning*. Its early black-and-white episodes have distinct affinities both with the gritty

Granada Television's *Coronation Street*, 25 years old and still running

northern 'New Wave' movies and with Hoggart's *Uses of Literacy*, of which initially it seemed almost to be a consciously dramatised version. *Coronation Street* is not film, apart from the occasional location insert, but it is important to any consideration of the last twenty-five years of British cinema, for what it represents. Its longevity and sustained popularity indicate the kind of hold which genre television can exert upon domestic British audiences; it serves as an example of the consistent way in which commercial television has disarmed critics by taking over their kind of ground; and it has been a modest training-ground for talent: director Michael Apted and writer Jack Rosenthal are two of those who did spells on *Coronation Street* before moving on to single plays, and subsequently into cinema.

The same sort of pattern can be seen on a larger scale in the development of British television fiction since the late 1950s across a range of different types of programming. Among these are (a) the law and order series, a genre as endlessly and richly renewable as the Western: an important landmark here is the BBC's North of England police series *Z Cars*, particularly in its dynamic early years from 1962; (b) the high-prestige but by no means elitist tradition of

221

original drama produced electronically (live transmission progressively giving way to videotape). Institutionalised by ATV's Armchair Theatre in 1956, this was sustained in a succession of ITV and BBC slots: it developed later than the American 'Golden Age' of studio drama, but lasted much longer, and is still not quite defunct; (c) the TV 'play' made on film pioneered by the producer-director team of Tony Garnett and Ken Loach with some dramas of tremendous vigour and public impact like *Cathy Come Home* (1966) and *The Big Flame* (1969); (d) an extremely wide range of multi-episode modern fiction (video or film, adaptation or original, ITV or BBC), broadly taking over the structure first used in *Quatermass* in 1953. Sometimes characterised as TV novels, these include multi-author series with a team of writers but a strong continuity and coherence, such as *Helen, a Woman of Today* (1973); original works by such writers as the novelist Frederic Raphael (the six-part *The Glittering Prizes*, 1976); and adaptations of contemporary novels such as Piers Paul Read's *A Married Man* (1983) and, most spectacularly, Granada's 14-part rendering of Paul Scott's Raj Quartet, *The Jewel in the Crown* (1983). Finally, (e) there is the solid genre of literary and historical *period* drama, ranging from the almost annual new versions of Dickens or Jane Austen to the sixty-eight episodes of *Upstairs Downstairs*. And, in addition to all this fiction, the documentary mode and spirit have been almost completely taken over by television, and interestingly extended in the direction both of drama-documentary and of *vérité* filming.

Such an account lapses easily into a numbing catalogue, but it does need setting out, in view of the fact that TV's past even now remains relatively unchronicled, and is not often correlated with film history; it at least indicates something of the sheer range of ambitious work which British television has produced over twenty-five years, work which has compared very favourably with the cinema's output both in attractiveness to British audiences and in the satisfactions it afforded its makers. Many directors, and even more writers and producers, found it considerably more worthwhile working for TV companies and audiences than trying to put together projects for what remained of the British cinema. The stronger the pull of television became, the more that cinema was weakened, which in turn further strengthened the pull of television.

Until recently, this process operated in a fairly ruthless one-way fashion, with television draining off from any actual and potential British cinema much more than it gave. One factor was the way it paid generally low sums for the right to screen cinema films, and presented them (BBC especially) with some care, a strategy which, given the tatty state of most cinemas, lessened the attraction of a night out. Admittedly, TV did give back certain materials and personnel. A cluster of TV spin-offs did well at the domestic box-office from time to time: *Quatermass* had again been the prototype, but the most regular spin-offs were situation comedies like *Till Death Us Do Part* (1968) and *The Lovers* (1973). Various film-makers made short-term or long-term moves from TV to cinema, sometimes extending cinema's thematic or stylistic range in useful ways: examples here would include directors Jack Gold and Ken Loach, the writer Colin Welland (*Chariots of Fire*), and the Monty Python team. A recent group of directors, from backgrounds in TV advertising or drama, have, like Dick Lester earlier, moved across more permanently, often to base themselves in America as much as in Britain: Alan Parker, Ridley Scott, Michael Apted, Hugh Hudson. None of this has seriously redressed the balance of power or helped to recreate any solid cinematic base.

A more significant base may be provided by the varied co-production arrangements that have followed the establishment in 1982 of Channel 4 Television. For the first time, television has been helping to fund films that will have a cinema release, and something of the flexible interaction long since established in, for instance, Germany and Italy has been introduced in Britain. Some of the details and implications of this recent shift in relations are discussed elsewhere in this book by Robert Murphy, by Sylvia Harvey, and by John Caughie. The point to note here is the extent of the shift in attitudes that has taken place over the years, which has probably been more extreme and interesting in Britain than anywhere else.

As recently as 1961, the British Film Institute's regrettably short-lived TV magazine *Contrast* described the novelist J. B. Priestley as 'the only major English writer to accept television as part of his world, not just part of his cook's'.[15] This nicely evokes a common attitude of the time, which has its parallel in those British 'New Wave' films referred to earlier. If Alan Sillitoe or Tony Richardson employed cooks, one feels it was only for their benefit that they would have wanted a set in the house. A quarter of a century on, it would be hard to find a novelist who has not written for, or who could not easily be imagined writing for, television, in a non-slumming spirit. Likewise, the particular kind of animus against television displayed by those films discussed above has passed. In sum, cinema's relation to television has moved on from one of fascination and fear, through scorn, then envy, to a complex co-operation whose results it is, in 1986, rather too early to predict.

Notes

1   Figures from *BBC Annual Handbook*, London, BBC, 1985, p. 139.

2   Tony Garnett is quoted on the title page of Alexander Walker's *Hollywood England* (London, Michael Joseph, 1974), a detailed and indispensable account of the British film industry in the 1960s. Walker tells the full story of *Tom Jones* in Chapter 7.

3   Total cinema admissions in the UK fell from, to the nearest million, 1,285 million in 1953 to 357 million in 1963 (i.e. to 28 per cent of the 1953 figure): Department of Trade and Industry figures, quoted by Linda Wood, *British Film Industry*, BFI Information Guide no. 1, 1980. The relation of film and TV statistics is discussed by John Spraos in *The Decline of the Cinema* (London, Allen & Unwin, 1962), especially Chapter 1, 'The Influence of Television'.

4   Stuart Hood, *On Television*, London, Pluto Press, 1980, Chapter 1 especially.

5   On Ealing and television, see Charles Barr, *Ealing Studios*, London, Cameron and Tayleur/David and Charles, 1977, pp. 180–1.

6   Richard Hoggart, *The Uses of Literacy*, Pelican edition, 1958; on brass bands, see p. 119.

7   See C. H. Rolph, *The Trial of Lady Chatterley,* Harmondsworth, Penguin, 1961.

8   Hoggart, *The Uses of Literacy*, Chapter 7, 'Invitations to a Candy Floss World: the Newer Mass Art'. Cf. *Report of the Committee on Broadcasting,* London, HMSO, 1962, Cmnd. 1753, p. 34.

9   1962 *Report*, p. 35.

10 On this film and on the work of Stewart McAllister within the documentary film movement, see Dai Vaughan, *Portrait of an Invisible Man* (London, British Film Institute, 1983), which also refers to the relation between the Free Cinema group and Jennings, pp. 177–9.

11 H. V. Kershaw, *The Street Where I Live,* St. Albans, Granada, 1981, p. 143.

12 *Report of the Committee on the Future of Broadcasting*, London, HMSO, 1977, Cmnd. 6753, p. 146.

13 1977 *Report*, p. 148.

14 For interviews with Grigsby and with Forman, see Eva Orbanz, *Journey to a Legend and Back: the British Realistic Film*, Berlin, Edition Volker Spiess, 1977, pp. 100–16.

15 *Contrast*, vol. 1, no. 1, Autumn 1961, p. 74.

Sylvia Harvey
THE 'OTHER CINEMA' IN BRITAIN
UNFINISHED BUSINESS IN OPPOSITIONAL AND INDEPENDENT FILM, 1929-1984

Defining the 'other cinema'

This chapter is concerned with the images and sounds, movements and voices, marginalised from the mainstream of British cinema. It involves not only a search for the silenced and the absent, and an attempt at filling in the gaps of established film histories; it also involves a questioning of the definitions and purposes of the cinema itself, and of its broader social and cultural role. This broader frame of reference includes questions about the ways in which audio-visual tales have been told, and images produced: by whom, for whom, and with what purpose?

There are several 'other cinemas' in Britain. One is the voice of the inter-war middle classes, developing the language of social democracy within, for example, the Grierson documentary school. A second is the voice of a radicalised section of the new middle class of the post-war period, critical of both the ideological content and the aesthetic strategies of mainstream film and television. In the late 60s this voice creates an 'independent' cinema movement. A third, more difficult to identify and define, is the voice (or voices) of the working class, traced across the changes in the structure and composition of that class in the inter-war and post-war periods. After a century of universal literacy and just over half a century of universal suffrage, these voices have been grossly under-represented both in print and in audio-visual culture.[1] This third 'other cinema' must be taken to include the voices and demands of a range of oppressed social groups, including women and black people who have struggled in productive, critical and difficult alliance with (but also in) the working-class movement, for radical social change. The relationship between 'voice' and 'class' is a complex one, and it should not be assumed that the class origin of a film-maker determines the aesthetic or class character of his/her film, or that in any one film only one of these three voices can be present. A rather more complex set of relationships is predicated here, but not rendered theoretically explicit in the space available.

In a necessarily brief and selective account of these 'other cinemas' I shall concentrate on two periods and movements. One is the workers' film movement of the 1930s, opposed to the policies of the National government and to the capitalist economic and social system. The second is the independent film movement that emerged from an experimental, fine art context in the late 1960s, and entered the world of television in the early 1980s through the new fourth television channel, with its statutory obligation to 'encourage innovation and experiment in the form and content of programmes'.[2]

It is important to see the emergence of the workers' film movement in the 30s, and its developments both in exhibition and production, in the context of the explicit film censorship regulations of the time. The main fear of the bourgeoisie controlling British economic and political life in the 20s and 30s was of the consequences of the Russian Revolution in 1917. Controlling an economic system based on the subordination and exploitation of labour, they had good reason to fear the taking of state power by a workers' party, the establishment of a new type of state, the Soviet Union, and the impetus that this had given to the spread of socialist and communist ideas among European workers. For the bourgeoisie, a small and powerful minority confronted for the first time in 1917 by a major challenge to its power, the fear of revolution in Britain was exacerbated by the General Strike of 1926, the Wall Street Crash of 1929, and the severe capitalist economic crisis of the 30s. From this perspective, and with universal suffrage only a recent phenomenon, freedom of thought for the majority of people was a luxury not to be tolerated. The social and political purposes of the British Board of Film Censors (BBFC) regulations become clear in this context: they were a response to what was perceived to be a real danger, a real threat, that the popular cinema might become an agent in the development and transformation of popular political consciousness. The achievements of this process of censorship are apparent in the 1937 report of Lord Tyrrell, President of the BBFC, in which he notes that there was not 'a single film shown to-day in the public cinemas of this country which dealt with any of the burning questions of the day'.[3]

It may be worth noting here, as an example of this process, that the film script treatment of Walter Greenwood's famous novel *Love on the Dole* (which was first published in 1933, and taken to be a clear and powerful working-class statement of a very general experience of unemployment and hardship) was turned down by the BBFC in 1936. Eight years were to elapse between the novel's publication and the time it first became available to filmgoers in 1941.[4] In making such decisions, the censors extrapolated from the BBFC regulations. In 1931, the list of forbidden subjects included the following:

> relations between capital and labour . . . inciting of workers to armed conflict . . . industrial violence and unrest; conflicts between the armed forces of a state and the populace . . . scenes showing soldiers or police firing on defenceless population . . . objectionably misleading themes purporting to illustrate parts of the British Empire, [or representing] British possessions as lawless or iniquitous.[5]

Such regulations are among the many and varied forms of censorship (and they vary in character in the inter-war and post-war periods) which subordinate and marginalise those 'other' forms of audio-visual production that it is the purpose of this chapter to explore. The focus of the chapter, therefore, is on the achievements of the relatively powerless and the relatively silenced within cultural history.

Cinema, Culture and Class

A brief and selective overview of the activity of working-class cultural producers in the inter-war and post-war periods may be useful here. The richness and diversity of work produced by working-class writers in the 30s was not matched by comparable achievements in the cinema. Compared with cinema, the means of production for *writing* (though, perhaps more importantly, not the social preparation and impetus to produce) are obviously relatively easy to acquire. Where working-class life was represented as part of the content of *film* stories, it tended to be stereotyped or trivialised or rendered comic; viewed very much from the outside.

British cinema of the 30s offered a limited range of working-class themes: the descent into hell story (*Doss House*, John Baxter, 1933); the representation of education as the only sort of one-way ticket *out* of hell available to a special sort of working-class man (*The Stars Look Down*, Carol Reed, 1939 – also notable for its misogynist view of working-class women, for the extraordinarily unrealistic casting of Michael Redgrave as the miner's son, and for the comment of a contemporary critic and film-maker, Paul Rotha, that it was 'the first film which had a chance to touch the conscience of the middle class'[6]); or the cheerful musicals of George Formby and Gracie Fields.

The range of subject and treatment in the working-class novel of the period is striking by contrast: from Lewis Grassic Gibbon's trilogy *A Scots Quair* (1932–4) to the mining novels of Walter Brierley

(*Means Test Man*, 1935) and Lewis Jones (*Cwmardy*, 1937), and the work of a group of Liverpool writers – the tragic and ferocious expressionism of James Hanley's *The Furys* (1935) and the montage techniques of Jim Phelan's *Ten-a-Penny-People* (1938). In addition, many of these writers published poems and short stories in magazines like *The Adelphi, Left Review* and *New Writing* (edited by John Lehmann). There is no doubt, however, that the control of publishing (including left-wing publishing) was in the hands of middle and upper middle-class people – among them some of the rebel sons and daughters of the bourgeoisie. It was difficult, or impossible, for working-class people to take control, as of right, of the means of cultural expression. They were constantly in the position of being given a space, a voice, with all the associated problems of cultural paternalism and class ventriloquism that this activity of permitted and regulated entry suggests – particularly in the case of entry into such forms of expression as the novel, a form developed and refined by bourgeois writers for two centuries. The outsider position of working-class writers at this time is well summarised by Sid Chaplin, miner, poet and novelist: 'This effort to give people a voice was of course greatly assisted by a generation of left-wing public schoolboys, like John Lehmann, Cyril Connolly, Reginald Moore, and so on.'[7]

The situation was similar in the various organisations of the workers' film movement in the 30s, which were predominantly staffed and run by middle-class men. It is important, however, to make a distinction between, on the one hand, the members and organisers of the Workers' Film Society, of Kino, of the Workers' Film and Photo League, and of the Progressive Film Institute, many of whom were members of the Communist Party, and, on the other hand, those who worked within the state-sponsored documentary film movement. The group who worked with John Grierson at the Empire Marketing Board and subsequently at the General Post Office – financed by the 'National' governments of the 30s – regarded themselves as socialists but were not involved in working-class struggles. They represented British social reality within a social democratic, consensual frame of reference, and were not willing, or not permitted, to present contemporary reality in terms of a fundamental conflict of interest between two classes, exploiters and exploited. It has often been remarked that Griersonian documentaries (*Coalface*, for example) present the dignity and heroism of labour. But this is an investigation of social anthropology, a view from above and outside, a middle-class journey into the 'darkest England' of the working class. Or, as Grierson himself put it, this was a project to 'travel dangerously into the jungles of Middlesbrough and the Clyde'.[8] In these images of silent and muscular bodies at work we may find the traces of what Richard Hoggart was later to identify as the middle-class admiration for 'the remnants of the noble savage'.[9] These are images produced of, but not for, working-class people. Raymond Williams has offered a precise account of the social function of this type of representation as a subsection, or late arrival, within the long history of bourgeois realism: '. . . the extension to working-class life, the realisation of something that is exotic to the audience. There is a sense in which what was earlier called the drama of "low life" is a minor intention of bourgeois drama itself, where "to see how the other half lives", as it was often put, was in itself. . . a particular form of entertainment.'[10]

Important though the work of Grierson and his school is for the development of the language of documentary film, this group of films, their aesthetic structure and their social function, can be sharply distinguished from films like *Bread* (1934), *Jubilee* (1935) and *Hunger March* (1934), produced by Kino. In contrast to the cultural paternalism of Griersonian documentary, addressed to and confirming the superior position of a middle-class audience, some working-class writers of the post-war period addressed themselves specifically to the needs of a working-class readership. Thus Alan Sillitoe, author of the very popular *Saturday Night and Sunday Morning* (published in 1958 and produced as a film in 1960), noted his intention 'to write a book around a man who had never read a book in his life. I hoped that such a person of this group who could read (but had not so far been bothered to read a book) would be induced to read this one; because it was in some way about himself' (interviewed in the *Daily Worker*, 28 January 1961).

It is this intention to represent the world *for* a working-class readership or audience that subsequently marks the work of a generation of writers for television. They include Ken Loach and Tony Garnett as the director-producer team for *Cathy Come Home* (BBC, 1966), *The Big Flame* (BBC, 1969), *Rank and File* (BBC, 1971), *Days of Hope* (BBC, 1975); Ken Loach as director of *Which Side Are You On?* (Channel Four, 1985); Jim Allen, the scriptwriter for *The Big Flame, Rank and File, Days of Hope*, as well as for *The Spongers* (BBC, 1978) and *United Kingdom* (BBC, 1981); Trevor Griffiths, who moved from theatre to television to write *All Good Men* (BBC, 1974), *Bill Brand* (Thames, 1976), *Country* (BBC, 1981) and *Oi for England* (Central, 1982); Barry Hines, who wrote *The Price of Coal* (BBC, 1977) and *The Gamekeeper* (BBC, 1980); and Alan Bleasdale, writer of *Boys from the Blackstuff* (BBC, 1982). The few working-class writers who developed in the 70s in the much more marginal 'independent' film sector were able to combine writing and directing. They include

Doll's Eye (1982)

Jan Worth, *Doll's Eye* (British Film Institute and Channel Four, 1982); Mick Eaton, *Darkest England* (Channel Four, 1984); Phil Mulloy, *Through an Unknown Land* (Channel Four, 1984); and Richard Anthony, *After the Ball* (Yorkshire Arts Association and Channel Four, 1985).

The social base of the 'independent' film movement that emerged in the late 60s lay predominantly in the new middle class – a class able to benefit from the opportunities for advancement opened up by the post-war capitalist boom, by the expansion of the state and of public sector employment, and by the greater availability of higher education (in 1939 there were some 69,000 places in higher education; by 1977 there were 400,000[11]). In addition, through the avenues opened up by college and polytechnic film courses and by the regional film workshops, a few film-makers from working-class families entered this independent sector. It is important to note, but not to overstate, the significance for general cultural development of these changes in educational provision. By the late 1970s only a minority of 18-year-olds (about 14 per cent) were able to enter full-time education; and the proportion of children of unskilled manual workers entering university actually decreased from its pre-war level.[12]

Unlike their counterparts staffing the 'creative grades' in the mainstream film and television industries, the independent film-makers of the post-1968 generation were radicalised within the framework of the politics of the 'New Left': the politics of the Campaign for Nuclear Disarmament, of opposition to the war in Vietnam and to the policies of the Heath, Wilson and Callaghan governments (as well as to Stalinism and its legacy); a policy of support for national liberation struggles in Asia and Africa, and for the new women's, black and gay movements and the ecology movement. This New Left created a paradoxically non-aligned political space outside both the Labour and Communist parties, and, by and large, apart from any involvement in labour movement organisations. The period of New Left, middle-class vanguardism found its cultural expression in cinema in the independent film movement, opposed to the aesthetic and political orthodoxies of established film and television, and committed to the creation of a 'parallel' or 'alternative' cinema.

The return to the 30s

The dissidents of the 70s, refusing the existing practices of the audio-visual sphere and seeking to build alternatives, began a scrutiny of British cinema history, looking for antecedents, for other moments of opposition. It was this search for suppressed but useful histories (the desire to 'seize hold of a memory as it flashes up at a moment of danger'[13]) that resulted in the investigation and recovery of the workers' film movement of the 30s.[14]

By the late 70s, this 'return to the 30s', to a period of worldwide capitalist recession, was clearly a response to contemporary circumstances of recession, de-industrialisation and mass unemployment. This recovery of a film culture has not been a simple one, and involves assessment of two 'other cinemas' of the time: the Griersonian documentary model on the one hand, and the various organisations of the communist-inspired workers' film movement on the other.

The British Board of Film Censors' 1931 list of forbidden topics provides a useful point of reference for such an assessment. Five years after the General Strike of 1926, the BBFC regulations forbid subjects which deal with the 'relations between labour and capital', or with 'industrial violence and unrest'; they also ban subjects which give 'a false impression of the police forces in Britain', or which reflect badly upon 'the administration of British justice'.[15] In the same year, 1931, Grierson and Robert Flaherty were working on *Industrial Britain,* a film which is true to Grierson's general project of showing 'the ardour and bravery of common labour',[16] but where not a trace of capital or of the effects of capitalist ownership is to be found.

Also in 1931, Ralph Bond, a member of the Communist Party and a founder member of the Federation of Workers' Film Societies (FOWFS, founded in 1929), was writing in *The Plebs*: 'We can and we must fight capitalist influences in the Cinema . . . by exhibiting the films of the only country where the workers are the ruling class, and by making our own films . . . to aid and encourage the workers in their fight against capitalism.'[17] Bond's recommendations were already being carried out by Atlas Films, which had been set up to act as distributor and supplier to FOWFS. In 1930, Atlas released *Glimpses of Modern Russia* and two issues of *Workers' Topical News* (all three were silent films). These newsreels represented a variety of militant activities within the working-class movement. They included rallies of the National Unemployed Workers' Movement (ill-regarded by Ramsay MacDonald's Labour government of 1929–31), and May Day demonstrations where the slogans were clearly critical of the inaction of the Labour government in the face of rising unemployment: 'Underclad, Underfed, Under the Labour Government', 'We refuse to starve in silence', 'All Power to the Workers of the World'. It was precisely ideas of this kind which the BBFC was determined to keep off the public cinema screens; and Atlas films could only be shown under private club or society conditions – the FOWFS had been set up explicitly to avoid the existing censorship regulations. In respect of the BBFC policy of preserving the good name of the British Empire, one other slogan recorded for later generations in the *Workers' Topical News* is worth noting: 'Fight to Release British and Colonial Political Prisoners'. In 1934 Grierson produced, and Basil Wright directed, *Song of Ceylon*, a celebration of Britain's imperial trading relations; also without doubt *aesthetically* a very important film. But Grierson seems to have been quite unaware of, or unconcerned about, the kinds of brutality endemic to the colonial relationship, and to have seen the celebration of Empire as a legitimate and noble aim of the documentary film. He writes approvingly in a 1937 essay of the aim of the Empire Marketing Board: 'to bring the Empire alive in contemporary terms, as a commonwealth of nations and as an international combine of industrial, commercial and scientific forces.'[18]

The two alternative cinemas of the 30s were also sharply differentiated in respect of their treatment of the issue of justice at home in

Alternative cinema in the 30s: Chamberlain as mannequin in *Hell UnLtd.*
(1936)

Britain. Criticisms of police brutality towards the hunger marchers,
and such denials of civil liberties as the attempts made by the police
and the Home Office to ban the screening of *Battleship Potemkin* at a
miners' hall in Jarrow, led in 1934 to the founding of the National
Council for Civil Liberties.[19] The issue of real attacks on the liberties
of working-class people is not on the agenda of the state-funded
Grierson school. Casual, state-licensed brutality unleashed on
second-class citizens, and the recurrent class bias in the administration of justice, were left to be represented by the chronically
underfunded film-makers of organisations like Kino and the Workers' Film and Photo League (both founded in 1934).[20] One example
of this would be the short fiction film *Bread* (1934, silent) produced
by the London Production Group of Kino together with members of
the Workers' Theatre Movement.

Bread was photographed by Sam Serter, who had attended the
International Workers' Theatre Olympiad in Moscow in 1933, and
was aware of developments in Soviet cinema. He had attended a
lecture given by Eisenstein in London in 1929, and traces of the
montage methods of Eisenstein can be discerned in the film. It is not
typical of the largely documentary output of the radical film
movement of the time, being more highly crafted and constructed,
though not as aesthetically advanced as two of the most famous films
of the period: *Hell UnLtd.* (1936, silent; Helen Biggar and Norman
McLaren, Glasgow School of Art), and *Peace and Plenty* (1939,

233

sound, Ivor Montagu and Kino). The central character of *Bread*—
Tom – is refused Means Test assistance and unable to feed his family.
He stands outside a shop window full of bread, and images flash,
almost subliminally, through his mind, including an image of a First
World War memorial on his housing estate. Desperate, he smashes
the window, takes the bread, then is chased by a policeman, arrested
and tried. In court (and contrary to the rules of representation
specified by the BBFC) the magistrate's leniency with a group of
upper-class students who have overturned an apple barrow and
'playfully' used the fruit to bombard each other, is contrasted with
the severity of the sentence against Tom. With Tom in prison, and
through the mediating device of an ironic title, 'No need to starve',
the film then cuts into a documentary sequence showing hunger
marchers bearing the banners of the National Unemployed Workers'
Movement, and advancing towards the camera. The financial
poverty of the radical film movement made it impossible for the
experiments of interweaving fictional and documentary materials in
this film to be seriously developed into a school of film-making. None
the less, the realism without defeatism of this film, together with the
caustic wit of *Peace and Plenty* and the passionate surrealism of *Hell
UnLtd.*, make these films worth remembering and studying.

Throughout this decade the high costs of production mean that
radical film-making was undertaken only with the greatest difficulty.
The first organisations of the workers' film movement existed to
exhibit and distribute films (largely Soviet ones), rather than to
produce them. This importation and dissemination, through the
workers' film societies, of Soviet films also serves as an important
reminder of the cultural internationalism of the decade and the high
esteem in which the Soviet Union was held.

It is also important to note (especially if any comparisons are to be
made with the independent movement of the post-war period) that
the radical workers' films organisations of the 30s were closely tied to
the major working-class political parties: the Labour Party and
(much more actively involved in political and cultural work) the
Communist Party. This close relationship of cultural work and
political parties (a relationship explicitly refused by Grierson[21]) is
one of the distinctive features of the decade, and it provided a vital
framework, both supportive and critical, for the cultural producers.
In the short history of representative democracy, political parties
have been the chief organisational forms through which class
interests and political mandates have been expressed.

In the second half of the 30s, political life in Britain was dominated
by the increasingly dangerous international situation – the rise of
fascism and attacks on workers' organisations in Germany, Italy and

Spain. The radical film organisations of the time provided important alternative sources of information to those offered by the official newsreels with their few 'clearly defined and monotonous categories – Sport, Royalty, Military'.[22] So the Progressive Film Institute (PFI), for example, founded in 1935 to import and distribute Soviet films in 35mm (and attempting to make inroads into the independently owned commercial cinemas as their counterparts, Kino, worked to develop an alternative 16mm circuit), also distributed *Free Thaelmann!* (1935). Commissioned by the Relief Committee for the Victims of German Fascism, this film was promoted as part of the international campaign to obtain the release of the leader of the German Communist Party, imprisoned by Hitler. After the revolt of the fascist generals under Franco in 1936, and the beginning of the Civil War in Spain, the PFI made some twelve films in support of the Republican side,[23] helping to create the context in which large numbers of working-class men in Britain volunteered to fight with the Republicans in the International Brigade. The production and energetic promotion of these films can be compared with similar campaigns in Britain in the 70s and 80s in defence of workers' organisations and parties in Latin America. The threat to democracy from fascist generals, and from United States military intervention (in Chile with the coup in 1973; in Nicaragua after the Sandinista victory in 1979; and in El Salvador), has been the subject of films distributed by Educational Television Films (ETV) and by The Other Cinema. As in the case of contemporary campaigns, the films of the 30s were used both for educational and fund-raising purposes; it was estimated, for example, that *Defence of Madrid* (1936) raised over £6,000 in aid for Spain.

The development of non-commercial 16mm film exhibition circuits in the 30s created important alternative means for the dissemination of ideas expressed through an audio-visual medium, and such work continued into the post-war period. However, it is important to get some sense of the relative scale of activities in comparing the 30s with the present. The single most important factor here is probably the development of a mass audience for television in the post-war period. Throughout the 50s, as more and more families acquired television sets, figures for cinema attendance declined drastically. In 1936 Kino had estimated that 1,000 screenings had reached a total of nearly 250,000 people in the course of the year; by contrast, in 1983 *The Cause of Ireland* (Platform Films, 1983), a film made from a perspective highly critical of the role of the British state in Northern Ireland and focusing on the views of working-class people, reached through *one screening* on Channel Four Television an estimated audience of 294,000.[24]

The Modern Independent Movement, 1966–79

The 30s have rightly been called the 'decade of defeat' for the working-class movement. It was a period in which the electoral weakness of the Labour and Communist Parties allowed the two 'National' governments of the time to manage a capitalist crisis largely in the interests of the capitalist class. The result was widespread deprivation and suffering; it was followed during the war years (1939–45) by a growing popular determination that this war was being fought both against fascism and for a better Britain, for an end to insecurity, hunger and want. The spirit of 'no return to the 30s' was given tangible, material form in the great capitalist economic boom of the post-war years; a qualitatively better standard of living for the majority in Britain became the guarantee of an end to the nightmare of the 30s. Those guarantees were to end, for an increasing number, with the economic crisis of the 70s, and with the opening of the 1979 Thatcher government offensive against the existing mixed economy, social democratic consensus of the welfare state, and against the organisations of the trade union movement. This offensive, in Britain, on behalf of the restructuring of the international capitalist economy, was to result in the deliberate creation of a pool of 4 million unemployed by 1984.

The emergence of the modern independent film movement needs to be understood in the context of the economic changes and the social policies of the post-war years. The policies were those of a social democratic consensus, adhered to over three decades by both Labour governments (1945–51; 1964–70; 1974–9) and Conservative governments (1951–64; 1970–4). At least up to the early 70s, these were decades of economic expansion and paternalistic social reform. Many of the ideals of the consensus – of a social order achieved through the rational planning of experts, operating above mere class interests, and of an informed and equal citizenry – were already manifest in the 30s documentary films of the Grierson school. The historian Arthur Marwick refers to this phenomenon as the consolidation of 'middle opinion' in the 30s, and its effective victory and implementation in the post-war years.[25] In post-war practice, social democratic policies for meritocratic advancement through an expanded educational system offered to the existing middle class, and to a minority of the working class, the chance of a better life. The fundamental relations of power and wealth were left unchallenged. Included within these policies was a system of state subsidy for predominantly middle-class cultural activities (and, specifically, for film production), made available, under pressure, by the British Film Institute, the Arts Council of Great Britain and, from the early 70s, the Regional Arts Associations.[26]

236

The origins of the modern independent film movement can be traced to the founding in 1966 of the London Film-makers' Co-operative. Ten years later the founding conference of the Independent Film-makers' Association (IFA) was to define independence in terms of three connected policies: an avoidance of the constraints which 'big private capital' was believed to impose, a rejection of the aim of 'making unchallenging films to attract large audiences immediately', and a commitment to 'the preservation and development of critical thought'.[27] An increasing interest in the film medium in Colleges of Art produced a cluster of film-makers who found the aesthetic constraints of the Hollywood-dominated industry and its English variants intolerable. Influenced by alternative traditions, including the American 'underground' and New Cinema and the European avant-gardes of the 20s, they developed a critique of both the practices and the products of the mainstream industry, and established production facilities at the Co-op which (including the use of an optical printer) ensured that they could retain control over, and experiment with, all the stages of the production process. With a general commitment to experimental and avant-garde practices in image production, they believed that the full development of the potential of the film medium lay outside its commercial exploitation; the producers and investors who controlled the industry would not permit serious and sustained experiment in the development of audio-visual languages.

The Co-op was also important for providing the cultural space within which the issue of modernism and its relations with cinema could be placed on the agenda. This became especially important in relation to the importation and screening of films by Jean-Luc Godard and by Jean-Marie Straub and Danièle Huillet, figures who became very influential in the development of a generation of younger film-makers in Britain in the 70s.[28] Like all research and development projects, the Co-op has been vulnerable to the charge of producing elitist, irrelevant or esoteric work. But, in the long term, and in so far as its members have been seriously experimenting and grappling with the ways in which meaning has and can be produced through particular combinations of images and sounds, their films may continue to be useful to new entrants into the audio-visual sphere. One of the explanations for the actual cultural marginalisation of the Co-op may be the rather conventional notions of theatrical drama that tended to predominate in TV drama, together with the high degree of division of labour in TV which has tended to separate writers from access to the means of audio-visual expression.[29]

The Co-op provided the cultural framework for the work of film-makers like Malcolm LeGrice and Peter Gidal who have explored both the specific material properties of the film medium, and the extremely limited ways in which it has been historically developed, within the constraints of a capitalist industry. The relatively early emergence and subsequent dominance of particular forms of narrative cinema have been explored by film-makers like LeGrice, and by theorists and film-makers Noël Burch, Laura Mulvey and Peter Wollen. A systematic investigation and practical taking apart of traditional narrative is apparent in such work as *After Lumière, L'Arroseur Arrosé* (LeGrice, 16 mins., 1974) and *Riddles of the Sphinx* (Mulvey and Wollen, 92 mins., 1977), though the latter is more drawn to the utilisation and transformation of narrative forms than to their abolition. Peter Wollen's critical writings were also very influential in developing the loose alliance of political and avant-garde film-makers that characterised the early period of the Independent Film-makers' Association (founded in 1974). Wollen speaks of a 'bridge between two types of film-making' in an interview in the magazine *Afterimage* (no. 6, Summer 1976, a special issue on independent cinema).

A second important factor in the development of the independent film movement was the setting up, in the late 60s and 70s, of a number of radical film production collectives. These included Cinema Action (London, 1968; films for the labour movement on the subjects of housing, industrial relations, strikes and occupations against factory closures and redundancies, the Republican movement in Ireland, the miners' strikes of 1972 and 1974);[30] Amber Films (Newcastle upon Tyne, 1969; films documenting the lives of working people in the North-East of England); the Berwick Street Collective (London, 1972; films about Ireland and the unionisation campaign of women night-cleaners); Liberation Films (London, 1972; films on community action, and 'trigger' films designed to stimulate discussion in an educational context);[31] the London Women's Film Group (London, 1972; films about the involvement of women in the 1926 and 1972 miners' strikes, and about the 1970s campaigns for equal pay and abortion rights);[32] the Newsreel Collective (London, 1974; films about 'the daily lives and struggles of working people', including the subjects of abortion rights, women's health care, racism and teenage sexuality).[33]

These groups and their films emerged from the political context created by the development of the New Left, and in the aftermath of the events of May 1968 in France. Their ideological formation is complex and contradictory: the product of Cold War politics and left vanguardism, also able at times to reproduce the uncritical, social democratic celebrations of labour of the Grierson school, praising the humanity of the subordinate but leaving the dominators invisible.

Fly a Flag for Poplar (1974), made by the production collective Liberation Films

Some of the films received state subsidy; others were made very cheaply by film-makers who were unemployed or working part-time in the industry to subsidise their other film work. From the late 70s, more and more independent film-makers sought to enter the union (the Association of Cinematograph, Television and Allied Technicians, ACTT), many being admitted into the newly established 'grant-aided' category within the union. This unionisation was itself stimulated by a desire on the part of independent film-makers to be more organisationally effective, and to be involved in struggles being conducted within the mainstream of the industry, including the 1973 ACTT campaign for the nationalisation of the industry. Unionisation was also facilitated for a period in the late 70s by an increase in state subsidy and (more significantly in the short term) by the availability of funding from the new Channel Four Television: the new channel began broadcasting in November 1982.

Most of the early production groups were established in London. But from the mid-70s a network of regional film and video workshops was developed, mostly on the basis of state subsidy from Regional Arts Associations. Production centres were set up in Edinburgh,

Newcastle upon Tyne, Liverpool, Leeds, Sheffield, Nottingham, Manchester, Norwich, Bristol, Birmingham, Belfast, Cardiff and elsewhere.[34]

Discussions by the radicalised middle-class film-makers of the late 60s focused on the need to create an alternative, 'counter' or 'parallel' cinema opposed to both the aesthetics and politics predominant in the mainstream of the industry. But the movement tended to be isolated both from other cultural developments (from discussions within the new 'fringe' theatre movement, for example, and from radical writers and producers in television) and from day-to-day involvement in working-class political parties and organisations. It was correspondingly heavily involved in the new 'issue politics' of the time; but it becomes easier to see, with hindsight, that like the non-aligned left more generally it had very few working-class participants. In this, it shares many of the problems of the intellectual left of the time, and in some cases was characterised by a phenomenon outlined by Raymond Williams in a 1977 essay as:

> that contempt of people, of their hopelessly corrupted state, of their vulgarity and credulity by comparison with an educated minority, which was the staple of cultural criticism of a non-Marxist kind and which seems to have survived intact, through the appropriate alterations of vocabulary, into one fashionable form of Marxism which makes the whole people, including the whole working class, mere carriers of the structures of a corrupt ideology.[35]

In this respect, the method of a vanguardist 'political modernism' espoused by some independent film-makers is ambivalent. Its positive (and rightly anti-populist) aspect lies in its refusal to reproduce those characteristics of a dominant film language that render it incapable of representing reality in its complexity and contradictoriness. Its negative aspect lies in its propensity to challenge the audience with the sort of unremitting difficulty and uncompromising complexity likely to drive them from the cinema.[36] Of course, it matters very much who is, in theory and in practice, being addressed by the film. There is an established tradition in twentieth-century art, traceable back to the Dadaists, of addressing the bourgeoisie with a view to shocking and alienating them. There is also a tradition of addressing a middle-class audience with a view to arousing their philanthropic concern (thus Paul Rotha's comment about *The Stars Look Down* being able to 'touch the conscience of the middle class'); but in a way that basically confirms the spectator class in its own position of superiority. Any radical political modernism has to address the fundamental question: 'who is able to transform the world, and how might they be addressed in such a way as to help them in that process of struggle and change?'

The centrality of modernist ideas in 70s debates about independent cinema drew upon the anti-realist film theory developed in the journals *Screen* and *Afterimage*. A rejection of cinematic illusionism and of the mechanisms of what was believed to be an escapist process of identification, together with a rejection of traditional narrative forms, was at the heart of these debates. Such ideas fostered a self-consciousness about the means of representation, about the actual image-making processes to be employed by the film-maker which, at best, mark an advance from the theory and practice of the film-making of the 30s radical tradition. The possibilities, dangers and limitations of the various methods of communication had become more apparent.

An interest in questions of form was thus widespread – at best genuinely useful in developing new methods, at worst merely formalist. These interests were sometimes expressed in terms of the Godardian injunction not just to 'make political films' but to 'make films politically', and they are apparent in a cluster of films produced in 1978–9 which may be taken to summarise a certain stage of development within the independent film movement: *Telling Tales* (Richard Woolley, 88 mins., 1978); *In the Forest* (Phil Mulloy, 80 mins., 1978); *News and Comment* (Frank Abbott, 35 mins., 1978); *Thriller* (Sally Potter, 33 mins., 1979); *Often During the Day* (Joanna Davis, 15 mins., 1979); *Song of the Shirt* (Sue Clayton and Jonathan Curling, 135 mins., 1979); *Taking A Part* (Jan Worth, 45 mins., 1979). All seven films, whether in fiction or documentary mode, fragment the continuous flow, the organic unity of narrative. They assemble and juxtapose episodes or fragments, with a view to producing a critical and analytical account of their subject. They all, to differing degrees and in more or less cautionary ways, draw attention to the process of representation itself, indicating to the audience the kinds of work normally concealed in illusionist cinema.

Telling Tales, in interweaving the lives of a bourgeois and a working-class couple, draws attention to the way that tales are told in the struggle between the classes and between the sexes, and emphasises that such tales have a purpose and a function; they are intended to affect the outcome in any situation of conflict and tension. *Thriller* is likewise concerned with the purposes and social function of story-telling, taking as its basic text Puccini's opera *La Bohème,* with its two versions of femininity – pathetic victim and lively 'bad girl' – and analysing and reworking it from a feminist perspective.

Some of the films make apparent the actual process through which images are produced. *News and Comment*, in critically examining television's techniques for news production, shows both the original, 'factual' film image and the process whereby the film editor works on and contextualises such images. *Song of the Shirt*, with a series of fluid camera movements through deep space, moves on to and away from the surface planes of a variety of graphic, photographic and video images; the illusionist quality of these images and their authority as credible accounts of the past are dissolved before our eyes. *Often During the Day*, a study of the facts and feelings of domestic labour, frames the characters in its final, live action sequence at just above waist level, thereby both defying and drawing attention to normal conventions of framing. *Taking A Part* incorporates the voice of the director and offscreen comments at the beginning of the take, and involves one of the characters in recording the 'slate' at the beginning of the take and in conversation with the invisible camera-person.

None of the films provides traditional forms of identification. The three peasants, two men and a woman, who are the central characters in Phil Mulloy's both ferocious and poetic account of English history, *In the Forest*, travel across time and space from the early medieval period to the nineteenth-century Peterloo massacre, with no respect for the conventions of naturalistic narrative. They are emblematic and typical rather than individual; they are not realised in terms of personal psychology and motivation. It is deliberately left unclear in *Taking A Part* whether the two characters are actresses or real people speaking of their own lives; this device both breaks normal patterns of identification and voyeurism, and foregrounds social issues and realities rather than personalities.

As a group, these films also raise questions of interpretation, authenticity and class 'voice'. In *Taking A Part* there are two quite distinct, implicitly counterposed working-class voices with different views of the world. *Telling Tales* registers differences of interest between male and female working-class voices. *Song of the Shirt* presents voices of resignation, of anger and of analysis. *In the Forest* juxtaposes two voices of history: one a conservative account of English history in terms of progress and harmony, the other a voice that interprets historical fact in terms of oppression and exploitation.

Some of these films have been screened on Channel Four Television, and all are available in distribution by organisations that have, in different ways, continued the cultural work of 30s organisations like Kino and the Progressive Film Institute. *Often During the Day* is distributed by Circles, one of a number of feminist distributors. Most are available through The Other Cinema, which

Making films politically: *In the Forest* (1978)

was established out of debates in the late 60s on the need to form institutions for an alternative or parallel cinema. The 1972 catalogue of The Other Cinema notes its commitment to making available the work of film-makers who 'seek to change people's perceptions of political, social or personal situations, often with the aid of new film forms'. At worst, these films offered themselves as product within a radicalised middle-class enclave; at best, they presented a challenge to the existing state of things, contributing to the creation of a cinema space in which society is represented and interpreted so that it can also be changed.

Independence in the 80s: Film, Video, Television

The two most important factors for the development of independent film in the 80s have been, at the political level, the break with consensus and the major right-wing offensive initiated by the

Thatcher governments of 1979 and 1983; and, at the economic level, the advent of Channel Four Television and the appointment (as a result of a long and intensive campaign by the Independent Film-makers' Association) of a Commissioning Editor with responsibility for funding independent film.

A decade of working and campaigning within the independent film sector resulted in the production of a number of films by women, including: *Maeve* (Pat Murphy and John Davies, 110 mins., 1981); *Doll's Eye* (Jan Worth, 80 mins., 1982); *Bred and Born* (Mary-Pat Leece and Joanna Davis, 1983); *The Gold Diggers* (Sally Potter, 90 mins., 1983); *Give Us a Smile* (Leeds Animation Workshop, 12 mins., 1983); *Red Skirts on Clydeside* (Sheffield Film Co-op, 40 mins., 1984); *Property Rites* (Heather Powell and Carola Klein, 1984). All these films share the theme of woman as investigator, and in some of them women characters are also cultural producers: Maeve is a photography student, Jane in *Doll's Eye* and the central character in *Property Rites* are journalists; *Bred and Born* and *Red Skirts* have central figures who are researchers, investigating and writing or making films about women's social situation and role in history. There is a potential danger with this theme that the film may overemphasise the importance of the role of the cultural producer. *The Gold Diggers* continues some of the concerns of *Thriller* in investigating the parts allocated to women in traditional film narrative, and women's place in relationships of power and wealth. In two of the films, *Maeve* and *Doll's Eye*, the protagonists are clearly working-class women. In the former, Maeve returns to her home in Belfast to rethink and argue about the place of women in the Republican movement; in the latter, the lives of middle-class and working-class women in conditions of economic recession, and their demands for independence, are contrasted. *Property Rites* and *Give Us a Smile* explore the issues of rape and violence against women, and consider the social function of pornography and of sensationalist news reporting of rape cases.

The early 80s also saw the development of work by black film-makers and film workshops, often arising out of and building upon work in other cultural areas – in theatre, in local journalism and radio, in community campaigns and politics. This work is already extreme-ly diverse stylistically, and includes: *Burning an Illusion* (Menelik Shabazz, 107 mins., 1981); *On Duty* (Cassie McFarlane, 1984); and *Territories* (Isaac Julian, Sankofa, 1984). *Burning an Illusion* follows the development, change and radicalisation of a young woman as she witnesses the arrest, racist treatment and sentencing of her boyfriend. *On Duty* (based on a stage play and subsequently developed as a film, shown on Channel Four) juxtaposes fictional

Rethinking the place of women: *Maeve* (1981)

reconstruction of real events and documentary interviews with a woman working in the National Health Service who is fighting the privatisation of her job. *Territories* is a highly self-conscious work within the modernist tradition, which explores through a variety of sardonic, detached, passionate and lyrical modes existing and dominant media representations of the black community. Both *Burning an Illusion* and *On Duty* explore the experiences that activate, and the processes that transform, 'non-political' working-class women.

Although Channel Four Television has become a major transforming factor in the independent film sector, providing both production finance and the opportunity of reaching much larger audiences than was possible through the established methods of film distribution, other important work has developed, on video and outside the remit of either state or commercial television finance. 1983–4 saw the commissioning of independent film and video-makers' work by both trade unions and local councils. In 1983, for example, the Birmingham Film Workshop, in conjunction with the local Trade Union

Resource Centre, produced for the National and Local Government Officers' Association the tape *Put People First*, as a part of the union's national campaign against privatisation. And Leeds Animation Workshop was commissioned by Sheffield City Council to make the short animated film *Council Matters* (1984), as part of the campaign against government cuts in local authority spending. The most important, ambitious and underfunded project was the production of the Miners' Campaign Videotapes. A series of tapes under the title 'Coal not Dole', this material was produced as part of the support and campaign work for the 1984–5 miners' strike, filmed by a large number of groups and individuals all round the country, edited in London, and distributed by regional film workshops and by the National Union of Mineworkers.

It is important in comparing the work of the 30s radical film organisations with that of the modern independent film movement to realise the differences of scale involved. A far greater volume and diversity of work has been produced in the modern period, and some of this work has gained access to the significantly larger audiences reached by the new fourth television channel. In addition, and quite

Black film-making: community politics in *On Duty* (1984)

apart from the independent film movement, a rich variety of radical work by writers struggling to represent the world in ways useful to working-class viewers has appeared on television. In 1974, for example (the year of the founding of the Independent Film-makers' Association), John McGrath's stage play *The Cheviot, the Stag and the Black, Black Oil*, written for the 'fringe' theatre group '7: 84', was produced for television. Its critical history of the underdevelopment of the Scottish Highlands is still a remarkable achievement. It succeeds in developing new and original forms in television, and in developing these to communicate a clear and passionate analysis.

It would be appropriate to conclude this chapter with a brief consideration of three films produced from within the independent film movement – three films of Thatcher's Britain. All of them return in different ways to the unfinished business of the 30s: to the issues of unemployment (and the economic system that creates it), class difference, power and powerlessness. But in also representing the new consciousness, demands and activity of women, they add a significant new item to that 30s agenda.

After the Ball (Richard Anthony, 1984; financed by Yorkshire Arts Association and screened on Channel Four in 1985) explores the situation of a man at breaking point after a full year of unemployment. His wife's response is more robust, more determined, more political. At the end of the story the man's feelings of numbed, alienated detachment are transformed, suddenly, into a moment of angry and violent self-expression which results in his arrest. What happens next is left for the audience to imagine.

Through an Unknown Land (Phil Mulloy, Channel Four, 1984) operates in the generic territory of the road movie, and updates Priestley's 1934 *English Journey* from a working-class perspective. The film breaks with established narrative conventions in attempting a difficult mixture of naturalism, symbolism and stylisation *Doll's Eye* (Jan Worth, British Film Institute and Channel Four, 1982) also makes use of some unfamiliar methods (unfamiliar to television, though familiar from the modernist strand of the independent sector): an episodic structure, emblematic settings, stylised dialogue.

The central characters in *Doll's Eye* and *Through an Unknown Land* (Jackie and Pete) are, at the end, unemployed, restless and angry. But both films have to some extent identified the sources of power which cause the experience of unemployment and of a world hostile to the interests of the protagonists. This is done through the device of the male switchboard voices in *Doll's Eye*, voices which control the world of big business and employment. In *Through an Unknown Land* the causal factor is identified through the introduction of a new type of businessman, Eurocrat and aristocrat Lord

Arlingham, whose company dealings result in the redundancy of Pete's mother. And the film adds further frames of reference and explanation in representing the latter-day imperialism of Britain's war in the Falklands/Malvinas and in making a brief mention of Britain's continuing colonial relationship with Ireland. The journey to the Second World War aircraft museum evokes the memories of Pete's father and mother, and through these the film is able to refer to the troubled significance, for working-class people, of the 1945 Labour election victory. The image of Pete's return home at the end, to his parents and girlfriend, has a powerful resonance, representing forms of class solidarity both across the generations and between men and women. But, as *Doll's Eye* emphasises in making central the new demands and expectations of working-class women, the space and significance of the home has changed and is changing. The space of the home begins to be dynamically interrelated with the outside world, the world of politics and class struggle. The concluding image of *Doll's Eye* represents a young woman who is in neither trade union nor political party, but whose determined step and forward movement seem to anticipate the activity of those 'non-political' working-class women who were to become an energising force at the heart of the 1984 miners' strike, and at the heart, therefore, of the practical, political opposition to Thatcherism.

It is in such extensions and reworkings of the agenda of the 30s that a modern radical cinema must return to the unfinished business of that decade, with a new sense of purpose, a new clarity and a new force.

Notes

1　For a discussion of this inadequate representation see Ken Worpole, *Dockers and Detectives – Popular Reading: Popular Writing* (London, Verso, 1983), and *Reading by Numbers: Contemporary Publishing and Popular Fiction* (London, Comedia, 1984); Raymond Williams, 'The Welsh Industrial Novel' in *Problems in Materialism and Culture* (London, Verso, 1980); Dave Morley and Ken Worpole (eds.), *The Republic of Letters: Working Class Writing and Local Publishing* (London, Comedia, 1982). For a comparable argument in respect of theatre, see John McGrath, *A Good Night Out – Popular Theatre: Audience, Class and Form* (London, Eyre Methuen, 1981).

2　Simon Blanchard, 'Where Do New Channels Come From?' in Simon Blanchard and David Morley (eds.), *What's This Channel Four? An Alternative Report,* London, Comedia, 1982, p. 22.

3　Nicholas Pronay, 'The First Reality: Film Censorship in Liberal

England' in K. R. M. Short (ed.), *Feature Films as History*, London, Croom Helm, 1981, p. 124.

4   Tony Aldgate, 'Ideological Consensus in British Feature Films, 1935–1947' in Short (ed.), *Feature Films as History*, p. 101.

5   Pronay, 'The First Reality', p. 120.

6   Paul Rotha, *The Film Till Now*, London, Hamlyn, rev. ed., 1967, p. 559.

7   Michael Pickering and Kevin Robbins, 'The Making of a Working Class Writer: An Interview with Sid Chaplin' in Jeremy Hawthorn (ed.), *The British Working Class Novel in the Twentieth Century*, London, Arnold, 1984, p. 146.

8   Quoted by Stuart Hood, 'John Grierson and the Documentary Film Movement' in James Curran and Vincent Porter (eds.), *British Cinema History*, London, Weidenfeld and Nicolson, 1983, p. 107.

9   Richard Hoggart, *The Uses of Literacy*, Harmondsworth, Penguin, 1958, first published 1957, p. 16.

10   Raymond Williams, 'A Lecture on Realism', *Screen*, vol. 18, no. 1, Spring 1977, p. 68.

11   John Stevenson, *Social Conditions in Britain Between the Wars*, Harmondsworth, Penguin, 1977, p. 36.

12   Details of these figures are given in Rick Rogers and Anna Coote, 'Class After Class: Part One', *New Statesman*, 30 April 1982, p. 10.

13   Walter Benjamin, 'Theses on the Philosophy of History' in *Illuminations*, London, Fontana, 1973, p. 258.

14   See, for example, Bert Hogenkamp, 'Film and the Workers' Movement in Britain, 1929–1939', *Sight and Sound*, vol. 45, no. 2, Spring 1976; articles by Bert Hogenkamp and Ralph Bond in Jon Clark, Margot Heinemann et al. (eds.), *Culture and Crisis in the Thirties*, London, Lawrence and Wishart, 1979; Don Macpherson (ed.), *Traditions of Independence: British Cinema in the Thirties*, London, British Film Institute, 1980.

15   Pronay, 'The First Reality', p. 120.

16   Forsyth Hardy (ed.), *Grierson on Documentary*, London, Faber, 1979, p. 76.

17   *Traditions of Independence*, p. 141.

18   *Grierson on Documentary*, p. 78.

19   For details of the Jarrow case, see articles by Ivor Montagu and others reprinted in *Traditions of Independence*, pp. 111–15.

20   For detailed discussions of the work of these organisations, see Terry Dennett, 'England: The (Workers') Film and Photo League', *Photography/Politics: One*, London, Photography Workshop, 1979; Paul Marris, 'Politics and "Independent" Film in the Decade of Defeat' in *Traditions of Independence;* Trevor Ryan, ' "The New Road to Progress": The Use and Production of Films by the Labour Movement, 1929–39' in *British Cinema History*; and the forthcoming book on the workers' film movement in Britain by Bert Hogenkamp.

21   *Grierson on Documentary*, p. 78.

22   Ralph Bond, 'Cinema in the Thirties: Documentary Film and the Labour Movement' in *Culture and Crisis in the Thirties*, p. 245.

23   Ryan, ' "The New Road to Progress" ', p. 120.
24   Viewing figures provided by Channel Four Television.
25   Arthur Marwick, 'Middle Opinion in the Thirties: Planning, Progress and Political "Agreement" ', *English Historical Review*, vol. 79, April 1964.
26   Various attempts have been made to democratise arts funding. See, for example, the correspondence between the Federation of Worker Writers and Community Publishers and the Arts Council of Great Britain, cited in Morley and Worpole (eds.), *The Republic of Letters*, p. 134; the account offered by a Labour Minister for the Arts, Hugh Jenkins, in *The Culture Gap: An Experience of Government and the Arts*, London, Marion Boyars, 1979; and developments in arts funding policy at the Greater London Council in the early 80s, outlined in a variety of policy documents.
27   From 'Independent Film-making in the 70s: An introductory discussion paper from the Organising Committee for the IFA Conference held in May 1976', available from the Independent Film and Video-makers' Association (IFVA), 79 Wardour Street, London W1V 3PH. The IFA (from 1983, the IFVA) was founded in 1974.
28   An important discussion of these developments, together with a critique of some of the more idealist elements within the modernist and related 'structural-materialist' project, is to be found in Peter Wollen's essays: 'Godard and Counter Cinema: *Vent d'Est*' (1972), 'The Two Avant-Gardes' (1975), and ' "Ontology" and "Materialism" in Film' (1976), all reprinted in Wollen, *Readings and Writings: Semiotic Counter Strategies*, London, Verso, 1982. See also Malcolm LeGrice, *Abstract Film and Beyond*, London, Studio Vista, 1977; Peter Gidal (ed.), *Structural Film Anthology*, London, British Film Institute, 1976; collected essays in *Film as Film: Formal Experiment in Film, 1910–1975*, catalogue for the exhibition 'Film as Film', London, Arts Council of Great Britain, 1979. See also essays by Anne Cottringer, 'On Peter Gidal's Theory and Definition of Structural/Materialist Film', Laura Mulvey and Peter Wollen, 'Written Discussion', and Mike Dunford, 'Experimental/Avant-Garde/Revolutionary Film Practice', all in *Afterimage*, no. 6, Summer 1976.
29   For a critique of both naturalism and the dominance of theatrical models in television, see John McGrath, 'Television Drama: The Case Against Naturalism', *Sight and Sound*, vol. 26, no. 2, 1977.
30   See David Glyn and Paul Marris, 'Seven Years of Cinema Action', *Afterimage*, no. 6, Summer 1976.
31   For further details see Rosalind Coward (ed.), *Liberation Films Distribution Catalogue*, London, Liberation Films, 1978.
32   For further details of these films and others by the Berwick Street Collective and the Newsreel Collective, see Sue Clayton (ed.), *The Other Cinema: Women's Movement Film Catalogue*, London, The Other Cinema, 1981 (?).
33   Ibid., p. 20.
34   For further details see the annual British Film Institute Yearbook; the *Regional Film Directory* (ed. Frank Challenger, Stafford, West Midlands Arts, 1984); *Independent Film Workshops in Britain 1979* (ed. Rod Stoneman, Torquay, Grael Communications, 1979); *The New Social Function of*

Cinema: Catalogue British Film Institute Productions, 1979–1980 (eds. Rod Stoneman and Hilary Thompson, London, British Film Institute, 1981). See also the text of the important new ACTT agreement, *ACTT Workshop Declaration* (London, ACTT, 1984). For further details of organisational developments within the independent sector, see Simon Blanchard and Sylvia Harvey, 'The Post-War Independent Cinema – Structure and Organisation' in *British Cinema History*.

35   Raymond Williams, 'Notes on Marxism in Britain since 1945' in *Problems in Materialism and Culture*, p. 241. See also Williams' discussion of 'issue politics' in 'Problems of the Coming Period', *New Left Review*, July-August 1983, p. 13. For discussions of the development of 'New Left' politics into the Labour Party and into local government, see *Who's Afraid of Margaret Thatcher? In Praise of Socialism*, Ken Livingstone in conversation with Tariq Ali, London, Verso, 1984; and Ken Livingstone, 'Renaissance Labour Style', and Beatrix Campbell, 'Politics, Pyramids and People', both in 'Labour and the People' debate, *Marxism Today*, vol. 28, no. 12, December 1984.

36   For further discussion of these issues, see Sylvia Harvey, *Independent Cinema?*, Stafford, West Midlands Arts, 1978, and 'Whose Brecht? Memories for the 80s', *Screen*, vol. 23, no. 1, May–June 1982.

My thanks to many people who helped in various ways with the production of this chapter (but who may not agree with it): Charles Barr, Simon Blanchard, Charlotte Brunsdon, Sergio Bustamante, John Corner, Jonathan Curling, Richard Dyer, Richard Hines, Stanley Forman, Bert Hogenkamp, Tony Kirkhope, Jan Worth. I should also like to thank Elaine Burrows and Jackie Morris of the National Film Archive, and staff of the British Universities Film and Video Council. The 1984–5 Miners' Strike made possible the development of some of the ideas expressed here.

Alastair Michie

SCOTLAND: STRATEGIES OF CENTRALISATION

One cannot look at Edinburgh without being conscious of a visible crack in historical continuity. The actual town, the houses, streets, churches, rocks, gardens, are still there; but these exist wholly in the past. That past is a national past; the present, which is made up of the thoughts and feelings and prejudices of the inhabitants, their way of life in general, is as cosmopolitan as the cinema.

Edwin Muir, *A Scottish Journey*, 1935

The main thrust of this chapter is, using Scotland as a test-case, to study the part played by cinema in the drawing together of disparate communities under one banner; to focus on the ambivalent attitude shown to the 'provinces' by British cinema, and the way this contributes to the wider hierarchical interplay of 'sameness' and 'difference' through which, as Foucault describes it, societies simultaneously unify and disperse their heterogeneous elements. While the otherness summoned by gender and skin colour may be more immediate and universal, if we look closely we find that regional differences play an equally important part in the construction of identity. Jokes, as ever, provide a rough measure of this dependence, where we find sex and colour matched gag for gag by variations on the theme of 'There was once a Scotsman, an Irishman and an Englishman . . .', from which we can be assured that the Englishman will walk away confirmed in his generosity and intelligence.

No doubt we could trace such stereotypes back to their historical source, so that, for example, Scottish stinginess relates to their pioneering status in world banking. Though space obviously limits such a study, it is important to keep in mind that this limiting of available discourses is anchored in history and that the relationship of the terms depends on the power structure functioning at the time of origin. For Scotland, the dourness, the whisky drinking, the fanatical religion, have all been torn from history and allowed to float through layer upon layer of myth, until they attained their current status as 'natural' common-sense identifications. Two recent books above all have opened up the rich subject of 'Scottishness' in a cogently analytical way, and this essay is much in their debt: they are Tom Nairn's wide-ranging political and cultural study *The Break-Up of Britain,* and *Scotch Reels,* edited by Colin McArthur for the Edinburgh Film Festival's 1982 event of that name dealing with film and TV representations of Scotland.[1]

Cinema is, of course, a particularly effective purveyor of regional myth and uniter of nations. Nowhere, perhaps, is Kuleshov's 'creative geography' capable of being put to better use than in the construction of a fictional national whole. The camera scans the horizon, sucks in faces, towns, factories, even histories – everything – and reshapes it. Film can, quite literally, place two houses, in reality hundreds of miles apart, alongside one another. Through the mechanisms of narrative and the power of the look, it can create that strange land, so familiar and yet so different, real and yet non-existent, a mythical container of contradictions – a United Kingdom. It is this that we shall tackle, adopting (rather like Einstein reviewing the universe) a peripheral viewpoint. Our aim is to challenge the security with which we speak of a British cinema. As a means of opening up a larger mechanism – *British* nationalism – and observing how it works, Scotland certainly provides a useful lever. Its unique position as almost a nation-within-a-nation, with its autonomous legal, religious and educational structures, as well as a long individual cultural heritage, offers us a strong totality to hold against the larger British identity in which it is subsumed, and which its quasi-autonomy serves to perpetuate.

Loss of control

It is the commercial aspect of film, however, that establishes the priorities governing production decisions and is responsible for putting on the screen the shadows that captivate and mesmerise us. By being made in such an environment, motion pictures naturally support dominant thought patterns and are especially noncritical of the economic system that nurtures them.[2]

A comprehensive history of early Scottish cinema has still to be written, but from the 'fragments' that remain we can put together a picture of a people losing control of their own film representation from the word go.[3] A centralisation of production control in the south of England – a process whose consolidation it is beyond the scope of this essay to trace – helped to determine the various internal strategies that were to operate in individual films.

In hindsight, the earliest exhibitions of cinema in Scotland were ironically appropriate in terms of both product and place. The first flickering on Scottish screens was at the Empire in Edinburgh on 13 April 1896, when the already much-travelled Lumière actualities, *Arrival of the Paris Mail, A Practical Joke on the Gardener, Building a Wall*, etc., were projected from one of the brothers' machines in a setting (one of many rising under the same inscription across the land) which proclaimed an imperial Britain. Although in those days the sun may never have set on the British Empire, on this occasion poor lighting made the show a rather dim disappointment. Consequently, what might be termed the first 'successful' display of moving pictures north of the border occurred six weeks later at the Glasgow Skating Palace, on 26 May, when a South African entrepreneur, A. M. Hubnar, offered a selection of English actualities: *Arrival of the Calais Express, Blackfriars Bridge* and *The Blacksmith's Shop*, among others, projected from an R. W. Paul machine. It was this very strangeness, the imported quality of the entertainment, that was offered as a selling point, with the show being advertised as 'Direct from . . .' and 'The rage of . . . LONDON!'.

If the Edinburgh première venue revealed the imperialist framework that film was entering, the Glasgow location supplied an absurdly apt realisation of the representational constraints waiting to snatch up a seventh art. Known popularly as the Bannockburn Panorama, the Skating Palace had its walls and halls adorned with archetypal 'Tartan' paintings and paraphernalia commemorating the famous battle. This shrine to Tartanry is only one link in a long chain that runs through Scottish cinema, frequently strangling it. It is the discourse of shortbread tins and whisky advertisements; the lone piper whose lament is heard the world over. Historically, it is the means by which any potential rebellion has been turned backwards to a wallowing in past glories and to a celebration of Scottish heroes as brave, bonny but impractical dreamers. This procedure, fuelled by Sir Walter Scott, was one to which cinema was to contribute substantially.

Film technology and material all arrived from abroad and came in foreign hands. To be sure, there was seemingly nothing at this stage to stop a domestic industry taking over the means of production, but it is important to note that the vital initial investment in the image, and the popular paradigm of images, had been set. Thus it is not so surprising to find Hubnar returning a year later with a Lumière lookalike, *The Departure of the Columbia from Rothesay Pier*, or that the *Glasgow Herald* in November 1896 should carry this review:

The cinematograph continues the chief attraction. There are in all a dozen pictures thrown on the screen each of which is a wonder in itself. Nothing could be finer than the representation of the Gordon Highlanders leaving Maryhill barracks. The picture lasts several minutes, and was repeatedly applauded as the swinging gait of the Highlanders stirred the patriotism of the audience.

– a clear display of the imperial ends to which a combination of Tartanry and a naive pleasure in the projection of movement could be adapted.

Closely akin to this was a fascination with anything royal (1897 was Victoria's Diamond Jubilee), which has persisted to the present day, where cameras roll at the slightest hint of activity at Balmoral Castle. It is not surprising, then, to discover that the smash hit of 1900 was *The Prince of Wales in Edinburgh*. More intriguing still is a film from six years on, *Aberdeen 1906*, as it is now titled. This had originally just been basic newsreel footage depicting crowds, coaches and the inevitable Highland regiment attending the Prince of Wales' visit to Marischal College. As Méliès was to find with the coronation of Edward VII, no cameras were allowed inside to film the event (it is doubtful if there would have been sufficient light), but, where the French pioneer simply restaged his event himself, this moment was not to be reconstructed for another fifty years. In 1956 the Scottish Film Council decided to rework the material into a brief narrative, adding stills, bagpipe and crowd noises, and a voice-over from none other than Tom Fleming, subsequently, as BBC commentator, the voice behind so many royal pageants, including, most recently, the marriage of the present Prince of Wales (himself the author of an arch piece of Tartanry, *The Old Man of Lochnagar*).

But it was the search for exploitable narratives, rather than actuality (royal or otherwise), that saw the full-blooded filmic appropriation of Scotland. In the rapid cinematic colonisation of literature, Scott and Stevenson were prize territories. So, from the former we find: '*Quentin Durward*: Pathé, February 1912. *Lady of the Lake*: Vitagraph, August 1912. *Ivanhoe*: Imp, July 1913; Zenith, July 1913. *Heart of Midlothian*: Hepworth, April 1914'; while from the latter we have: '*Dr Jekyll and Mr Hyde:* Nordisk, September 1910; Imp, June 1913; Kineto, June 1913. *Treasure Island:* Vitagraph, April 1908. *The Black Arrow*: Edison, January 1912, and *The Suicide Club*: B & C, July 1914.'[4] All have enjoyed a succession of subsequent remakes. This provided perhaps the most direct entrance for Tartanry into Scottish film images, and a continued search for successful stories would similarly herald in the Kailyard School via adaptations of Barrie and later Buchan. The Kailyard tradition is an opposite and complementary phenomenon to Tartanry. In the words of Cairns Craig, it presents

> not the Scotland of romantic glamour, but a Scotland of parochial insularity, of poor, humble, puritanical folk living out dour lives lightened only by a dark and forbidding religious dogmatism. [. . .]
>
> Tartanry and Kailyard, seemingly so opposite in their ethos, are the joint creations of an imagination which, in recoil from the apparently featureless integration of Scottish life into an industrial culture whose power and identity lies outside Scottish control, acknowledges its own inability to lay hold of contemporary reality by projecting itself upon images of a society equally impotent before the forces of history.[5]

By the end of the Great War more and more Scots seemed to share Hugh MacDiarmid's view that England had lost its glory and that union with a decaying neighbour might be no longer desirable. Typically, this discontent produced a new literary movement, even a new language (MacDiarmid's neo-lowlands), but very little effective political action. By now, however, the mass of the population spent much more time in movie houses than in bookshops, and what they got there was an imported culture. It was, no doubt, cold comfort to the nationalists that England had suffered just as drastically as a result of America's new-found status as a creditor nation, by which it had been able to corner the world's film markets. The final nail in the coffin came in 1929, with the arrival of Al Jolson in *The Singing Fool* at the Glasgow Colosseum. With the conversion to sound, Scotland lost any immediate hope of entering production autonomously, with costs escalating and movie houses across the country having to struggle to adapt and even stay open.

It was precisely at this point, significantly, that Scotland's independent film culture took root, with the formation of the Glasgow Film Society in 1929. In addition to a chain of such societies, there followed the establishment of the Scottish Film Council (1934), the Scottish Central Film Library (1939), and, in 1947, the Edinburgh Film Festival, which at least in its early years had a strong documentary input.[6] If Scotland was busy trying to counterbalance the external domination of commercial cinema, England produced films that simultaneously highlighted the rifts in the union and attempted to weld them back together. Having noted the centralisation of production power, it is to these strategies of centralisation within the films themselves that we must now turn.

Screening Scotland: poster for *Ivanhoe* (1913)

Tight Little Island

There is a danger when dealing with the later 'core' texts in the debate about Scottish cinema that a pseudo-genre is constructed, the 'Scottish film', with its own iconography of kilts, claymores, whisky bottles, undertakers, Bible punchers, etc., which is totally detached from any exigencies of production and so tends to wander willy-nilly across studio and geographical boundaries. The resultant analyses resemble a poor piece of Freudianism, whereby a stock of fixed, determined symbols is created with the same meaning irrespective of the analysand. We should, rather, be following Freud's methodology of dream-work, determining how the individual dreamer (studio) utilises an available vocabulary of motifs.

Not to labour the point, but simply to give an example of the difficulties involved, it is interesting to look at the meanings produced from one motif, a telephone, in two different production contexts. As Colin McArthur has described in his iconography of the gangster film,[7] telephones repeatedly represent a threat of violence, as in the classic example of the abusive calls to the detective's wife in Lang's *The Big Heat* (1953). However, in a contemporary Ealing film, *The Maggie* (1954), or the more recent 'after Ealing' *Local Hero* (1983), the telephone becomes a comic instrument conveying meanings of 'insularity', as American businessmen struggle with public call-boxes in the back of beyond. Again, the same call-box serves to signal national oppositions in *A Canterbury Tale* (1944), as the American sergeant battles with the English 'A' and 'B' button system. While each of these examples has a common foundation in the term 'communication', it is the subtle shades of difference evoked by each context, the specific work of each 'dream', that must concern us. The same applies to the larger space of narrative, where we must try to avoid the empty reductionism of a perpetual sacrifice on the oedipal altar, and, instead, trace how and why such strategies are employed in each situation.

What follows is a series of 'working notes' approaching some of the ways in which the techniques of cinema serve both to isolate and to retrieve one region, Scotland, in a national matrix. If a particular region is to be utilised as 'different' it must first be fenced off, put into cinematic quarantine. The isolated community, shut off from 'reality', detached from history, recurs throughout Scottish films. But this similar representation can be arrived at by a number of diverse routes. Although we are primarily concerned with British productions, *Brigadoon* (1954) provides a useful starting point for examining some of the factors that must be taken into account.

The village of Brigadoon, reappearing every hundred years, is the shut-off community *par excellence*: the dream world pulled out of history, waiting to be stumbled upon by outsiders lost in the mist. It is the same mist that led the ship on to the rocks in *Whisky Galore* (1949), that Danny and Mac are delayed by before reaching the fishing village in *Local Hero*, and that has served to dislocate countless communities in cinema. It provides, of course, a neat combination of cinema language and scenery, justifying the recognisable 'dream dissolve' by climate. But, while these factors might allow us to catalogue *Brigadoon* as 'Scottish', they also label it as a 'Hollywood Musical' and a 'Vincent Minnelli Film'. Its blatantly

Just another dream land: musical Scotland in Minnelli's *Brigadoon* (1954)

'staged' appearance, the play between illusion and reality, makes it a key text in any auteurist study of Minnelli's *mise en scène*. In the process, Scottish music, dancing, costume and scenery are all sucked up in the musical's thirst for novelty, for new dressings for the same old love story. Scotland falls under the same process that swallowed up most of the South Pacific, the Bavarian Alps, the Himalayas and most of the world outside of and including Burbank: just another dream land employed by the genre.

By contrast, Ealing's *Whisky Galore* and *The Maggie*, while offering similarly cut-off, mist-enshrouded communities – in one case an island, in the other a boat – both disjointed by the arrival of foreigners, do so as a result of different production pressures. Talk of closed, eccentric (literally 'off-centre') communities in British cinema, and one is immediately thrown up against Ealing. For, in films like *Passport to Pimlico* (1949), *The Titfield Thunderbolt* (1953), *The Bells Go Down* (1943), and a host of others, the same process is at work, whereby 'One "village" stands for a city, a nation, of interlocking communities, just as a small detachment of firefighters stands for a nationwide service.'[8] The isolated communities of

Whisky Galore and *The Maggie* clearly fit this model. What is interesting is the damage done to the Ealing discourse by its association both with Scotland and with a particular – Scottish – director: Alexander Mackendrick. Both films are pervaded by a blacker humour (continued in Mackendrick's later, English-based film *The Ladykillers*, 1955) whereby the central 'aliens' are quite viciously humiliated: laughed at, not with.

Whisky Galore follows the oft-trod narrative path towards a resolving marriage. What is interesting is the nature of the 'blocks' to that wedding that, by denying immediate closure, drive the story. The island of Todday is internally split by two obsessions, familiar in the discourses of Tartanry and Kailyard: whisky and presbyterianism. These the islanders have managed to resolve by conflating them in their basic rituals of birth, marriage and death. Dr Maclaren (James Robertson Justice) celebrates the delivery of twins with a glass of whisky; old Hector needs just one last dram before he can die peacefully; and, a central point in the narrative, to have a wedding there must be a *reiteach* (a wedding party), and to have the *reiteach* there must be a large jug of whisky. The impossibility of retrieving the life-giving whisky from the sunken vessel on the Sabbath (which must be kept holy) would not, in itself, have blocked the wedding, merely have delayed it by a day. It is the introduction of a third obsessional term in the equation that upsets the mythical equilibrium of the island. This third term is the English Home Guard Captain, Waggett.

Sir Stephen Tallents, in his plan for the 'Projection of England' in the 1930s, numbered among the qualities of the English to be celebrated: 'Parliamentary institutions (with all the values of a first edition). In national affairs – a tradition for justice, law and order . . . In sport – a reputation for fair play.'[9] Waggett is the personification of these values taken to a farcical extreme. He sees his duty as protecting the ship (its name symbolic of those parliamentary institutions, 'The SS Cabinet Minister') from what he sees as potential anarchists, in the name of law and order. All this irrespective of the fact that the ship will sink anyway. At one point he even laments a failed attempt to teach the local children football (a case of 'coals to Newcastle' if ever there was one), in which they deliberately kicked each other and then kicked the ball into the sea: 'They're so unsporting. They don't do things like the English. We play the game for the sake of the game, other nations do it for the sake of winning.' It is his total failure to understand the community, and his obsession with the letter of the law rather than the spirit, that leads to his exclusion from their world. With his evacuation, balance returns.

Pivotal to the film's double-play is the role of the English sergeant, Fred. He is the audience's guide through the island from the moment we 'arrive' with him on the steamer. Though Charles Barr has suggested that it is Basil Radford's Waggett who represents the typical Baldwinesque Englishman,[10] I feel that he is too excessive a character, not 'placid' enough to fulfil this function, which belongs, surely, to the sergeant. Not too bright, but honest, fair-minded without being gullible, he supplies the voice of moderation, of consensus. It is his inverse trajectory to Waggett's – inclusion against exclusion – that we are watching. This inclusion is achieved by a remarkable series of 'conflationary' strategies whereby Fred's marriage to Peggy is linked with the wedding of George (a native islander) to Peggy's sister Catriona. Two in particular stand out. Firstly in the preparation scenes before the party we have three shots that turn the foursome into a twosome: George brushing his hair cuts to Fred brushing his boots; which cuts to the final shot of the two sisters fighting over a mirror. Nearer the end of the film there is a brilliant revolving shot of all four dancing in a circle round the camera, whereby their faces, looking directly at us, merge into one. It is at this point, when Fred is fully accepted by the community, that Waggett is fully rejected, as a laugh is carried and amplified from his wife, to the party-goers and finally out to us, completing another circle of complicity. The excesses of the islanders are played off against those of the Captain, and an essentially 'English' consensus of behaviour is established in the sergeant.

The situation in *The Maggie* is slightly different. Once again we have the balanced community, now held even closer as the island becomes a boat. Their stability is again threatened, this time by the lack of money for vital repairs. Once more the chance of removing this lack, by getting a cargo fee, is threatened by an outsider: the rich American businessman Calvin B. Marshall (Paul Douglas). Like Waggett, Marshall is led a merry dance by the 'wily' Scots, and humiliated at every turn. But because the film lacks a mediatory figure like Fred, he is not finally expelled. Arriving at the ceilidh, suitably sore of foot and head, he stands in the symbolic doorway, from which, unlike his English forerunner, he is invited in. He learns, himself, that the slower pace of Kailyard life is not so bad after all, and his acceptance is signalled by a change from streamlined suit to chunky-knit sweater (a shift followed thirty years later by Mac, the American of *Local Hero*). In this instance the 'wedding' turns out to be a symbolic one, where a rocky romance ends with the Clyde puffer, née 'Maggie', becoming 'The Calvin B. Marshall'. The consensus offered by this film, made five years later, when American multinationals were increasing their activities in Scotland, is one that

Community and consensus: the English sergeant joins the Scottish dance in
Whisky Galore (1949) . . .

suggests a people saying to a dominant commercial force (much as
countless film women do to their husbands), 'You can buy me out,
but do it slowly'.

The Ealing influence can be seen in the films of the state-aided
independent production company Group 3 (1951–5), of which
Michael Balcon himself was chairman: repeatedly, the small com-
munity is foregrounded. Two of the dominant Board members were
Scots, John Grierson and James Lawrie, and three films from the
Group's limited output are set in Scotland: *You're Only Young
Twice, Laxdale Hall* and *The Brave Don't Cry* (all 1952).

The first is an adaptation from a play by Grierson's friend from
Glasgow University, James Bridie, celebrating the juvenile highjinks
of undergraduates from that same university at the expense of a
puritanical Head. *Laxdale Hall* is a limp successor to *Whisky Galore*.
A number of Scottish villagers refuse to pay road tax for a road they
deem unworthy of the name. Whitehall officials (Raymond Huntley
and a very young Fulton Mackay – the old man in *Local Hero* – here
playing a rare romantic lead) arrive to sort the matter out and

persuade the villagers to move to an industrial town. Added to this is
the threat posed by professional poachers from Glasgow draining the
Laird's loch. The film is remarkable in the way that it manages to
place that *English* landowner (Ronald Squire) at the heart of the
community, and establish him as the accepted voice of consensus
opposed to the excesses of the Whitehall delegate, without ever
questioning his (historical) right to be there. The one saving grace of
this otherwise predictable Highland yarn is a scene in which
characters from *Macbeth*, local amateur thespians, rampage around
the loch in search of the poachers during a storm. Both these films,
sadly, in their refusal to leave the shelter of a familiar representational
harbour, reveal the financial insecurity of the Group – never
wholeheartedly supported by the industry and unable, or unwilling,
to afford a risk.

There survives, however, one film that does some justice to the
potential of associating the leading figures of documentary and of
Ealing. Directed by Philip Leacock, who had started in documentary and was to move on to success with *The Kidnappers* (1953; a film

... and the American businessman joins the ceilidh in *The Maggie* (1954)

dealing with another isolated Scottish community, the pioneers in Nova Scotia), *The Brave Don't Cry* continued the tradition of showing closed societies, but on this occasion tied it to the lived experience of a mining village. Here the community is allowed to stand on its own two feet, with no pretensions to 'representing the nation'. Grierson took a close personal interest in the film (later admitting it to be his favourite) and his influence is clear both in the choice of subject, with its echoes of a film society favourite, Pabst's *Kameradschaft* (1931), as well of the documentary movement's own *Coalface* (1935), and in the way a low budget is turned to stylistic advantage in the low-key shooting and acting. Indeed, as Colin McArthur points out,[11] it is only in the one area in which the film has a weather-eye on the box office – the casting – that it falters. For, although the presence of the drafted-in star, John Gregson, may have calmed the accountants, his *deus ex machina* status sticks out awkwardly. There is a striking parallel between the positions of Gregson as star saving the film and Gregson the ex-miner returning, rather oddly, as management saving the day. The resultant 'all pull together' effect, denying class difference, is disturbing, but *The Brave Don't Cry* sticks in the memory both for its haunting, stark images of miners leaving for work, and because it is such a rare beast – a Scottish film that is not 'about' Scotland.

Mention of Grierson inevitably invites discussion of the documentary film movement, and it is worth looking back to consider the influences behind that movement and how they led it to become one of the major builders of a centralised consensus in Britain. In its own structure, the group was a testimony to the pull of the centre, with diverse regional talents gravitating to London. While Grierson himself, as a result of his world travels, had developed a healthy dislike of the then dominant modes of representation, the man who was to give him the chance to develop alternative forms was also to tie them to an established imperialist enterprise. Stephen Tallents of the Empire Marketing Board had one prime concern and that was for 'The Projection of England': Parliament, Navy, cricket, Dickens, you name it, he wanted it on the screen. This, combined with the institutional financial structure they served, explains why the movement drifted from a desire to portray the wo:king classes to an involvement with the furthering of the national wealth. Their concerns became, in essence, national concerns, so that a project that began with the words, 'I was very interested in putting the working classes on the screen',[12] ended with the epitaph: 'Documentary built up a true conception of practical internationalism, in which national characteristics and national achievements were seen to form the best basis for the interchange of ideas and the promotion of mutual understanding between peoples.'[13] As far as the regions were concerned, it signalled the arrival of more film vans from London coming to 'creatively' pick and choose which parts of their 'actuality' could be incorporated in the 'reproduction' of a national image.

Though the national unification project was really to take off during the war (as we would expect), a number of the films of the 1930s suggested techniques that would be useful. High on the list is *Night Mail* (1936), directed by expatriate Scot Harry Watt, and probably the most widely seen and discussed of all the GPO Unit's productions. Here, the central device of a train travelling from London northwards to where 'All Scotland waits for her;/ In the dark glens, beside pale-green lochs,/ Men long for news', was a way of linking diverse communities around one aspect of similarity. It was a journey not confined to documentary. Robert Donat had made it the previous year, as Richard Hannay in Hitchcock's *The 39 Steps* (as, in the same role, would Kenneth More in 1960 and Robert Powell in 1978); so did Wendy Hiller, the new post-war woman in search of herself on the Hebrides in Powell and Pressburger's *I Know Where I'm Going* (1945); and many others would purchase the same ticket on the Northern Line. Where in *Night Mail* Scotland is one of many regions drawn together by way of a repeated work process (loading the mail), poetic rhythm, and melody (courtesy of Auden and Britten respectively), in the fiction films it provides a 'dream country', a Brigadoon at the end of the line, preferably arrived at through fog or thunderstorm, in which problems ranging from marriage to murder can be resolved with the return of a happy couple.

Harry Watt was to retrace this journey, not on a train but with lorries carrying balloons to Edinburgh, while filming *Squadron 992* at the start of the war. But it is in the work of another documentarist during these years that we find the encapsulation of all our strategies of centralisation. Humphrey Jennings had already shown an interest in the nation as a whole in his work for Mass Observation, with the charting of a day in the life of a nation, Coronation Day, 12 May 1937; but it was in his now famous wartime films, notably *The First Days, Listen to Britain, Heart of Britain* and *A Diary for Timothy*, that he developed an individual, poetic technique for joining disparate community activities into a unified whole, finding the deeper structures of 'sameness' within 'difference'. Jennings in fact engages more with Wales and the North of England than with Scotland, and he is in any case considered in detail elsewhere in this volume, but the strong 'geographical' dimension in his work, as he searches for a literal and metaphorical 'Heart of Britain', should be noted here.

Jennings illustrates the process by which, for Grierson himself and for the documentary movement generally, the conflicting pressures

Journey to Scotland: Robert Donat leads Madeleine Carroll through the glens in Hitchcock's *39 Steps* (1935)

of working-class representation and of national projection eventually saw the triumph of the latter. Grierson's career is a map of growing national responsibility. Having moved from the Empire Marketing Board, and the GPO Film Unit, to become chairman of the National Film Board of Canada, he returned after the war to work for Films of Scotland: 'Founded in a deliberate attempt to use film for national purposes, the Films of Scotland Committee was, for Britain, unique. Nowhere, as in Scotland, was there a body using the cinema to maintain the national will and benefit the national economy.'[14] In his biography of Grierson, Forsyth Hardy entitled the chapter on Grierson's Scottish sojourn 'The Heart is Highland', and it is an odd measure of the way the movement had shifted from its original intentions that, while Grierson was in Scotland working for Group 3, two of the few remaining 'disciples', Edgar Anstey and Stewart McAllister, were also north of the border, working as producer and associate producer respectively on a British Transport Film, *The Heart is Highland* (1952), an up-market travelogue joining all the old chestnuts – whisky, lochs, Glamis Castle, etc. – in an attempt to boost the tourist trade.

Documentary did not, of course, have a monopoly on wartime unification strategies; the commercial studios were equally busy turning out national pictures. While it is beyond the scope of this chapter to outline all of these, there is one strategy that was particularly powerful in the drawing of the regions into a consensus – the training film. A full analysis of this genre has yet to be produced, but its ideological force is more than hinted at in the slide from films of post-Vietnam neurosis, *The Deer Hunter, Apocalypse Now* and *Coming Home,* to training films like *Private Benjamin, Stripes* and *An Officer and a Gentleman*, in an America moving from post-Watergate uncertainty to Reaganite nationalism. As regards wartime Britain, the two key examples are Carol Reed's *The Way Ahead* (1944) and Leslie Howard's *The Gentle Sex* (1943).

Where, normally, we carry around at least a dual citizenship, as part of a locality and part of a nation, in wartime huge sections of the population are literally transported from the former into rapidly constructed strongholds of the latter. For those not drafted directly, there awaits the film of the process waiting to draw them in. *The Way Ahead* is such a film. In brief, it is the story of a platoon of men from diverse backgrounds who go through an army training course and come out the other side to acquit themselves with honour in North Africa. Scotland is represented by John Laurie, who played the puritanical crofter in the original *39 Steps* and later became popularly known for his role in the long-running TV series about the Home Guard, *Dad's Army*. Where, in an actual camp, diversity is hammered out by blind discipline, in the cinema it is performed by the 'rules' of narrative identification. Central to this is the role of David Niven (already bearing a cultural load of 'Englishness' from previous films; later, ironically, to star in Korda's 1948 film *Bonnie Prince Charlie*), as the modest, fair and caring South of England officer leading the men. His values are very much those of Tallents, and the film's trajectory is to persuade the men, and us, to accept those values. Again we find the train journey, on which the men first meet, supplying a swift device for unification, as each man quickly summarises his background (for Laurie it is as a tractor-driving farmer); one character, a travel agent, is even able to spell out the details of all the train lines and timetables that knit the country together.

The Gentle Sex relies just as heavily on this device, beginning in a railway station where the girls, recruits to the Auxiliary Territorial Service, all meet under the male gaze and patronising commentary of Leslie Howard. Like Launder and Gilliat's *Millions Like Us*, also from 1943, but without the same sharp awareness of class, gender and regional divisions, it follows the girls' absorption into a consensual view of Britain, united against Nazism (wartime, of course, increasing the definition of identity by *inter*national contrasts). To this end, a key scene in the film, suitably conducted in the guard's van of a train, has Lilli Palmer, an escapee from the Nazi annexation of Europe, attacking one girl's suggestion that Britain could make profitable use of German efficiency. Audience and characters are carried down south, secure in their national persona.

New Directions?

So far this account has focused mainly on the two most celebrated of 'serious' British film producers, Balcon and Grierson, and the way they dealt with Scotland. In the work of a third such producer working in a nationalistically British way, David Puttnam, one finds the familiar interweaving of eccentric, isolated communities and national pride: again, Scotland is central.

Local Hero (1983) is in many ways a continuation of Bill Forsyth's personal comedy of role reversal, the girl/boy inversion of *Gregory's Girl* (1981) becoming the Scots/American inversion of the later film. We have already discussed some of the familiar motifs operating in the film; while the comedy lies in upsetting the usual opposition of insular, backward Scots against jet-setting Americans, it still relies on that limited paradigm for its laughs. It is tied as much to the Kailyard model it seeks to parody as was George Douglas Brown's novel, *House of Green Shutters*. The end result is a doubly distanced film: where its predecessors, *Whisky Galore*, *Brigadoon* and so on, built a nostalgic picture of a lost way of life, *Local Hero* creates a nostalgia for those self-same films. It is a frightening sign of how history is carried away into myth.

If the Puttnam/Forsyth collaboration produced another isolated community, Puttnam's earlier *Chariots of Fire* (1981), directed by Hugh Hudson, supplied a remarkable resurrection of the unification strategy. Ed Carter has shown how the film's claims to be showing history 'simply as it was' are far from justifiable;[15] what interests me is the way it has used its biographical raw material to fashion a nationalist message. *Chariots of Fire* is a film about 'races' in both senses of the word. We find Scotland again constructed in terms of Presbyterianism and scenery, with the evangelist Liddell running for Christ across the Highlands. His training programme is paralleled (cinematically by a cross-cutting sequence in the middle of the film) with that of Harold Abrahams, a Cambridge undergraduate. Abrahams, however (echoing Waggett in *Whisky Galore*), is not allowed to occupy the space of 'Englishness' in the film, both because of his Jewish background, and, mainly, because he is too excessive in his attempts to be the Gilbert and Sullivan Englishman; in short, he tries

United Kingdom: Scotland (Ian Charleson) wins for Britain in *Chariots of Fire* (1981)

too hard. He serves as a narrative balance – English excess versus Scottish (religious) excess – to Liddell. This opposition is subsumed in the term 'British' as both are chosen for the Olympic team pitted against the Americans, who are portrayed, once more, as the super-efficient, modernised training experts. But it is only when Liddell refuses to run in the heats of the 100 metres on the Sabbath – a recall of the Sabbatarianism in *Whisky Galore* – that we discover our point of consensus in the film, our middle line, our Sergeant Fred, in the 'amateur' Englishman Lord Andrew Lindsay (Nigel Havers). Lindsay does not show Abrahams' excessive desire to win, and is consequently willing to back down and let Liddell avoid a religious crisis and run in the 400 metres instead. Both are thus enabled to go on to beat the Americans and stand in a self-congratulatory pyramid of success – one matched only by the Oscar-waving scenes that followed in Hollywood as Colin Welland, the film's scriptwriter, declared that 'The British are coming!'.

Where the popular debate that followed the film's commercial success was primarily concerned with whether the British *were* coming, and if so how best to capitalise on it, the 1982 'Scotch Reels' event at the Edinburgh Film Festival was questioning what exactly *British* meant. It was no longer a matter of how films expressed a British *Volksgeist*, but rather why they failed to voice a genuinely Scottish one. Indeed, it was not the films alone but the entire Scottish film culture that came under criticism for its lack of self-definition and achievement. It was as a result of this investigation that the strategies of centralisation discussed here began to be laid bare. The classification of a superficial Scottish iconography proved less important than the uncovering of the deeper structural operations forming a narrative, poetic, or rhetorical unity disguised as a national unity. It would be unfair to chastise Scottish film-makers like Grierson, Mackendrick or Forsyth for remaining tied to the old discursive positions, since, as Tom Nairn said of the literary figures before them, it was impossible for them to work in any other mode. They all received their training elsewhere and, while typically each has voiced a yearning to return and portray their lost homeland, they have all been forced to produce their work within the confines of externally constructed production bases: the Empire Marketing Board, Films of Scotland, Ealing, Group 3 and, most recently, Goldcrest.

Although Scotland has provided a useful model for other peripheral studies, the practical application of these discoveries seems to have contracted beyond the neo-nationalist boundaries envisioned by Nairn towards a far smaller alternative scale of production based on the community. From the Rio cinema in Hackney to the Tyneside Festival and Northern Trade Films in Newcastle, a host of local film projects have been organised to meet the requirements of specific communities (a shift aided to a large extent by both the availability of relatively inexpensive video technology, whose capital outlay can be recouped with smaller audiences, and the support of local authorities offering financial assistance despite increasing restrictions on their activities by central government). In this context, films are selected for production or exhibition depending not on their ability to invoke supposedly 'universal' human truths or stylistic significance, but on their relevance to the community. This may indicate the most productive way ahead.

Notes

1   Tom Nairn, *The Break-Up of Britain,* London, New Left Books, 1977; Colin McArthur (ed.), *Scotch Reels,* London, British Film Institute, 1982. See also John Brown, 'Land Beyond Brigadoon' in *Sight and Sound*, vol. 53, no. 1, Spring 1984.

2   Thomas Guback, 'Hollywood's International Market' in Tino Balio (ed.), *The American Film Industry*, Madison, University of Wisconsin Press, 1976, p. 140.

3   Some useful material can be found in the special issue of the *Educational Film Bulletin,* September 1946, celebrating fifty years of Scottish cinema.

4   Rachael Low, *History of the British Film 1906–1914,* London, Allen & Unwin, 1949.

5   *Scotch Reels,* pp. 7 and 11.

6   For a more extensive chronicling of dates in Scottish film culture, see the list drawn up by Jim Hickey in *Scotch Reels,* pp. 70–2.

7   Colin McArthur, *Underworld USA*, London, Secker & Warburg/ British Film Institute, 1972.

8   Charles Barr, *Ealing Studios,* London, Cameron & Tayleur/David & Charles, 1977, p. 34.

9   Stephen Tallents, *The Projection of England,* London, Faber, 1932.

10   Barr, *Ealing Studios,* p. 109.

11   *Scotch Reels,* pp. 56–7.

12   Elizabeth Sussex, *The Rise and Fall of British Documentary*, Berkeley and London, University of California Press, 1978, p. 11.

13   Basil Wright, *The Long View,* London, Secker & Warburg, 1974, p. 110.

14   Ibid., p. 200.

15   Ed Carter, 'Chariots of Fire' in *Jump Cut*, no. 28 (1982), pp. 14–15.

Elaine Burrows

LIVE ACTION
A BRIEF HISTORY OF BRITISH ANIMATION

A cartoon was originally a design, drawn on stiff paper, for other artistic works such as tapestries and stained glass. By the 19th century it had come to be a satirical sketch in a newspaper or a magazine. By the 20th century the satirical edge had become unimportant, and a cartoon was simply a visual joke. This notion of cartoons as comic strips, or 'the funnies', is the one that has been most closely associated with the animated film cartoon; ideas of fine art or politics have become almost completely lost for the general audience. Although in the early years of animation many films were based on the work of newspaper cartoonists, and could have developed with a stronger satirical line, animation's most consistent appeal has always been its ability to represent wildly surreal activities in which objects, animals, and people can be squashed, broken up, reconstituted, and meta- morphosed into other things.

Animation is extremely labour-intensive and, consequently, very costly when compared to modest-budget live-action cinema. It is regrettable – though perfectly understandable in the context of cinema as industry – that financial constraints have usually inhibited experimentation and/or the production of 'non-commercial' films. While governments may be willing to fund wartime propaganda, manufacturers to pay for advertising and promotional films, or well- established studios to set up subsidiary units to produce series of entertainment shorts, there is rarely much money for animators to make more adventurous films, either for their own artistic pleasure, or in the interests of minority social or political causes. In Britain, it has been impossible for major studios to fund animation to the same extent that, for example, Warner Bros did in the United States. Nor has a British animation studio ever had the extraordinary entrepren- eurial abilities of the Disney organisation.

The content of animation films has also been problematic. Apart from the surreal comedies, many films have been based on magical or fantastic stories, folk tales, and so on, where the unique abilities of animation to produce transformations impossible to achieve in live-action cinema have been its greatest asset. Unfortunately, this asset has also been a great liability: fairy stories and folk tales have long been regarded as a proper diet for children, and animation has, in consequence, been dismissed not only as 'funny cartoons' but, quite unnecessarily, as children's films.

It is probably for these reasons that animation has, until very recently, been ignored or marginalised by film critics and historians alike.[1] The few histories of animation that do exist have been mostly of the 'fanzine' variety, with lots of pictures and minimal information. This is unfortunate: the history of animation is analogous to that of live-action cinema in many respects, and the study of animation could surely yield complementary theoretical and historical insights about the cinema. Like live-action, animation has had its evolving 'codes', and its pioneers; it has gone through phases of development and experimentation, both artistic and technical; it has been used for entertainment, as instruction, and as propaganda; it has had its own studios and companies, and it has been part of the output of major live-action organisations; there are animators who work with money from outside agencies, and there are those who struggle to maintain their independence and political integrity; animation has had its own stars.

Animated cinema in Britain dates back, in one form or another, to the very early days of the moving picture. Because animation is based on single-frame, step-by-step motion, the apparent movement of inanimate objects, without human intervention, could be achieved by the same 'trick' photography as was employed by Méliès and his contemporaries. Arthur Melbourne-Cooper's *Matches Appeal* (c. 1899) exploited this principle in a simple advertisement for Bryant and May's matches, asking cinema patrons to send boxes of matches to the British troops in South Africa. The film employs matchstick characters which move around and chalk up the words of the message on a board. Not only is *Matches Appeal* possibly the first British animated film; it is also the first in a line – which extends forward to the present day – of films financed by commercial (or, more rarely, cultural) sponsorship.

Melbourne-Cooper made a number of animated and trick films during the next fifteen years, and also produced live-action shorts, both fiction and non-fiction. This was a rare combination. Most of the 'animators' who started work in Britain before the First World War were lightning cartoonists, with established careers in the music hall, or illustrators who produced film-enhanced lightning cartoons from their own newspaper and magazine work. In most cases, of course, the actual animation was done by others, but the artists were given the credit.

A few people began to produce films of jointed cut-outs and puppets, but the first British film to consist entirely of separate drawings was *The Hand of the Artist*, made by Walter Booth in 1906. Booth made his films for distribution by existing companies such as Paul, Kineto, and Urban, who could afford to finance his work from their profits.

The First World War gave British animation a new impetus. Not only did the government realise the potential that animation had for instructional films, but the lightning cartoonists had vital political subjects to tackle. A number of new animator-artists began work as the demand for films increased. Lancelot Speed started, in 1914, his eight-part *Bully Boy* series for Neptune Films; these were a mixture of lightning sketches and cut-outs, commenting on the attitudes and activities of the 'Bully Boy' Kaiser, and on topical wartime events. When Neptune and the series folded, Speed made some films for release by Jury's Imperial Pictures, such as *The U-Tube* (1917) and *Britain's Honour* (1919). He went on to be 'adviser' on the *Wonderful Adventures of Pip, Squeak and Wilfred* series (1921), adapted, like many other films of the period, from the work of newspaper and magazine artists, in this instance A. B. Payne of the *Daily Mirror*.

Dudley Buxton, already well known as a cartoonist and lightning sketch artist, made three *War Cartoons* in 1914. In the following year, he and Anson Dyer produced alternate issues of *John Bull's Animated Sketch Book*. This series ran for more than twenty issues, on into 1916, each issue consisting of several items made by cut-out and lightning sketch techniques. Buxton and Dyer (who was a genuine 'cartoonist', having started his artistic career as a designer specialising in ecclesiastical stained glass) moved together to Kine Komedy Kartoons. Among Buxton's work after this was the *Memoirs of Miffy* series (1920) which was notable for using the more advanced 'cel' technique invented in America in 1915 by Earl Hurd and William Bray. Although British cinema in general suffered from a wartime influx of American films, it was, in addition, British film-makers' reluctance to move from cut-out to cel which held back British animation for several years.[2]

In 1924 and 1925, more than twenty films were made, by the cel method, of the adventures of G. E. Studdy's cartoon character, *Bonzo*. It would be instructive to look at both *Bonzo* and *Pip, Squeak and Wilfred* in the context of discussions of 'stars', since these characters were – until very recently – virtually the only ones in British animation to have any kind of life outside their screen

Lancelot Speed and *Bully Boy* (1914)

activities. In the last few years, however, characters like Danger-mouse and SuperTed, designed for children's films, have been promoted through comic strips and toys. The reverse is also beginning to happen as manufacturers have started to commission animated films as part of their marketing strategy for new toys.

Anson Dyer's career in animation is a story of success against the odds, trying, as he did, to maintain the artistic integrity of his work, while being forced, for financial reasons, to accept commissions for advertising films. After the war, he made three 'Uncle Remus' stories as *Phillip's Philm Phables* (1919). For Hepworth, he produced a series of Shakespearian parodies called *Cartoon Burlesques* (1919–20), some films of his own creation, *Bobby the Scout* (1921), and children's films like *Little Red Riding Hood* (1922).

Hepworth's bankruptcy in 1924 might have put an end to Dyer's financial stability, but fortunately Archibald Nettlefold, who bought out Hepworth's Walton Hall studios, decided to keep on the animation unit. Dyer should have been able to claim credit for the first British animated feature, but Nettlefold insisted on breaking down *The Story of the Flag* (1927) into separate parts for its release, thinking that it would not be a commercial proposition as a feature. It was Nettlefold, however, who raised enough money to fund Dyer's Anglia Films (1935), Britain's first full-time animation studio. *You're Telling Me* (1937), sponsored by W. D. & H. O. Wills, was not simply an advertisement for Capstan cigarettes, but also showed the inside of the studios, the animators at work, and some of the actual animation process. This was Dyer's first Technicolor film, the 3-strip Technicolor process having been contracted solely to Disney between 1933 and 1935. The first British animated Technicolor short had been *Fox Hunt*, made by Anthony Gross and Hector Hoppin for London Films in 1935; all other British colour animation up to this date had been made in more limited 2-strip systems.

Dyer went on to make a series of Stanley Holloway/Marriott Edgar monologues like *Sam and His Musket* (1935) and *Three Ha'pence a Foot* (1937). He also made commercially sponsored advertising films like *All the Fun of the 'air* (1935) and *The King with a Terrible Temper* (1937) for Bush Radio, and *Red, White and Blue* (1938), produced by Publicity Pictures for Hanson's Coffee Essence.

It was Publicity Pictures that produced, with the Film Society, Len Lye's *Tusalava* (1929). Lye went on to work at the Empire Marketing Board and GPO Film Units, under John Grierson. Grierson was exceptional in recognising animation as an integral part of film-making, being influenced in this, perhaps, by his interest in Soviet cinema: he encouraged the experimental work of Len Lye and Norman McLaren, and also employed Lotte Reiniger on a number of promotional shorts. Reiniger had been making silhouette films in Germany since the early 20s, mainly based on Perrault stories or operas. At the GPO she made *The Tocher* (1938), based on an old Scottish tale, and a number of other, somewhat whimsical films for telegrams, Post Office Savings, and so on.

Lye worked in the tradition of the German school of abstract/ avant-garde film-makers like Richter and Fischinger. Chief among his experiments was the technique of painting directly on to the film frame, as in *A Colour Box* (1935), and in combining this technique with abstract images and live-action in films like *Rainbow Dance* (1936) and *Trade Tattoo* (1937). He also worked in puppet animation on *The Birth of the Robot* (co-directed with Humphrey Jennings in 1936), and in stop-frame on *N. or N. W.* (1937). Norman McLaren also worked with a number of different techniques, employing a collage of live-action and stop-motion on *Camera Makes Whoopee* (1936) and the anti-war film *Hell UnLtd.*, made the same year (while he was still at art school) in collaboration with Helen Biggar. *Love on*

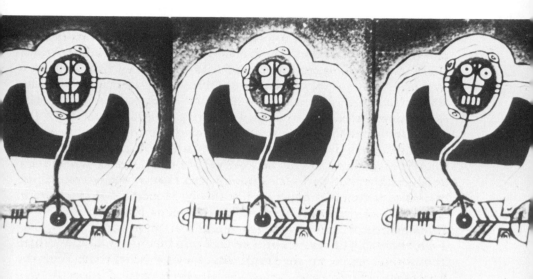

Frames from Len Lye's *Tusalava* (1929)

the Wing (1938), a superb example of painting onto film, set to music
by Jacques Ibert, was, however, banned by its producers, the GPO,
because of its sexual imagery. McLaren's later work was mainly
produced outside Britain, usually for the National Film Board of
Canada. However, he did design and animate *Around is Around* and
Now is the Time . . . for the 1951 Festival of Britain, and showed that
animation and stereoscopy are an ideal combination – something
more or less ignored by proponents of the 3-D film at the time.

The GPO encouraged the experimental work of its animators in a
way that has rarely happened before or since, but at the same time it
expected them to assist in the more mundane processes of producing
animated diagrams and the like, in order to explain to the public such
things as *How the Telephone Works* (1938). These kinds of film were
the forerunners of a multitude of wartime educational and
propaganda productions, with many government departments commissioning, through the Ministry of Information, films on 'why one
should . . .' be thrifty, save scrap, or buy war bonds.

A great many of these films were made by Halas & Batchelor.
Founded in 1940, the company made as its first film *Pocket Cartoon*,
a political satire on which Alexander Mackendrick collaborated.
Halas & Batchelor were put under contract to the Ministry of
Information to produce humorous propaganda shorts like *Filling the
Gap* and *Dustbin Parade* (both 1942), and an hour-long diagram/
model film for the Admiralty (the company's first feature-length

277

production) called *Handling Ships* (1945). Government sponsorship continued in the post-war reconstruction period with the *Charley* series (for various government departments via the Central Office of Information), and with films on topics like health education. In 1948, Halas & Batchelor made another hour-long film, *Water for Firefighting*, for the Home Office. In 1950, the company began its long and fruitful association with commercial and scientific sponsors with *As Old as the Hills* for the Anglo-Iranian Oil Company. At the same time it was making short fictional and abstract films like *Magic Canvas* (1948) for general audiences. For the Festival of Britain, Halas & Batchelor produced the four-part series *Painter and Poet*, which combined the talents of contemporary artists like Henry Moore and Ronald Searle with those of poets (present and past) such as Kathleen Raine and William Cowper. In 1953, they made their first puppet film, *The Figurehead*, a 3-D version of *The Owl and the Pussycat*, and a third sponsored feature, for the Admiralty, *Coastal Navigation*. With the experience of three full-length productions behind them, it was hardly surprising that Halas & Batchelor should be the company to make Britain's first full-length animated entertainment film, *Animal Farm* (produced by Louis de Rochemont), which appeared in 1954.

Despite winning acclaim at home and abroad, *Animal Farm* was not given a full general release. Nor was *Ruddigore*, Halas & Batchelor's subsequent entertainment feature (1967). Much British animation, of course, has been made for sponsors and the non-theatrical circuit (and latterly for advertising and television), but for other kinds of work the question of how to obtain adequate theatrical exhibition has been a permanent problem.

For many years, this kind of exhibition was tied to the circuit system in which producers and/or distributors had direct links with particular cinema chains. Because British animation was made almost completely independently of the major film companies, the films had no easy access to these chains. In contrast, Warner Bros. animation could readily be seen, alongside Warners' features, at ABC (now EMI) cinemas. The Disney organisation established themselves in Britain by releasing their films – including the nine features made between 1938 and 1953 – via RKO and the Rank/Gaumont cinemas. When RKO folded in 1953, Disney took over distribution for themselves and could be assured of a place in those same cinemas. In addition, newsreel cinemas tended to buy packages of American-made films and not trouble to book films on an individual basis. Art houses simply ignored most things that didn't come from Eastern Europe. Even today, when TV companies like Channel 4 are sponsoring animated films, they seem to have little interest in marketing the products.

Halas & Batchelor's *Animal Farm* (1954)

The one serious effort by a major figure in the British film industry to promote animated film production was unfortunately short-lived. Wanting to set up a British rival to the immensely successful Disney organisation, J. Arthur Rank established an animation unit in 1945, with studios at Moor Hall, Cookham. In charge of this G-B Animation was American-born David Hand who, at Disney, had directed *Snow White and the Seven Dwarfs* and supervised *Bambi* and *Victory Through Air Power*. With Ralph Wright and John Reed, Hand produced wartime training films, advertising and instructional shorts, and, in 1947, for overseas distribution by the British Council, a featurette about Magna Carta. G-B Animation then turned its attention to two popular series: *Animaland* (released between 1947 and 1949), which introduced such characters as Zimmo the Lion and Ginger Nutt the Squirrel; and *Musical Paintbox* (1948–9), depicting the songs, legends, scenery and historical personages of the British Isles. The films were not strong enough to compete abroad, and the relaxation in 1948 of government controls on imported films set them, on their home ground, against large numbers of stockpiled American productions, with dispiriting results – exactly as happened with their live-action counterparts. G-B Animation became a financial liability, and Rank closed the unit in 1950.

Numerous smaller companies had started up in the 1940s. British Animated Productions (with an ex-Fleischer employee, George Moreno, as producer); British Industrial Films, run by John Curthoys, and linked with his Analysis Films and the Anson Dyer studio; the British Instructional Films animation unit, headed by Helen Dunt, who later created the animation department of Associated British-Pathé; Diagram Films; the Mack Cartoon Unit; Pinschewer Films; Signal Films – these were among the many studios which survived for a longer or shorter time by turning out advertising, industrial, and educational films, all financed by outside sponsorship, with varying degrees of artistry.

The company which came nearest to challenging Halas & Batchelor's supremacy in the field of sponsored films was Larkins, also founded in the early days of the Second World War. Appointed director there in 1941 was Peter Sachs who, like Halas, had worked with George Pál in the 30s, and who had come with W. M. Larkins from Analysis Films. Also on the Larkins staff were Denis Gilpin, Richard Taylor, and Beryl Stevens, and their close association with the Film Producers' Guild enabled them to draw on the expertise of the member companies for whom they, in turn, made shorts and animated inserts. Wartime government sponsorship enabled them to produce films like *Summer Travelling* and *War in the Wardrobe* (both 1945, for the Ministry of War Transport and the Board of Trade respectively). After the war, the Central Office of Information and the British Council commissioned a series based on traditional English songs like *Widdicombe Fair* and *The Lincolnshire Poacher* (both 1949). In the same year Larkins made *T for Teacher*, which the Tea Bureau hoped would invigorate the British preoccupation with making a good cup of tea. In the 1950s, industrial sponsorship funded such films as *Balance* (1951, re-edited as *Enterprise*, 1954) for ICI, and *Full Circle* (1953), for the Anglo-Iranian Oil Company. A series of overseas promotional films for Barclays Bank, starting with *Put Una Money for There* (1958, for West Africa), helped to make them one of the most sought-after studios for advertising by industrial and commercial companies.

As such companies began to lose interest in animated promotional films, there came a new momentum from the need for advertising for the new independent television network. The first night of ITV transmission included a number of animated advertisements. One, for Crompton's Bulbs, was from Biographic, a company formed in 1954 by ex-Larkins staff Bob Godfrey and Keith Learner, later joined by Vera Linnecar and Nancy Hanna.

The demand for advertising films increased tremendously, and the consequence was that new companies sprang up as they had done in the 1940s. Encouraged by the prospect of an expanding market, the American UPA company (formed by ex-Disney employees) opened a branch in London. Their interest did not last, however, and when they withdrew, their representative George Dunning was free to start his own company, TV Cartoons, in partnership with John Coates (1957). Dunning's own experimental work, like *The Flying Man* (1961) and *Damon the Mower* (1972), was extremely influential on British animation, helping to expand film-makers' horizons and encourage them to try new techniques. TVC's production of the Beatles' film, *Yellow Submarine* (1968), while traditional in some respects, has an extravagance of colour and design rarely seen since the revolutionary days of the 1930s.

With most of Britain's animators working on commissions from television for advertising and entertainment shorts, there was a dearth of more personal projects in the late 1950s. Something of a renaissance began with the arrival from Canada of Richard Williams. His film *The Little Island* (1958), a very funny but also deeply serious half-hour allegory about non-communication between people of inflexibly dogmatic attitudes, won a British Academy Award. Williams managed subsequently to succeed where Anson Dyer had failed. Although, like most British animation studios, the Richard Williams Company survives on money from promotional and advertising films (the first of their more than 2,000 advertisements was *Guinness at the Albert Hall,* 1962), they have always managed to remain artists, to experiment with new styles and techniques, and to persuade their sponsors to go with them rather than to hold them back. Some of their best-known productions are title sequences for films like *The Charge of the Light Brigade* (1968) and *Murder on the Orient Express* (1974).

It was in 1968 that art schools and colleges began to include animation in their syllabuses. Until this time, it had been impossible to get training other than with an animation studio, and even then it was rare to get instruction as opposed to work experience. These art school courses have had a beneficial effect on the quality of work being produced in Britain, as students learn more about what has been achieved in the past, study principles of narrative and ways of relating sound and image, and are encouraged to employ more personal styles. Student work is now of such a high standard that advertising agencies have occasionally commissioned films from the colleges.

One thing that colleges cannot often afford to provide is access to computers. This will not be of much concern to some people since there has always been a fear that animation might, as a result of the introduction of computer technology, become the province of

Richard Williams' *The Little Island* (1958)

engineers rather than artists. It is to be hoped that these fears will not
be realised; there is already criticism of many animators' work being
all style and no content, and to find that style itself was becoming
simply a matter of more and more complex computer tricks would be
very disheartening. As it happens, many British companies are using
computers creatively, developing styles that are complemented
rather than controlled by the new technology. A good example is
Cucumber Studios, who realised the potential of computers very
early in their work. Their *Accidents Will Happen* (1979) is a
successful combination of modernist, geometric design and com-
puter-assisted animation.

Accidents Will Happen was set to a song by Elvis Costello, and was
one of the first animated films made to promote pop music. Record
companies provided a new source of sponsorship money for animation, until their attention turned to the pop video. *Bring it all Home*
(1980), by Derek Hayes and Phil Austin, who had made the futuristic
Max Beeza and the City in the Sky (1977) while still at the National
Film School, was set to a Gerry Rafferty song produced by Liberty
United Records. *Seaside Woman* (Oscar Grillo, 1980) was financed

by Paul McCartney's MPL Communications for a Linda McCartney song. (MPL's most recent production is *Rupert and the Frog Song,* directed by Geoff Dunbar in 1984.)

Seaside Woman won awards at Cannes, Chicago and Zagreb, but was attacked in some quarters for its racist imagery. So, too, was *Sunbeam*, a slick 30s pastiche made by Paul Vester's Speedy Cartoons company in 1980. Socio-political issues, other than those promoted by the government, have largely been ignored by animators; ignorance of or disregard for current debates has enabled film-makers to perpetuate old stereotypes in the name of 'humour'. One of the worst offenders has been Bob Godfrey, with films like *Henry 9 Till 5* (1970) and *Dream Doll* (1979). It is true, of course, that advertising relies heavily on stereotypes; sexism, in particular, is rampant in all forms of promotional material. No doubt financial pressures have an effect on animators, making them unwilling to bite the hands that feed them by taking a strong line on such issues. It is

Max Beeza and the City in the Sky (1977)

also true that, because 'It's only a cartoon', many people who would be critical of similar images in photographs or live-action films tend not to notice, or turn a blind eye to, animated images.

Some animators, feminists in particular, have started to redress the balance, firstly by ensuring that their work does not contain stereotypes, and secondly by dealing with issues outside the common run of animated films. They have been able to do this because they rely on cultural rather than commercial organisations for their basic funding. Vera Neubauer's *The Decision* (1981), for example, was funded by the British Film Institute's Production Division. It looks at the myths and realities of married life, and becomes a critique of the many earlier films based on fairy-story and folk tale themes. Leeds Animation Workshop, currently funded through the BFI's Regional Division, has made films on social issues such as state-supported child care (*Who Needs Nurseries? We Do!*, 1975) and violence against women (*Give Us a Smile*, 1983).

Cultural sponsorship has also encouraged a renaissance of 'art' and experimentation. The Arts Council can claim credit for Tony White's *Hokusai: An Animated Sketchbook* which, seven years in the making, was the British Academy's Best Factual Short Film of 1978. The Arts Council also sponsored Geoff Dunbar's *Lautrec* (awarded the Palme d'Or at Cannes in 1975) and *Ubu* (which won the Golden Bear at Berlin in 1979). The Greater London Arts Association put money towards the Quay Brothers' *A Fratricide/Ein Brudermord* (1981). Later examples of the Quays' disturbing puppet films, such as *The Cabinet of Jan Svankmajer* (1984), have been financed by Channel 4 Television.

Despite the myth that 'animation is for children', there have, until relatively recently, been few serious attempts to make films specifically aimed at children. In the last few years, however, companies like Cosgrove Hall (now a subsidiary of Thames Television) have begun to move in this direction. Cosgrove Hall has produced films in a variety of techniques for series like *The Adventures of Captain Kremmen* (1979) and *Dangermouse* (1980), and longer films such as *The Wind in the Willows* (1983). Bob Godfrey (who showed his true capabilities with *Great!*, a film about Isambard Kingdom Brunel which, among many other awards, won the Oscar for Best Short Film of 1975) has recently turned his attention to *Henry's Cat* (1983 and 1984, with a third series in progress), curiously enough a spin-off from *Henry 9 Till 5*. The Welsh company Siriol has made for Welsh Channel 4 Television the *SuperTed* series (1983) and a series called *Wil Cwac Cwac* (1985).

Channel 4 Television is the most recent of the many sponsors on whom British animators have always had to depend for financial viability. It is unfortunate that the sponsors' efforts (with the partial exception of Channel 4's contribution to the funding of the Cambridge Animation Festival) have not helped much in the exhibition of animation; unless the films appear on television, they are virtually unavailable. Even then, British material represents only a small proportion of the films screened. It is paradoxical that, when the excellence of the work of British animators is demonstrated nightly in television advertising, and when British films take prizes at all major film festivals, there should still be such a disregard for them in the minds of distributors and exhibitors.

If more work could be done on documentation and research, then perhaps animation would achieve the kind of respectability that live-action cinema now enjoys. A better educated audience might increase the demand for good animated films, and distributors and exhibitors would therefore be encouraged to make more films available. This, in turn, would help the animators' financial situation, making them less reliant on commercial sponsorship, and enabling them to spend time on personal, artistic, and even politically committed projects.

Notes

1   A rare exception is Rachael Low, who has dealt with various aspects of animation in the 1914–18, 1918–29, and the two 1930s non-fiction volumes of her *History of the British Film*. More specialist sources of information on British animation (though not in the context of British cinema as a whole) are Denis Gifford's articles for the *World Encyclopedia of Cartoons* (1980), and Ralph Stephenson's *Animation in the Cinema* (1967, new edition in 1973 as *The Animated Film*). *Animator's Newsletter*, now called *Animator*, has carried a series of articles, "The Shadows Move', on the history of British animation by Ken Clark, and articles by Ken Clark and others about various aspects of the industry.

2   In 'cel' animation, moving images are drawn frame-for-frame on transparent celluloid sheets. The backgrounds and any other non-moving parts of the image remain unchanged. The transparent 'cels' are photographed in sequence over the non-moving images. In this way, a greater flexibility of movement can be achieved than would be the case with cutouts, but less work is required than if the whole frame, including static elements, had to be redrawn each time.

Robert Murphy

RIFF-RAFF
BRITISH CINEMA AND THE UNDERWORLD

Between the wars, the pattern of crime in Britain changed considerably. The traditional criminal craftsmen – the cracksman, the creep, the cat burglar – were eclipsed by smash-and-grab raiders and motor bandits. The old 'rough house' gangs which had terrorised the poorer districts of Victorian cities were subdued by an increasingly powerful police force, but in their place arose more sophisticated criminal gangs such as the Darby Sabini mob and the Messina Brothers, who paid protection money to the police out of the fat profits they made from illegal gambling and organised prostitution. Little of this found its way into British films. Anything that depicted a real-life crime or realistically represented criminal techniques, any mention of drugs or prostitution, any attempt to look at crime from the criminal's point of view, any portrayal of sordidness or brutality – all were rigorously excluded by the British Board of Film Censors. Take, for example, *The Blue Café*, a play dealing with a Soho café, the headquarters of 'Blackie Hyam's dope-peddling racket' and featuring 'decadent society folk, prostitutes, and the riff-raff of Soho'. A shocked censor reported in 1933 that, 'The whole story centres round the dope traffic. The language and morals are impossible. Under no circumstances could we pass a film based on this play.'[1]

Edgar Wallace had set something of a fashion for gangster plays with *On the Spot* – which opened in the West End in April 1930 and ran for a year – but the dominant strand of crime fiction in the interwar years was the intricately plotted murder mystery exemplified by the writings of Agatha Christie, Dorothy L. Sayers, Anthony Berkely and John Dickson Carr. Brock Williams' scenario for *The Thirteenth Candle*, submitted to the BBFC in 1933, with its timeless country-house setting, its gallery of stereotyped characters, and its unlikely solution to an improbable murder, encapsulates the essentials of the genre. In the language of the BBFC scenario report:

286

Sir Charles Merton is discovered just after dinner one evening in his own house, stabbed with a stiletto.

He was an unpopular individual and apparently a good many people had some sort of motive of [sic] getting rid of him. Captain Blyth an old friend of Lady Merton's had been dining that night and Sir Charles had been grossly rude to him. It transpires that Sir Charles had instructed his lawyer to prepare a new will vindictively cutting out Lady Merton. The lawyer incidentally was losing his job as agent for a very big estate. The butler was under notice to leave. After everybody in turn was suspected, Captain Blyth traces the way the crime was committed, by fusing of a wire in the table candelabra, which broke an electro-magnetic circuit suspending the stiletto from the ceiling, the work of Dobin the chauffeur, because Sir Charles was flirting with his girl.[2]

Predictably the BBFC found nothing to object to, but the 'whodunnit' in its pure form was too bloodless and unemotional to have very wide cinematic appeal. The novels of Edgar Wallace, with their fast, action-packed plots, their excursions into the bizarre and the exotic, their gibbering monsters and fiendish master criminals, provided more appropriate screen material. Between 1925 and 1939 over fifty films were made from Wallace plays and novels.

In their passage into film there was a tendency to play up the fantastic elements of Wallace's stories. *The Terror* (1938), *The Dark Eyes of London* (1940), and *The Door With Seven Locks* (1946) are as much horror as crime films. Locked-room mysteries like *The Clue of the New Pin* (1929), and 'old dark house' stories like *The Frightened Lady* (1932), are as remote from the realities of real-life crime as the adventures of Lord Peter Wimsey, Hercule Poirot and Dr Gideon Fell. Yet Wallace did have extensive knowledge of the police and the underworld. Much of the attraction of novels like *The Squeaker*, of the Mr J. Reeder stories, and of his six-times-filmed play *The Ringer*, lies in the skill with which Wallace incorporates realistic detail into his feverishly melodramatic plots.

Towards the end of his life Wallace became fascinated with the American crime scene. His play *On the Spot* concerned the Capone-like activities of an American gangster (played by Charles Laughton), and his novel *When the Gangs Came to London* hypothesised an American take-over of the London underworld. *On the Spot* was submitted to the BBFC six times between 1931 and 1937 before being filmed in Hollywood as *Dangerous to Know*.[3] *When the Gangs Came to London* was submitted only once; as with Grierson Dickson's similar *Soho Racket*, the reaction of the Board was so hostile that further attempts must have appeared futile.[4] The Americanised underworld of Graham Greene's *Four Dark Hours* did eventually reach the screen as *The Green Cockatoo* in 1940, three years after it had been made, but by then it had been reduced to a conventional crime melodrama.

Wallace died in 1932, but he had started a vogue for writing in colloquial American which was taken up with considerable commercial success by Peter Cheyney and James Hadley Chase. Their pidgin American now reads grotesquely, but American influences – particularly the writings of Theodore Dreiser, Upton Sinclair, Ernest Hemingway and Dashiel Hammett – had a more fruitful effect on working-class novelists like James Hanley, George Garrett and Jim Phelan, and on the school of low-life writing which began to emerge in the mid-1930s.

Walter Greenwood spans both fields with *Love on the Dole* (1933) and the Soho melodrama *Only Mugs Work* (1938). *Love on the Dole* was quickly adapted for the stage, and repeated attempts were made to film it. Rioting unemployed, the dominant shadow of the bookmaker over the down-trodden working-class community, and a heroine driven by poverty into prostitution, proved unacceptable to the BBFC until 1941, when its anguished message about the evil effects of unemployment had become redundant. Greenwood entered the film industry in 1935, scripting the George Formby vehicle *No Limit*. With the exception of the unusual *Chance of a Lifetime*, his scriptwriting over the next twenty years was on comedies and conventional thrillers. *Only Mugs Work*, like *Love on the Dole*, was successfully dramatised, but there is no evidence of any attempt to turn it into a film.

Just as significant were the four novels by James Curtis published in the late 30s – *The Gilt Kid* (1936), *You're in the Racket Too* (1937), *They Drive By Night* (1938), and *There Ain't No Justice* (1938). The protagonists of all four novels are solidly situated in a semi-criminal working-class setting, despise and distrust the police – who are shown as violent and unpredictable – and accept brutality as a part of everyday life. As the titles suggest, this is a rough and sordid world with no room for moral or any other scruples. Refreshingly, though, there is none of the 'bully worship' which George Orwell saw as a distastefully fascistic strand in the writing of Wallace, Cheyney and Hadley Chase.[5] Curtis' heroes are small men with as little sense of their own superiority as Hammett's Sam Spade.

They Drive By Night was picked up soon after publication by Warner Brothers, adapted by Derek Twist, and made into a film at their Teddington studio. It was favourably received both critically and commercially. Even Aubrey Flanagan, London correspondent of the *Motion Picture Herald*, was thrilled into uncharacteristic enthusiasm:

They Drive By Night (1938): Ernest Thesiger as the psychopathic killer

'This canvas of rain and wind-swept highways, of dingy snack bars and hard-boiled Cockney artisans, is both fascinating and convincing: the low life element has seldom if ever been handled with more naturalness and sympathy, whether by directorial treatment or individual portrayal.'[6] There were, of course, censorship problems. In Curtis' novel Shortie Matthews, the hero, is a small-time criminal released from jail on the morning another man is hanged. After being coolly received by his former friends, he visits his girl-friend, a prostitute, only to find her strangled with a silk stocking. Fearing that he will be suspected of her murder, he goes on the run and after various adventures finishes up in Sheffield, where he rescues a 'road girl' from rape by two middle-class motorists. Partly because she believes in his innocence, partly through sheer exhaustion, Shortie gives himself up at a police station in a small northern town. He is beaten up to extract a confession, but the real murderer is caught and Shortie happily resigns himself to a twelve-month stretch for assaulting the police.

Twist's adaptation removed those aspects most likely to upset the censors – the prostitutes become dance hostesses, there is no police brutality, the middle-class rapists are reduced to a lecherous lorry driver – but the film remains remarkably true to Curtis' vision of life in the lower depths. Director Arthur Woods makes full use of Warner Brothers expertise with rain-swept streets and atmospheric night photography to give the film a grittiness and power quite unusual in 30s British cinema. Molly the 'road girl', in her new vocation as dance hall hostess, becomes responsible for trapping the murderer – Ernest Thesiger's chillingly sinister psychopath – and there is a pointed contrast between the resourcefulness which Molly and Shortie show in spite of being undernourished, undereducated and constantly exposed to the elements, and the degenerate middle-class murderer, his luxury flat awash with cats and morbid books.

While *They Drive By Night* was being filmed at Teddington, another of Curtis' novels, *There Ain't No Justice*, had been discovered by Michael Balcon's protégé Pen Tennyson, who persuaded Balcon to let him film it as his directorial debut. The differences between film and novel are no greater than with *They Drive By Night*. Tommy Mutch, the hero, is provided with a nice girl-friend to contrast with the goodtime girl who tempts him from the straight and narrow; and his sister gets involved with a thief, instead of dying from the consequences of a back-street abortion. Tommy himself is changed more radically. As played by Jimmy Hanley, he is a rough but kindly working-class boy who becomes a boxer in order to raise enough money to marry but walks out in disgust when he realises the boxing world is crooked. In the book he is less endearing – a callow, slightly stupid fighter with ideas above his station. When he realises he has been duped, he beats the promoter to a pulp and continues his career as a battered, cynical bruiser slugging out his fury against the world. The working-class community he inhabits is claustrophobic, mean and, above all, boring. 'Sunday afternoons were dull, Tommy was sitting in front of the kitchen stove reading the News of the World; Elsie was reading Peg's Paper; Ernie was trying to get Radio Luxemburg; Mrs Mutch was darning socks; Lily was playing on the floor; Fred Mutch was out with his pigeons. He had a race on that afternoon and might pick up twenty five bob.'[7] Seen through Ealing's rosy glasses this becomes warm, cosy, jovially human, with everybody helping each other and getting together in the pub to sing 'Knees Up Mother Brown'.

They Drive By Night and *There Ain't No Justice* are the most prominent examples of a flowering of low-life movies at the end of the 30s. Among the others are Lawrence Huntington's *Bad Boy* (1938; re-issued as *Branded*); two films produced by Joseph Somlo – *On the Night of the Fire* (1939, Brian Desmond Hurst) and *A Window in*

London (1939, Herbert Mason) with Sally Gray and Michael Redgrave; Oswald Mitchell's *Night Journey* (1939); Walter Summers' *Traitor Spy* (1940) with its conventional plot enlivened by remarkable night-club sequences and a spectacularly melodramatic ending; Roy William Neill's *His Brother's Keeper* (1939); and Norman Lee's *Murder in Soho* (1939), with Jack La Rue and Sandra Storme. But the war shifted the focus away from the underside of British society. With everyone pulling together, film producers felt a duty to concentrate on positive, optimistic subjects. Tennyson went on to *The Proud Valley*, where the striking miners come together with the bosses to save the pit, and then to the naval propaganda of *Convoy*. He was killed in an air crash in 1941, and Ealing was not to return to the low life until 1947 and *It Always Rains on Sunday*. Arthur Woods, too, was killed in the war, his last film – ironically – a Lord Peter Wimsey mystery, *Busman's Honeymoon*.

One might expect that the development of a community spirit – and the conscription of large numbers of criminals – would result in a fall in the crime rate. But war conditions created their own opportunities for crime. Bombing raids left shops and homes open to the elements, and looting was more of a problem than the authorities were prepared to admit. Black market activity was a thorn in the side of the government from the beginning of the war. The Ministry of Information encouraged popular comedians like George Formby, Will Hay, and Elsie and Doris Waters to appear in films where they exposed black marketeers just as they had triumphed over saboteurs and fifth columnists. The problem was kept within bounds during the early years of the war when there was strong moral condemnation of those who seemed to be undermining the war effort, though the fines imposed by magistrates (themselves often traders and shopkeepers) on traders and shopkeepers found guilty of black market dealing were often derisory, and the market towns around London – Chelmsford, Braintree, Watford, Maidstone and especially Romford – attracted hordes of London dealers who would exchange their gowns, cloth, and manufactured goods for agricultural produce with no regard whatever for the rationing system.

With the end of the war the situation worsened. The dire economic situation made austerity inevitable, but it seemed an unfair price to pay for victory. The Labour government did at least ensure that the burden was not borne entirely by the poor and underprivileged. Currency restrictions prevented the rich from running off to their traditional holiday haunts, and *The Times* mournfully recorded the disgrace of Lady Daphne Crommelin Russell (daughter of the Duke of Bedford), Mrs Mathilde Collins (of Regent's Park), John A. Sleight (Chairman of the United Hunts Club) and a variety of company directors, factory owners, debutantes and distinguished ex-servicemen, all found guilty of currency offences, often in collusion with the unsavoury international racketeer Black Max Intrator.[8]

Even the government was tainted with corruption. In the dying months of 1948 the headlines were filled with the proceedings of the Lynskey Tribunal set up to investigate the connection between two junior ministers – John Belcher and George Gibson – and Sidney Stanley (alias Sid Wulkan alias Solomon Kohhsyzcky), self-confessed king of the contact men, 'those tactful guides through that no-mans-land where the new world of the planned society met the old world of big – and sometimes curiously ill-defined – business: where the England that queued met the England that did not queue.'[9] Sidney Stanley and Black Max Intrator were the most illustrious members of what seemed to be a new category of criminal: the spiv.

> A spiv, it was agreed, was a relentless opportunist who earned his living by not working, preferably within the law. In fact they were not averse to a touch of crime, provided it looked (and perhaps felt) like something else, just as they didn't mind driving lorries as long as their clothing vividly proclaimed that they weren't lorry-drivers. They never planned their opportunities, as criminals did; they merely took them, snatched and improvised, inventing as they went along.[10]

David Hughes, writing in the 60s when crime was once again coming into fashion, relentlessly romanticises the spivs, seeing in them rather than in the bureaucratic Labour government the authentic voice of the working class. 'The spivs, flashily displaying all the suppressed energies of the back streets, were an unconscious dramatic protest, a form of civil disobedience that millions of English people found endearing.'[11]

In fact, contemporary attitudes were much more ambivalent. The thrill of obtaining illicit goods had to be balanced against the constant need to 'keep in' with all the right people. According to journalist Arthur Helliwell, by 1947 Britain had become 'the land of the well-greased palm. We've developed into a nation of bribers. Everyone is on the game, from the big shot who buys the motor dealer's wife a fur coat and gets delivery of a new car in a week, to the housewife who slips the fishmonger a packet of cigarettes after the queue has gone.'[12] Undoubtedly, though, the flashily dressed spivs who serviced the black market did capture the public imagination. Helliwell became Britain's best read columnist when he began charting the activities of Pop-up Ted, Wicked Bill, Playful Pluto, Ben the Bandit and Long-Nosed Jerry, habitués of the sleazy cafés of

Notting Hill and the Elephant and Castle. There was nothing particularly new about Helliwell's spivs: similar characters could have been found in low-life novels and criminal autobiographies of the 30s. The spiv was merely the dress-conscious wide boy strolling lazily into the limelight. As such, he was not always harmless and lovable. Most of Helliwell's information was colourful gossip which flattered the vanity of the spivs and didn't interfere with business. Serious newspaper investigation could be dangerous – to both sides. In March 1947 press attention was drawn to the Messina brothers, a well-established gang of pimps and racketeers. Helliwell's colleague Duncan Webb kept on their trail for the next three years, and in September 1950 began a series of exposés which forced the police to act. He was threatened and attacked several times.[13]

Towards the end of the war the cinema began to revive its interest in the underworld. Sidney Gilliat's *Waterloo Road* (1945), like other wartime realist films, features a cosy working-class family, with Beatrice Varley the kindly, worn-out mother, George Carney the pigeon-fancying father, and John Mills the soldier son. However, there is a fly in the ointment – Ted Purvis, who runs the local pin-ball saloon. Purvis is flashily handsome with brilliantined hair, a sharp suit and a spotted bow-tie. He is cruel, vicious and thoroughly unscrupulous but, as played by Stewart Granger, the dashing hero of *The Man in Grey, Fanny by Gaslight* and *Madonna of the Seven Moons,* he is a very real temptation to Mills' young wife, confined to a drab existence with her bickering in-laws. The reviewers call him 'the local pin-table king', 'an amorous artful dodger', 'a handsome small-time racketeer'. Though the term had not yet come into general circulation, he is the screen's first fully-fledged spiv.

Granger's performance could hardly escape notice, but the seeds sown by Ted Purvis were slow to germinate. It was over a year before another spiv movie appeared: John Harlow's low-budget quickie *Appointment With Crime.* Gritty and fast-moving, it attracted general critical approval and there were generous comparisons between William Hartnell's thin-lipped, hard-boiled hero and James Cagney.

Both *Waterloo Road* and *Appointment With Crime* seemed to exemplify what was best in British cinema – the ability to make films cheaply which unravelled powerfully dramatic plots within a recognisably authentic world. But concern over the glamorising of crime and the reluctance of many critics to accept films regarded as sordid and violent meant that many of the subsequent spiv movies were received with hostility. The arrival of nine spiv movies within fourteen months – *Dancing With Crime* (June 1947), *They Made Me a Fugitive* and *Black Memory* (July 1947), *It Always Rains on Sunday*

293

Spivs: Stewart Granger, with Joy Shelton, in *Waterloo Road* (1945)

(November 1947), *Brighton Rock* (December 1947), *Night Beat* (February 1948), *Good Time Girl* (May 1948), *A Gunman Has Escaped* (June 1948) and *Noose* (August 1948) – seems to have reduced some critics to hysteria. For Arthur Vesselo,

> *They Made Me a Fugitive* might have come straight out of a German studio of the 'twenties. Half-a-dozen other recent British films, superficially perhaps not quite so obviously in this class, have nevertheless an unpleasant undertone, a parade of frustrated violence, an inversion and disordering of moral values, a groping into the grimier recesses of the mind, which are unhealthy symptoms of the same kind of illness.[14]

Vesselo associated *They Made Me a Fugitive* with the 'morbid burrowings' of a cluster of gloomy melodramas that had appeared in the first half of 1947. Fred Majdalany in the *Daily Mail* was more specific:

> I deplore the picturesque legend that is being created round that petty criminal fashionably known as the spiv. The spiv as stylised by the writers and caricatured by the actors seems to be a mixture

of delightful Cockney comedian and pathetic victim of social conditions. For myself, I find the activities of sewer rats – in or out of a sewer – of strictly limited interest.[15]

The *News of the World* critic, before the end of the same film, 'sought escape into the sunshine, desperately longing to encounter again the simple sentimentalities of *The Courtneys of Curzon Street*'; the *Sunday Dispatch* critic claimed to have vomited at the sight of *Good Time Girl*. It is difficult to disentangle irredeemable inanity from justified complaints about social irresponsibility. Richard Winnington thought that the possibility of a relevant and progressive cinema was being sacrificed to the interests of crass commercialism. Answering a reader's letter asking 'why films cannot be made that depict ordinary men and women enjoying and enduring the normal ups and downs of life', he argued that 'to do just that by using every known development and thrusting about for new forms in which to dress the familial and the universal is the main purpose of the cinema. It

Spivs: William Hartnell and friends in *Appointment With Crime* (1946)

requires a concentration of imagination and courage'. This was felt to be singularly lacking in an industry where 'outside the six or so leading virtuosi and the languishing documentary concerns, hacks and adventurers hold sway over unhappy writers among whom there is to be felt the lack of a primary vocational urge towards the cinema.'[16] This laudable commitment of the film critics to ordinary people, to 'the England that queued', has to be balanced against a narrow prurience more intolerant even than that of the BBFC. While the latter were prepared to regard a tidied-up version of James Hadley Chase's best-seller *No Orchids for Miss Blandish* as 'no worse than other gangster films', critical outrage at what they considered 'nauseating muck' and a 'wicked disgrace to the British film industry' led to the film being banned by local authorities in many parts of the country.

The scenario for *They Made Me a Fugitive* passed through the hands of Colonel A. Fleetwood Wilson, one of the new recruits at the BBFC.[17] He thought it unpleasant but could see no grounds on which he could turn it down. Jackson Budd's novel *A Convict has Escaped* (1941), on which the film is based, concerns the attempt by a young South African serviceman, on the run from Dartmoor, to piece together the details of a crime he can only dimly remember but of which he is convinced he is innocent. With the help of a young prostitute and a sympathetic Scotland Yard detective, he succeeds in clearing his name. Cavalcanti and scriptwriter Noel Langley retain only the central premise of a convict on the run for a crime he did not commit, and a sequence where a middle-class lady attempts to make a devil's pact with the desperate convict to do away with her drunken husband. The hero becomes Clem Morgan (Trevor Howard), a drunken ex-RAF officer who misses the excitement of war and is persuaded to join a black market gang run by a loud, friendly super-spiv Narcissus (Griffith Jones). They operate from the Valhalla funeral parlour, dispatching and receiving coffins laden with ciga-rettes, whisky, nylons and – to Clem's alarm – drugs. Distrustful of this 'amateur', Narcy successfully frames him and steals his girl. Sentenced to fifteen years in Dartmoor, Clem is goaded by Narcy's rejected girl-friend (Sally Gray) into escaping. In a melodramatic shoot-out in the funeral parlour, Clem manages to kill Narcy, who with his dying words swears to the police that Clem is guilty of the crime for which he has been framed.

The novelty of casting the villain in the contemporary guise of a spiv seems to have triggered off wholly inappropriate reactions from the critics. The metamorphosis of Griffith Jones from a foppish juvenile lead in pictures like *The Four Just Men* and *The Wicked Lady* into a character whose handsome, jovial exterior conceals a soul as

'An inversion and disordering of moral values': *They Made Me a Fugitive* (1947), with Trevor Howard and Sally Gray

black as soot is indeed striking, but the film can no more be accused of treating him sympathetically than any other melodrama where a larger than life villain overshadows the other characters. Made for Nat Bransten's Alliance Company – the offspring of a short-lived alliance between RKO and the Rank Organisation – at the small Riverside studio at Hammersmith, *They Made Me a Fugitive* successfully combines the urgency and atmosphere of a Warner Brothers 'off the front page and on to the screen' drama with the black humour and quirky characterisation of Hitchcock's 30s thrillers.

Dancing With Crime, also from Alliance, was a less prestigious affair, though John Paddy Carstairs directs young hopefuls Richard Attenborough and Sheila Sim with aplomb, and Brock Williams turns his hand to the seedily glamorous world of the Palais de Danse with as much proficiency as he had to the murder of Sir Charles Merton. *Black Memory*, scripted by John Gilling and directed by Oswald Mitchell, begins with a prologue wherein a mob attack a shop and, in a murky alley, a dimly glimpsed assailant beats up the pawnbroker who owns it. Danny Cruff's father is hanged for the murder, and when his mother expires with grief Danny is sent to an approved school. A number of years later he returns to the area, an upright young man though haunted by the 'black memory' of his father's crime. He meets Johnnie (Michael Medwin), a school-fellow who used to bully and torment him. Johnnie, now a sneeringly vicious spiv, attempts to coerce Danny into helping with a warehouse robbery. Helped or hindered by other members of the small, tight-knit working-class community, Danny manages to bring about the downfall of his tormentor and at the same time to clear his father's name. Made on a shoestring budget at the tiny Bushey studio, the film makes the most of Gilling's spirited dialogue, and Medwin gives the definitive rendering of the low-ranking spiv with his pushed back trilby, double-breasted suit, dark shirt, spotted tie and big ideas.

Low-budget, unpretentious, and solidly on the side of law and order, *Dancing With Crime* and *Black Memory* failed to arouse critical ire. *It Always Rains on Sunday,* made at Ealing, the studio best favoured by the critics, and directed by promising young director Robert Hamer from a popular novel by Arthur La Bern, presented a more difficult problem. Ostensibly it seemed to carry out Richard Winnington's wish of looking at the ups and downs in the lives of ordinary people. But as a realistic display of East End life in 1947, the film diligently depicts a whole range of spivs. There are the Hyams brothers: Morry (Sydney Tafler), music shopkeeper, bandleader and inveterate womaniser, and his brother Lou (John Slater), a classic East End Jewish wide boy with smart suit, fixed smile and a string of tempting offers to pretty young women prepared to play the game. On a lower level there are the three smalltime crooks (John Carol, Jimmy Hanley, Alfie Bass), desperately trying to rid themselves of a lorry-load of ill-gotten roller-skates. Finally, there is Tommy Swann (John McCallum), the convict on the run around whom the narrative revolves. Wet, dirty and violent, he is shown in flashback to have been as smooth and as smart as Lou Hyams.

This accumulation of spivvery provoked Caroline Lejeune, doyenne of British film critics, into an attack on the 'adulation of the spiv' as the cult of an 'unfit and mannered minority' who were 'sadly misinterpreting the temper of the people'.[18] But it was Lejeune who was in the minority. *It Always Rains on Sunday* was one of the most successful films of the year and many critics broke ranks to support it. Vesselo argued that to object to a picture of Bethnal Green because it included aspects of low life was taking the argument too far, and Dilys Powell was won over by 'an amused, a devoted attention to the tiny decorations of the everyday, to the chattering neighbour, the darts game and the black cat brushed with an exasperated gesture off the sofa-head. These trifles mark the difference between the studio set and the room lived in.'[19]

Like Curtis in the 30s, La Bern was discovered simultaneously by two studios. While Ealing was filming *It Always Rains on Sunday*, Gainsborough prepared *Good Time Girl* based on La Bern's novel *Night Darkens the Street*. It ran into censorship problems and was not released until May 1948, thus catching the backwash of the *No Orchids* affair. Its range of spivs was more extensive even than that of *It Always Rains on Sunday*: Jimmy Rosso, Peter Glenville's snivelling, vulgar, Latin waiter; Maxie (Herbert Lom), the night-club owner 'with a connoisseur's intolerance for clumsy sinning'; race-track gang leader Danny Martin (Griffith Jones again); and two violent American deserters played by Bonar Colleano and Hugh McDermott. As the title indicates, though, the main focus of attention is the female equivalent of the spiv, the good-time girl, a species which with their 'bleached or brassy hair, greasy scarlet mouths done up from corner to corner, no eyebrows to speak of, painted nails, blue shadows on their eyelids . . .'[20] seemed to threaten the moral fibre of the nation.

A year or so earlier, Jack Lee's dramatised documentary *Children on Trial* had attempted to examine seriously the problems of juvenile delinquency. La Bern's novel is both more sensational and more hard-hitting. Lee shows the probation service and approved school system as kindly, caring, and considerate of the individual problems of the teenagers who have 'gone off the rails'. In *Night Darkens the Street*, La Bern's heroine, Gwen Rawlings, is convicted of an offence she is innocent of by a priggishly unsympathetic court; her probation officer is an incompetent hypocrite; and the approved school to which she is sentenced is run by a sadist with a staff of leering bullies.

In *Good Time Girl*, the principal of the approved school is well-intentioned but, with her limited resources, unable to prevent bullying and petty tyranny; and the story is narrated by a sympathetic magistrate (Flora Robson) – albeit the one who finds Gwen guilty of a crime she did not commit – as a warning to the potentially wanton Diana Dors. Predictably, there were accusations that the film celebrated the good-time life which ostensibly it condemned.

Some critics expressed similar disapproval of *Brighton Rock*. Richard Winnington saw the film as merely 'a child's guide' to the metaphysical subtleties of the book, and Reg Whitley in the *Daily Mirror* indignantly complained that the novel's religious symbolism had been replaced by 'false, cheap, nasty sensationalism'. As with *It Always Rains on Sunday*, though, the film's realism won it some support. To Margaret Lane in the *Evening Standard*:

> The people may be sordid, but they are real. Their mouths go dry, their pulses beat like ours. The bed creaks, the pillows are dirty in their naked ticking, the mobster's girl gets up with hair unbrushed

and last night's make-up cracking on her face. Oh yes, it is all terribly sordid, but it is so true that one begins to feel a kind of elation, and the elation lasts to the very end of the picture, and in the final moment is unexpectedly shot through with pity and tenderness. One comes away both sobered and exalted as from a tragedy.[21]

The Boultings made clever use of their Brighton locations, and, for the first half of the film at least, Attenborough's seventeen-year-old gangster is genuinely frightening. But the atmospheric realism of the film subtly undermines Greene's symbolism. We see too much of the world outside Pinky's head to get involved in his metaphysical torments. The film succeeds almost in spite of its ambitions towards profundity.

While *They Made Me a Fugitive* and the first wave of spiv movies were drawing the fire of the critics, Richard Llewellyn's play *Noose* was attracting big audiences to the Saville Theatre. In 1937, two years before he found fame and fortune with *How Green Was My Valley*, Llewellyn had submitted a story to the BBFC called *Murder in Soho*. It centred on the activities of 'Knucks' Luciani, a Soho gangster who draws his profits from forgery, smash and grab raids, drug trafficking and prostitution. The heroine, Dora, a freelance prostitute sick of being intimidated, enlists the help of 'Squeaks' Hoyle, an ex-heavyweight boxer. 'Squeaks' persuades the shop-keepers and restaurateurs of Soho to pay him £5,000 if he can rid them of Luciani. This he manages to do by recruiting a team of bruisers who are bigger and stronger than the gangsters and thus able to batter them into submission. Unsurprisingly the BBFC in 1937 found this 'quite prohibitive',[22] but the rise of the black market in the 40s made a more acceptable facet of the underworld available. Prostitution and drug trafficking could be toned down in favour of unprohibited subjects like smuggling and warehouse theft. When Llewellyn's play was submitted in 1947, the censors made only minor objections to 'vulgarity', 'brutal fighting' and 'women in their undies'.

Despite the stylish direction of Edmund T. Greville, *Noose* hangs together poorly as a film. 'Squeaks' has become Captain Jumbo Hoyle (Derek Farr), a Bulldog Drummond-like ex-commando prone to remarks such as 'it's a bit galling to have to spend six years of your life clearing out a couple of stinkers over there and then to come back and find one in your own back yard.' The other three major characters carry more interesting connotations. Luciani (now Sugiani) was played on stage by Charles Goldner, a specialist in oily but generally benevolent Italian roles. For the film he was replaced by the infinitely more menacing Maltese-born Hollywood actor,

Brighton Rock (1947): Richard Attenborough (right) as Pinky

Joseph Calleia. With his heavy-jowelled moodiness, his big black fedora and his violent relations with women, Sugiani began to look very much like real-life vice-king Eugene Messina. The heroine Linda Medbury (Carole Landis, who had committed suicide by the time the film was released) is upgraded from whore to fashion correspondent, brought over from America to write about Dior's New Look. The New Look became a major issue in the spring and summer of 1948, with opponents appealing to the President of the Board to regulate the length of skirts to prevent wastage of material. *Noose* has it both ways. Landis/Medbury is impatient of fashion writing when women are being exploited by pimps and black marketeers, but throughout her battle with the mobsters she totters round on high heels, all flounces, peplums, hobble skirts and absurd little hats.

Landis' fashion-conscious investigator is complemented by Nigel Patrick's charismatic spiv, Bar Gorman. Gorman is at the opposite pole to Griffith Jones' Narcy – a spiv with a heart of gold, always ready with a flashy smile and a pound of black-market tea for the flower-seller or the seamstress. With pencil-thin moustache, carnation and camel-hair coat he is elegant rather than flashy and even manages to be stylish in his threats. 'You're a smashing looker, ducks,' he tells the interfering Medbury. 'You've got these and those, all in the right place. But there's a big difference between now and then. They might – slip a bit.' As Sugiani's front man he combines the non-stop patter of a street-market salesman with the power and patronage of a benevolent Godfather.

With the exception of Richard Widmark's Harry Fabian in *Night and the City* and Welles' international racketeer Harry Lime in *The Third Man*, Bar Gorman is the last of the original and significant spivs. Ironically, Patrick eventually crossed over to play a police inspector in Basil Dearden's *Sapphire*. Dearden was Ealing's most ostentatious director. His earlier achievements included the Hearse Driver episode in *Dead of Night*, the morbidly intense *Frieda*, and Ealing's one venture into Technicolor costume drama, *Saraband for Dead Lovers*. In 1950 he directed *Cage of Gold* which, with its ex-RAF officer villain, lies on the peripheries of the spiv cycle; in 1952, *The Square Ring*, a compendium of boxing stories scripted by Robert Westerby; and in 1955 *The Ship That Died of Shame*, where ex-officers seek to recapture wartime thrills by turning to smuggling. His main contribution to the spiv cycle, though, was the anti-spiv movie *The Blue Lamp*.

The Blue Lamp was the top box-office film of 1950, and the character of George Dixon, the elderly, kindly copper who falls victim to Dirk Bogarde's cowardly young thug, was revived as the star of the television series *Dixon of Dock Green*, which was to run for twenty-five years. Shifting attention from the spiv to the policeman, the film was welcomed by the critics as a return to social responsibility, and 'an overdue apology for that flat-footed squad of "What's all this 'ere?" semi-comic policemen who have plodded through so many British films.'[23] In fact the idea of sympathetically depicting the life of the ordinary policeman had been attempted two years earlier in the worst of the spiv movies, *Night Beat*, which tells the story of two ex-commandos, Andy (Ronald Howard) and Don (Hector Ross). At a loss for what to do once they have been demobilised, they join the police. Andy falls among spivs and good-time girls, and before long is implicated in murder; Don is quickly recruited by Scotland Yard. The life of the ordinary policeman comes across as cold, wet and dull, which is not what the young recruits have been led to expect. Andy's father, a country copper for fifty years, had presented a more idyllic picture: 'I never had much money but there's not many as I'd change my lot with. I've three villages in my section. I've me marrows and me roses and 4,000 folk big and small, to count as friends. That may sound soft to you youngsters, but on that score I reckon myself a rich man.' It is a resonant image, which *The Blue Lamp*, with its star-gazing, choir-

Racketeers: *Noose* (1948)

singing policemen, audaciously transfers from country village to inner-city working-class community. As Charles Barr points out, Mitchell (Jimmy Hanley), the new recruit, is absorbed into a family and the whole premise of the film 'rests on a daydream of universal benevolence'.[24]

The Blue Lamp can be seen as doing for the police what *The Way Ahead* did for the army, *The Way to the Stars* for the RAF. But the image of a benevolent police force would not have been acceptable to a mass audience twenty years earlier. To the middle classes the policeman was a social inferior whose usefulness in preventing burglaries had to be balanced against his nuisance value with regard to motoring offences. Among working-class people the police were generally regarded with suspicion, in the rougher areas with fear and derision.

It was the black market and the changing pattern of crime that allowed a change of image. At its height between 1946 and 1948, the black market touched most people in one way or another, and for those few who were tempted permanently into the orbit of crime there were millions more who shrank back from this contact with the underworld. The knowledge that society wasn't as safe and ordered as it seemed made people receptive to the idea of the police as a reassuring, protective force, keeping the unruly elements firmly but tolerantly under control. In such a world the role of the spiv had to change. Actors like Michael Medwin and Alfie Bass in the television series *The Army Game*, and George Cole in Launder and Gilliat's St. Trinian's films, developed the spiv into a comic figure – a cheeky, flashy, lovable rogue. By the time of *The Blue Lamp* the vicious young hoodlums depicted by Medwin in *Black Memory* and by Attenborough in *Brighton Rock* have been identified as something different from the spiv: a 'youth problem'. The spiv-like denizens of race-track and billiard parlour have reverted to their proper place as underworld professionals, contemptuous of the amateur who is stupid enough to upset the status quo by killing a copper.

The spiv cycle faded with the 40s, but British low-life films continued unchecked. The new 'X' certificate made it possible to film those Soho melodramas which had proved unacceptable in the 30s, and a host of Hollywood policemen, gangsters and private dicks became embroiled in the British underworld to further the interests of prolific 'B' movie producers like Hammer and Anglo-Amalgamated in the American market.

Comparisons between the British spiv cycle and American *film noir* are inevitable but unhelpful. The spiv films have no *femmes fatales*, atmospheric low-key lighting is incidental rather than integral, and there is little sense of the times being seriously out of joint. Even *Brighton Rock*, most doom-laden of the cycle, has a happy ending. If one is to look for British *film noir*, then a more fruitful area to explore would be the series of 'morbid' films which have in common an interest in psychology and neurosis – films such as *Wanted for Murder* (1946, Lawrence Huntington), *Daybreak* (1946, Compton Bennett), *The Shop at Sly Corner* (1947, George King), *The Upturned Glass* (1947, Huntington), *Dual Alibi* (1947, Alfred Travers), *Temptation Harbour* (1947, Lance Comfort), *Frieda* (1947, Basil Dearden), *Mine Own Executioner* (1947, Anthony Kimmins), *Obsession* (1949, Edward Dmytryk), and *For Them That Trespass* (1948, Alberto Cavalcanti); and, alongside these, the 'man on the run' films with their haunted, fugitive heroes – *Odd Man Out* (1946, Carol Reed), *Take My Life* (1947, Ronald Neame), *The October Man* (1947, Roy Baker), *My Brother's Keeper* (1948, Alfred Roome), and *Man on the Run* itself (1949, Huntington). But that is another story.

Notes

1   British Board of Film Censors, Scenario Reports 1933, p. 125.
2   Ibid., p. 131.
3   Jeffrey Richards, *The Age of the Dream Palace*, London, Routledge & Kegan Paul, 1982, p. 114. Richards' exploration of the BBFC scenario reports is useful and revealing.
4   BBFC Scenario Reports 1932, p. 94.
5   George Orwell, 'Raffles and Miss Blandish' (1944) in *Collected Essays, Journalism and Letters*, London, Secker & Warburg, 1968, vol. 3, pp. 212–24.
6   *Motion Picture Herald*, 28 January 1939.
7   James Curtis, *There Ain't No Justice*, London, Jonathan Cape, 1937 p. 50.
8   *The Times*, issues of 1 June 1947, 10 June 1947, 3 December 1947.
9   Harry Hopkins, *The New Look*, London, Secker & Warburg, 1963, p. 101.
10 David Hughes, 'The Spivs' in Michael Sissons and Philip French (eds.), *Age of Austerity*, Harmondsworth, Penguin, 1963, p. 87.
11 Ibid., p. 105.
12 *The People*, 9 March 1947.
13 Geoff Dench, *Maltese in London*, London, Routledge & Kegan Paul, 1975, pp. 68 70.
14 *Sight and Sound*, vol. 16, no. 63, Autumn 1947.
15 *Daily Mail*, 27 June 1947.
16 *News Chronicle*, 17 January 1948.
17 BBFC Scenario Reports 1944, p. 88a.
18 *Observer*, 20 November 1947.
19 *Sunday Times*, 20 November 1947.
20 Ethel Mannin, *The People*, 16 March 1947.
21 *Evening Standard*, 9 January 1948.
22 BBFC Scenario Reports 1937, p. 23a.
23 *Star*, 20 January 1950
24 Charles Barr, *Ealing Studios*, London, Cameron and Tayleur/David and Charles, 1977, p. 83.

THE FILM SOCIETY, 1925-1939

Jen Samson

Historical research on the cinema tends to privilege film production, with the result that other practices within the institution of cinema, notably distribution and exhibition, find themselves relegated to back-row seats. A detailed history of the Film Society is absent from publications on British cinema which, at most, mention it only in passing.

The seminal and pioneering work of the Film Society gave rise to a specific structure of independent film exhibition in Britain and formed the basis of what we now call the independent cinema circuit. The new and controversial foreign films which the Film Society imported into Britain during the late 1920s and throughout the 1930s not only increased esteem for the medium among the intelligentsia, but also had an effect on the development of British film production. In addition, it initiated the rapid growth of the film society movement nationally.

The creation of a minority film culture in Britain owes much to Ivor Montagu. Early in 1925, Montagu, on his way back from Berlin where he had been sent by *The Times* to write on the German film industry, met the actor Hugh Miller, who had been making a film in Germany. Between them they decided to try to set up a film society in London to exhibit foreign films hitherto unavailable in Britain. Their idea was based on the Stage Society, founded in 1899, which promoted unseen works by playwrights such as Shaw, Ibsen, Strindberg, Cocteau and Pirandello. These plays, either for reasons of censorship or because they were thought to be uncommercial, had no other way of being performed. The Stage Society organised performances on Sundays, for a private audience, when commercial theatres were closed. More often than not, these were single performances.

A party at Iris Barry's home was to provide the ideal opportunity for Montagu and Miller's idea to come to fruition. Iris Barry, who was at this time film critic of the political weekly the *Spectator*, invited the following: Ivor Montagu; Hugh Miller; Adrian Brunel, film director at Gainsborough Pictures; Walter Mycroft, film critic of the *Evening Standard*; Frank Dobson, sculptor; and Sidney

Bernstein, film exhibitor (later to become Chairman of Granada Television). Twenty-one-year-old Montagu became Chairman of this group, which constituted the Film Society's first Council. Miss J. M. Harvey (recommended to the Society by Hugh Miller), was the secretary and organisational linchpin until 1935. Miss Harvey's own business – 'Concert Direction and Representative for Dramatic Artists' – enabled her office at 56 Manchester Street, Marylebone, to become the official Film Society address. The name originally chosen by the Council was, significantly, 'Independent Film Theatre Ltd', but this name was unavailable because at the time Independent Films Ltd was a cinema proprietor.

In 1972, the Arno Press published an 'unauthorised' set of Film Society programmes. This volume refers to the Society as the London Film Society – a name it never had. It was, after all, *the* Film Society. Nothing like it had existed in Britain before. Paris had Le Vieux Colombier, which exhibited art films and avant-garde works not distributed in the rest of the country. Now London had the Film Society.

At 2.30 p.m. on Sunday 25 October 1925, at the New Gallery Kinema in Regent Street, the first Film Society screenings took place, with 1,400 people in attendance. Lord Ashfield, who had connections at the New Gallery, knew Ivor Montagu's father, Lord Swaythling, and this acquaintance secured the use of the cinema free of charge for Film Society screenings. The arrangement is indicative of the informal way in which the Society operated throughout its existence. As a non-profit-making limited company, the Council had to rely on its members' travels abroad to borrow prints for the shows. Independent film-makers such as Len Lye, whose film *Tusalava* was first shown at the Film Society, and Lotte Reiniger, specialist in 'silhouette' films, became friends of individual Council members. Innumerable letters were written making requests, and international arrangements, to obtain films 'which were in some degree interesting and which represent the work which has been done, or is being done experimentally in various parts of the world. It is in the nature of such films that they are (it is said) commercially unsuitable for this country; and that is why they become the especial province of the Film Society.' Money was only ever spent on the preparation and English titling of borrowed copies, on musical scores, on full orchestras, and on payment of any duty imposed by Customs.

The first programme serves as a convenient example to illustrate the way in which selections were made by the Council. (In what follows, dates attached to film titles refer to the completion date of the film, not to its Film Society screening.) First to be screened were Walter Ruttmann's experimental *Absolute Films, Opera 2, 3 and 4*

(1923–5), which were described as 'studies in pattern with drum accompaniment'. Second was a 1912 Essanay Western, *How Bronchu Billy Left Bear Country*, starring G. M. Anderson, the first cowboy star. Third was Adrian Brunel's short pastiche film *Typical Budget*, made at Gainsborough in 1925 but still not released or even trade-shown. Top of the bill was Paul Leni's German expressionist film *Waxworks* (1924), the merit of which was said to be 'architectural' rather than 'dramatic'. Finally, a 1916 Chaplin film, *Champion Charlie*, was shown, all Council members evidently being keen Chaplin fans.

As this suggests, programming was a matter of finding a mix of experimental or avant-garde works, revivals of old favourites no longer to be seen elsewhere, and new films from abroad that had no other means of distribution in Britain. Films were chosen not on a basis of profitability or audience potential, but because the Film Society was founded 'in order that works of interest in the study of cinematography, and not yet easily accessible, might be made available to its members'.

During the fourteen years of its existence, the Film Society screened approximately 500 films from 18 different countries, mainly in two large West End cinemas in London. By November 1929 the Sunday afternoon shows had become so popular that the Society had to move its screenings from the New Gallery to a larger cinema, the Tivoli Palace in the Strand. The following six years proved the most successful, in terms of attendance figures, but by October 1935 the screenings had returned to the New Gallery, where they stayed until the war brought an end to the Society in 1939.

Over the years, experimental and avant-garde works such as Germaine Dulac's *La Coquille et le Clergyman* (1929), Viking Eggeling's *Symphonie diagonale* (1918), Alberto Cavalcanti's *Rien que les heures* (1926), Walter Ruttmann's *Berlin* (1927), and Man Ray's *Emak Bakia* (1926) played alongside early American silents (Mack Sennett, Charlie Chaplin, Buster Keaton, D. W. Griffith, Mary Pickford) and Walt Disney cartoons. Non-feature British films like John Betts' *Sport and Interest in a Fresh Light* (1926), the pioneering science films made by British Instructional and New Era in the *Secrets of Nature* series (1922–33), and Adrian Brunel's burlesques, played with European, American, Japanese and Soviet features that are now regarded as classics of world cinema – films such as Jean Renoir's *Nana* (1926), Ernst Lubitsch's *The Marriage Circle* (1924), John Ford's *The Informer* (1935), Carl Dreyer's *La Passion de Jeanne d'Arc* (1928), Jean Vigo's *Zéro de conduite* (1933) and *L'Atalante* (1934), Fritz Lang's *Dr Mabuse, the Gambler* (1922) and *Testament of Dr Mabuse* (1933), Alfred Hitchcock's *The Lodger*

Kinugasa's *Crossways* (1929), shown at the Film Society and the first Japanese film to be seen in Europe

(1926), Joris Ivens' *The Bridge* (1928), *Rain* (1929) and *Philips Radio* (1931), Teinosuke Kinugasa's *Crossways* (1929), the first Japanese film to be seen in Europe), Erich von Stroheim's *Greed* (1923), and G. W. Pabst's *The Joyless Street* (1925), with Garbo in her first major role.

The Pabst film prompted the following letter from an indignant member in January 1927:

Dear Sirs, Yesterday morning I had an interview with Miss Harvey and gave her very clearly to understand the surprise and dismay with which I had witnessed the performance on Sunday. To have assured one's friends that the Society was out to improve the tone of film performances and then to take a niece for the first time to prove my assertions not unnaturally prompted the query whether I subscribed to the Society in order to see such films as *The Joyless Street*. Is it possible that the Council take their own women folk to such a performance?

The extent to which the Society was providing an entirely new and alternative kind of programming was apparent to all. The hostility expressed by some of its own members was less threatening, though, than the hostility the Society received from both the trade and the censors. In its founding stages, influential names were sought by the Council to ensure respectability and acceptance: George Pearson (film producer), Julian Huxley (biologist), J. B. S. Haldane (biochemist), Lord Swaythling, H. G. Wells and George Bernard Shaw were all registered as original subscribers. Members of the Society from the film world and elsewhere also included the Hon. Anthony Asquith, Lord David Cecil, Roger Fry, J. Maynard Keynes, Dame Ellen Terry, Ben Webster, Michael Balcon, John Gielgud, Ivor Novello, and Victor Saville. Undoubtedly, such names helped to secure a future for the Film Society. An understanding that Society screenings would escape the censor if held on Sundays proved, however, to be wrong. Whereas plays performed at the Stage Society, to a private audience on Sundays, did not have to be submitted to the Lord Chamberlain for approval, the cinema did not escape the censor in quite the same way. A law introduced in 1909 to protect audiences against fire resulted in every cinema performance having to be issued with a licence by a County Council, in this case the London County Council. Although a licence was granted to the Film Society to show uncensored films under club conditions on Sundays, it was not issued without a battle, and one that periodically had to be refought.

The trade's reaction to the Film Society was one of caution and mistrust. Society screenings were seen by the trade both as a commercial threat and as an implied criticism of their own work. Adrian Brunel's employers even insisted that he resign from the Council for fear that his association with the Society would damage the reputation of the films he made for Gainsborough. The trade also found it impossible to understand why anyone would want to show *only* films that distributors were not interested in buying themselves. The same attitude was to be found in the Soviet Union when Montagu was there in 1926 on a zoological expedition. In vain he tried to persuade the studios to lend him prints of the new films by Pudovkin and Eisenstein; not until 1928–9 did he succeed in obtaining prints for the Society of Pudovkin's *Mother* (1926) and *The End of St Petersburg* (1927).

Some of the press reacted to the screenings with claims that the Society had been formed to 'communise the country'. Legal battles ensued, and press hostility continued throughout the 1930s. Among the first ever screenings of Soviet films in Britain were: Eisenstein's *Battleship Potemkin* (1925), Vertov's *Man With a Movie Camera* (1928) and *Enthusiasm* (1931), Ilya Trauberg's *The Blue Express* (1929), Kozintsev and Leonid Trauberg's *New Babylon* (1929),

Kuleshov's *The Great Consoler* (1933), Raizman's *The Last Night* (1937) and Legoshin's *Lone White Sail* (1938).

Explorations of different kinds of programming resulted in events such as the one on 16 March 1930 devoted solely to women directors. It included films by Mary Field, Lotte Reiniger, Dinah Shurey, Dorothy Arzner, Germaine Dulac, and Olga Preobrazhenskaya. On 28 October 1934 a programme was compiled to show four different kinds of non-commercial films: a Hector Hoppin and Anthony Gross experimental animation film, *Joie de vivre* (1934); a fictional short film by Ernst Angel, *Der zerbrochene Krug* (1934); a GPO Film Unit experiment in sound, the documentary *Weather Forecast* (1934); and a full-length educational documentary, *Deutschland zwischen gestern und heute* (1934). Technical innovations in sound and colour were studied, and at least two 'study groups' were set up which involved members' participation. The first, led by Eisenstein when he was in London in 1929, consisted of six two-hour lectures on different aspects of montage. Hans Richter taught the second study group, also in 1929, when he helped members to produce an 'abstract film' called *Everyday*.

By 1929, not only had film societies started to form in other cities, but a number of groups within the Labour movement had become involved in the production, distribution and exhibition of films. These last were specifically political interventions. Ivor Montagu's letter of resignation from the Council of the Film Society in November 1929 highlights the crucial ideological differences between the original Film Society and the workers' film societies to which, in part, it gave rise. Montagu said that he had recently become vice-chairman of a Workers Film Federation, whose object was 'avowedly political', and while he was ready to help the Society 'in any matters upon which I may be consulted, it is possible that my position as Chairman, or even member, of the Council may lead to misunderstanding prejudicial to the Society's interest.'

The split between the Film Society's 'aesthetic' and 'technical' study of film as an artistic medium, and the workers' film societies' understanding of film as a productive political tool, provokes some interesting theoretical questions, although these questions are beyond the scope of this account of the Film Society's activities. While the Film Society never wanted to be directly involved in film production itself (other than to provide one opportunity for its members to make a film), it would nevertheless be misleading to suggest that it had no influence at all on film production. As we have seen, a major concern of the Society was to screen films in order that style and technique could be studied. This concern is evident in the Society's programme notes which accompanied each screening and which consistently drew attention to formal experiment. Speculatively, I would argue that the Film Society was seen by many as a training ground, a way of learning about new film techniques. In an attempt to encourage attendance by those already working in the industry, the Society organised a cut-rate annual subscription for film technicians. A range of volunteers, continuing the work originally done by Brunel and Montagu in their Dansey Yard cutting room, helped with the technical preparation of programmes, thus learning skills of titling and cutting: among those involved were Jock Orton, Ian Dalrymple, Angus Macphail, Sidney Cole, Bill Megarry and Frank Wells (son of H. G.).

Many others were to serve on the Council before 1939, some of whom were either already working in the film industry or were to become important names in British cinema: men like Thorold Dickinson, Anthony Asquith, John Grierson, and Basil Wright. The links that can be made between some of the people involved in organising the programmes, the kinds of films they screened, the film-makers themselves, and those who attended the Society's screenings, not only enable us to understand the special structure of the Film Society and the way in which choices and decisions were made, but also indicate a likely effect on British film production.

Three among many kinds of 'cross-fertilisation' can be picked out. First, that between Soviet cinema and the British documentary movement, many of whose personnel were either Council members or ordinary members of the Society (Grierson, Wright, Arthur Elton, Cavalcanti, Sidney Cole). Grierson's own film *Drifters* and Eisenstein's *Battleship Potemkin* (previously banned) had their first British showing together in a Film Society programme in November 1929, and the Society continued with regular screenings of films from both sources. Second, between Hitchcock and Montagu, and thus, whether directly or indirectly, between Hitchcock and Pudovkin, whom Montagu translated and brought over to lecture, and whom Hitchcock always cited as a key early influence. As a result of contacts through the Society, Michael Balcon asked Montagu to do some re-editing on *The Lodger* to help its chances of commercial distribution: this led to an extended collaboration with Hitchcock on films like *The Man Who Knew Too Much* (1934) and *The 39 Steps* (1935). Third, on a different level, in 1930 Iris Barry went to New York, where she was soon to set up the Film Library at the newly established Museum of Modern Art.

The programme notes for the first show had stated that 'the Society is under no illusions. It is well aware that *Caligaris* do not grow on raspberry bushes and that it cannot, in a season, expect to provide its members with an unbroken succession of masterpieces.'

Once a month, for eight months of the year, four or five films not shown elsewhere had to be located and acquired for Film Society shows. If there was a fear at the start of the venture that enough worthwhile films might not exist, by 1939 there were many other cinemas looking for similar material. The Academy Cinema in Oxford Street, for example, opened in 1931 and specialised in Soviet, German and other European art films.

In 1925 there were no film institutes, film archives or film festivals. Serious newspaper criticism of film did not exist; nor did specialised cinemas for minority audiences, film libraries, or educational attention to film. By 1939 all these things had been established. Moreover, there was now a national network of film societies and workers' film societies, which meant that to a large extent the work of the Film Society was being successfully continued by many different groups in various parts of the country. The beginning of the war necessitated, at the very least, a temporary shut-down of Film Society activities. And a decision was taken to disband the Society, with the hope that others would continue to provide alternative structured programming for minority audiences.

A note on sources

Quotations from Film Society documents are taken from the material on the Society held in the Special Collections room of the British Film Institute Library.
Further material can be found in the following books and articles:
Don Macpherson (ed.), *British Cinema: Traditions of Independence*, London, British Film Institute, 1980.
Ivor Montagu, *The Youngest Son: an Autobiography*, London, Lawrence and Wishart, 1970.
Caroline Moorehead, *Sidney Bernstein: a Biography*, London, Jonathan Cape, 1984.
Screen, vol. 13, no. 3, Autumn 1972, interview with Ivor Montagu.
Sight and Sound, vol. 44, no. 4, Autumn 1975, 'Old Man's Mumble: Reflections on a Semi-Centenary' by Ivor Montagu.
Film Dope, no. 11, interview with Thorold Dickinson.

FITZ
THE OLD MAN OF THE SCREEN
Denis Gifford

It was 1960 and I was busily compiling the list of films which would eventually become *The British Film Catalogue 1895–1970*. I had assembled a list of titles from the old company catalogues kept by the National Film Archive, and to fill in some names of the unlisted actors and film-makers of the early period I tried to contact the remaining pioneers. One, once found, usually led to another, and so it was that a chain of Hepworth relations and employees led me to the most remarkable, delightful, and certainly oldest man I have ever met: Lewin Fitzhamon.

'Fitz', as he liked to be called, and as he was known throughout the British film industry, was a once hale and still hearty old chap; once big, always bald, and now half-blind, although the great shaggy eyebrows must have been partly responsible for this. Amazingly, and unlike most other Hepworth alumni, he lived not in the depths of Surrey but upstairs at Burleigh Mansions in Charing Cross Road. Handy for me, but heartbreaking for him, for he had been born a countryman and green fields, dogs, and especially horses were the love of his life.

I visited Fitz frequently, and we became good friends, even though he tended to address me in his letters as 'Beloved pest'. For more than a year we went through his career, sometimes on tape, sometimes by correspondence. More than once I talked him into writing his autobiography, and more than once he made a start. But, of course, he grew tired, older, sicker. Then, one day, I called in to see him. He was in bed. He gave me a gummy smile, popped his eyeballs, called out 'Cup! Cup! Cup!' as he did to Tariff his horse to get it to gallop towards the camera, and died.

Fitz's film career actually began as early as 1896 when a music hall showman, François Xaintrailles, took a short scene of Fitz raising his hat outside the Middlesex Music Hall. The film was too scratchy to be shown. His first film proper was a sequence from one of his music hall sketches, *Briton vs Boer* (1900). Fitz played the Boer. It was advertised as 'Two Minutes of White Heat Excitement taking place on the Open Veldt'. In fact, it was shot on a golf course. Fitz left the theatre in 1904 to become the Stage Manager to the Hepwix Manufacturing Company of Walton-on-Thames, the family film concern run by Cecil Milton Hepworth. As a contract employee he wrote, stage-managed, directed, and acted in around two films a week for eight years. In a note on his memoirs he wrote: 'The writer of these reminiscences believes that he was the first professional producer of a film in any country.'

Here are some extracts from Fitz's unfinished manuscripts. Cecil Hepworth called his autobiography *Came the Dawn*. Fitz called his *Early Morning Mists*.

On the Stage

The writer of this started his theatrical career about 1887 at the Theatre Royal, Margate. Miss Sarah Thorne owned the theatre, and ran a dramatic school there. It was celebrated in its day; there is hardly a person alive now who remembers her name. The writer was contemporary with Arthur Bourchier and the Vanbrugh girls: inclination turned more to stage management than acting, and he became subsequently Stage Manager to Willie Edouin (of *Our Flat* fame) at the Strand Theatre, and Harris at the Adelphi, and afterwards to Messrs Conquest and Leonard at Rotherhithe, where he produced a number of Mr Leonard's melodramas.

A Literary Career

I was also an occasional contributor to a now defunct paper called *The Globe,* and the sporting *Pink 'Un*. I wrote proverbs for them, like 'It's a long lane which has no public house in it!' While doing all this I perpetrated a couple of novels, *The Rival Millionaires* and *The Vixen*, published by Ward Lock. So you see I was a busy man: if you were to search the record of the Albert Hall, you will find that a Mrs Walter Wood gave shows there, which I produced.

Meeting Mr Hepworth

I had just finished a tour with Conquest and Leonard, and had to wind up. And about this time Cecil Hepworth was making 'sketch films' or 'incidents'. In those days there were no catalogues, and Hepworth used to get his scenarios typed up by Ethel Christian Ltd. One day he was bemoaning the fact that he could not get a fellow after his own cast of mind to produce films for him. Ethel Christian said, 'Why, I know the very fellow you want!' That was how I eventually went down to Walton-on Thames. [Ethel Christian was an actress in Fitz's touring sketch company. She has billing in *The First Shot*, played at the Bedford in October 1899. She may also have been the first Mrs Fitzhamon. When 'resting' she ran a typing agency for the theatrical profession.] There was a cordial interview at the office of the Hepworth Manufacturing Company in Cecil Court, just off Charing Cross Road, where it was settled that this feller should have a shot at it.

The Studio at Walton
The game at first was to submit a scenario. If approved, you gathered your little company together and took train one fine morning (and don't you forget it, it had to be a *fine* morning!) to Walton-on-Thames. There you went through a new experience: acting without an audience, without any 'working-up process', having to keep within the focus of a cold, unsympathetic camera, and perhaps beginning in the middle of the story. You can't imagine what a ghastly business it was for an ardent actor who liked 'taking the stage' and working himself up to a rumbustious state, to be constantly reminded to 'keep in the picture', or to 'cut it short, the film's running out!' There was never any enthusiasm at Hepworth-on-Thames!

I remember that they had a set out of *Alice in Wonderland* (1903): the tea-table scene, Alice with the Mad Hatter, the White Rabbit, and the Dormouse. It seemed frightfully tame to a bloke accustomed to the action in Drama and Farce! In fact, the whole place seemed queer after the Theatre, with its scenery, flies and traps. It was just a bare set of boards in a back garden of a villa in Hurst Grove. The stage for the interior sets was in the garden of 'the works', and your first impression was that you had strayed into an undertaker's premises. Even when the sun shone it was a gloomy place, and the entire lack of enthusiasm was depressing. The villa itself housed all the cameras and implements of the coming trade. The scenery was just one interior painted a dismal grey, and the staff consisted of Cecil Hepworth himself, John and Claude Whitten the cameramen, and May Clark, the daughter of the owner of the boathouse at Walton-on-Thames. May became film cutter and cashier and actress and general utility. The front bedroom upstairs was used as drying rooms for the positives, which hung in loops from hooks on wires across the ceiling. The bathroom was the dark room and laboratory.

Fitz takes charge
It was a rum change for a fellow accustomed to crowded Music Halls, or to touring all over England, to find himself in a quiet, sleepy place like Walton, where nothing ever happened. That, however, was about to be changed, and Walton was to wake up and find itself infested with wild and woolly creatures who delved into every alley,

stopped every bus, held up the traffic with the authority of pantomime policemen, and found that crowds collected like magic! Walton became the first Film Town of England.

First the blighter who caused all the commotion had to get himself lodgings, and damned cramped and uncomfortable they were. The only thing I can remember about the sitting room is that it had a glass case of water, seaweed, shells and minnows. It was soon littered with papers, manuscripts, and props! Then I had to find a carpenter. The top back bedroom became his shop. Then I sought out a property man. Skerrett was the first. He was a retired policeman and not active enough. He was succeeded by Bob Boucher. Skerrett's first job was collecting a hamper full of feathers! He became one of our Policemen.

My days were very full. I was generally up at six. It was not long before I found the riding school and hunting stables at Weybridge. They belonged to Weekes. He had been in the Dragoon Guards, and made a fine policeman, besides being useful in any Western pictures, of which we did one or two. I do not think it was long before I acquired my cottage. It was a large cottage with stabling, a big yard and a garden, the whole surrounded by a wall. With my dogs it was a safe place for keeping our valuable props.

I had a few days roaming the country as soon as I was settled in Walton. I used to get to know the farmers, and particularly get pally with the police; Hepworth was no good at that sort of thing. I was busy in the pubs, too; you had to make pals of everyone! Having acquired the cottage, life became as interesting and exciting as in my riding and stage-managing days. Gradually 'Tariff' the horse, 'Tiger' and the other dogs were added to my establishment.

Making a Film

The stories were very simple, such as could be told by a few words thrown upon the screen. The first people I got to help me were, naturally, those who had been with me on tour, like Tom Mowbray, Fred Dark, and Dolly Lupone. We depended a good deal on local talent, for in those early days film-making was an adventure, not a business – for me, at any rate.

When I went to Hepworth's I had the field to myself. Whoever was there before me had gone. Yet there are some items in the Hepworth catalogue which ring a bell. The explanation is this. In those far-off days film was imperfect; it often broke or faded, the negative particularly. It was one of my jobs to retake a scene, perhaps improve on it. Sometimes we would put a new trick in, for the early films were mostly trick subjects. I was a man after Cecil's own heart: I should think we were the trickiest pair of tricksters that ever concocted a film.

317

'In those early days film-making was an adventure': Lewin Fitzhamon's *Father's Lesson* (1908)

Now as to the first ever ... [Fitz's first film for Hepworth is uncertain; his memory varied from time to time.] It is safe to say that the first film, if you can call 250-feet a film, was *The Ratcatcher's Daughter*. [There is no such title in the Hepworth catalogue; it was probably a working title.] Dorothy Lupone was the ratcatcher's daughter, the audience being told that the father was about to be trapped by a gamekeeper, with the help of a policeman (Fred Dark in this case). Dolly pretended to be lost, made a scene with the policeman, weeping copiously, and so distracted his attention. She clung to him, so the policeman took her back home, home being an appalling interior, more like a prison cell than anything, but it was the only one we'd got!

Mrs Sebastian Smith was the policeman's wife. I feel pretty sure of this, as this was my first meeting with her, on that primitive platform in the back garden. She gave Dolly a good supper. Supper was intercut with snaps of the poacher selling his hares and pheasants. We didn't bother about dissolves in those early days. Dolly then had to escape. She had a good pair of legs and was not averse to showing them. She climbed out of a window, apparently down a rain pipe (a pole with one or two supports), on to a tree branch, and presently rejoined her parent in their hovel – the same scene as the policeman's room, but no pictures or furniture, only straw.

A Dissolve and Day for Night

Now then, as to our second ever. This was Dorothy Lupone again, and I'll bet you the title on the Hepwix Films synopsis was the same as our christening, *Robbing the Hen Roost*. [Fitz loses his bet: again, the title is not listed.] Lupone was a young gipsy. I believe this must have been the first time I met the gipsies; we made use of a passing caravan. I got quite friendly with a lot of them, in time. Well, Dolly was a gipsy who raided a farm and stole eggs.

Now I do believe this was the first time a dissolve was attempted, from Dolly's pretty face to a nest of eggs. I can't remember whether it was successful or not. A lot of boards had to be pulled away to let in the light on the nest. I don't think it occurred to anyone to have a nest built in the open. By the way, everything was taken in broad sunlight, and stained blue for a 'night effect', like when Dolly escaped out of a window and down the tree.

When Dolly came out of the hen house with her catch, the alarm was given by an apparently ferocious dog. Attached to his kennel he leapt in the air barking, warning of the intruder. At the rehearsals, tempting morsels were thrown to the dog, some on a string, so that he leapt up to catch them. When the camera was in motion, one only had to go through the same motion. The finale was A.1. for those days. All the feathered tribe was collected into a corner, the dog was incited, a window opened. The whole collection in the corner was roused to a furious flutter, the dog barked ferociously, chickens and feathers were thrown into the melée from behind the camera. It made a good finale.

Sunday: the day of rest

Must have a pause here to recollect what we did on Sunday. I know for certain that all the morning I wrote films, or revised films sent in by the public, who received six shillings, eight shillings, or ten shillings for a plot. Besides my films I wrote *Ariadne, Daphne* and *Kyrene*, but do you think I could get Hepworth to produce them, though they are full of tricks? Too advanced, I suppose. Why on earth does someone not produce them today?

Inserting a close-up

In *What the Curate Really Did* (1905) Claude Whitten was the curate. He was just the type, with a dear, gentle face. One of the three gossipers was Mrs Sebastian Smith; another, a Miss Aitken, who had been an actress and was living in retirement at Shepperton. It was while the gossipers were round the tea-table that I suggested to Hepworth that we should take a close view of Miss Aitken: her face was alive with malicious invention! It came out a ghastly, snarling mask – some unforeseen shadow cast by scenery, I believe. We often moved up the camera afterwards, but out of doors.

Filming the Topicals

John Whitten, the cameraman, and I did a lot of topical work. A review in Hyde Park by Queen Victoria in a barouche drawn by four horses. She had an Indian servant behind her, holding a sunshade. One opening of Parliament. An Oxford and Cambridge Boat Race, but I lost John in the crowd so that I did not have much to do with the film! Several Derbies. This was a regular thing. We would have three cameras working, one at Tattenham Corner. We were there for the Derby when a Suffragette rushed into the horses.

Camera Tricks

Invisibility (1909). This was really Cecil Hepworth's film. He was awfully clever with tricks. If you photograph black on black, nothing shows; that was the principle. A movable, three-sided cupboard was made. It was lined with black velvet. First I was filmed in this with a sardonic grin on my face. Dissolve: an ancient skeleton (it had been knocking about the place for years) took my place. Dissolve: and then your Fitz clothed in black tights, jersey and helmet of black suede took the skeleton's place, the left hand lightly dipped in whitewash. Fitz raised his left arm and scratched his tight-fitting helmet. Dissolve: the scene, a counting house, and an official counting piles of money and notes. Dissolve: to an eye – not mine – rolling! Dissolve: now the table has been moved to the cupboard. The hand stretches out and annexes a bundle of notes. Dissolve: back to the counting house. The official aghast to find his notes have vanished. Dissolve!

My Best Actor

The best actor I ever had or knew was Tariff. Show him a camera and he knew that something frisky was expected from him. Then there is the secret magic a man must possess so that the animal trusts him and knows what he must do. But did Tariff act? When galloping full tilt down a lane, with stirrups flying in the air – for simplicity and directness there is no human to touch an animal! The next best actor I handled was Tom Mowbray, the best actress, Dolly Lupone, then Alma Taylor.

Note: An incomplete filmography of Lewin Fitzhamon, listing 379 of his films, is in Denis Gifford's *Illustrated Who's Who in British Films*, published in 1979 by Batsford Books, London.

HUMPHREY JENNINGS
SURREALIST OBSERVER
Geoffrey Nowell-Smith

Humphrey Jennings was by vocation an intellectual. By profession he was, for the most fertile period of his career, a film-maker. He also attempted a career as a painter, but was never good enough or fashionable enough to make a living at it. He is mainly remembered today for a small number of documentary films, mostly made during the war and in collaboration with Stewart McAllister. Many of his intellectual interests are in fact expressed in these films – which is a contributory reason for their being more memorable than most other documentary films from the same period. But in other respects the range of interests proved too broad to be contained in the body of work – films, photographs, paintings, poems, prose – that he left behind him at his untimely death in 1950.

Received wisdom has it that Jennings was something of a dilettante, who never really found his way until disciplined by the pressure of working collaboratively in documentary and under the imperatives of wartime. He is seen as part of the documentary 'movement', and yet somehow to the side of it, never quite fitting in either personally or artistically. Needless to say this view emanates from within the documentary movement itself, the source of many questionable received doctrines about British film history. It is a view which has prevailed because of its simplicity. It offers a standpoint from which to view a multi-form activity and give it some sort of sense and context. Without such a standpoint, attempts to assess the range of Jennings' concerns tend to lack focus. His work outside documentary has a personal, biographical unity and, studied on that level, a high degree of interior coherence. But it has always proved hard to fit into a coherent external context. A minor painter, a very minor poet, an innovative photographer who nevertheless left no legacy, a historian whose major work was never completed, an organiser of Surrealism and Mass Observation, he belongs as a footnote in various histories; only in documentary does he figure as a protagonist.

And yet documentary – the documentary of the documentary movement of the 1930s and 40s – is perhaps the worst possible context in which to study his work. It also provides a most unreliable standpoint from which to form a judgment. The reason for this has partly to do with Jennings' own career and preoccupations, which are easily misrecognised within the documentary context; and partly to do with a fundamental flaw in the documentary standpoint itself, as a result of which he is simultaneously absorbed and rejected, accommodated and pushed to one side.

Thanks in particular to John Grierson, the documentary movement was very good at seizing the limelight and at promulgating a version of things which both validated its own practice as 'documentary' and established a hierarchy of values for assessing cinema in general. The general hierarchy of values, which combined 'art' and 'realism' as two main pinnacles and pushed 'entertainment', together with 'fantasy', 'escapism' and 'aestheticism', down into the foothills, does not have many adherents today; but on the whole the self-valorisation of documentary, although marginalised, has not been explicitly challenged.[1]

In this self-valorisation, two notions emerge as central. First, that documentary was what the documentary movement did. And second, that documentary was a vehicle for improvement. A third notion, which in practice was less central though it was very important for the theory, was that the basic mode of documentary was realist. The documentary movement was dedicated to improvement at an ideological level; its practitioners were almost all reformists or meliorists of one kind or another. It also needed the rationale of 'usefulness' to get sponsors to put money into the films. But it was always prepared to compromise the idea of realism as an aesthetic at an everyday level – if the idea of an abstract film could be sold to the General Post Office as a way of advertising lower postal rates, so much the better. Deeper down, however, most of the documentarists fell in with certain beliefs about reality and its representation which made some version of realism the preferred mode of documentary narration. Although the production of the documentary movement is extremely varied, time and again the same basic form of filmic construction recurs, a form which has become canonical in cinema and is perpetuated, in hackneyed form, in contemporary television.

Jennings was involved with the documentary movement briefly in 1934–5 and then again from 1938 through to the end of the Second World War and beyond. Many of the films he made for documentary producers of necessity fall into line with the (fairly flexible) orthodox practice of the movement. But at no time did he share the governing presumptions of the movement. He was unorthodox, and the unorthodoxy shows. Politically and ideologically he was not a meliorist or even a reformist. He was disparaging of realism, and of the practice that went with it. To be understood in the documentary context, therefore, his films have to be read against the grain, as exceptions to an assumed norm. But if the documentary context, with all its associated ideological baggage, is removed, and another context substituted, their project becomes clearer. They are not exceptional documentaries, for ever hovering on the edges of ordinary practice and about to take flight into a realm coyly and unconvincingly referred to as poetry, but films of a different type.

Rather than with the documentarists proper, Jennings gains from being situated in the context of experimental film and of the European avant-gardes – or what was left of them after the initial impetus ran out in the early 30s. This is not to say that he was not a documentarist; clearly he was, both institutionally and in his attachment to an idea of documentation. But he shares with Vertov, Ivens and Moholy Nagy – and with the Buñuel of *Las Hurdes* – the quality of not being defined by the documentary mode as such and of stretching beyond it into areas of filmic experiment whose rationale is not that of social documentary. Situated alongside Vertov's *Enthusiasm*, Moholy Nagy's *Marseille vieux port* or Ivens' *A Valparaiso* (rather than *Night Mail, Housing Problems* or *Industrial Britain*), his films enter into sharper focus, and their espousal of distinctly aesthetic values seems less a distraction and more central to their purposes.

Correspondingly, the cultural context in which the films require to be read is that of the modernist experiment in which Jennings was most actively engaged in the years between his two periods of employment as a documentary film-maker.[2] Modernism in Britain was not strong, and operated in a space circumscribed by the aestheticism of Bloomsbury on the one hand and the utilitarianism of enlightened commercial patrons on the other. Its status as a radical movement was further diminished by the adherence of the majority of left writers and artists to the canons of realism (socialist or otherwise). Within this restricted space Jennings played an important and underestimated role, both as a cultural entrepreneur and as an artistic innovator. If this role has never been properly recognised it is because the tendencies to which he was attached, and which provided his main formative experience, had little sequel and were more or less obliterated in the 'settlement' that took place after 1945. Jennings' wartime films are, in fact, one of the few recognised monuments of the 1930s modernism to which he was attached – though it is not as modernism that they are recognised.

Jennings' main areas of activity in the crucial years 1935–8 were two, Surrealism and Mass Observation. In 1936 he was an organiser of the International Surrealist Exhibition in London, and around that time he was practising painting and photo-collage in a broadly Surrealist mode. In 1937 he was one of the founders of Mass Observation, and editor (with Charles Madge) of *May 12th*, a record of mass observers' reports on the day of George VI's Coronation. In the same period he read first Freud and then Marx, and began the research into industrialism which was to culminate in the great compilation of texts to which he gave the title *Pandaemonium*.[3] Also in this period he evolved, not exactly a theory of documentary, but a set of ideas around the practice of documenting, including photographic and cinematic documents as well as the written and spoken word.

Such a confluence of interest – Walker Evans with André Breton, Marx and Freud with T. S. Eliot – seems surprising, and it is hard to see immediately how they could be accommodated together. Surrealism and Mass Observation in particular are incongruous bedfellows. But it is worth remembering that the first 'manifesto' of Mass Observation – a letter in the *New Statesman and Nation* signed by Tom Harrisson, Jennings and Charles Madge – was quite surrealist in its orientation, and culminated in a list of topics for investigation which could have come straight from the pages of *La Révolution Surréaliste* – a magazine which, for its part, was also renowned for promoting investigations into bizarre areas of human conduct. As it happens, Harrisson himself, rather than Jennings, was responsible for the surreal elements of the manifesto, and (according to Madge) Jennings, the only real surrealist in the group, was not in favour of their inclusion.[4] In general, however, Jennings seems to have felt no contradiction in his own practice between his activities as Surrealist and as Mass Observer. He crossed easily from one to the other, and retained a loyalty to each even as he moved on to yet another stage of development.

What enabled him to hold such diverse ideas and practices together was a version of the modernist conviction that twentieth-century life was not amenable to treatment in artistic discourses inherited from previous centuries – whether the composed rhetoric of classicism or the elitist individualism of romanticism. He fought hard to establish the originality and essential modernity of Surrealism against attempts to reduce it to symbolism or any form of latter-day romanticism.[5] He was less interested in the sociological and purely observational side of Mass Observation than in the opportunity he saw in it of democratising the discoveries of Surrealism and of representing popular subjectivity dialectically and in unromanticised form. At the same time he was interested in the resonance of objects and of objectivist representation, whether wilfully artistic (as in New

Deal photography) or non-artistic (as in newsreels). In photographs, in Mass Observation reports, and in the multi-layered but elliptical style of Eliot's *Waste Land*, he found a capacity to connect to modern experience lacking in conventional expressive forms (including those, such as the 'proletarian novel', favoured by many of his radical contemporaries).

His development through the 1930s shows an increasing radical-isation, but one at variance with that of the orthodox left, whose rhetoric he distrusted. From 1938 onwards, however, the extremism of 1936–7 is attenuated. He becomes less cosmopolitan and more sensitive to the specifics of national/class/regional experience. 1938 was the year of the *Anschluss* and of Munich, a year in which the advance of fascism escalated into wars of national conquest. For Jennings it was the year in which a popular-national thematic emerges in his writing. It was also the year in which he re-entered salaried employment in the GPO Film Unit.

The first film of any consequence he made for the GPO was *Spare Time* (1939), a film about working-class leisure set in Sheffield, South Lancashire and South Wales. This was a project that he hijacked and turned into something very different from the anodyne proposal that had been knocking around the Unit offices at the time of his arrival.[6] *Spare Time* is sometimes referred to as Jennings' 'Mass Observation' film, so it is worth pointing out not only that Mass Observation had nothing to do with the making of it, but that Jennings at the time had no longer any formal connection with the movement. More importantly, the film eschews the very feature of Mass Observation practice which most interested Jennings – the representation of popular subjectivity – and instead is resolutely objectivist. More important still, however, is the film's deviation from documentary movement norms. It is in a sense a very pure documentary film – in the sense, that is, of being a film that documents. But in order to achieve that objective, that purity, it neglects – even repudiates – the established codes of documentary narrative construction.

Orthodox documentary narrative construction is formed around three elements: a seen object which attests to the 'documentary' reality of the film; codes of framing, lighting, etc., and also music, which add levels of connotation and emotivity; and a use of the spoken or written word, generally in the form of commentary, to establish meaning. Crudely, the object assures you that what you see is real; the music and *mise en scène* guide emotional response; and the commentary tells you what to think. Not all documentary films, fortunately, are quite so crude (though some of Jennings' own, such as *A Defeated People*, 1945, come perilously close), but an overall

325

shaping within these broad parameters is essential to the narrativised realism which is the hallmark of official documentary.

Clumsily, and perhaps not always with full consciousness, *Spare Time* violates the codes. The commentary is laconic – six sentences, totalling one hundred words in all. A brass band, a kazoo band and a Welsh choir, introduced on screen but continuing as sound-over, provide almost the entire soundtrack, offering a perfunctory association with the images. The *mise en scène* is rudimentary, almost minimalist, with lighting limited to the basic necessity of enabling shooting to take place in conditions which a still photographer could cope with but not (at the time) the cinema. In fact, all the shots have the look of still photography about them. They are snapshots, but snapshots that happen to move. Their movement is sufficient, but only just, to disturb the documented pastness which is the hallmark of the still photograph. But only in rare moments is it sufficient to produce the present-ness and anticipated future of cinematic narration.

More than anything else it is the uncinematic, snapshottish quality of the images that marks *Spare Time* as a different sort of document from the documentary model. Refusing to narrativise, it also refuses to ennoble. It is a film about the servitude and grandeur of working-class leisure under capitalism. But what is grand and what is servile is left to be inferred. Neither the picture, nor (until the very end) the commentary, offers any guidance. Then, at the close of the film, as a miners' cage descends into the pit, the commentary voice (Laurie Lee) says, 'As things are, spare time is a time when we have a chance to do what we like, a chance to be most ourselves.' As things are . . .

Jennings never made another film like *Spare Time*. All his subsequent films are more cinematic. But alongside those – *Heart of Britain* (1941), *Family Portrait* (1950) – which fall back into documentary narrative modes, stand the films which exploit cinematic resources more radically and which stretch the mode to which formally speaking they belong. To this latter, more important category belong the acknowledged successes of *Listen to Britain* (1942), *Fires Were Started* (1943) and *A Diary for Timothy* (1945), as well as those less acknowledged – *Words for Battle* (1941), *The True Story of Lili Marlene* (1944), *The Silent Village* (1943).

What separates these films from *Spare Time* is the coming of the war on the one hand, and Jennings' partnership with Stewart McAllister on the other. Through McAllister, Jennings discovered editing; and, through editing, cinema. His association with other members of the GPO (soon to become Crown) Film Unit – for example with sound recordist Ken Cameron – also forced him to acquire what he had never acquired as a self-taught painter, which was a real sense of

326

Snapshots that move: *Spare Time* (1939)

technique. All the films of the 40s show a high level of technical accomplishment, sometimes (as in *Listen to Britain*) executed in a bravura mode but sometimes (as in *The Silent Village*) used protectively, to enable the film to get away with risks in its narrative construction. Through McAllister, too, Jennings was enabled to perform the most difficult trick of all, that of combining two seemingly antithetical features of cinema, its ability to invent and create through juxtaposition and overlay and its anchorage in a given reality, without falling into the compromise formation of cinematic real*ism*.

All this would have been impossible, however, had it not been for the war. Among its other effects, the war liberated documentary from its need to find a purpose. Both before the war and again after, documentary had to align its own intrinsic purposes with a purpose defined from outside. An example of this can be found in Edgar Anstey's *Housing Problems* (1935), in which the denunciation of existing housing conditions is made possible only by the promise of a solution, in the form of better conditions on the horizon thanks to enlightened planning and (in particular) the efforts of the Gas Company. No solution, no sponsor; no sponsor, no film. Much of the insipid meliorism of documentary output in the 30s derives from the need to respect this equation.[7]

The war swept the equation away. Documentary no longer had any need to equate its purposes with the requirement of finding an audience or sponsor. The purpose became the war effort, for which there was no simple formula. Of course, a lot of films were made to simple practical formulae, and Len Lye was put to work on useful subjects like how to make a meat pie without meat. But propaganda purposes could not be so easily defined, and Crown in particular was free to undertake a range of subjects unconstrained by a quantifiable need. Jennings more than anyone profited from the freedom thus provided, which included a freedom of formal experiment as well as freedom (within obvious limits) of content.

Jennings' wartime films show a remarkable variety of form. Most are non-fiction, but two are, in different ways, 'fictional'. Of the latter, one – *Fires Were Started* – is a narrative feature, though shot and edited in a largely documentary manner and very closely based on ordinary facts. The other – *The Silent Village* – is ostentatiously counter-factual: it is based on real events, but events which took place in a different country from the one where the film is set. The film is set in Wales, under hypothetical Nazi rule, and recounts events leading up to a massacre modelled on the one that took place at Lidice in Czechoslovakia after the assassination of Deputy Reichsprotektor Heydrich.

The non-fiction films also differ among themselves, particularly in the role assigned to commentary. One or two have the conventional 'voice of Truth' commentary, of the type which classically typifies British documentary but which the documentarists themselves were increasingly eager to get rid of (the tendency, not shared by Jennings, was to replace it with staged dialogue). In *Heart of Britain* the commentary is at times embarrassingly sententious, but in *The True Story of Lili Marlene* Jennings evades the problems of the distant and authoritative voice by having the narrator (Marius Goring) appear on screen and keeping the words of the commentary (which are interspersed by bits of face-to-camera testimony and re-enacted broadcast) modest and investigative in tone. In *A Diary for Timothy*, the break with 'voice of Truth' commentary is even more radical. The commentary (originally written by E. M. Forster) is ruminative and question-posing, and the image track takes up the questions in a contrapuntal or dialogistic mode, not so much answering as counter-questioning the questions of the commentary.

More interesting still are two films which do not have commentary. One of these – *Words for Battle* – does indeed have an off-screen voice (Laurence Olivier's), but the words spoken are all quotations from literary texts or speeches. Here conventional roles are reversed (as in a sense they also are in *A Diary for Timothy*), since it is now the image which 'comments' on the text, amplifying its meaning. The relationship between image and text is at the outset little more than mutually illustrative, but as the film progresses it becomes more dynamic. The final text is Lincoln's 'Gettysburg Address' and the scene Parliament Square in London: 'and that government of the people, by the people and for the people . . .' Olivier declaims. Then a pause (probably lengthened by McAllister during the sound-edit), and an armoured car enters frame right, before the voice continues: '. . . shall not perish from the earth.' The effect here is no mere illustration of Lincoln's famous (too famous) words, but the generation, through montage, of a cluster of ideas around democracy and armed defence; and it all happens in a moment, both chilling and exhilarating, which no amount of verbal explication can re-create.

Listen to Britain, finally and as is well known, has no spoken words on the soundtrack at all. (The voice-to-camera introduction preserved on release prints is an extraneous addition, for export

Words for Battle (1941)

distribution purposes.) Every meaning in the film, therefore, is produced by the juxtaposition of image with image and with musical or natural sound. Many tributes have, rightly, been paid to the extraordinary bravura of this film, for which McAllister shared the directing and editing credit. It would be superfluous to add to them here.[8]

More important than the purely formal differences between the films, however, is the political division between the earlier films and the later ones, which affects their form as well as their content. Broadly speaking, the division is before and after Stalingrad. The films of 1940, 1941 and even 1942 are premised on the danger of defeat. They aim to create an image of a diverse but united nation, whose multiple sources of energy are being harnessed to a single, life-and-death struggle. 1942 marks the beginning of a relaxation: America's entry into the war after Pearl Harbor and the British-led victories in North Africa made eventual victory seem more likely. But it was not until early 1943, when the Germans were checked at Stalingrad and Zhukov's forces began the massive roll-back which was to bring the Russians to Berlin, that German defeat came to seem a real possibility.[9] Then, with the Allied landing in Sicily later that year, it finally became possible to think of the war being won and a battle engaged for winning the peace.

The ideological shift that took place across a wide spectrum of British society about 1943 has been brilliantly chronicled by Angus Calder in *The People's War*.[10] Briefly, the issue was whether, after the hardship and struggle of war, the British people would allow their country to revert to being what it had been like before. The work of Jennings and of other documentarists is more than just a barometer of this shift: documentary film was in fact an agent both of producing the cohesion called for at the beginning of the war and of questioning it as the possibility of peace became imminent.

In *Words for Battle* and *Listen to Britain* in particular, Jennings applies the cultural knowledge and understanding he began to acquire in the late 30s to an idea of the British nation (or nation-people, to use Gramsci's phrase). The idea expressed in both films is of an industrial nation, still attached both nostalgically and projectively to rural values; a nation divided regionally and by differences of class and culture; but also one capable of holding together its contradictions and divisions in the face of external threat. The idea is consonant with Churchillian national rhetoric, but by no means equivalent to it; it both holds more together and shows more awareness of its own instability. The absence of commentary in *Listen to Britain* is crucial to the holding in place of the many facets of Jennings' 'national-popular' idea. The famous 'cutting on a chord' between Flanagan and Allen in the works canteen and Myra Hess playing Mozart with the RAF orchestra in the National Gallery is an example of an associative montage which calls into play more ideas and in a more open-ended manner than a commentary could deal with. A commentary would inevitably have fixed certain meanings and eliminated others, whereas it was essential that meaning be left open and especially that the union of popular and high culture and their possible divergence be held in the balance, possibilities glimpsed rather than realities asserted. Commentary, too, would either have to express or not to express further aspects of the film's associative chain, such as the fact that both Bud Flanagan and Myra Hess were Jewish – one native, the other a refugee.

With *A Diary for Timothy,* made during the closing stages of the war in Europe though not released until after the Labour election victory and VJ day, the provisional holding together of diversity and contradiction gives way to a separation of elements. The elements are broadly the same – they are personified as a farmer, a miner, a railwayman and an RAF pilot of middle-class background. But the theme of the film is not present unity but the modified social relations into which the elements and their personifications could be expected to enter in the future world of the peace.

Like the earlier films, however, *A Diary for Timothy* holds a precarious balance. It is unequivocal in its assertion that Britain is a class society and that the balance of class forces must change in a popular and socialist direction. But it is imbued with a deep and challenging scepticism about change being accomplished. Acute tension is present in small details: while the commentary evokes ideals of reconstruction, a pane of glass smashes, as if to say that reconstruction will not be easy, may even be sabotaged.

Shortly after the end of the war, Jennings left the Crown Film Unit. His last film for Crown was *The Cumberland Story,* released in 1947. Thereafter he made only two more films, though he was involved in a number of abortive projects and was location-scouting for a new project at the time of his death. In the absence of films to direct he returned to drawing and painting, elaborating a new composite style and often reworking images from one medium into another. The later drawings and paintings (or those that can be presumed to be later; they are not always easy to date) show in particular a reflorescence of rural themes that had never been far from the surface in his work generally and which perhaps represented for him an element of nostalgia.

It has been suggested that Jennings suffered a loss of creativity in the post-war years, and it is certainly the case that nothing he

331

produced after 1945 is of the stature of his earlier work: his best paintings remain those of his surrealist period in the 30s and his best films are the wartime ones. More than a loss of creativity, however, he suffered a loss of context. Documentary continued, but as a handmaiden to post-war social democracy, with both its social and its aesthetic radicalism stripped from it. The intellectual history of the post-war period has yet to be written; perhaps the reason for its absence is that it would be both difficult and depressing to write. The aftermath of war seems to have produced an exhaustion not in individuals (who remained productive) but in ideas to work with. Unlike the countries of occupied Europe, which experienced intellectual and cultural renewal with resistance and liberation, the post-war settlement in Britain was barren. Artistic production did not cease (in the cinema, the presence of films like *Dead of Night* and *A Matter of Life and Death* is testimony to this). But for many artists, and especially for those who had been most radical in the 30s and during the war and who had the deepest investment in social and cultural change, the post-war settlement offered only the most elusive and unreal of promises. Among these, unfortunately, was Humphrey Jennings.

Notes

1 The closest attempt is in Don Macpherson (ed.), *Traditions of Independence: British Cinema in the Thirties*, London, BFI, 1980.

2 Jennings' involvement with modernism is charted in David Mellor, 'Sketch for an Historical Portrait of Humphrey Jennings', in Mary Lou Jennings (ed.), *Humphrey Jennings: Film-maker, Painter, Poet*, London, BFI in association with Riverside Studios, 1982, pp. 63–72.

3 This has now finally been published: *Pandaemonium: The Coming of the Machine as seen by contemporary observers*, edited and introduced by Mary Lou Jennings and Charles Madge, London, André Deutsch, 1985.

4 30 January 1937. Reprinted in *Humphrey Jennings: Film-maker, Painter, Poet*, pp. 16–17. The topics to be investigated by 'mass observation' include 'The aspidistra cult/Anthropology of football pools/Bathroom behaviour/Beards, armpits, eyebrows . . .' I am grateful to Charles Madge for his help in supplying background information about Jennings' career in the 30s.

5 See in particular, *Humphrey Jennings: Film-maker, Painter, Poet*, p.14.

6 See Dai Vaughan, *Portrait of an Invisible Man: The Working Life of Stewart McAllister, Film Editor*, London, BFI, 1983, pp. 42–3.

7 This should not be taken as a criticism of commercial sponsors, or of film-makers who accepted sponsorship. The need for a 'solution' is a question of narrative logic, and the same considerations would apply if the

film had been produced by and for a political organisation – though the 'solution' would have been different.

8   The best account is in Vaughan (op. cit.), pp. 83–100. Among others who have written eloquently about Jennings' films it is worth citing: Lindsay Anderson ('Only Connect', *Sight and Sound*, vol. 23, no. 4, April–June 1954, reprinted in *Humphrey Jennings: Film-maker, Painter, Poet*, pp. 53–9); Eric Rhode (*Tower of Babel: Speculations on the Cinema*, London, Weidenfeld and Nicolson, 1966); Jim Hillier (in Lovell and Hillier, *Studies in Documentary*, London, Secker & Warburg/BFI, 1972); and Elizabeth Sussex (*The Rise and Fall of British Documentary*, Berkeley and London, University of California Press, 1976).

9   That Stalingrad was the turning point was widely felt at the time, not just in Russia itself but in Britain and throughout occupied Europe (where the BBC Overseas Service was a major source of information and inspiration). Jennings' own sense of the importance of the Russian front is evident from the commentary to *The True Story of Lili Marlene* and from a letter to his wife of 3 September 1943 (published in *Humphrey Jennings: Film-maker, Painter, Poet*, p. 36).

10   Angus Calder, *The People's War*, London, Jonathan Cape, 1969.

PAUL ROBESON
THE BLACK MAN AS FILM HERO
Jeffrey Richards

It is customary to see the British cinema's attitude to race in the 1930s in the context of what I have called 'the cinema of Empire', a cinema that celebrated the glories of British Imperial rule and the concept of 'The White Man's Burden'.[1] But there was an alternative view, and it was to be found in the British films of Paul Robeson. Robeson declared: 'There is no such thing as a non-political artist. The artist must elect to fight for freedom or for slavery.'[2] He became a 'political artist' during the years in which he lived and worked in Britain, from 1928 to 1939.

By any definition, he was a remarkable man. Born in Princeton, New Jersey, he won a scholarship to Rutgers University, where he became an All-American footballer as well as graduating with honours. He had intended to take up law, but drifted into acting and singing. He established himself on the American stage, particularly through parts in Eugene O'Neill's plays *All God's Chillun Got Wings* and *The Emperor Jones*, but found the strict racial segregation in American society a restraining influence on his career. When he went to England to appear in *Showboat*, he found the atmosphere there freer, and decided to settle in London. He achieved considerable success on the London stage and became enormously popular as a singer in concerts, on records and on radio.

In this way he provided himself with a platform for the views he was formulating. First, in his own words, he 'discovered Africa' and became an advocate of blacks returning to their 'roots'.[3] He studied and wrote about African culture and language. In an article entitled 'I Want to be an African', written in 1934, Robeson argues the need to rediscover the African heritage. 'In my music, my plays, my films, I want to carry always this central idea: to be African.'[4] He stressed that Africans should master European technology but retain their own cultural identity.

He also came to believe in the solidarity of the working classes of the world, both black and white – what he called in his autobiography 'the oneness of humankind'.[5] Throughout the 30s he was active in left-wing causes. He joined the Unity Theatre in 1938 to act in Ben

334

Bengal's *Plant in the Sun*, a powerful plea for trade unionism. He toured the provinces singing to the workers, insisting on a cheap ticket policy. He visited Spain, and gave concerts in Britain in support of the Republican cause during the Civil War. Most important of all, he discovered in the Soviet Union his ideal workers' state and promptly sent his son there to be educated.[6]

Robeson turned to the cinema as the most influential mass medium of the age to translate his views to a wider audience. He believed that with a few honourable exceptions (*Hallelujah, Imitation of Life, The Emperor Jones*), Hollywood films had never done justice to the black person: this he attributed to Hollywood's fear that 'the Southern States . . . might not patronise realistic films about coloured folk'.[7] Robeson could in fact never have achieved the status he sought in the Hollywood of the 1930s. *The Emperor Jones* (1933), in which he played the title role of the negro railway porter who becomes the ruler of an island, was an independent production made in New York; although praised by the critics, it received only limited distribution and made little money. Robeson's only Hollywood performances were in supporting roles as the faithful, bale-toting 'darkie' of the Deep South, part of Hollywood's generalised stereotyping of blacks as 'toms, coons, mulattoes, mammies and bucks'.[8] In *Showboat* (1936), Robeson gave a powerful rendition of 'Ole Man River', but had little else to do. Then he was part of an embarrassing shanty-town sequence in the all-star *Tales of Manhattan* (1942). In a world where Stepin Fetchit's slow-witted menial and Hattie McDaniel's beaming maid were the favoured archetypes, there was no room for black heroes.[9]

In Britain, in contrast, Robeson made six films, all of which were built round him and his talent. His size, massive and compelling, his warming smile, his innate dignity, the powerful and emotional naturalism of his acting, the magnificent bass-baritone voice, all proclaimed him a star, unquestionably the most important black star since the 19th-century American tragedian Ira Aldridge, who had also sought in Britain and Europe the recognition denied to him in his own country. In his British films, Robeson was invariably given top billing, above the title. This was in itself an achievement, and something which accorded with his aim: he set out to play distinctively African heroes because of his belief that he needed to help his people to overcome a deep sense of inferiority, and to demonstrate that blacks were equal to but different from whites.[10]

Robeson's first attempt to play an authentic African leader and also to bring African culture to the screen misfired. He signed to play Sanders' faithful ally Chief Bosambo in Alexander Korda's production *Sanders of the River* (1935), on the basis of the documentary

335

footage of African tribal life and customs which director Zoltan Korda had brought back from a field trip to Africa. Robeson declared: 'I wanted to show that, while the imperialists contend that the Africans are "barbarians and uncivilised", they have a culture all their own, and have as much intelligence as any other people.'[11]

Robeson was top-billed over Leslie Banks, who played the title role, and he sang four songs, based on authentic tribal chants recorded in Africa and westernised by composer Mischa Spoliansky. But the finished film appalled Robeson, who later described it as 'a piece of flag-waving in which I wasn't interested'.[12] He walked out of the première and refused to work for Korda again. He also insisted in future on having approval of the final cut of his films. *Sanders of the River*, which told how Commissioner Sanders and Chief Bosambo suppressed a tribal uprising in Nigeria, was a hit with both the public and the newspaper critics in Britain, but it was roundly attacked both by left-wing and black organisations in Britain and America. Robeson defended himself by saying that the Imperialist slant had been introduced in the cutting and in scenes in which he did not appear. This is not entirely convincing, since Robeson himself in one of his songs hymns the praises of the Commissioner ('Sandi the strong, Sandi the wise'). Nor is there any sign of awkwardness or embarrassment in his virile, charismatic and engaging performance. But there is no doubt that his presence, role and songs all provide a powerful endorsement of the British Imperial mission.[13]

However, he made two valuable contacts on *Sanders*: Major Claude Wallace, the technical adviser, and Dorothy Holloway, Korda's casting director. Together they wrote for Robeson a new script, *The Song of Freedom*. Directed in 1936 by J. Elder Wills for the small independent Hammer company, this film was in a sense Robeson's answer to *Sanders of the River*, and his first systematic attempt to dramatise his own ideas. He said it was 'the first picture to give a true picture of many aspects of the life of the coloured man in the West. . . . This film shows him as a real man with problems to be solved, difficulties to be overcome.'[14]

Robeson played John Zinga, descendant of the ancient kings of Casanga but now working as a London docker. The opening scenes show Zinga and his wife (Elizabeth Welch) integrated into the dockland community and accepted as equals by the white workers; but Zinga, feeling himself to be African, longs to return to his roots. This is made possible when he is discovered singing in a pub and transformed into an international opera star. White-suited and solar-topeed, almost like a black Sanders, he finds the island of Casanga run by witchdoctors and sunk in superstition, savagery and disease. Eventually he breaks the power of the witchdoctors and begins the

Paul Robeson in *The Song of Freedom* (1936)

introduction of Western technology and medicine, while assuring the natives that they will retain their own culture and identity. It was an honourable and well-intentioned film which, despite passages of conventional melodrama, stressed the central elements of the Robeson world-view (the validity of African culture, the return to African roots, the international solidarity of the workers).

For his next film, Robeson returned to a big studio (Gaumont British) for a screen version of the Rider Haggard classic, *King Solomon's Mines* (1937). For all that it is the story of a group of white explorers in search of the fabulous mines, this is unlike other versions in centring squarely on Umbopa, a character whom Robeson was happy to play, seeing him 'not just as a splendid savage but a man of real thoughts and ambitions'.[15] Robeson's Umbopa is indeed just that. Not only is he mentor, protector, adviser and guide of the English adventurers, he also uses them to further his own restoration to the throne of the Kukuana. Once he reaches Kukuanaland, Umbopa effectively takes charge of the expedition. He rescues the whites when they are trapped in the mines by the evil witchdoctor Gagool. The film closes with Umbopa, now ruler of an independent Kukuanaland, shaking hands with Allan Quatermain and seeing the whites off with a rendition of the most popular of three Spoliansky songs, 'Mighty Mountain'.

It was for another independent company (Buckingham) that Robeson starred in *Jericho* (US title, *Dark Sands*, 1937), a vigorous and enjoyable melodrama directed by the American Thornton Freeland and shot partly in superb North African locations. It provided Robeson with his first opportunity actually to visit Africa, and gave him the novel role of a black American soldier. Jericho Jackson is not only a soldier but also a college graduate, an athlete, a scholar and a medical student. This might not have been remarked on if the super-hero had been white; here, he is black, and furthermore is given a comic white sidekick (Wallace Ford) who dies saving his life. The film is also remarkable in that it features a black American regiment on a troop-ship bound for Europe in 1917. Jericho establishes his heroic credentials by rescuing his comrades when the ship is torpedoed. But when he accidentally kills a bullying sergeant and is sentenced to death, he is forced to flee to North Africa.

Like *Song of Freedom*, *Jericho* is almost a riposte to *Sanders of the River*: it has its own Sanders figure in Captain Mack, the white commander of the black regiment, who describes the blacks as 'children' and treats Jericho as his head prefect. Played by the British-born actor Henry Wilcoxon without a trace of an American accent, he conforms exactly to the stereotype of the white Imperial hero. After Jericho's escape, he is cashiered and imprisoned. Jericho meanwhile establishes himself as the ruler of an Arab tribe, to whom he brings unity, justice and Western medicine. When, eventually released, Mack tracks him down, he is so impressed that he decides to leave Jericho in his Saharan kingdom rather than attempt to return him to America.

After these chieftain roles, Robeson returned to the docks for his next film, J. Elder Wills' *Big Fella* (1937). Praising his 'intelligent acting and superb singing', the trade paper *Kinematograph Weekly* noted that Robeson 'partnered by Elizabeth Welch . . . carries the slight but amusing story and converts it into entertainment of immense family and general appeal'.[16] Ostensibly based on the novel *Banjo* by the Jamaican writer Claude MacKay, it took only the setting (the Marseilles waterfront) and the leading character (a musical black vagabond, here renamed Joe) from its source. Like *Jericho*, Joe is given a white sidekick and functions as an equal in the working-class community of the Marseilles waterfront. Joe befriends a runaway white boy and takes a steady job to support him, thus recovering his self-respect. Some critics complained that he was demeaning his race by playing such a lazy, shiftless character, but Robeson pointed out that the story was about Joe's regeneration and he wanted his characters to be human rather than superhuman.[17]

Although *Big Fella* stressed the theme of black and white working-class solidarity, it was Robeson's final British film, *The Proud Valley* (Ealing Studios, 1940), that explored this theme in most detail. Based on a real character working in the Welsh mines, the story was written specifically for Robeson by the left-wing producer Herbert Marshall, who had produced *Plant in the Sun,* and his wife Alfredda Brilliant. As directed by Pen Tennyson, it emerged as one of the most committed films of the era.

The film sought to do justice to the aspirations both of the working class and of the black man in Britain. It faced head-on the subjects of conditions in the mining industry, racial prejudice and unemployment. Robeson is David Goliath, an unemployed stoker, who gets a job down the mines. He overcomes initial prejudice to become an accepted member of the community; but the pit is closed down, and he joins a deputation of miners who march to London to protest to the owners. It is re-opened to assist the war effort, but David is killed in an accident, sacrificing his life to save the new friends he has made. Despite the climactic tragedy, the film's mood is one of essential optimism as David is integrated into the community and as the community itself is integrated into the nation with the onset of war.

The impact of Robeson's films is likely to have been greater in Britain than in his native America, for the simple reason that they were more widely shown in Britain. Only *Sanders of the River* and *King Solomon's Mines* were widely shown in the United States. *Jericho* and *The Proud Valley* had limited showings. *The Song of Freedom* and *Big Fella* were not shown at all. In Britain, they were all widely shown and, except for *Big Fella*, were several times re-issued in the 1940s, giving them an unusually long lifespan. But even the despised *Sanders* may have had some beneficial effect in America. For Robeson declared in an interview in 1936:

> On many occasions people would come up to me in small towns, where formerly I could have walked unrecognised on the streets, congratulate me on my performance as Bosambo and tell me that the film had given them new ideas about the African Negro. Most of them confessed that before seeing the picture they had regarded the Negro as a violent savage, having gleaned their notions of him from such films as *Trader Horn* and the Tarzan adventures, in which the natives were depicted as paint-daubed, gibberish-mouthing, devil-worshipping creatures. But they had come to see him as a man with lucid emotions and a code and language of his own.[18]

In Britain, where the coloured population was small during these years, he is likely to have achieved his greatest impact on white audiences. Since the prevailing stereotypes of blacks in films were variations on subservience and villainy, his most notable achievement was perhaps to create a distinctive and dominant black hero. His hero was either a wise and just African ruler (*Sanders of the River*, *King Solomon's Mines*, *Jericho*) or a working-class stalwart (*Big Fella*, *The Proud Valley*) or both (*The Song of Freedom*). For all the criticism of *Sanders*, for all Robeson's subsequent pessimism about his ability to get his ideas across in films, his British film career does constitute an important and honourable episode in the struggle to obtain racial equality both in Britain and America.

Notes

1   Jeffrey Richards, *Visions of Yesterday*, London, Routledge & Kegan Paul, 1973, pp. 2–220.
2   Paul Robeson, *Here I Stand,* London, Dobson, 1958, p. 60. For a full account of Robeson's life and career, see Marie Seton, *Paul Robeson,* London, Dobson, 1958.
3   Philip S. Foner (ed.), *Paul Robeson Speaks: Writings, Speeches, Interviews 1918–74*, London, Quartet, 1978, pp. 351–2.
4   Ibid., p. 91.
5   Robeson, *Here I Stand*, pp. 56–7.
6   Foner, op. cit., p. 95.
7   *Film Weekly*, 23 May 1936.
8   The classifications are those of the black writer Donald Bogle in his book *Toms, Coons, Mulattoes, Mammies and Bucks*, New York, Viking, 1973.
9   For a detailed and thoughtful account of Hollywood's depiction of blacks in this period, see Thomas Cripps, *Slow Fade to Black: the Negro in American Film 1900–1942*, New York and London, Oxford University Press, 1977.
10   *Spectator,* 15 June 1934.
11   Foner, op. cit., p. 107.
12   Ibid., p. 121.
13   For a detailed discussion of *Sanders of the River*, see Anthony Aldgate and Jeffrey Richards, *Best of British*, Oxford, Blackwell, 1983, pp. 13–27.
14   *Film Weekly,* 23 May 1936.
15   Seton, op. cit., p. 108.
16   *Kinematograph Weekly*, 24 June 1937.
17   *Film Weekly*, 23 May 1936.
18   Ibid.

DIANA DORS
Christine Geraghty

'That great swatch of stuff to one side of her ear which resembles cotton with a light dusting of candy is her hair. The underslung pout apparently made of foam rubber is her lip. In spite of her highly unlikely appearance, she is natural, friendly and polite.'

(Daily Express, 5 September 1956)

Throughout the 50s, the British press wrested with the contradictory phenomenon of Diana Dors: the sex symbol whose appearance they mocked, the girl from a railway town who earned more than a Cabinet Minister, an acknowledged self-publicist who was frank and humorous in her dealings with reporters, an actress who drew attention to her major serious performance by gliding down a Venetian canal in a mink bikini.

Dors' name in the 50s was inextricably linked with those of Monroe and Bardot, and she was often seen as Britain's answer to them. It may be useful to look at what the three had in common as 50s sex symbols before looking more specifically at Dors herself. The sex symbol, like any star, is constructed not only out of film and pin-up material but also out of the drama of her off-screen life. In the case of Monroe, Bardot and Dors, the tissue of love affairs, scandals, marriages and divorces provided much of the material of their star images. At the crux of this construction of a sex symbol are the contradictory ideas of vulnerability and knowingness which allow the female star to be perceived as sexually active and challenging but not held responsible for how she behaves.

The knowingness of the sex symbol is demonstrated in the calculation of her appearance – the degree of cleavage revealed, the raising of the skirt, the different shades of blonde. These are bodies quite clearly on display, and their physical attributes are even itemised as if they have become separate objects – Bardot's pout, Dors' lip, Monroe's wiggle. The glamour with which such stars are associated is tied up with this knowingness: a deliberate dressing up, an emphasis on expense and sensuality – diamonds, sequins, furs – very different from the dress of other female stars of the period, such

341

as Doris Day. In the film narratives, the characters they play tend to be surrounded by incompetent and inadequate men. While the male characters are necessary to the plot, it is the female body which is directly presented to the cinema audience in poses which recall the static images of the pin-up.

But if, on the one hand, these sex symbols are knowing and even calculating, they are redeemed by their vulnerability and suffering. They may appear to use men through their sexuality, both in their films and in their off-screen lives, but it is as if their sexuality is something which flows through them and is beyond their control. This side of the sex symbol is associated with a certain childishness which is partly indicated by an emphasis on being natural and direct – Bardot's tousled hair and bare feet express this, as does Dors' down-to-earth manner. It is also present in the characters they play – most literally represented in Carroll Baker's *Baby Doll*, but clear also in Bardot's Juliette (in *Et Dieu créa la femme*) and Monroe's Lorelei (in *Gentlemen Prefer Blondes*). Such representations redefine the star image in terms of a different set of problems – Monroe's troubled lack of confidence, Bardot's refusal to accept French society's norms – asserting a vulnerability through which their private lives could be understood. It is striking that Dors, Monroe and Bardot all, at various points, had husbands who were publicised as greatly influencing or even controlling their wives' careers. The stormy and often destructive life of the sex symbol is generally accepted as a sign of the excessive female sexuality embodied in these stars. If it cannot be controlled by men, it certainly cannot be controlled by the women themselves. The sex symbol cannot be held personally responsible for what happens; nevertheless, it is clear that she cannot avoid the outcome of unleashing such a force. The end of their careers – Monroe's death, Bardot's retreat into obsessive privacy, Dors' bankruptcy and decline – can then be satisfactorily explained in terms of reaping the whirlwind.

No single sex symbol will fit this knowingness/vulnerability axis in the same way. Dors, Bardot and Monroe were of different nationalities, from different backgrounds, and worked in different film industries. Nevertheless, the way in which Dors can be set against this paradigm helps to identify her particular star image.

Certainly Dors seized with relish the glamorous end of the spectrum. A *Daily Mail* reporter in 1956 described her as 'coruscating with purple sequins, topped with white fur and tinkling with the chunkiest jewellery seen outside the Congo.' She was seen to spend more lavishly – on clothes, on cars (including a powder-blue Cadillac), on houses. She was presented as being precociously sexual, entering a beauty contest at the age of thirteen 'without parental or

Yield to the Night (1956)

school blessing' (*Daily Mail*, 5 May 1956) and winning a prize. 'I was
very advanced,' she said later (*Time*, 10 October 1955). At fifteen, she
had a film contract and had appeared in a number of films. At
nineteen, she was married and owned a second-hand Rolls Royce.
Such precocity could lead to absurd situations. On one celebrated
occasion, when she was taken to court for non-payment of rent, the
judge noted that she was a minor and ruled that it was the duty of the
court to protect infants. This was promptly translated into headlines,
suitably accompanied by revealing photographs: 'Judge says this
baby needs protection.'

Certainly in the mid-50s Dors was seen as knowing rather than
vulnerable. The 'baby' was understood to be vastly experienced. It
was part of the Dors image that she enjoyed her own appearance and

343

used it to challenge others. 'I might as well cash in on sex now while I've got it,' she is quoted as saying by several reporters. 'It can't last for ever.' 'What merchandise!' was another of her comments about herself, 'And boy, how it sells' (*Time*, 10 October 1955). She later maintained that 'I was the first sex symbol this country ever had. Before me female stars were either pretty or matronly. Sex was just an incidental – best left to the Continentals' (*Daily Express*, 30 January 1966). She also presented her sexuality as a challenge to the Establishment – her extravagant spending on luxuries was raised in the House of Commons – and to the British film industry. 'As for British directors,' she remarked in the same interview, 'they are afraid of sex. Probably not inwardly but it appears that way.'

The press, though they faithfully reported Dors' publicity-conscious exploits, didn't know quite what to make of her. One way of handling her was to treat her literally as a commodity to be sold in the national interest, one whose visible assets could, in a metaphor of the time, be transformed paradoxically into invisible earnings. 'She has made of the unlikely commodity of sex appeal a British export,' wrote a *Daily Mail* reporter in 1956, and went on to compare her to Rolls Royce, Dunhill and Savile Row as upholders of British goods abroad. There are occasions, however, when hostility to her emerges, expressed through grotesque descriptions of her appearance. The reviews of *Yield to the Night* (1956) in particular contrast her appearance as the condemned murderess with her normal star image, and prefer her stripped of her glamour. The *Financial Times* reviewer commented that 'Dressed in her finery, Miss Dors had previously suggested some frivolously inflatable beach toy or, as the French may have discovered, a possible blonde sister to the pneumatic Michelin Man.' Alan Brien in the *Evening Standard* described her as possessing 'a torso like a figure of eight cut out of eiderdown' and commented that 'that vanishing chin, those caterpillar lips and the acid-drop eyes have about them a Hogarthian earthiness.' It is dangerous to assume that film reviews speak for audiences, but such remarks are striking in their own excess and seem to express a hostility to a female star who appears to control and enjoy her image as a sex symbol.

But throughout her career the Dors image was also marked by the vulnerability which is the reverse side of the sex symbol's knowingness. Her first husband was presented in the press as a publicity seeker who used her for his own ends. The marriage ended in violence and divorce, and subsequent relationships proved equally difficult, particularly when her third husband, Alan Lake, served a prison sentence. For most of her career Dors was characterised as having bad judgment in emotional matters – a fault she readily admitted – and no financial sense. 'Men were my downfall,' announced the headline to an interview in the *Sunday Express* in 1978. When her film star career ended in the 60s, Dors was forced into tours of working men's clubs, trading on her sex symbol past. When she died in 1984, she had made something of a comeback as a character actress and a television personality, but one of her obituaries (in the *Daily Telegraph*) still described her story as 'that of a little girl whose dream of becoming a Hollywood star turned into a nightmare'.

Nevertheless, Dors was always marked as a survivor. There was a toughness and humour about her which was missing from Monroe and Bardot and which the British press with characteristic chauvinism ascribed to her nationality: 'something of a British institution, like the Albert Hall, an edifice she will be the first to tell you she now solidly resembles' (*Sunday Express*, 17 September 1978). But her capacity to survive may also be understood in class terms. British female stars in the late 40s and early 50s – Margaret Lockwood, Phyllis Calvert, Jean Kent, even Googie Withers – were middle-class in performance, accent and role. Dors, although her drama school voice sometimes betrayed her, was given working-class roles and played them with gusto. In *Good Time Girl* (1947) she portrays with sullen defiance the girl whom the probation officer tries to save; in *Dance Hall* (1950) she stands out from the gentility of the other girls; in *Yield to the Night* her lack of pretensions is specifically set against the upper-class arrogance of the woman she kills.

In such films Dors evades middle-class moral judgments. The sullenness and obstinacy which are as much part of her roles as the humorous resignation she also displayed signify characters who want more from life than their apportioned lot and resent others who have escaped boredom and poverty. Her sex symbol career spanned a period of change from the austerity and rationing of the late 40s to an emphasis on domestic spending in the 50s and on women as crucial spenders. By emphasising both glamour and toughness in her reworking of the sex symbol paradigm, Dors embodied both the down-to-earth recognition that money was crucial to getting on and the heady notion that it could all be thrown away on having a 'good time'. For film audiences in the 50s, she could be seen as one of 'us', not one of 'them'; and her performance, in and out of the films, could be enjoyed the more because of it.

345

DIRK BOGARDE

Andy Medhurst

Dirk Bogarde's place within British film history is simultaneously central and problematic. Few other British stars have received such critical acclaim, few have so dominated box-office and popularity polls, but the critical and popular reputations rest on different, almost mutually exclusive sets of films. The popular Bogarde, the screen idol Bogarde, belongs to the 1950s, to genre films, to Rank, to *Doctor in the House, The Wind Cannot Read* and *A Tale of Two Cities*. The Bogarde of critical respectability belongs to the 60s and 70s, to art cinema, to 'independence' and 'integrity', to *The Servant, Accident,* and *Death in Venice*. Bogarde, according to critical orthodoxy, is the pin-up who matured into an actor, or rather the reluctant pin-up who was really an actor all along, if only he could find films worthy of his talent. In this sense, he has been constructed as the star who transcended British cinema, who escaped from its cramped, domestic mediocrity into the wide open spaces of the international art film.

Clearly, this will not do. One does not have to be nationalistic to see the crudity and misrepresentation that underpin a comment such as David Thomson's, in his *Biographical Dictionary of the Cinema*, that Bogarde 'quickly became one of the leading men of British cinema: the worst fate that could have befallen him and one which has marked him for life, no matter how much he has striven to overcome it.'[1] Here, British cinema is posited as a cross between a leper's bell and an albatross, with Bogarde one of its more lamentable casualties. No, this will not do at all.

We need to see Bogarde's 50s and early 60s films in context, not place them in some twisted teleology that reduces them to an extended apprenticeship. Bogarde's roles in that period offer a particularly illuminating way into understanding the general condition of British film-making. If he seems uneasy or misplaced in the generic rigidity of his Rank films, we need to ask why that should be the case, not simply assume that they are 'bad' films. In this essay I want to offer a reading of Bogarde's career (for a star's career is a text to be read as much as a film is) which focuses on his difference from the norms of British male stardom. An understanding of the difference will bring the norms more clearly into view. Thus I would hope that a study of Bogarde has a wider relevance.

It would be disingenuous, however, to pretend that I approach Bogarde from a purely detached academic standpoint. I would not have been drawn to study him closely had I not begun from a position of intense admiration. This needs to be said, since it should not be forgotten that the fascination with a star image is probably the most seductive method that narrative cinema has developed in order to catch and bind its audience. After that initial pull, though, certain star images begin to set off resonances that have deeper social implications. Hence what I have come to value in Bogarde, what I find compelling in a wider sense, is how his star persona serves as a register of social tensions, more precisely how those tensions cohere around the problem of masculinity. Bogarde's image, both in screen performances and the equally important off-screen publicity material, can, I think, be read as a series of attempts to find a new way of representing male sexuality. This is all the more creditable, all the more impressive, given the precise film-historical and social-historical context of the early 1950s. One only has to set Bogarde against his contemporaries, the likes of Kenneth More and Richard Todd, to notice some significant differences. Unlike them, Bogarde seems always unhappy with existing norms of masculinity. Where they embody restraint, he strives for excess. Where they remain calm in a crisis, Bogarde goes to pieces.

These remarks are of course generalisations, and Bogarde did appear in a number of films which were just as emotionally constricted as those inhabited by More and Todd. The key Bogarde films, however, are those that are sites of deviation, and the most startling of these remains *The Blue Lamp* (Ealing Studios, 1950). A crucial film in many respects, it now looks less like an advertisement for the Metropolitan Police than a troubled examination of post-war male youth. It is also the film that secured Bogarde's stardom, and it is not hard to see why.

The most interesting opposition in the film is not that between law and crime in abstract terms, or that between Jack Warner and Dirk Bogarde, although this furnishes the film's central iconic moment when Bogarde shoots Warner dead; it is the contrast between Bogarde and Jimmy Hanley, who plays the young constable. *The Blue Lamp* must have been uncommonly sure of the rightness of its ideological project (that the police uphold the law, that the law preserves decency and the 'British way of life'), because it seriously asks its audiences to side with Hanley and to favour him over Bogarde. Looked at today, however, this contest is absurdly one-sided. Where Bogarde's performance stands as compelling, thrilling, and above all erotic, Hanley is drab, bland, and neutered. His position in the narrative is as Warner's symbolic son (replacing the real son who died in the war, just to load the dice even further) but the film neglects to give him any independent life, any hint of sexuality. He doesn't even have a nice, bland Ealing girlfriend. Bogarde, however, is violently sexual, so much so that it is hard not to see his real crime as eroticism rather than murder. As in the American *film noir*, with which *The Blue Lamp* has some distant similarities, sexual and legal transgression are conflated, and this is achieved principally through the intensity of the transgressor's performance. Where *The Blue Lamp* is strikingly unusual is that the transgressive sexuality is male, and that the intensity is Bogarde's. Most of Bogarde's later art films drew on a seam of erotic cruelty (*Accident, The Night Porter, Providence*), but this did not have to be drawn out by 'great directors'; it is already there, fully fledged and in context twice as powerful, in this Ealing film directed by Basil Dearden. (It is worth noting, however, that when in his autobiographies Bogarde lists those directors he most respects, Dearden is always there, alongside the more predictable Losey and Visconti.)

The other central tension in British cinema, besides sexuality, is class, and *The Blue Lamp* is also pertinent here. Erotic cruelty was not new to British films; in the 1940s it had been the property of James Mason. Yet where Mason's successes had been mostly in historical or aristocratic roles, Bogarde's appropriation of the thrilling sadist persona is urban, contemporary and working-class. It is, then, less distanced and more radical, more of a challenge to the norms of British screen masculinity.

Such was the impact of *The Blue Lamp* that Bogarde feared being typed in young thug or spiv roles. ' "Save Me From Spivs" by Dirk Bogarde' is the title of one early 50s fan magazine article. His contract with Rank, however, meant that the sheer volume of films he appeared in prevented him being fixed entirely in one genre. Hence he appears in typically 50s war films and domestic comedies (*The Sea Shall not Have Them*, 1954, and *For Better for Worse*, 1954, can serve as indicative titles for each type) where it is, admittedly, hard to discern any groundbreaking portrayal such as that in *The Blue Lamp*. Bogarde was the leading romantic hero of the period, but while the films fuelled that image, the accompanying fan material is less straightforward. On the one hand, fan articles such as 'Save Me From Spivs' made it clear that Bogarde was beginning to chafe at the limitations of the parts he played; on the other, the visual iconography of the Bogarde pin-ups increasingly departs from the standard representations of the male star. There is a general tendency in the 50s for British male stars to be shown as country gentlemen, sporting tweeds and jodhpurs and living in rural comfort.[2] Bogarde fits in with this trend, but, with hindsight, can be seen to be playing with its codes, quietly mocking its absurdities while the Richard Todds went along with them wholeheartedly. Increasingly through the 50s, the stress is on Bogarde's house, and on Bogarde as home-maker. These articles can often only be described as camp. Two quotations should give the flavour of what I mean: 'He also likes to tinkle on the spinet for his own amusement, dreaming back to Victorian days when some gracious lady in a crinoline and long curls swished around the family drawing-room and finally parked herself on the stool and made music';[3] or 'Dirk does not mind muddy shoes leaving their mark on the floor, so long as it is the kitchen floor and not the carpet in the front hall. . . . The guest bedroom he designed in pink, cream and grey. . . . For his study he chose man-sized armchairs. . . .'[4] It is impossible to think of such things being written about other male stars of the period; even in the prime of his romantic hero phase, Bogarde's star image is at some level opposing itself to traditional masculinities. The wit with which the ideal-home articles are written also makes them less problematic, from today's stand-point of sexual politics, than his alluring brutality in *The Blue Lamp*.

The undertones of camp sometimes even make their way through to the Rank genre romances. *Campbell's Kingdom* (1957) is a kind of British attempt at a Western, with Bogarde going to Canada to search for oil and fight off the heavies (led by Stanley Baker) who try to force him to leave. Bogarde's progress in the film is realised through iconography. He arrives in the snowy Canadian shanty town, fresh from London, wearing a camel-hair overcoat and beige woolly gloves, and only manages to take on the villainous gang by switching to plaid shirt, black boots, and a bizarre leather wrist-strap. If the narrative's ideological project is to show how Bogarde 'becomes a man', then the performance and its toying with the signifiers of masculinity take on a potentially subversive role. *Campbell's Kingdom,* however, dwindles away into mainstream heroics of so predictable a pattern that Bogarde can do nothing but go along with them.

There are three later films, Bogarde's most fascinating since *The Blue Lamp*, which do succeed in imploding their generic constraints, and which do so by moving into the area which can be seen in retrospect as the logical conclusion of Bogarde's testing of masculine parameters – namely, homosexuality. It is possible to hunt out distant hints of homosexuality in many Bogarde films: war films, almost by definition, rely on at least some degree of close bonding between men, and *Hunted* (1952) and *The Spanish Gardener* (1956), of the non-war films, are also open to such readings, but it is on the

349

Changing images of Bogarde: *The Blue Lamp* (1950) ...

unofficial 'trilogy' of *Libel* (1959), *The Singer not the Song* (1960), and, especially, *Victim* (1961) that I want to concentrate.

When the British cultural hegemony was demanding social realism, working-class actors, factories and seedy pubs, *Libel* flourished its theatrical origins, its Establishment credentials (directed by Anthony Asquith when those were the days of Tony Richardson), its gallery of character actors (Robert Morley and Wilfrid Hyde-White, among others), and its unashamed melodrama. It was wholeheartedly derided by critics. Now, it looks like a dazzling fusion of courtroom tension, family melodrama, sexual ambiguity, and class conflict, with elements of the war film and Hammer horror. And at the centre of this stands Bogarde. He plays three parts, as the plot is to do with doppelgängers and mistaken identities, but he plays one of the parts (Frank Welney) as, almost but not quite blatantly, homosexual. The fact that the character Welney seems to desire is his double means that Bogarde desires Bogarde, which I suppose adds narcissism to an already spicy psychoanalytical brew. I mention *Libel* here largely because it is a film that cries out for re-evaluation (and psycho-analytical approaches would be the most fruitful) and also because it gives Bogarde his best opportunity since *The Blue Lamp* for his unique combination of compelling acting and interrogation of masculine norms.

The Singer not the Song features Bogarde as a Mexican bandit, wearing leather trousers and riding a white horse, involved in a torrid love-hate relationship with an Irish priest played by John Mills. That mere plot description ought to signify why I include it here. Clearly a less serious film than *Libel*, it is also, in the final analysis, a less interesting one. Bogarde aside, it lacks the conviction that would make it a homoerotic *Duel in the Sun* (John Mills looks as though he wishes he were somewhere else throughout the film). It is, however, tempting to see it as Bogarde's full-bloodedly camp revenge on the generic crudities of *Campbell's Kingdom* and its ilk.

... *Victim* (1961)

Victim is Bogarde's finest achievement since *The Blue Lamp*, and the two make suitable bookends for the British 50s phase of his career. Both were made by the producer-director team of Michael Relph and Basil Dearden, and in both a carefully wrought ideological project is wrecked by Bogarde's intensity. In the earlier film, his attractiveness (in all senses of the word) undercuts the surface eulogy to law and order. In *Victim*, he turns a cautious plea for sexual tolerance into an eroticised melodrama. *Victim*'s intentions were to support the recommendations of the Wolfenden report, which advocated the partial decriminalisation of male homosexual acts, but the emotional excess of Bogarde's performance as the homosexual barrister pushes the text beyond its liberal boundaries until it becomes a passionate validation of the homosexual option. Simply watch the 'confession' scene for proof of this.

Bogarde's shift in direction in these films can perhaps be put into context by mentioning again the wider cultural shift into social realism. Bogarde had made his mark in the early 50s by being a signifier of difference, an alternative masculinity. In *The Blue Lamp* and the other spiv films, this meant adopting an assertive, aggressive heterosexuality, to contrast strikingly with the restraint and lack of display that was the British screen's male norm. By the early 60s, however, aggressive heterosexuality had returned, and in more convincingly working-class ways than Bogarde had ever managed. To maintain difference, to keep searching out new models of male sexuality, Bogarde's move into openly or covertly homosexual characterisations was in some ways an inevitable step.

It was also bound up with Bogarde's age. *Victim*'s immediate achievement, in terms of his career, was to lose him the young fan following he had built up during the 50s. He was playing not only a homosexual, but a middle-aged homosexual, and this sudden refusal of teenage appeal freed Bogarde to undertake more personally motivated projects. *Victim*'s own narrative can be enticingly related to the effect the film had on Bogarde's career. Two elements of the plot invite such a reading. Firstly, the fact that Boy Barrett has kept a scrapbook of newspaper cuttings about Melville Farr (Bogarde). This is distinctly odd – it's a well-filled scrapbook, but when did the popular press ever pay so much attention to barristers? Film stars, on the other hand. . . . Thus when Barrett, on the run from the police, tears up the scrapbook and tries to flush the pieces down a public toilet (I'll not dwell on the Freudian implications of the locale), we can easily see this as the Bogarde star image (the stuff, one presumes, of so many 1950s teenage scrapbooks) being consigned to a very graphic oblivion. Secondly, Farr's speech about how he intends to go into court as himself, a public figure, in order to highlight the legal oppression surrounding male homosexuality, can clearly be seen to parallel Bogarde's decision to play such a part. *Victim* is, if nothing else, a film that advocates coming out.[5]

It is at this point that many critics would step in to argue that *Victim* marks Bogarde's liberation from mediocrity, that the portrayal of Farr paves the way for the greater achievements of the later art films. I would prefer to argue that after *Victim*, Bogarde never again made such an interesting film. He may have found his later work more personally satisfying, as his elegant and informative autobiographies bear witness, but critical analysis can never simply accept an artist's own self-estimation. Bogarde's later films lack that sense of social tension that makes *The Blue Lamp, Libel,* and *Victim* so challenging and so important. They become, increasingly, vehicles for his undoubted actorly skills, reaching with *Death in Venice* (1971) a peak of virtuosity in a vacuum. Pleasures exist in such films (*Providence,* 1977, particularly), but they lose their sense of social moment. They cease to be interventions into a national film culture, and not only by virtue of their 'international' label. The British art films Bogarde made in the 60s are equally culpable in their striving after significance.

The Servant (1963) and *Accident* (1967) seem to me to be so much less rich than the best of Bogarde's earlier work. Their very reservedness shrieks of pretension; they seem determined to seek approval according to literary notions of value. Their vaunted complexity remains fixed at the level of their narrative enigmas, and their vicious misogyny cannot claim the excuses of generic determinism available to *The Blue Lamp.* The very fact that *The Servant* was heralded as (yet another) breakthrough into maturity should be enough to send those of us familiar with the various false dawns of British cinema rushing back to the reassuring immaturity of melodrama. Of course, Bogarde's performance in both *The Servant* and *Accident* is breathtaking, but his surroundings have taken on a repellent quality.

I don't want to suggest that there is nothing of any worth after *Victim.* Bogarde's career has enough ups and downs to wreck the smug neatness of any such assertion. Two 1963 films fascinate (and outshine their contemporary *The Servant*). *The Mind Benders* is the third great Bogarde/Relph/Dearden collaboration, and its bleak acccount of academia and neurosis has far more complexity than the grinding elusiveness of *Accident.* And *I Could Go On Singing* contains one of the finest Bogarde performances; he is, inevitably, outshone by Judy Garland, but the film can also be seen in terms of the homosexual subtext of his work.[6]

Dirk Bogarde, then, is one of the signposts of tension in the British cinema of the 1950s and early 1960s. That period has for too long been the butt of gibes about sexlessness and tedium. Bogarde, like in her very different way Diana Dors,[7] indicates the underside of emotional repression, the sneer or the pout that disturbs the stiff upper lip. His best work thrives on the existence of repressive ideologies, since then he has something to chip away at, to worry, to rub against. That rub, that friction generates the spark of significant interest, and the spark illuminates. Bogarde in *Victim* and *The Blue Lamp* achieves the rare power of genuine subversion in popular culture, and it is this achievement which matters – far, far more than his ventures into minority art.

Notes

1   David Thomson, *A Biographical Dictionary of the Cinema,* 2nd edition, London, Secker & Warburg, 1980, p. 54.
2   On the visual iconography of male stars of this period, see Andy Medhurst, 'Can Chaps be Pin-ups?', *TEN–8*, no. 17, 1985.
3   'Dirk Bogarde' in *'Girl' Film and Television Annual*, no. 1, 1956.
4   Maud Miller, 'My Friend Dirk Bogarde' in *'Girl' Film and Television Annual*, no. 5, 1960.
5   For further discussion of *Victim*, see Richard Dyer, ' "Victim": Hermeneutic Project', *Film Form*, no. 2, 1977; and Andy Medhurst, ' "Victim": Text as Context', *Screen*, vol. 25, nos. 4–5, 1984.
6   On the gay relevance of *I Could Go On Singing,* see Richard Dyer, 'Judy Garland and Gay Men' in *Heavenly Bodies,* London, BFI, 1986.
7   See Christine Geraghty's article on Dors in this volume.

MANDY
DAUGHTER OF TRANSITION
Pam Cook

Mandy, a film about a deaf child's struggle to enter 'normal' society, was shot at Ealing in 1951 and released in July 1952. It is commonly identified as a film 'authored' by Alexander Mackendrick, an Ealing director who worked against the grain of the studio's preference for safe subject matter and a realist aesthetic. It is, equally, a key film of the early 1950s, appearing at an important moment for Britain, Ealing, and British cinema. 1951, the year of the Festival of Britain, which celebrated the achievements of the outgoing Labour government, was also the year of *The Lavender Hill Mob* and *The Man in the White Suit*, described by Charles Barr as the last of the 'buoyant' Ealing comedies.[1] 1951 was a turning point for the film industry in general: the 'X' certificate was introduced in an attempt to stem the decline in cinema audiences by moving into sensational and previously forbidden areas of sex and violence, under pressure on the one hand from the influx of 'Continental' sex films and European art cinema, and on the other from competition for audiences from television.

It is simplistic to pin down a shift in social climate to a single year, but it does seem that 1951 can be seen as a pivotal year for British society, marking a shift from a period of post-war austerity, presided over by a Labour government dedicated to welfare capitalism, to the consumer boom of the 50s managed by a new tough breed of Conservatives. The shift can also be characterised in terms of changing national values, community spirit giving way to individualism and an increasing emphasis on the private domain of home and family. Culturally, the British dedication to high art values of 'quality', 'taste' and 'realism' was to be assaulted by the influx of American consumer goods and popular culture, scandalising intellectuals from both left and right.

None of these shifts was particularly sudden: the seeds of Americanisation, and of greater laxity in moral values, for instance, were obviously already there during the war and post-war years; and when the Conservatives came to power in 1951, they did so by a narrow margin, suggesting that there was no major swing to them, and that the post-war Labour government's commitment to gradual-ism and reformism may have helped pave the way to Conservative victory and an ideology of 'classlessness' and consensus. However, it would also be a mistake to characterise the shift as entirely smooth. This transitional period was marked by a proliferation of competing ideologies, testifying to a national uncertainty about traditional values and their effectiveness in the post-war Britain of new technologies, egalitarian social democracy, and sexual emancipation. The social democratic rhetoric of radicalism, of a social revolution achieved painlessly, masked a suspicion of new ideas and a cautious attachment to traditional structures. The Festival of Britain itself perhaps exemplifies these contradictions – on the one hand celebrat-ing the benefits of the Welfare State and nationalisation, and calling up the New Commonwealth as an ideal family of nations; on the other, promoting a particular style of living, a superficial 'Scandin-avian' modernism which could easily be imposed upon traditional structures of home and family.[2]

Ealing had flourished during those years when the values of community and co-operation, which were to come under pressure in the 50s, were mobilised in the interests of national unity. In a way, it came to represent those values itself, becoming something of a national institution. When faced with the decision either to exploit changing values, as Hammer did subsequently, or to accommodate them, Ealing took the latter road, producing a series of staid, normative comedies and dramas which have come to be seen as representative of the studio's 50s output. In this linear version of events *Mandy,* which appeared in 1952, fits neither into Ealing's buoyant period, nor into the 50s consensus films. Thus it stands out as an isolated work, a powerful masterpiece which paradoxically marks the beginning of the studio's decline. But it seems less exceptional if considered as, precisely, a transitional film, an attempt by Ealing to negotiate a shifting terrain at a time when its future was uncertain; an attempt, perhaps, to take on board changing values, to explore and even exploit them, and finally to project an Ealing version of Britain in transition which would show the future as developing gradually from the past. In this sense, *Mandy* could be seen as exemplary, not only of Mackendrick's authorial concerns, but also of the relationship between social, cultural and economic factors at the particular historical moment of its production.

Mandy was promoted by Ealing as having its inspiration in a social problem – the institutionalised care of deaf and dumb children – and as using a real institution – the progressive Royal Residential School for the Deaf in Manchester – as a model. At the same time, the film was described by the studio as a powerful and moving human drama based on a novel which had been serialised for BBC radio's 'Woman's Hour'. Here are the first indications of an attempt to straddle contradictions. The appeal to a notion of documentary social realism both recalls a respected tradition of British 'quality' cinema and capitalises on an emerging genre of 'social problem' pictures. The social realist mode also connotes the realm of the public. This appeal to 'quality' confers respectability on the melodramatic/women's picture aspect of the film – its blatant appeal to the private, personal realm of the emotions in order to capture an audience and manipulate its responses. (This was a direction often taken by mainstream British cinema in the 50s – see the combination of melodrama and social realism in *Yield to the Night,* 1956, and *Woman in a Dressing Gown,* 1957, for example.) The tension between public and private, the shifting boundaries between them, is a major theme in *Mandy,* intersecting with the tension between past and future and worked through in terms of different institutional spaces (home/garden vs. school/playground/park).

Ultimately, these tensions are resolved by finding a new balance between the conflicting terms, and a space which lies somewhere between the basic oppositions, representing a compromise. Certain characters represent the poles of the oppositions: Mandy's grandparents stand for the old, traditional, monogamous middle-class family; Mandy herself, Kit (her mother), and Searle (headmaster of the school for the deaf) stand for the new, democratic, egalitarian ideal; Harry (Mandy's father) vacillates between the two, caught in his own resistance to change. This resistance is echoed in Ackland, representative of the institutional old guard on the school's governing body, in conflict with the progressives, Jane Ellis and Searle. The drama of shifting attitudes and ideas is worked through in Kit and Harry's relationship, torn apart by the conflict: the melodramatic mode evokes the power relations at stake in the private space of the family, the private pain of transition, while the social realist mode is used to depict power relations in the institutional hierarchy. Importantly, the public and private overlap – in the close relationship that forms between Kit and Searle, for instance, and in the scheming one between Ackland and Harry. These areas of overlap provide another locus for the playing out of the drama of shifting boundaries: Kit and Searle must sacrifice their relationship, Harry must disentangle himself from Ackland so that a new balance between old and new, public and private, can be found, and new boundaries drawn. The value of progressive ideas has been proved, but only in so far as they put pressure on established, traditional structures to change – a truly reformist, gradualist philosophy.

The point of this account of *Mandy*'s thematic and narrative structure is not to reduce it to an impoverished schema, nor to prove that the film is reactionary, or reformist rather than radical. I want to argue that the film is contradictory, that in negotiating sets of competing and conflicting ideologies it produces a vision of Britain which is at once forward-looking and backward-looking – looking forward, that is, to a new egalitarian society in which boundaries of class and sex are broken down, and looking backward to traditional structures in order to preserve them. *Mandy* projects a picture of a nation on the brink of change, from which it ultimately draws back, sadly unable to rise to the challenge. Ealing itself was in the same position.

To explore this contradiction further, I'd like to look at the film more specifically in terms of the way it mediates post-war ideologies of femininity and the family, particularly those of mother and child. The war years had encouraged economic and sexual emancipation for women, a situation not entirely reversed in the post-war reconstruction period, when labour shortages meant that women, including wives and mothers, were required for certain forms of work. However, in the post-war period women's main role in society was seen as lying within the family, a trend which continued into the 50s as the economic boom made housewives increasingly important as purchasers and consumers. Nevertheless, the active social role envisaged for women during the war years continued in the post-war vision of a democratic and egalitarian society. Women had their own clearly defined contribution to make to the building of this new society, primarily as housewives and mothers. But if femininity was defined mainly in terms of hearth and home, which many feminists would now see as essentially oppressive and limited, it was also seen as having a positive effect on the overbearing, aggressive aspects of masculinity, softening it, making it more tolerant and flexible. There was a merging of masculinity and femininity in which each could benefit from taking on certain qualities of the other. This egalitarianism extended to the family too, which was no longer envisaged as authoritarian and patriarchal, but as a partnership of equals, albeit with clearly defined, different roles.

The emphasis on the family had repercussions for women; their employment, indeed all activities outside the home, had to be fitted round their primary role as housewives and mothers. During this period new meanings were attached to motherhood.[3] The war years had given rise to anxieties about the lives of mothers and children, about the depleted population, the declining birth-rate, and the detrimental effects of evacuation and institutional care on young children separated from their mothers. Studies during and after the war began to address the importance of the emotional and psycho-

Tensions: the family in *Mandy* (1952)

logical well-being of the child, stressing the mother-child relationship and relegating fathers to shadowy, background figures.
Paradoxically, the stress on the presence of the mother both confined
the mother to the home and gave a new status and power to
motherhood itself. Simultaneously, female sexuality was increasingly defined as active. The Kinsey Reports of 1948 and 1953, given
wide publicity in Britain as well as in the United States, suggested
that women's sexual needs were more diverse and demanding than
had generally been thought, and, moreover, that they did not fit
neatly into the assumptions underlying the heterosexual couple
relationship. As if to counterbalance the threatening implications of
such evidence, traditional notions of the family as a site for
reproduction were rejigged to accommodate these disturbing new
ideas. On the one hand, the family became a central organising
principle in the new British society, and on the other, it was posed as
the place where conflicting ideologies of parenthood, childcare and
sexuality would be battled out and finally contained.

Against the background of these shifting definitions of femininity
and the family, Ealing films in general subscribed to traditional

ideologies.[4] Criteria of realism, quality and taste dominated the studio's output, producing a repression of certain questions, particularly those of female sexuality – though the films of 'maverick' directors Robert Hamer and Alexander Mackendrick have been identified as focusing on such issues in interesting ways. Thus *Mandy* can be seen as exceptional in dealing quite directly with problems of sexual desire and restraint in the 'new family' of post-war and 50s Britain. Nevertheless, like Mackendrick's preceding film, *The Man in the White Suit* (1951), it remains pessimistic about the possibilities for radical change, in spite of, even perhaps because of, its apparently positive 'happy ending'.

In its construction of femininity, *Mandy* draws on post-war images of the New Woman – equal to, but different from, men. It centres, as we have seen, on the relationship between Kit and Harry, Mandy's mother and father. Phyllis Calvert's performance as Kit recalls the parts she played as an active and desiring mother in Gainsborough women's pictures of the 40s (*Madonna of the Seven Moons, They Were Sisters*), where the woman's desire was validated, as long as it did not transgress the social and moral order. Nevertheless, the focus on feminine desire in these films produced contradictions: the inevitable repression of desire consequent upon sacrifice of self-interest to a higher moral order frequently produced tragic scenarios in which loss remained more palpably significant than the victory of the social order. In *Mandy*, Kit's desire manifests itself primarily in relation to her struggle on behalf of her child, though she and her husband Harry have a passionate and, for Ealing, highly charged sexual relationship. The problem posed, and finally worked through in the film, is how far the acting out of each of the major characters' desires is for the good of the child, and therefore for the future health of society. It is significant that Mandy is a girl, for what is also at issue is the role of women in the new Britain – indeed, the film opens with Kit's voice-over asking explicitly what Mandy's future prospects might be. Mandy's entry into society is blocked by her father's self-interested pride and authoritarian attitudes.

Harry's patriarchal attitudes must change if Mandy is to play an active role in society, and it is primarily Kit's acting out of her own desire which brings about such a change. In the process, the traditional bourgeois family is split. Kit and Mandy are reconstituted as a single parent family, finding in Searle a surrogate father-figure who has many of the attributes of a mother. Kit temporarily takes over control of the family, becoming more 'masculine', while Harry must become, like Searle, more 'feminine'. The boundaries of sexual difference are significantly shifted, hence the apparent optimism of the happy ending.

It becomes clear, however, that this shift is heavily circumscribed. The incipient love affair between Kit and Searle is curtailed, the alternatives to the monogamous, heterosexual family unit – the 'extended' family, the single parent family, the state institution as family in the form of the residential school – are all found to be inadequate, or rather, are seen as intermediate stages in the progress towards the 'new', reconstituted heterosexual monogamous family; no longer quite so patriarchal, the power relations altered to take account of the 'equal but different' status of the mother, allowing Mandy to run out from the private, enclosed space of the family to join the rest of society. Restraint and curtailment are marked in the closing moments of the film. As Mandy runs to join the other children, Harry holds Kit back from following her: a tiny gesture, but significant enough to be repeated, and undermining the 'happy ending' with a question – with the father now back in control, the mother held in place, just how egalitarian is the new social order?

It is not reading too much into this small gesture, I think, to see in it a pessimism about the nature of reformism which makes *Mandy*, finally, less a celebration of the New Britain than a critique of the gradualist philosophy underlying its vision of change.

Notes

1   Charles Barr, *Ealing Studios*, London, Cameron and Tayleur/David and Charles, 1977.
2   Elizabeth Wilson, *Only Halfway to Paradise*, London, Tavistock, 1980.
3   Maggie Millman, *What is a Family?*, booklet accompanying the Channel 4 series *Flashback*, 'What is a Family? Images from the 20th century', first transmitted in February 1984, London, Eyre and Spottiswoode, 1984.
4   John Ellis, 'Made in Ealing', *Screen*, vol. 16, no. 1, Spring 1975.

THE SHIP THAT DIED OF SHAME
Jim Cook

Throughout the 1950s, as the radical moment of 1945 and Labour's landslide victory solidified into Tory rule, 'Butskellite' consensus,[1] and a reformed capitalism, 'the War' came to be seen in quite complex terms as the period before 'now'. For all its very real traumas, it came to assume a fixed point in people's consciousness as a time when purpose and a sense of national identity were unproblematic, opposed to 'now' with its conflicting and confusing claims on loyalties. In this context, *The Ship That Died of Shame* (directed by Basil Dearden for Ealing Studios in 1955) is an exemplary film of its time, not only activating memories but, through its narrative structure, constructing and expressing a striking critique of such nostalgia and the drives which fuel it.

In outline, its story is simple enough. After a 'good war' in command of a motor gunboat, blighted only by the death of his wife, Commander Bill Randall (George Baker) loses contact with his two close companions: Hoskins (Richard Attenborough), his second-in-command, and Birdie (Bill Owen), their engineer. Unable to settle down after the war and without suitable employment, he accepts Hoskins' offer of re-forming the team, rescuing the gunboat from the breaker's yard, and embarking on a little light smuggling. At first the adventures and thrills seem to replicate the war, but the increasingly criminal nature of the work breaks into this fantasy, and the film ends with a literal break with the past as, in their flight from the police, the boat smashes on the rocks. This essay is concerned with *how* the film tells this story.

It is difficult not to describe the opening scenes of *The Ship That Died of Shame* in terms of dreamlike picaresque. Opening shots behind the credits of a motor gunboat, number 1087, scything through choppy seas effortlessly connote the war, excitement and action – associations quickly disturbed by a fading down of the 'natural' sounds and their replacement with plaintive music and the ruminative voice-over of Bill telling us that 'the beginning, like almost everything else about me, went back to the war'. Then, it was good: there was the team of George Hoskins and Bill Randall and Birdie, with clear objectives (kill Jerry) and a strong camaraderie and harmony of purpose centred on 'her' (1087): a harmony threatened only occasionally, and then not for long, by George's moral flightiness over the accuracy of their toll of 'hits'.

Gunboat 1087 is not the sole recipient of skipper Bill's love, however. There is also Helen, Mrs Randall (Virginia McKenna), a wife with whom he has spent only three days and whom we disturbingly first see, like his objects of attack, through Bill's binoculars. Borrowing a friend's cottage for effectively their first time together, Helen feels troubled – 'as if we were doing something wrong' – and panics in the shadows as she loses her bearings and her sense of where Bill is. This sense of the frailty of the future is then overridden by fulfilled sexual desire and a post-coital construction of what we are fighting for expressed in extreme personal terms. For Bill, 'Since I've known you there seems to be a purpose in things – even in this damned war'; to which Helen admonishingly replies, 'Don't ever do anything silly with that ship of yours, will you?' After the quiet sensuality of these scenes, there follows the violent harmony of a night battle, the run for home, and an attack by a stray German plane. Returning to the cottage, Bill finds Helen dead, killed in an air-raid. For the rest of the war 'there seemed nothing else in life, only the ship'. In time, the war ends, and instead of victory celebrations there is a long scene of 1087 going to her last anchorage – a 'funeral' at which all due rites are observed and which seems in some way to stand in for the repressed memory of Helen's death.

With the war over, the tone of the film alters considerably as the narrative shifts from 'then' to an account of events leading up to the film's 'now' of 1955; although in fact precise chronology is left vague. Just as Bill is experiencing the difficulties of post-war adjustment with the collapse of his boat-building enterprise, he meets up again with (is picked up by?) George, appropriately at a Services Club reunion, where anything George might have to offer seems a better bet than the dispirited staring into beer and mournful renditions of 'We'll Meet Again' which characterise the occasion. What in fact George does have on offer is, through some modest smuggling, the promise once again of action and adventure, the reunion of the old firm of Hoskins, Randall and Birdie, and, crucially, the reincarnation of 1087 as their smuggling vessel. Visiting the mudflats where the boat is beached, Bill murmurs, 'It's her, all right', and George, leaning insinuatingly against him, follows up his advantage with, 'We'd certainly be doing her a favour getting her out of this graveyard.'

From this point, our engagement with the film is governed by a complex narrative tension between what one might call a 'realistic' level and a 'metaphoric' level. On the side of realism, grounded in the film's present and in the development of the narrative, a number of questions and anxieties present themselves. Is George to be trusted? Will the innocent Bill be able to prevent himself and the loyal but hapless Birdie from getting more involved in serious smuggling? On the side of metaphor, rooted in the past and acting as a brake on narrative development, is a more fundamental anxiety: how far does the 'mess' they are drifting into imply not merely criminality punishable by man-made law, but also a more fundamental dereliction, as Bill ignores the moral imperative issued during the war by Helen about not doing anything silly with the ship? It is this tension, always implying more at stake in the narrative's unfolding than is actually articulated, which gives the film its peculiar intensity and power to disturb.

Initially the tension is controllable, playful even, as when the wily old customs man (Bernard Lee) boards the boat, senses that something is going on (he can always tell a 'wrong 'un'), but is outwitted by the team as Bill in particular quick-wittedly creates a diversion. But such individual initiative derived from the past is no match for the long-term deviousness of George, who after a sea battle encounter with the 'enemy' – here, more professional smugglers – promptly turns round and does a deal with them.

It is at this point that the dense and allusive pessimism of the film becomes very clearly marked, as the realistic and metaphorical levels start to butt against each other. In one scene, where George proposes his deal to the professionals' leader (a chilling performance by Roland Culver as the 'Colonel'), a hitherto unspoken cynical misogyny comes to the surface. In the next scene, while George sups with the devil, we find Birdie and Bill cleaning 1087 and wondering 'if she's happy in her new job'. In fact, 'she', the principle of honour and virtue, now proceeds to react against the drift towards moral anarchy, and, shortly after the discovery that the cargo has escalated from wine and watches to forged currency, the ship's engines unexpectedly and inexplicably stop. The two levels are now riding very close to each other, and to the characters' consciousness. George to Birdie: 'I'd put you on a charge for this [the engine breakdown] if we were still in the Service.' Birdie: 'There's lots of things would be different, sir, if we was still in the Service.'

The most extreme difference between the traditions of the Service and their current work, between the two kinds of dangerous 'job', is embodied in the human cargo the men are committed to carrying: he is revealed to be a child-killer on the run, and it is this that finally explodes any fantasy of sustaining past heroics and camaraderie. As at so many points in the film, the visual style during these sequences is highly expressive as well as functional: unlike the 'pure' darkness of

After the war: *The Ship That Died of Shame* (1955)

the war night battle scenes through which their victories could shine,
here the night is sinisterly foggy as the sad-looking figure – echoes of
the Nazi banality of evil – erupts from the shadows of a hideous past
and on to the boat.

Of course, once their cargo's identity is known as the violator of
families and the future, there is no way that even George's amoral
pragmatism can contain the group. The way 'the old firm' finally
splits up, however, is significant: George accuses Bill of 'softness
right from the start' and links this with 'brooding about how happy
you might have been with what's-her-name, Helen'. This direct
reference to 'the ideal' – that is, to both precisely what it is for Bill that
allows him to construct a continuity between 'then' and 'now' *and* to
its regressive, repressive edge – unleashes Bill's only act of spontaneous physical violence. To counter this mounting hysteria, the figure
of the wise, simple customs officer now reappears, but his gut-
instinct morality (to Birdie of George: 'Until I saw your boss and how
he looked it was only suspicion') is brutally overridden by the
Colonel, who shoots him. In the final confrontation at sea, with Bill
and Birdie now fighting George and the Colonel, it is as though the

film is unable realistically to prise the characters free from the moral chasm into which they have fallen, and must itself simultaneously invoke the metaphorical level and spectacularly destroy it in order to close the narrative. Thus it is only through the ship's 'intervention' – stopping her engines and then righting herself in the storm as George goes overboard – that the 'heroes' are saved. As the ship breaks up on the rocks, Bill, literally cast free/adrift, finally recalls Helen's admonition and tells Birdie, 'Well, we did do something silly, useless, futile, pathetic.' Final dissolve to 1087 at war: 'And so she gave up and died in anger and in shame. Yes, she had her pride.'

Unlike contemporary reviews of the film which, sensing the two levels at which it works, tended to regard it as broken-backed,[2] I have tried to argue for the pleasures of reading between these levels and to see them as both held together and kept apart by the obsessive equation of a good past with 'her' – Helen, 1087, England (?). Drawing its overtly social and pessimistic anxieties about post-war reconstruction perhaps from Nicholas Monsarrat, author of the original novel (as of *The Cruel Sea*), the film overlays them with deeper worries, possibly from the more 'metaphysical' concerns of the playwright John Whiting, who worked on the script. At all events, the conscious worries of 'Where did it all go wrong?' and even 'Was it all worth it?' are not answered through a social account of post-war British society. Rather, the concern with a lost moral decency and pride is ultimately located in Bill's confused and impotent male sense of the loss of 'her' – the erotic and the sensual. Read this way, 'the beginning' does not just go 'back to the war', but more precisely it is located in that wartime moment of sexual fulfilment for Bill and Helen which the film records but is unable thereafter quite to accommodate.

Overall, because its criticism of nostalgia is far more intricate than any simple realist comparison between the good old days and post-war conditions could have been, *The Ship That Died of Shame* becomes, like *Mandy*, a particularly interesting example of a film which in fact says more than it seems to be saying. Consciously concerned about the continuing value of masculine heroics and the war, its particular form of narrative organisation results in the film not only offering a critique of such looking back in others, but also finding itself neurotically locked into a past where only the erotic can come to signify completion and fulfilment, and from which the only escape can be through violence and excess.

Notes

1   Butskellism: a portmanteau word formed from the names of two successive Chancellors of the Exchequer, the right-wing Socialist Hugh Gaitskell and the left-wing Conservative Rab Butler, to denote a particular form of 1950s political consensus.

2   The anonymous reviewer for the British Film Institute's *Monthly Film Bulletin* called it 'a sentimental fantasy tacked on to a basically conventional thriller'.

FRENZY
A RETURN TO BRITAIN
Peter Hutchings

Frenzy (1972) was the fifth of the six films Hitchcock made for the Hollywood studio Universal, following *The Birds, Marnie, Torn Curtain* and *Topaz* and preceding his final film, *Family Plot*. It was also his last British film (and his first British film since *Stage Fright* in 1950). The two previous films, *Torn Curtain* and *Topaz*, had been disappointing both critically and commercially, and Hitchcock, who was seventy years old when he made *Topaz*, was beginning to be considered worked-out, finished as a major director.

His return to Britain to make *Frenzy* was a wise career decision: a move from large budgets to a relatively small one, and a public relations coup by one of cinema's greatest showmen and self-publicists. In coming to Britain he guaranteed himself substantial press coverage, giving the press what he always tried to give his audience – a good story, the story of the local boy made good. On another level, the return to Britain at this point in his career can be seen as Hitchcock, after the experimentation of the earlier Universal films, returning to more familiar territory – London and the murder thriller – but still carrying over some of that inventive experimentation and self-reflexivity. Clearly the film can be placed firmly within the obsessive concerns of Hitchcock's work as a whole – the Wrong Man idea, the formation of the couple (foregrounded in this film by the depiction of the marriage bureau), and even old chestnuts like the transference of guilt. However, the film has, I believe, significance outside these immediate concerns of authorship: in particular, for its illumination of the relation of Hitchcock's cinema, and the type of cinema he represents, to British cinema and British film culture as it had developed, in his absence, since the Second World War.

Any outline sketch of British film history must identify the war as a central dividing and defining moment. With the war comes documentary as an important force (though of course its origins go further back), and with it, crucially, a critical privileging of realism which has been with us ever since. After the war we find a wide variety of British cinematic 'genres' which are themselves very rigorously divided, defined and valued through a realism/non-realism distinction. On the realist/Good Taste side we have Ealing, Free Cinema and the British New Wave; on the non-realist/Bad Taste (and also, significantly, immensely successful) side we find Gainsborough melodramas (which begin during the war), Hammer (beginning more or less with the success of *The Quatermass Xperiment* in 1954, consolidated three years later by *The Curse of Frankenstein*) and *Carry On* (a series commencing with *Carry On Sergeant* in 1958 and, like Hammer, petering out in the 1970s). Falling somewhere in between we have post-war war movies. A rigid dichotomy is discernible here, both in the way in which film production is organised in terms of various genres, and more especially in criticism, criticism as a hierarchical system of valuing films with 'realism' firmly embedded at the top.

Significantly, Hitchcock left Britain in 1939, thereby missing out on this critical privileging of realism, which was probably just as well considering the sort of films he had made and would go on to make. One can offer here as an interesting parallel the career of Michael Powell, a British non-realist director who stayed behind, whose position within mainstream cinema became increasingly marginalised in the 50s with his ballet/opera films (at a time when Hitchcock was making his 'great' movies with the likes of James Stewart and Cary Grant), and whose career was eventually brought to a virtual halt by the controversy surrounding the release of *Peeping Tom* in 1960.

What I want to suggest here is that *Frenzy* can, in a way, be seen as a compendium of post-war British cinema, of all those 'genres' mentioned above and a few more besides, so that, rather than being some curious and almost senile anachronism (which was how it was seen by more than one British critic[1]), *Frenzy* gives us a Hitchcock making up for lost time, so to speak, with some interesting implications for the way in which we understand British cinema. I don't mean to imply by this that Hitchcock himself, consciously or unconsciously, designed the film this way, but rather that inscribed within the film is a familiarity with various aspects of British cinema and some of the issues and institutions with which it deals; an explication of these various elements can point to a different idea of cinema from that which has been prevalent in Britain since the war.

Our first link with Ealing can be found via the several references, mainly derogatory, made by critics at the time of *Frenzy*'s release to its *Dixon of Dock Green* style of dialogue. (Dixon first appeared in *The Blue Lamp*, an Ealing film of 1950, before being resurrected in 1955 for the long-running BBC TV series.) Another reference lies in the way in which the film centres itself on a small community (Covent Garden) existing within a larger community (London/England) in the fashion of, say, *Passport to Pimlico* (1949). One can note in this respect the high-angle master shot of Covent Garden, near the beginning of the film, which signifies Covent Garden as an area complete and separate in itself – a shot that would not be out of place in films like *Passport to Pimlico* or, to give a wartime example, *The Bells Go Down* (1943).

One finds echoes of Gainsborough melodrama, Hammer and some aspects of Powell and Pressburger in the evocation of the city as the site of libido, where the streets of London, to quote directly from the film, are littered with 'ripped whores', metaphoric or otherwise. A fairly random parallel from a Gainsborough melodrama could be the opening scenes of *Fanny by Gaslight* (1944), the setting here being a respectable city house that stands directly over a brothel called The Shades. Interestingly, Hammer released their Ripper movie, *Hands of the Ripper* (surely one of their most notable and underrated achievements) the year before *Frenzy*. Hammer's streets of London in this film, perhaps not unexpectedly, are on occasion quite literally littered with ripped whores, as well as a few symbolic ones (the Ripper's ideology in this instance equating sexually active women with prostitutes) as Jack the Ripper's daughter inherits her father's legacy.

Jack the Ripper himself (who is mentioned in the opening sequence of *Frenzy*) is, of course, a crucial aspect of this idea of the city as a site for the activities of the libido. (The British/Canadian co-production of 1978, *Murder by Decree,* is a particularly fine recent example of a mining of this rich and still relatively unexplored vein of British culture, with in this case Victorian sexual repression in the guise of Sherlock Holmes versus uncontrolled and violent male sexuality in the guise of Jack the Ripper.) It is significant in this light that the first necktie murder in Hitchcock's film is greeted with the comment that 'It's *another* necktie murder', a line repeated in newspaper headlines several times throughout the film. One can link this with the reaction to the Glueman in Powell and Pressburger's 1944 film *A Canterbury Tale*, the news of whose nocturnal activities – pouring glue into young girls' hair during the blackout – is greeted with the remark 'The Glueman's out *again*'. *Again* and *another*: two signifiers of indefinite repetition, in a situation where repeated acts of psychopathic violence have become an integral part of the British way of life, so much so that in one of *Frenzy*'s famous set-pieces – the camera held on the exterior of the marriage bureau while we wait for the secretary to find the body inside – the two women who hear the secretary's scream exhibit only temporary surprise before walking on as if nothing important or out of place has actually happened (as indeed it hasn't for this type of film).

Return of the native: Hitchcock in Covent Garden during the filming of *Frenzy* (1972)

Other echoes of British horror in this film include the presence of Anna Massey, who also appears in *Peeping Tom*, and Jon Finch, who began his film career only two years before *Frenzy* with two films for Hammer (*The Vampire Lovers*, *The Horror of Frankenstein*). And the freeze-frame on Brenda Blaney's eyes staring into the camera as she dies can be read as a reconstruction of what Mark Lewis sees through his deadly camera in *Peeping Tom*, or, if one is not willing to go that far, as at least showing a similar awareness of the potential aggression of the camera as exhibited by Powell in his 1960 landmark film.

British comedy also finds a place in *Frenzy*. Note, for a start, the mere presence of Rita Webb (as the killer's mother) and of Bernard Cribbins (perfectly cast against type, as the pub landlord) – two minor comic icons of British popular culture. The scene in the hospital where Blaney escapes with the aid of his fellow prisoners/patients is particularly reminiscent of the several *Carry On* films set in hospitals (their equation of hospital with prison becoming literal in *Frenzy*). Moreover, the concept of a marriage bureau populated by an unmarried, matronly figure (Joan Sims, perhaps?) and a sexually repressed/spinsterish assistant is very *Carry On* in its potential, if not in its actual execution in this film. Significantly or otherwise, the *Carry On* team had already given us their marriage bureau film two years previously, in 1970, with *Carry On Loving*.

As for Free Cinema and the British New Wave, one of the most noteworthy previous cinematic excursions to Covent Garden was of course Lindsay Anderson's Free Cinema documentary *Every Day Except Christmas*, a lauding of the working class from a middle-class perspective. Richard Blaney is himself very much in the tradition of British cinematic heroes that began with the British New Wave and in particular with Albert Finney's Arthur Seaton in *Saturday Night and Sunday Morning* – surly, tending to inarticulacy, striking out blindly at the world around them – although Blaney is shifted somewhat in terms of time (from the 50s to the 70s), of location (from the North to London) and of class (from working-class factory worker to ex-RAF squadron leader), so that only the attitude, the posturing of the British working-class hero of the late 50s period, is preserved. On a broader level, and referring back to the 'Angry Young Man' phenomenon which, to a certain extent, generated the British New Wave, Blaney's relationship with his ex-wife, his taking out on her his own frustration and sense of failure, is similar to Jimmy Porter's relationship with his wife, Alison, in Osborne's *Look Back in Anger*. Blaney's RAF friend, incidentally, goes under the name of Johnny Porter. These references to the RAF also give us a link with British war movies. Indeed one critic of *Frenzy* complained that its music sounded like a parody of the score for *The Dambusters*.

Finally, we can make connections with a significant group of British films made by non-British directors. An important aspect of British film production in the 1960s and early 1970s was the work of, among others, Losey, Kubrick, Peckinpah, Polanski and Antonioni. One can note in this respect (as did many British critics of the time) the fact that Jon Finch's most important role before *Frenzy* was as Polanski's *Macbeth*, and, more significantly, the way in which Hitchcock's film, through its nudity and rape, invites some kind of comparison (and certainly got it) with *Straw Dogs* and *A Clockwork*

Orange, both of which also feature rape scenes; that is, *Frenzy* locates itself in the wake of an expansion (albeit shortlived) of what could actually be represented on the cinema screen, the impetus for which came largely from 'foreign' directors, as if a concern with violence and sex was in some way un-British and alien (and Hitchcock himself made *Frenzy* as a tourist rather than as a permanent resident).

I think there are two things that can be said about this apparent compendium of post-war British cinema. First, that it points to a structuring element in British cinema/British Hitchcock which serves to distinguish it to a certain extent from its American counterpart, and that is class. Class is clearly of central importance to virtually all those areas of film-making outlined above – the inflexible, immutable class structures and evil aristocracy of Hammer, the working-class 'bias' of the New Wave, the middle-class officers and working-class other ranks of the post-war war movies, and so on. Class signals its presence in *Frenzy* from the very beginning, with an upper-class politician more concerned with the reputation of his club than the strangled woman – 'I say, is that my club tie?'

The second thing that can be said about this compendium is that it refuses to acknowledge the strict hierarchy of the British cinematic orthodoxy which places 'realism' firmly at its summit. Hitchcock's film leaps from one genre to another with a gay abandon belying his advanced years. It does not privilege one above others: they are all seen as the same, equal partners in this cinematic world. There is no hierarchy of discourses structuring this film: the humour, say, of the Oxford household meals is not subordinated to and placed within a realist discourse. This clearly links with Hitchcock's notion of cinema as artifice (and the increased foregrounding of artifice in his Universal films), and the concomitant idea that realism is an artifice as well, a construction for cinematic purposes. (Note here Hitchcock's advice – on an earlier return to Britain – concerning an Allied documentary about the Nazi death camps, to use long takes because they make the film *seem* more realistic: realism is something that is *constructed* through the camera rather than a quality somehow inherent in particular subject matters.[2]) *Frenzy*, then, does not place the various styles and genres it encompasses into a static, hierarchical order, but rather allows them to mingle in a way which might be described as democratic.

Frenzy was released in 1972, as the major American film companies were beginning to withdraw the investment from Britain that had helped its cinema to flourish throughout the 1960s. This withdrawal of American finance, along with other factors, was to lead to the near collapse of the British film industry, rendering the mid-70s a virtual silence, a silence eventually broken by the much touted renaissance, the crucial film being *Chariots of Fire*, a film about Britain winning through, as much about cinema as it was about the Olympics.

This renaissance, this conscious rebuilding of British cinema, resulted in a situation where for possibly the first time in the history of that cinema the types of film being made were determined by the critically dominant privileging of realism. In the past there had always been areas of cinematic activity which existed in defiance of critical good taste. The 'renaissance' is notable for the paucity of the fantastic/non-realist films which have for so long comprised a popular, if critically deprecated, aspect of British cinema.

Frenzy's position just before this collapse and subsequent reconstruction, its almost schematic running through of the various film-making practices, respectable and otherwise, of the post-war period, makes it, in a sense, a compressed, two-hour retrospective of post-war, pre-renaissance British cinema, and moreover a vision of British cinema as heterogeneous, a testament to its variety and vitality, and also a reminder of what has been lost in this cinematic rebirth – broad comedy, horror, melodrama, and 'bad taste' in general. The achievements of David Puttnam, Richard Attenborough and co. have been considerable, but a regeneration of British cinema must remain incomplete until those areas of cinema which have for so long underwritten the industry in terms of popularity have been acknowledged, not only in critical writing but also in the types of films that are being made.

Notes

1   Alexander Walker's review of *Frenzy* in the *Evening Standard* (25 May 1972) and George Melly's review in the *Observer* (28 May 1972) are fairly representative examples.

2   For a fuller discussion of this project, see Elizabeth Sussex, 'The Fate of F3080', *Sight and Sound*, vol. 53, no. 2, Spring 1984, pp. 92–7.

APPENDIX 1
90 YEARS OF BRITISH CINEMA

This appendix is in two sections: (1) an alphabetical listing of all British film titles (and some television programmes and films) which are mentioned, however summarily, within the text; (2) a short bibliography. Each section is deliberately limited in scope: the aim is to provide an appendix which is clear, manageable, and appropriate to this book, and which also indicates where to go in order to supplement it.

The alphabetical listing of titles provides basic credits only. For fuller credits (and capsule plot summaries) of all pre-1970 non-animated fiction films, whether listed here or not, see Denis Gifford's monumental *British Film Catalogue 1895–1970*. The most convenient source for post-1970 films (and indeed for a wider range of films, from 1934, than is covered by Gifford) is the British Film Institute's *Monthly Film Bulletin*. Other useful, variously selective, filmographical sources include: Raymond Durgnat, *A Mirror for England*; Rachael Low, *History of the British Film*, seven volumes, spanning 1896–1939, including two volumes on non-fiction films of the 1930s; David Pirie, *A Heritage of Horror*; Frances Thorpe and Nicholas Pronay, *British Official Films in the Second World War*; and the Museum of Modern Art's *Michael Balcon: The Pursuit of British Cinema*, for credits of all films produced by Balcon.

The sequence of data in the titles listing is as follows: title and date (normally the date of the first public screening); production company; director (D); producer (P); scriptwriter (S) and source, if any; main cast (C). Short films, television series and animated films are indicated in lower-case bold lettering. Only material produced exclusively for television is designated as television (TV): films produced by or with television companies for theatrical as well as domestic screening are not specially marked out in this list, although any television funding is noted in the credits.

Aberdeen 1906 (1906)
Scottish Film Council.
Re-edited version (1956) of 1906 actualities.

ACCIDENT (1967)
Royal Avenue Chelsea Col. D: Joseph Losey.
P: Joseph Losey, Norman Priggen. S: Harold Pinter, from novel by Nicholas
Mosley. C: Dirk Bogarde, Stanley Baker, Vivien Merchant.

Accidents Will Happen (1979)
Cucumber Studios for Rock Biz Pix for Radar Records. Col.
P: Kevin Attew. D/anim: Clive 'Rocky' Morton, Annabel Jankel. Mus: Elvis
Costello.

The Adventures of Captain Kremmen series (1979)
Cosgrove Hall for Thames Television. Col.
Part of the Kenny Everett Video Show.

THE ADVENTURES OF QUENTIN DURWARD (1956)
MGM British. Col/Sc. D: Richard Thorpe.
P: Pandro S. Berman. S: George Froeschel, Robert Ardrey, from novel by Walter
Scott. C: Robert Taylor, Kay Kendall.

THE AFRICAN QUEEN (1952)
Romulus/Horizon. Col. D: John Huston.
P: Sam Spiegel. S: Huston, James Agee, from novel by C.S. Forester. C: Humphrey
Bogart, Katharine Hepburn.

After Lumière (1974)
D: Malcolm Le Grice.

After the Ball (1984)
Banner. Col. D: Richard Anthony.
S: Anthony. C: Colin Henry, Carol Katessa, Mark Wright.

AFTER THE VERDICT (1929)
BIFD. D: Henrik Galeen.
P: I.W. Schlesinger. S: Alma Reville, from novel by Robert Hichens. C: Olga
Tschechowa, Warwick Ward.

ALFIE (1966)
Sheldrake. Col/Sc. D/P: Lewis Gilbert.
S: Bill Naughton, from his TV play. C: Michael Caine, Shelley Winters, Millicent
Martin.

ALFRED THE GREAT (1969)
MGM British. Col/Sc. D: Clive Donner.
P: Bernard Smith, James R. Webb. S: Webb, Ken Taylor. C: David Hemmings,
Michael York.

Algy, The Piccadilly Johnny (1900)
Gibbons Bio-Tableaux. D: Walter Gibbons.
C: Vesta Tilley (song synchronised to gramophone recordings).

Alice in Wonderland (1903)
Hepworth. D: Cecil Hepworth, Percy Stow.
S: Hepworth, from Lewis Carroll. C: May Clark, Hepworth, Mrs Hepworth.

ALL AT SEA (1939)
British Lion. D/P: Herbert Smith.
S: Gerald Elliott, Reginald Long. C: Sandy Powell, Kay Walsh.

ALL GOOD MEN (TV) (1974)
BBC. Col. D: Michael Lindsay-Hogg.
P: Graeme McDonald. S: Trevor Griffiths. C: Bill Fraser, Ronald Pickup, Jack Shepherd.

All the Fun of the 'air (1939)
Anson Dyer Cartoons for Bush Radio. Col.
Mus. arr: Jose Norman.

ANASTASIA (1956)
20th Century-Fox. Col/Sc. D: Anatole Litvak.
P: Buddy Adler. S: Arthur Laurents, from play by Marcelle Maurette and Guy Bolton. C: Ingrid Bergman, Yul Brynner.

Animaland series (1947-9)
G-B Animation (Rank). Col. Exec P/D: David Hand. Series D: Bert Felstead.
S: Peter Griffiths, Reg Parlett, R.A.G. Clarke. Anim: Stan Pearsall, Ted Percival, Bill Hopper, John Wilson, Chick Henderson, George Hawthorne, Betty Hansford.

Animal Farm (1954)
Halas & Batchelor for Louis de Rochemont. Col.
P/D: John Halas, Joy Batchelor. From novel by George Orwell.

ANOTHER COUNTRY (1984)
Goldcrest/NFFC. Col. D: Marek Kanievska.
P: Alan Marshall. S: Julian Mitchell, from his play. C: Rupert Everett, Colin Firth.

ANOTHER TIME ANOTHER PLACE (1983)
Umbrella in association with Rediffusion, Channel 4, Scottish Arts Council. Col. D: Michael Radford.
P: Simon Perry. S: Radford, from novel by Jessie Kesson. C: Phyllis Logan, Giovanni Mauriello.

APPOINTMENT WITH CRIME (1946)
British National. D: John Harlow.
P: Louis H. Jackson. S: Harlow, Michael Leighton, Vernon Sewell. C: William Hartnell, Robert Beatty.

ARMS AND THE MAN (1932)
BIP. D: Cecil Lewis.
S: Lewis, from play by George Bernard Shaw. C: Barry Jones, Anne Grey.

The Army Game (TV) (1957-62)
Granada comedy series.
C: Michael Medwin, Alfie Bass, Bill Fraser.

Around is Around (1951)
National Film Board of Canada in collaboration with the British Film Institute for the Festival of Britain. Col. P/D: Norman McLaren.

Arrival of the Calais Express (1896)
P: A.M. Hubnar.

As Old as the Hills (1950)
Halas & Batchelor for Anglo-Iranian Oil Company. Col.
P: John Halas. D/story: Allan Crick. Anim: Bob Privett, Vic Bevis.

AS YOU LIKE IT (1936)
Inter-Allied. D: Paul Czinner.
P: Czinner, Joseph M. Schenck. S: J.M. Barrie, Robert Cullen, from play by
Shakespeare. C: Elisabeth Bergner, Laurence Olivier.

AUTUMN CROCUS (1934)
ATP. P/D: Basil Dean.
S: Dean, from play by C.L. Anthony. C: Ivor Novello, Fay Compton, Jack Hawkins.

BABYLON (1980)
Diversity Music/NFFC. Col. D: Franco Rosso.
P: Gavrik Losey. S: Rosso, Martin Stellman. C: Brinsley Forde, Karl Howman.

BAD BOY (1938)
Radius. D: Lawrence Huntington.
S: Huntington. C: John Warwick, Kathleen Kelly.
Also known as *Branded*.

Balance (1951) see **Enterprise** (1954)

BAND WAGGON (1940)
Gainsborough. D: Marcel Varnel.
P: Edward Black. S: Marriott Edgar, Val Guest, from BBC Radio series. C: Arthur
Askey, Richard Murdoch.

BANK HOLIDAY (1938)
Gainsborough. D: Carol Reed.
P: Edward Black. S: Rodney Ackland, Roger Burford, Hans Wilhelm. C: Margaret
Lockwood, Hugh Williams, John Lodge.
US title: *Three on a Weekend*.

THE BARRETTS OF WIMPOLE STREET (1957)
MGM British. Col/Sc. D: Sidney Franklin.
P: Sam Zimbalist. S: John Dighton, from play by Rudolph Besier. C: Jennifer Jones,
Bill Travers, John Gielgud.

The Basilisk (1914)
Hepworth. D/S: Cecil Hepworth.
C: Tom Powers, Alma Taylor.

BATTLE OF BRITAIN (1969)
Spitfire. Col/Sc. D: Guy Hamilton.
P: Harry Saltzman, S. Benjamin Fisz. S: James Kennaway, Wilfred Greatorex, from
books by Derek Wood, Derek Dempster. C: Laurence Olivier, Robert Shaw,
Michael Caine.

BATTLE OF THE RIVER PLATE (1956)
The Archers. Col. D/P/S: Michael Powell and Emeric Pressburger.
C: John Gregson, Anthony Quayle, Peter Finch.

BEES IN PARADISE (1944)
Gainsborough. D: Val Guest.
P: Edward Black. S: Guest, Marriott Edgar. C: Arthur Askey, Jean Kent.

BELL-BOTTOM GEORGE (1943)
Columbia British. D: Marcel Varnel.
P: Ben Henry. S: Peter Fraser, Edward Dryhurst, John L. Arthur, Richard Fisher, Peter Cresswell. C: George Formby, Anne Firth.

THE BELLS GO DOWN (1943)
Ealing. D: Basil Dearden.
P: Michael Balcon, S.C. Balcon. S: Roger Macdougall, Stephen Black, based on book by Black. C: Tommy Trinder, James Mason.

BHOWANI JUNCTION (1956)
MGM British. Col/Sc. D: George Cukor.
P: Pandro S. Berman. S: Sonya Levien, Ivan Moffatt, from novel by John Masters C: Ava Gardner, Stewart Granger.

THE BIG FELLA (1937)
Fortune. D/P: J. Elder Wills.
S: Fenn Sherie, Ingram d'Abbes, from novel by Claude McKay. C: Paul Robeson, Elisabeth Welch.

THE BIG FLAME (TV) (1969)
BBC. D: Ken Loach.
P: Tony Garnett. S: Jim Allen. C: Norman Rossington, Godfrey Quigley, Peter Kerrigan.

The Big Swallow (1901)
Williamson. D: James Williamson.
C: Sam Dalton.

Bill Brand (TV) (1976)
Thames, 11-part drama series. Col. D: Michael Lindsay-Hogg, Roland Joffé, Stuart Burge.
P: Burge. S: Trevor Griffiths. C: Jack Shepherd, Cherie Lunghi, Alan Badel.

BILLY LIAR (1963)
Vic/Waterfall. Sc. D: John Schlesinger.
P: Joseph Janni. S: Keith Waterhouse, Willis Hall, from their own play and Waterhouse's novel. C: Tom Courtenay, Julie Christie, Ethel Griffies.

The Birth of the Robot (1936)
Shell-Mex. Col. P/D: Len Lye.
Col. decor and production: Humphrey Jennings.

Blackfriar's Bridge (1896)
P: A.M. Hubnar.

BLACK JACK (1979)
Kestrel/NFFC. Col. D: Kenneth Loach.
S: Loach, from novel by Leon Garfield. P: Tony Garnett. C: Jean Franval, Louise Cooper, Stephen Hirst.

BLACKMAIL (1929)
BIP. D: Alfred Hitchcock.
S: Charles Bennett, Benn Levy, from play by Bennett. C: Anny Ondra, John Longden, Donald Calthrop.

BLACK MEMORY (1947)
Bushey. D: Oswald Mitchell.
P: Gilbert Church. S: John Gilling. C: Michael Atkinson, Myra O'Connell.

BLACK NARCISSUS (1947)
The Archers. Col. D/P/S: Michael Powell, Emeric Pressburger.
From novel by Rumer Godden. C: Deborah Kerr, David Farrar, Kathleen Byron.

The Blacksmith's Shop (1896)
P: A.M. Hubnar.

BLEAK HOUSE (1920)
Ideal. D: Maurice Elvey.
S: William J. Elliott, from novel by Dickens. C: Constance Collier, Berta Gellardi.

The Blind Boy (1900)
Gibbons Bio-Tableaux. D: Walter Gibbons.
C: G.H. Chirgwin (song synchronised to gramophone recording).

BLIND DATE (1959)
Independent Artists. D: Joseph Losey.
P: David Deutsch. S: Ben Barzman, Millard Lampell, from novel by Leigh Howard.
    C: Stanley Baker, Hardy Kruger.

BLITHE SPIRIT (1945)
Two Cities/Cineguild. Col. D: David Lean.
P: Anthony Havelock-Allan. S: Noël Coward, from his own play. C: Rex Harrison,
    Constance Cummings, Margaret Rutherford.

BLOOD OF THE VAMPIRE (1958)
Artistes Alliance. Col. D: Henry Cass.
P: Robert Baker, Monty Berman. S: Jimmy Sangster. C: Donald Wolfit, Barbara
    Shelley.

BLOW-UP (1967)
MGM. Col. D: Michelangelo Antonioni.
P: Pierre Rouve, Carlo Ponti. S: Antonioni, Tonino Guerra, Edward Bond, from
    story by Julio Cortazar. C: Vanessa Redgrave, David Hemmings.

THE BLUE LAMP (1950)
Ealing. D: Basil Dearden.
P: Michael Balcon, Michael Relph. S: T.E.B. Clarke, Alexander Mackendrick, Jan
    Read, Ted Willis. C: Jack Warner, Dirk Bogarde, Jimmy Hanley.

Bobby the Scout series (1921-2?)
Hepworth. D: Anson Dyer.

THE BOFORS GUN (1968)
Everglades/Universal. Col. D: Jack Gold.
P: Robert A. Goldston, Otto Platschkes. S: John McGrath, from his own play.
    C: Nicol Williamson, Ian Holm, David Warner.

BONNIE PRINCE CHARLIE (1948)
London. Col. D: Anthony Kimmins.
P: Edward Black. S: Clemence Dane. C: David Niven, Margaret Leighton, Jack
    Hawkins.

Bonzo series (1924–6)
New Era. P: W.A. Ward. S: Adrian Brunel (on some items). Anim: Percy Vigas, H.
    McCready, M. Matheson, H. Brian White, M. Jork, Marjorie Drawbell, Charles
    de Mornay, P.G. Tobin, Kevin Moran, S.G. Castell, Sid Griffiths.

BOOM! (1968)
WFS/Moon Lake. Col/Sc. D: Joseph Losey.

P: John Heyman, Norman Priggen. S: Tennessee Williams, from his own play.
   C: Elizabeth Taylor, Richard Burton, Noël Coward.

BOTTOMS UP! (1959)
Transocean. D/P: Mario Zampi.
S: Michael Pertwee, Frank Muir, Denis Norden, from Muir and Norden's TV series
   Whacko! C: Jimmy Edwards, Martita Hunt.

BOYS FROM THE BLACKSTUFF (TV) (1982)
BBC, 5-part drama series. Col. D: Philip Saville.
P: Michael Wearing. S: Alan Bleasdale. C: Bernard Hill, Tom Georgeson, Michael
   Angelis, Peter Kerrigan.

BOYS IN BROWN (1949)
Gainsborough. D: Montgomery Tully.
P: Anthony Darnborough. S: Tully, from play by Reginald Beckwith. C: Jack
   Warner, Richard Attenborough, Dirk Bogarde.

BOYS WILL BE BOYS (1935)
Gainsborough. D: William Beaudine.
P: Michael Balcon. S: Will Hay, Robert Edmunds, based on characters created by
   'Beachcomber' (J.B. Morton). C: Will Hay, Ralph Lynn.

THE BRAVE DON'T CRY (1952)
Group 3. D: Philip Leacock.
P: John Grierson. S: Montagu Slater. C: John Gregson, Meg Buchanan.

BREAD (1934)
Kino Production Group/Workers' Film and Photo League.

BRED AND BORN (1983)
BFI/Four Corners. D: Joanna Davis, Mary Pat Leece.
P: Four Corners. C: Women from East End of London.

BRIDESHEAD REVISITED (TV) (1981)
Granada 13-part serial (film). D: Charles Sturridge, Michael Lindsay-Hogg.
S: John Mortimer, from novel by Evelyn Waugh. C: Jeremy Irons, Anthony
   Andrews, Diana Quick.

THE BRIDGE ON THE RIVER KWAI (1957)
Horizon. Col/Sc. D: David Lean.
P: Samuel Spiegel. S: Pierre Boulle, Carl Foreman, Michael Wilson, from Boulle's
   novel. C: Alec Guinness, William Holden, Jack Hawkins.

BRIEF ENCOUNTER (1945)
Cineguild. D: David Lean.
P: Anthony Havelock-Allan, Ronald Neame. S: Noël Coward, from his own play.
   C: Celia Johnson, Trevor Howard.

BRIGHTON ROCK (1947)
ABPC. D: John Boulting.
P: Roy Boulting. S: Graham Greene, Terence Rattigan, from Greene's novel.
   C: Richard Attenborough, Hermione Baddeley.

Bring It All Home (1980)
Animation City. D: Phil Austin, Derek Hayes.
version of the Gerry Rafferty song.

Britain's Honour (1919)
Jury. D: Lancelot Speed.

BRITANNIA OF BILLINGSGATE (1933)
Gaumont, D: Sinclair Hill.
P: Michael Balcon. S: Ralph Stock, from play by Christine Jope-Slade and Sewell Stokes. C: Violet Loraine, Gordon Harker.

Briton vs Boer (1900)
Birt Acres.
Actuality and staged scenes.

The Broken Melody (1896)
Esme Collings. D: Esme Collings from play by James Tanner and Herbert Keene.

Brookside (TV) (1982–)
Channel 4 TV serial, broadcast twice weekly.
P: Phil Redmond.

BROTHERS AND SISTERS (1980)
BFI. Col. D: Richard Woolley.
P: Keith Griffiths. S: Woolley, Tammy Walker. C: Sam Dale, Carolyn Pickles.

Bully Boy series (1914)
Neptune. P: Percy Nash (?). Anim: Lancelot Speed.

BUNNY LAKE IS MISSING (1965)
Columbia. Sc. D/P: Otto Preminger.
S: John Mortimer, Penelope Mortimer, from novel by Evelyn Piper. C: Laurence Olivier, Noël Coward, Carol Lynley.

Burlesque Attack on a Settler's Cabin (1900)
Warwick Trading Co. C: Dan Leno.

BURNING AN ILLUSION (1981)
BFI. D/S: Menelik Shabazz.
C: Cassie McFarlane, Victor Romero.

BUSMAN'S HONEYMOON (1940)
MGM British. D: Arthur Woods.
P: Harold Huth. S: Monckdon Hoffe, Angus Macphail, Harold Goldman, from play by Dorothy L. Sayers and Muriel St Clare Byrne. C: Robert Montgomery, Constance Cummings.

The Cabinet of Jan Svankmajer (1984)
Atelier Koninck for Channel 4. Col. D: Stephen and Timothy Quay.
P: Keith Griffiths.

CAESAR AND CLEOPATRA (1946)
Pascal/Rank. Col. D/P: Gabriel Pascal.
S: George Bernard Shaw, Marjorie Deans, from play by Shaw. C: Vivien Leigh, Claude Rains.

CAGE OF GOLD (1950)
Ealing. D: Basil Dearden.
P: Michael Balcon, Michael Relph. S: Jack Whittingham, Paul Stein. C: Jean Simmons, David Farrar, James Donald.

CAL (1984)
Enigma for Warner Bros. and Goldcrest. Col. D: Pat O'Connor.

P: Stuart Craig, David Puttnam. S: Bernard MacLaverty, from his own novel. C: Helen Mirren, John Lynch.

Camera Makes Whoopee (1936)
Glasgow School of Art. D/Anim: Norman McLaren.

CAMPBELL'S KINGDOM (1957)
Rank. Col. D: Ralph Thomas.
P: Betty Box. S: Robin Estridge, Hammond Innes, from Innes' novel. C: Dirk Bogarde, Stanley Baker, Michael Craig.

CAN'T STOP THE MUSIC (1980)
Allan Carr. Col. D: Nancy Walker.
P: Allan Carr, Jacques Morali, Henri Beloo. S: Bronte Woodward, Carr. C: Village People, Valerie Perrine, June Havoc.

A CANTERBURY TALE (1944)
The Archers. D/P/S: Michael Powell, Emeric Pressburger.
C: Eric Portman, Sheila Sim, Dennis Price, Sgt John Sweet (US Army).

CAPTAIN HORATIO HORNBLOWER RN (1951)
Warner. D/P: Raoul Walsh.
S: Ivan Goff, Ben Roberts, Aeneas Mackenzie, from novel by C.S. Forester. C: Gregory Peck, Virginia Mayo.

CAPTAIN KRONOS, VAMPIRE HUNTER (1972)
Hammer. Col. D/S: Brian Clemens.
P: Clemens, Albert Fennell. C: Hurst Janson, John Carson, Wanda Ventham.

CARAVAN (1946)
Gainsborough. D: Arthur Crabtree.
P: Harold Huth. S: Roland Pertwee, from novel by Eleanor Smith. C: Stewart Granger, Dennis Price, Jean Kent.

CARRINGTON V.C. (1955)
Remus. D: Anthony Asquith.
P: Teddy Baird. S: John Hunter, from play by Dorothy and Campbell Christie. C: David Niven, Margaret Leighton, Noelle Middleton.
US title: *Court Martial.*

CARRY ON CAMPING (1969)
Adder/Rank. Col. D: Gerald Thomas.
P: Peter Rogers. S: Talbot Rothwell. C: Sidney James, Kenneth Williams, Joan Sims.

CARRY ON LOVING (1970)
Adder/Rank. Col. D: Gerald Thomas.
P: Peter Rogers. S: Talbot Rothwell. C: Sidney James, Kenneth Williams, Hattie Jacques.

CARRY ON SERGEANT (1958)
Insignia/Rank. D: Gerald Thomas.
P: Peter Rogers. S: Norman Hudis, John Antrobus, from play by R.F. Delderfield. C: William Hartnell, Bob Monkhouse, Shirley Eaton.

Cartoon Burlesques series (1919-20)
Hepworth. D: Anson Dyer.
P: Cecil Hepworth.

CATHY COME HOME (TV) (1966)
BBC drama (film). D: Ken Loach.
P: Tony Garnett. S: Jeremy Sandford. C: Carol White, Ray Brooks.

THE CAUSE OF IRELAND (1983)
Platform Films for Channel 4 TV. Col. D: Chris Reeves.
P: Alan Fountain. S: Geoffrey Bell.

CHAMPAGNE CHARLIE (1944)
Ealing. D: Alberto Cavalcanti.
P: Michael Balcon, John Croydon. S: Austin Melford, Angus Macphail, John
    Dighton. C: Tommy Trinder, Stanley Holloway.

CHANCE OF A LIFETIME (1950)
Pilgrim. D: Bernard Miles.
P: Miles, John Palmer. S: Miles, Walter Greenwood. C: Basil Radford, Bernard
    Miles, Kenneth More.

THE CHARGE OF THE LIGHT BRIGADE (1968)
Woodfall. Col/Sc. D: Tony Richardson.
P: Neil Hartley. S: Charles Wood, John Osborne. C: Trevor Howard, Vanessa
    Redgrave, John Gielgud.

CHARIOTS OF FIRE (1981)
Enigma/20th Century-Fox. Col. D: Hugh Hudson.
P: David Puttnam. S: Colin Welland. C: Ben Cross, Ian Charleson, John Gielgud,
    Lindsay Anderson, Ian Holm.

Charley series (1948–50)
Halas & Batchelor for Central Office of Information. Col. P/D: John Halas, Joy
    Batchelor.
Anim: Wally Crook, Vera Linnecar, K. Williams, Bob Privett, P. Wright, J. Beaver,
    Jack King, Vic Bevis, Spud Murphy.

THE CHERRY ORCHARD (TV) (1981)
BBC. Col. D: Richard Eyre.
P: Ann Scott. S: Trevor Griffiths, from translation by Helen Rappaport of play by
    Anton Chekhov. C: Bill Paterson, Judi Dench, Anton Lesser.

THE CHEVIOT, THE STAG AND THE BLACK BLACK OIL (TV) (1974)
BBC drama. Col. D: John Mackenzie.
P: Graeme McDonald. S: John McGrath.

Children on Trial (1946)
Crown. D: Jack Lee.
P: Basil Wright. S: Lee, Nora Dawson.

CIRCUS OF HORRORS (1960)
Independent Artists. Col. D: Sidney Hayers.
P: Norman Priggen. S: George Baxt. C: Anton Diffring, Erika Remberg.

THE CITADEL (1938)
MGM British. D: King Vidor.
P: Victor Saville. S: Frank Wead, Emlyn Williams, Ian Dalrymple, Elizabeth Hill,
    John van Druten. C: Robert Donat, Rosalind Russell, Ralph Richardson, Rex
    Harrison.

THE CLAIRVOYANT (1935)
Gainsborough. D: Maurice Elvey.

P: Michael Balcon. S: Charles Bennett, from novel by Ernst Lothar. C: Claude Rains, Fay Wray, Jane Baxter.

CLIMBING HIGH (1938)
Gaumont. D: Carol Reed.
S: Stephen Clarkson, Lesser Samuels, Marian Dix. C: Jessie Matthews, Michael Redgrave.

A CLOCKWORK ORANGE (1971)
Warner. Col. D/P/S: Stanley Kubrick.
From novel by Anthony Burgess. C: Malcolm McDowell, Patrick Magee, Adrienne Corri.

The Clown Barber (1898)
Williamson. D: James Williamson.

THE CLUE OF THE NEW PIN (1929)
British Lion. silent. D: Arthur Maude.
P: S.W. Smith. S: Kathleen Hayden, from novel by Edgar Wallace. C: Benita Hume, Donald Calthrop, John Gielgud.

Coalface (1935)
GPO Film Unit. D: Alberto Cavalcanti.
P: John Grierson. S: Cavalcanti (verse: W.H. Auden).

Coastal Navigation and Pilotage (1953)
Halas & Batchelor for the Admiralty. D: Louis Dahl.
P: Allan Crick.

COCKLESHELL HEROES (1955)
Warwick. Col/Sc. D: José Ferrer.
P: Irving Allen, Albert Broccoli, Phil C. Samuel. S: Richard Maibaum, Bryan Forbes, from the book by George Kent. C: José Ferrer, Trevor Howard.

Colour Box (1935)
GPO Film Unit. D/Anim: Len Lye.

COMIN' THRO' THE RYE (1923)
Hepworth. D: Cecil Hepworth.
S: Blanche McIntosh, from novel by Helen Mathers. C: Helen Adair, Shayle Gardner.

THE COMPANY OF WOLVES (1984)
Palace. Col. D: Neil Jordan.
P: Stephen Woolley, Nik Powell. S: Angela Carter, Neil Jordan, from short story by Carter. C: Angela Lansbury, David Warner, Sarah Patterson.

THE CONSTANT NYMPH (1928)
Gainsborough. D: Adrian Brunel.
P: Michael Balcon. S: Basil Dean, Alma Reville, from play by Margaret Kennedy and Dean. C: Ivor Novello, Mabel Poulton.

CONVOY (1940)
Ealing. D: Penrose Tennyson.
P: Michael Balcon, Sergei Nolbandov. S: Tennyson, Patrick Kirwan. C: Clive Brook, John Clements.

Coronation Street (TV) (1960–)
Granada TV serial, broadcast twice weekly.
S: H.V. Kershaw, many others.

CORRIDOR OF MIRRORS (1948)
Apollo. D: Terence Young.
P: Rudolph Cartier. S: Cartier, Edana Romney, from novel by Chris Massie. C: Eric
   Portman, Edana Romney.

CORRIDORS OF BLOOD (1958)
Producers Associates (MGM). D: Robert Day.
P: John Croydon. S: Jean Scott Rogers. C: Boris Karloff, Christopher Lee.

Council Matters (1984)
Leeds Animation Workshop/BFI/Sheffield City Council.

A COUNTESS FROM HONG KONG (1966)
Universal. Col. D/S: Charles Chaplin.
P: Chaplin, Jerome Epstein. C: Marlon Brando, Sophia Loren.

COUNTRY (TV) (1981)
BBC drama. Col. D: Richard Eyre.
P: Ann Scott. S: Trevor Griffiths. C: Leo McKern, Deborah Norton, James Fox.

THE COURTNEYS OF CURZON STREET (1947)
Imperadio. D/P: Herbert Wilcox.
S: Nicholas Phipps. C: Anna Neagle, Michael Wilding.

THE CRIMINAL (1960)
Merton Park. D: Joseph Losey.
P: Jack Greenwood. S: Alun Owen, Jimmy Sangster. C: Stanley Baker, Sam
   Wanamaker, Margit Saad.

CROMWELL (1970)
Irving Allen. Col/Sc. D: Ken Hughes.
P: Irving Allen. S: Hughes, Ronald Harwood. C: Richard Harris, Alec Guinness.

THE CRUEL SEA (1953)
Ealing. D: Charles Frend.
P: Michael Balcon, Leslie Norman. S: Eric Ambler, from novel by Nicholas
   Monsarrat. C: Jack Hawkins, Donald Sinden, Stanley Baker.

A CUCKOO IN THE NEST (1933)
Gaumont. D: Tom Walls.
P: Angus Macphail, Ian Dalrymple. S: Ben Travers, A.R. Rawlinson, from play by
   Travers. C: Tom Walls, Ralph Lynn, Mary Brough.

The Cumberland Story (1946)
Crown. D/S: Humphrey Jennings.
P: Alexander Shaw.

THE CURSE OF FRANKENSTEIN (1957)
Hammer/Clarion. Col/Sc. D: Terence Fisher.
P: Anthony Hinds. S: Jimmy Sangster, based on novel by Mary Shelley. C: Peter
   Cushing, Christopher Lee.

Dad's Army (TV) (1967–77)
BBC ½-hour comedy series.
S: Jimmy Perry, David Croft. C: Arthur Lowe, John le Mesurier, John Laurie.

THE DAM BUSTERS (1955)
ABPC. D: Michael Anderson.
P: Robert Clark, W.A. Whittaker. S: R.C. Sherriff, from books by Paul Brickhill,

Guy Gibson. C: Richard Todd, Michael Redgrave.

THE DAMNED (1962)
Hammer. Sc. D: Joseph Losey.
P: Anthony Hinds. S: Evans Jones, from novel by H.L. Lawrence. C: Macdonald Carey, Shirley Ann Field, Alexander Knox.

Damon the Mower (1972)
TV Cartoons. Col. D: George Dunning.
Based on the poem by Andrew Marvell. Anim: George Dunning, Roy Evans, Jerry Hibbert.

DANCE HALL (1950)
Ealing. D: Charles Crichton.
P: Michael Balcon, E.V.H. Emmett. S: Emmett, Diana Morgan, Alexander Mackendrick. C: Natasha Parry, Petula Clark, Diana Dors.

DANCE OF THE VAMPIRES (1967)
Cadre/Filmways. Col/Sc. D: Roman Polanski.
P: Martin Ransohoff, Gene Gutowski. C: Jack MacGowran, Roman Polanski, Alfie Bass.

DANCING WITH CRIME (1947)
Coronet/Alliance. D: John Paddy Carstairs.
P: James A. Carter. S: Brock Williams. C: Richard Attenborough, Sheila Sim.

Dangermouse series (1980–)
Cosgrove Hall for Thames Television. Col. D: Brian Cosgrove.
P: Cosgrove, Mark Hall. S: Mike Harding, Brian Trueman.

DANGEROUS MOONLIGHT (1941)
RKO Radio. D: Brian Desmond Hurst.
P: William Sistrom. S: Hurst, Terence Young, Rodney Ackland. C: Anton Walbrook, Sally Gray.
US title: *Suicide Squadron.*

DARKEST ENGLAND (TV) (1984)
Victoria for Channel 4 TV. Col. D: Michael Eaton.
P: Felicity Oppé. S: Eaton. C: Mark Wing-Davey, Elvis Payne, Ken Campbell.

DARK EYES OF LONDON (1939)
Argyle. D: Walter Summers.
P: John Argyle. S: Argyle, Summers, Patrick Kirwan. C: Bela Lugosi, Greta Gynt.
US title: *The Human Monster.*

DARLING (1965)
Vic. D: John Schlesinger.
P: Joseph Janni. S: Frederic Raphael. C: Julie Christie, Dirk Bogarde, Laurence Harvey.

DAVID COPPERFIELD (1913)
Hepworth. D: Thomas Bentley.
S: Bentley, from novel by Charles Dickens. C: Kenneth Ware, Alma Taylor.

DAVID COPPERFIELD (1969)
Omnibus. Col. D: Delbert Mann.
P: Frederick H. Brogger. S: Jack Pulman, from novel by Charles Dickens. C: Robin Phillips, Ralph Richardson, Michael Redgrave.

DAYBREAK (1946)
Triton. D: Compton Bennett.
P: Sydney Box. S: Muriel and Sydney Box, from play by Monckton Hoffe. C: Ann Todd, Eric Portman.

DAYS OF HOPE (TV) (1976)
BBC drama, four films. Col. D: Ken Loach.
P: Tony Garnett. S: Jim Allen. C: Paul Copley.

DEAD OF NIGHT (1945)
Ealing. D: Alberto Cavalcanti, Charles Crichton, Basil Dearden, Robert Hamer.
P: Michael Balcon, Sidney Cole, John Croydon. S: Angus Macphail, John Baines, T.E.B. Clarke. C: Michael Redgrave, Googie Withers, Mervyn Johns.

DEATH LINE (1972)
KL. Col. D: Gary Sherman.
P: Paul Maslansky. S: Ceri Jones. C: Donald Pleasence, Christopher Lee.

DEATH ON THE NILE (1978)
EMI. Col. D: John Guillermin.
P: John Brabourne, Richard Goodwin. S: Anthony Shaffer, from novel by Agatha Christie. C: Peter Ustinov, Bette Davis, David Niven, Maggie Smith.

The Decision (1981)
British Film Institute. Col. P/D/Anim: Vera Neubauer.

A Defeated People (1946)
Crown. D: Humphrey Jennings.
P: Basil Wright. S: Jennings.

Defence of Madrid (1936)
Progressive Film Institute. D: Ivor Montagu.

THE DEMI-PARADISE (1943)
Two Cities. D: Anthony Asquith.
P/S: Anatole de Grunwald. C: Laurence Olivier, Penelope Dudley Ward, Felix Aylmer.
US title: *Adventure for Two*.

DEMONS OF THE MIND (1971)
Hammer. Col. D: Peter Sykes.
P: Frank Godwin. S: Christopher Wicking. C: Paul Jones, Gillian Hills, Patrick Magee.

The Departure of the Columbia from Rothesay Pier (1897)
P: A.M. Hubnar.

THE DEVILS (1971)
Russo/Warner. Col/Sc. D: Ken Russell.
P: Russell, Robert H. Solo. S: Russell, from play by John Whiting and novel by Aldous Huxley. C: Oliver Reed, Vanessa Redgrave.

A Diary for Timothy (1945)
Crown. D: Humphrey Jennings.
P: Basil Wright. S: Jennings and (commentary) E.M. Forster.

Dixon of Dock Green (TV) (1955–76)
BBC police series.
S: Ted Willis and others. C: Jack Warner.

DOCTOR IN THE HOUSE (1954)
Rank. Col. D: Ralph Thomas.
P: Betty Box. S: Richard Gordon, Nicholas Phipps, Ronald Wilkinson, from
  Gordon's novel. C: Dirk Bogarde, Kenneth More, Muriel Pavlow.

DOLL'S EYE (1982)
BFI/Channel 4. Col. D: Jan Worth.
P: Jill Pack. S: Jan Worth, Annie Brown, Anne Cottringer. C: Sandy Ratcliff,
  Bernice Stegers, Lynne Worth.

THE DOOR WITH SEVEN LOCKS (1940)
Rialto. D: Norman Lee.
P: John Argyle. S: Lee, Argyle, Gilbert Gunn, from novel by Edgar Wallace.
  C: Leslie Banks, Lilli Palmer.
US title: *Chamber of Horrors.*

DOSS HOUSE (1933)
Sound City. D: John Baxter.
P: Ivor Campbell. S: Herbert Ayres. C: Arnold Bell, Herbert Franklyn.

Down Exeter Incline (1898)
Warwick. Railway actuality footage.

DRACULA (1958)
Hammer. Col. D: Terence Fisher.
P: Anthony Hinds. S: Jimmy Sangster, from novel by Bram Stoker. C: Peter
  Cushing, Christopher Lee.

Dream Doll (1979)
Bob Godfrey/Zagreb/Halas & Batchelor. Col. D: Bob Godfrey, Zlatko Grgić.
Anim: Grgić, Turido Paus, Alistair McIlwain, Spud Houston, Tony Fish, Peter
  Hearn, Ted Rockley.

DREAMING LIPS (1937)
Trafalgar. D: Paul Czinner, Lee Garmes.
P: Czinner, Max Schach. S: Margaret Kennedy, Carl Mayer, from play by Henry
  Bernstein. C: Elisabeth Bergner, Raymond Massey.

THE DRESSER (1983)
Goldcrest/World Film Services. Col. D/P: Peter Yates.
S: Ronald Harwood, from his own play. C: Albert Finney, Tom Courtenay.

Drifters (1929)
New Era for Empire Marketing Board. D/P/S: John Grierson.

THE DRUM (1938)
London. Col. D: Zoltan Korda.
P: Alexander Korda. S: Lajos Biro, Arthur Wimperis, Patrick Kirwan, Hugh Gray.
  C: Sabu, Raymond Massey, Valerie Hobson.

DRY ROT (1956)
Remus. D: Maurice Elvey.
P: Jack Clayton. S: John Chapman, from his own play. C: Ronald Shiner, Brian Rix,
  Peggy Mount.

DTs or The Effect of Drink (1905)
Haggar and Sons. D: William Haggar.

DUAL ALIBI (1947)
British National. D: Alfred Travers.

P: Louis H. Jackson. S: Alfred Travers, Stephen Clarkson, Vivienne Ades.
C: Herbert Lom, Phyllis Dixey.

Dustbin Parade (1942)
Halas & Batchelor and Realist for Ministry of Information for Ministry of Supply.
D/S: John Halas, Joy Batchelor.
Anim: Halas, Batchelor, Wally Crook, Vera Linnecar.

EASY VIRTUE (1927)
Gainsborough. D: Alfred Hitchcock.
P: Michael Balcon. S: Eliot Stannard, from play by Noël Coward. C: Isabel Jeans,
Robin Irvine, Violet Farebrother.

THE EDGE OF THE WORLD (1937)
Rock Studios. D/S: Michael Powell.
P: Joe Rock. C: Niall McGinnis, Belle Chrystal, John Laurie.

EDUCATING RITA (1983)
Acorn. Col. D/P: Lewis Gilbert.
S: Willy Russell, from his play. C: Michael Caine, Julie Walters.

ELEPHANT BOY (1937)
London. D: Robert Flaherty, Zoltan Korda.
P: Alexander Korda. S: John Collier, Akos Tolnay, Marcia de Sylva, from novel by
Rudyard Kipling. C: Sabu.

ELSTREE CALLING (1930)
BIP. D: Adrian Brunel, Alfred Hitchcock, André Charlot, Jack Hulbert, Paul
Murray.
S: Brunel, Val Valentine, Walter Mycroft. C: Tommy Handley, Lily Morris,
Donald Calthrop.

THE ELUSIVE PIMPERNEL (1950)
The Archers/London. Col. D: Michael Powell, Emeric Pressburger.
P: Samuel Goldwyn, Alexander Korda. S: Powell and Pressburger, from novel by
Baroness Orczy. C: David Niven, Margaret Leighton, Jack Hawkins.

English Nell (1900)
Mutoscope and Biograph.
From play by Anthony Hope and Edward Rose. C: Marie Tempest, Ben Webster,
H.B. Warner.

Enough to Eat (1936)
Gas Light and Coal Co. D/P: Edgar Anstey, Frank Sainsbury.
S (commentary): Julian Huxley.

Enterprise (1954, re-edited from *Balance*, 1951)
W.M. Larkins Studio and Film Producers' Guild for ICI. Col. D: Peter Sachs.
S: Roger McDougall.

THE ENTERTAINER (1960)
Woodfall. D: Tony Richardson.
P: Harry Saltzman. S: John Osborne, Nigel Kneale, from Osborne's play.
C: Laurence Olivier, Roger Livesey, Shirley Ann Field, Joan Plowright.

ESCAPE! (1930)
ATP. P/D: Basil Dean.
S: Dean, from play by John Galsworthy. C: Gerald du Maurier, Edna Best.

THE EUROPEANS (1979)
Merchant Ivory/NFFC. Col. D: James Ivory.
P: Ismail Merchant. S: Ruth Prawer Jhabvala, from novel by Henry James. C: Lee Remick, Robin Ellis, Tim Woodward, Wesley Addy.

The Everhardts' Clever Hoop Manipulation (1902)
Warwick.
C: The Everhardts.

Every Day Except Christmas (1957)
Graphic for Ford Motor Co. D/S: Lindsay Anderson.
P: Leon Clore, Karel Reisz.

EXPERIENCE PREFERRED BUT NOT ESSENTIAL (1982)
Enigma for Channel 4. Col. D: Peter Duffell.
P: Chris Griffin. S: June Roberts. C: Elizabeth Edmonds, Roy Heather.

Fabian of the Yard (TV) (1955)
BBC police series (film).
C: Bruce Seton.

FAHRENHEIT 451 (1966)
Universal. Col. D: François Truffaut.
P: Lewis M. Allen. S: Truffaut, J-L. Richard, Helen Scott, David Rudkin, from novel by Ray Bradbury. C: Julie Christie, Oskar Werner.

THE FALLEN IDOL (1948)
London. D: Carol Reed.
P: David O. Selznick, Reed. S: Graham Greene, Lesley Storm, William Templeton, from short story by Greene. C: Ralph Richardson, Michèle Morgan, Bobby Henrey.

Family Portrait (1950)
Wessex, for Festival of Britain. D/S: Humphrey Jennings. P: Ian Dalrymple.

FANNY BY GASLIGHT (1944)
Gainsborough. D: Anthony Asquith.
P: Edward Black. S: Doreen Montgomery, Aimee Stuart, from novel by Michael Sadleir. C: James Mason, Phyllis Calvert, Stewart Granger.
US title: *Man of Evil*.

FAR FROM THE MADDING CROWD (1967)
Vic. Col/Sc. D: John Schlesinger.
P: Joseph Janni. S: Frederic Raphael, from novel by Thomas Hardy. C: Julie Christie, Terence Stamp, Peter Finch.

THE FARMER'S WIFE (1928)
BIP. D: Alfred Hitchcock.
S: Eliot Stannard, Hitchcock, from play by Eden Philpotts. C: Jameson Thomas, Lillian Hall Davies, Gordon Harker.

FIEND WITHOUT A FACE (1958)
MLC Producers. D: Arthur Crabtree.
P: John Croydon. S: Herbert J. Leder, from short story by Amelia Reynolds Long. C: Marshall Thompson, Kim Parker.

The Figurehead (1953)
Halas & Batchelor. Col. D: Allan Crick, Bob Privett.
S: Joy Batchelor, from ballad by Crosbie Garstin.

Filling the Gap (1942)
Halas & Batchelor/Realist for Ministry of Information for Ministry of Agriculture.
  D: John Halas, Joy Batchelor.
P: Frank Sainsbury. Anim: Halas, Batchelor, Wally Crook, Vera Linnecar.

Fire! (1901)
Williamson. D: James Williamson.
Documentary reconstruction.

FIRE OVER ENGLAND (1937)
Pendennis. D: William K. Howard.
P: Erich Pommer. S: Clemence Dane, Sergei Nolbandov, from novel by A.E.W.
  Mason. C: Laurence Olivier, Flora Robson.

Firemen to the Rescue (1903)
Hepworth. D: Cecil Hepworth.

FIRES WERE STARTED (1943)
Crown. D: Humphrey Jennings.
P: Ian Dalrymple. S: Jennings, Maurice Richardson. C: William Sansom, Fred
  Griffiths, and other members of the Auxiliary Fire Service.

The First Days (1939)
GPO. D: Humphrey Jennings, Harry Watt, Pat Jackson.
P: Alberto Cavalcanti. S: (commentary) Robert Sinclair.

The Flying Man (1961)
TV Cartoons. Col. P/D/Anim: George Dunning.
S: Stan Hayward.

FOR BETTER FOR WORSE (1954)
Kenwood. Col. D: J. Lee Thompson.
P: Kenneth Harper. S: Lee Thompson, Peter Myer, Alec Grahame, from play by
  Arthur Watkyn. C: Dirk Bogarde, Susan Stephen.

The Forsyte Saga (TV) (1967)
BBC drama serial, 26 episodes. D: James Cellan Jones, David Giles.
P: Donald Wilson. S: Donald Wilson, from novel by John Galsworthy. C: Kenneth
  More, Eric Porter, Nyree Dawn Porter, Susan Hampshire.

FOR THEM THAT TRESPASS (1948)
ABPC. D: Alberto Cavalcanti.
P: Victor Skatezky. S: J. Lee Thompson, William Douglas Home, from novel by
  Ernest Raymond. C: Stephen Murray, Patricia Plunkett, Richard Todd.

49th PARALLEL (1941)
Ortus. D: Michael Powell.
P: Powell, John Sutro. S: Emeric Pressburger, Rodney Ackland. C: Eric Portman,
  Laurence Olivier, Anton Walbrook, Leslie Howard, Raymond Massey.

THE FOUR FEATHERS (1939)
London. Col. D: Zoltan Korda.
P: Alexander Korda, Irving Asher. S: R.C. Sherriff, Lajos Biro, Arthur Wimperis.
  C: John Clements, Ralph Richardson.

FOUR IN THE MORNING (1965)
West One. D/S: Anthony Simmons.
P: John Morris. C: Judi Dench, Norman Rodway.

THE FOUR JUST MEN (1939)
Ealing. D: Walter Forde.
P: Michael Balcon, S.C. Balcon. S: Angus Macphail, Sergei Nolbandov, from novel
  by Edgar Wallace. C: Hugh Sinclair, Griffith Jones, Anna Lee.
US title: *The Secret Four.*

Foxhunt (1935)
London. Col. D/Anim: Anthony Gross, Hector Hoppin.

A Fratricide/Ein Brudermord (1981)
Koninck Studios for Greater London Arts Association and Embassy of the Federal
  Republic of Germany. Col. D/Anim: Stephen and Timothy Quay.
P: Keith Griffiths. Based on Kafka's *Ein Brudermord 1916–1917.*

Free Thaelmann! (1935)
Relief Committee for the Victims of German Fascism.

THE FRENCH LIEUTENANT'S WOMAN (1981)
Juniper. Col. D: Karel Reisz.
P: Leon Clore. S: Harold Pinter, from novel by John Fowles. C: Meryl Streep,
  Jeremy Irons.

FRENCH WITHOUT TEARS (1939)
Two Cities. D: Anthony Asquith.
P: David E. Rose. S: Terence Rattigan, Ian Dalrymple, Anatole de Grunwald, from
  play by Rattigan. C: Ray Milland, Ellen Drew, Roland Culver.

FRENZY (1972)
Universal. Col. D/P: Alfred Hitchcock.
S: Anthony Shaffer, from novel by Arthur La Bern. C: Jon Finch, Barry Foster,
  Anna Massey, Alec McCowen, Vivien Merchant.

FRIEDA (1947)
Ealing. D: Basil Dearden.
P: Michael Balcon, Michael Relph. S: Ronald Millar, Angus Macphail, from
  Millar's play. C: David Farrar, Mai Zetterling, Flora Robson.

THE FRIGHTENED LADY (1932)
Gainsborough–British Lion. D: T. Hayes Hunter.
P: Michael Balcon. S: Angus Macphail, Bryan Wallace, from play by Edgar Wallace.
  C: Cathleen Nesbitt, Emlyn Williams.
US title: *Criminal at Large.*

Full Circle (1953)
W.M. Larkins Studio and Film Producers' Guild for Anglo-Iranian Oil Company.
  D: Peter Sachs.
Anim: Nancy Hanna, Vera Linnecar, Bob Godfrey, Rosalie Marshall, Irene
  Castellanos.

THE GAMEKEEPER (TV) (1979)
ATV. Col. D: Kenneth Loach.
S: Barry Hines. C: Phil Askam, Rita May, Andrew Grubb.

GANDHI (1982)
Indo-British/Goldcrest. Col/Sc. D/P: Richard Attenborough.
S: John Briley. C: Ben Kingsley, Rohini Hattangady, Roshan Seth, Martin Sheen.

THE GAY LORD QUEX (1917)
Ideal. D: Maurice Elvey.

S: Eliot Stannard, from play by A.W. Pinero. C: Ben Webster, Irene Vanbrugh.

GENEVIEVE (1953)
Sirius. Col. D/P: Henry Cornelius.
S: William Rose. C: Dinah Sheridan, John Gregson, Kay Kendall, Kenneth More.

THE GENTLE SEX (1943)
Two Cities. D: Leslie Howard.
P: Howard, Derrick de Marney. S: Moie Charles, Aimee Stewart, Roland Pertwee, Phyllis Rose. C: Joan Greenwood, Rosamund John, Lilli Palmer.

GEORGE IN CIVVY STREET (1946)
Columbia British. D: Marcel Varnel.
P: Varnel, Ben Henry. S: Peter Fraser, Ted Kavanagh, Max Kester, Gale Pedrick. C: George Formby, Ronald Shiner.

GEORGY GIRL (1966)
Everglades. D: Silvio Narizzano.
P: Otto Plaschkes, Robert Goldston. S: Margaret Forster, Peter Nichols, from Forster's novel. C: James Mason, Alan Bates, Lynn Redgrave.

GERT AND DAISY CLEAN UP (1942)
Butchers. D: Maclean Rogers.
P: F.W. Baker. S: Kathleen Butler, H.F. Maltby. C: Elsie Waters, Doris Waters.

GERT AND DAISY'S WEEKEND (1941)
Butchers. D: Maclean Rogers.
P: F.W. Baker. S: Rogers, Kathleen Butler, H.F. Maltby. C: Elsie Waters, Doris Waters.

GET CRACKING (1943)
Columbia British. D: Marcel Varnel.
P: Ben Henry. S: L. du Garde Peach. C: George Formby, Dinah Sheridan.

THE GHOST GOES WEST (1936)
London. D: René Clair.
P: Alexander Korda. S: Robert E. Sherwood, Geoffrey Kerr, from story by Eric Keown. C: Robert Donat, Jean Parker, Eugène Pallette.

THE GHOST OF ST MICHAEL'S (1941)
Ealing. D: Marcel Varnel.
P: Michael Balcon, Basil Dearden. S: Angus Macphail, John Dighton. C: Will Hay, Claude Hulbert.

THE GHOST TRAIN (1927)
Gainsborough. D: Geza M. Bolvary.
P: Michael Balcon, Herman Fellner. S: Arnold Ridley, from his own play. C: Teddy Deakin, John Manners.

THE GHOST TRAIN (1931)
Gainsborough. D: Walter Forde.
P: Michael Balcon. S: Angus Macphail, Lajos Biro, from play by Arnold Ridley. C: Jack Hulbert, Cicely Courtneidge.

Give Us a Smile (1983)
Leeds Animation Workshop. P/D/S/Anim: Leeds Animation Workshop.

GIVE US THIS DAY (1949)
Plantagenet. D: Edward Dmytryk.

P: Rod E. Geiger, Nat Bronstein. S: Ben Barzman, John Penn, from novel by Pietro di Donato. C: Sam Wanamaker, Lea Padovani.
US title: *Salt to the Devil.*

The Glittering Prizes (TV) (1977)
BBC, series of six plays. D: Waris Hussein, Robert Knights.
P: Mark Shivas. S: Frederic Raphael. C: Tom Conti.

THE GO-BETWEEN (1970)
World Film Services. Col. D: Joseph Losey.
P: Robert Velaise, John Heyman, Norman Priggen. S: Harold Pinter, from novel by L.P. Hartley. C: Julie Christie, Alan Bates, Edward Fox.

THE GOLD DIGGERS (1983)
BFI/Channel 4. D: Sally Potter.
S: Lindsay Cooper, Rose English, Sally Potter. C: Julie Christie, Colette Laffont.

GONE TO EARTH (1950)
London. Col. D: Michael Powell, Emeric Pressburger.
P: David O. Selznick. S: Powell and Pressburger, from novel by Mary Webb. C: Jennifer Jones, David Farrar, Cyril Cusack.

GOODBYE MR CHIPS (1939)
MGM British. D: Sam Wood.
P: Victor Saville. S: Eric Maschwitz, R.C. Sheriff, Claudine West, Sidney Franklin, from novel by James Hilton. C: Robert Donat, Greer Garson.

GOOD MORNING BOYS (1937)
Gainsborough. D: Marcel Varnel.
P: Edward Black. S: Marriott Edgar, Val Guest, Anthony Kimmins. C: Will Hay, Graham Moffatt, Lilli Palmer.
US title: *Where There's a Will.*

The Good Old Days (TV) (1963–83)
BBC music-hall series.
P: Barney Colehan. C: Leonard Sachs.

GOOD TIME GIRL (1948)
Triton. D: David Macdonald.
P: Sydney Box, Samuel Goldwyn Jr. S: Muriel and Sydney Box, Ted Willis, from novel by Arthur La Bern. C: Jean Kent, Dennis Price, Flora Robson, Diana Dors.

THE GOOSE STEPS OUT (1942)
Ealing. D: Will Hay, Basil Dearden.
P: Michael Balcon, S.C. Balcon. S: Angus Macphail, John Dighton, Bernard Miles, Reginald Groves. C: Will Hay, Frank Pettingell.

Go to Blazes (1942)
Ealing. D: Walter Forde.
P: Michael Balcon. S: Angus Macphail, Diana Morgan. C: Will Hay.

Grandma's Reading Glass (1900)
G.A.S. D: G.A. Smith.

GREAT EXPECTATIONS (1946)
Cineguild. D: David Lean.
P: Anthony Havelock-Allan, Ronald Neame. S: Neame, Lean, Havelock-Allan, Kay Walsh, Cecil McGivern, from novel by Charles Dickens. C: John Mills, Valerie Hobson, Bernard Miles, Alec Guinness.

GREAT EXPECTATIONS (1975)
Transcontinental. Col. D: Joseph Hardy.
P: Robert Fryer. S: Sherman Yellen, from novel by Charles Dickens. C: Michael
   York, Sarah Miles, James Mason, Margaret Leighton.

Great – Isambard Kingdom Brunel (1975)
British Lion. Col. P/D: Bob Godfrey.
S: Richard Taylor, Godfrey, Joe McGrath, Robin Smyth, Paul Weisser. D. Anim:
   Jeff Goldner, Anne Jolliffe.

THE GREEN COCKATOO (1937)
New World. D: William Cameron Menzies.
P: Robert T. Kane. S: Edward Berkman, Arthur Wimperis, from story by Graham
   Greene. C: John Mills, Rene Ray.
Alternative title: *Four Dark Hours.*

GREGORY'S GIRL (1980)
Lake/NFFC/STV. Col. D/S: Bill Forsyth.
P: Davina Belling, Clive Parsons. C: Dee Hepburn, Gordon John Sinclair.

GRIP OF THE STRANGLER (1958)
MLC Producers. D: Robert Day.
P: John Croydon. S: Jan Read, John C. Cooper. C: Boris Karloff, Jean Kent.

The Grove Family (TV) (1953–6)
BBC weekly serial. D: Richard West.
P: John Warrington. C: Edward Evans, Sheila Sweet, Peter Bryant.

Guinness at the Albert Hall (1962)
Richard Williams. P/D: Richard Williams.

A GUNMAN HAS ESCAPED (1948)
Condor. D: Richard Grey.
P: Harry Goodman, Richard Grey. S: John Gilling. C: John Harvey, John
   Fitzgerald.

THE GYPSY AND THE GENTLEMAN (1958)
Rank. Col. D: Joseph Losey.
P: Maurice Cowan. S: Janet Green, from novel by Nina Warner Hooke. C: Melina
   Mercouri, Keith Michell, Flora Robson.

HALF A SIXPENCE (1967)
Ameran. Col/Sc. D: George Sidney.
P: John Darts, Charles H. Schneer. S: Beverley Cross, from novel by H.G. Wells.
   C: Tommy Steele, Julia Foster.

HAMLET (1913)
Hepworth. D: E. Hay Plumb.
P: Cecil Hepworth. S: from Shakespeare play. C: Johnston Forbes-Robertson,
   Gertrude Elliot.

HAMLET (1948)
Two Cities. D/P: Laurence Olivier.
S: from Shakespeare play. C: Laurence Olivier, Basil Sydney, Jean Simmons.

HAMLET (1969)
Woodfall. Col. D: Tony Richardson.
P: Leslie Linder, Martin Ransohoff. S: play by Shakespeare. C: Nicol Williamson,
   Anthony Hopkins, Marianne Faithfull.

Handling Ships (1945)
Halas & Batchelor for the Admiralty. D: John Halas, Allan Crick.
P/Anim: Halas. S: Crick.

The Hand of the Artist (1906)
Urban Trading Co. D/Anim: Walter Booth.

HANDS OF THE RIPPER (1971)
Hammer. Col. D: Peter Sasdy.
P: Aida Young. S: L.W. Davidson. C: Eric Porter, Angharad Rees.

A HARD DAY'S NIGHT (1964)
Proscenium. D: Richard Lester.
P: Walter Shenson. S: Alun Owen. C: The Beatles, Wilfred Brambell.

The Haunted Curiosity Shop (1901)
R.W. Paul. D: R.W. Booth.

The Heart is Highland (1952)
British Transport Films. Col. D: John Taylor.
P: Edgar Anstey. S: Morny McLaren.

The Heart of Britain (1941)
Crown Film Unit. D: Humphrey Jennings.
P: Ian Dalrymple. S: (commentary) Jack Holmes.

HEART OF MIDLOTHIAN (1914)
Hepworth. D: Frank Wilson.
S: Blanche McIntosh, from novel by Walter Scott. C: Flora Morris, Alma Taylor,
    Stewart Rome.

Helen A Woman of Today (TV) (1973)
London Weekend Television, 13-part series. Col. D: Herbert Wise and others.
P: Richard Bates. S: David Butler and others. C: Alison Fiske, Martin Shaw.

HELL DRIVERS (1957)
Rank/Aqua. D: C. Baker Endfield.
P: S. Benjamin Fisz. S: Endfield, John Kruse. C: Stanley Baker, Patrick McGoohan,
    Peggy Cummins.

HELL IS A CITY (1960)
Hammer. Sc. D: Val Guest.
P: Michael Carreras. S: Guest, from novel by Maurice Proctor. C: Stanley Baker,
    Donald Pleasence.

Hell Unltd. (1936)
Glasgow School of Art. D/Anim: Norman McLaren, Helen Biggar.

HELP! (1965)
Shenson. Col. D: Richard Lester.
P: Walter Shenson. S: Marc Behm, Charles Wood. C: The Beatles, Eleanor Bron,
    Leo McKern.

Henry's Cat series (1983–)
Bob Godfrey for BBC TV. Col. D: Bob Godfrey.
S: Godfrey, Stan Hayward.

HENRY V (1945)
Two Cities. Col. D/P: Laurence Olivier.
S: Olivier, Alan Dent, from play by Shakespeare. C: Laurence Olivier, Robert
    Newton, Leslie Banks.

397

HENRY VIII (1911)
Barker. D: Louis P. Parker.
P: Will Barker. S: from play by Shakespeare. C: Herbert Tree, Arthur Bourchier, Violet Vanbrugh.

Henry 9 Till 5 (1970)
Bob Godfrey. Col. D/P: Bob Godfrey.
S: Stan Hayward. Anim: Godfrey, Dennis Rich.

HIGH TREASON (1929)
Gaumont. D: Maurice Elvey.
P: l'Estrange Fawcett. S: Fawcett, from play by Noel Pemberton-Billing. C: Jameson Thomas, Benita Hume.

HIS BROTHER'S KEEPER (1939)
Warner. D: Roy William Neil.
P: Sam Sax. S: Neill, Austin Melford, Brock Williams. C: Clifford Evans, Tamara Desni.

Hokusai: An Animated Sketchbook (1978)
Tony White for Arts Council of Great Britain. D/P/S/Anim: Tony White.

HOLIDAY CAMP (1947)
Gainsborough. D: Ken Annakin.
P: Sydney Box. S: Sydney and Muriel Box, Denis and Mabel Constanduros. C: Jack Warner, Kathleen Harrison, Jimmy Hanley, Flora Robson.

HORROR OF FRANKENSTEIN (1970)
Hammer. Col. D/P: Jimmy Sangster.
S: Sangster, Jeremy Burnham, from novel by Mary Shelley. C: Ralph Bates, Kate O'Mara, Dennis Price.

HORRORS OF THE BLACK MUSEUM (1959)
Merton Park. Col/Sc. D: Arthur Crabtree.
P: Herman Cohen, Jack Greenwood. S: Cohen, Aben Kandel. C: Michael Gough, Shirley Ann Field.

HOSTILE WITNESS (1968)
Caralan/Dador. Col. D: Ray Milland.
P: David E. Rose. S: Jack Roffey, from his own play. C: Ray Milland, Sylvia Syms.

THE HOUND OF THE BASKERVILLES (1921)
Stoll. D: Maurice Elvey.
S: William J. Elliott, Dorothy Westlake, from novel by Arthur Conan Doyle. C: Eille Norwood, Hubert Willis.

Housing Problems (1935)
Gas Light & Coke Co. D/P/S: Edgar Anstey, Arthur Elton, Ruby Grierson.

HOW HE LIED TO HER HUSBAND (1931)
BIP. D: Cecil Lewis.
S: Lewis, Frank Launder, from play by George Bernard Shaw. C: Edmund Gwenn, Vera Lennox, Robert Harris.

HOW I WON THE WAR (1967)
Petersham. Col. D: Richard Lester.
P: Lester, Denis O'Dell. S: Charles Wood, from novel by Patrick Ryan. C: Michael Crawford, John Lennon.

How The Telephone Works (1938)
GPO Film Unit. D: Ralph Elton, Jack Chambers.

HUE AND CRY (1947)
Ealing. D: Charles Crichton.
P: Michael Balcon, Henry Cornelius. S: T.E.B. Clarke. C: Alastair Sim, Jack
   Warner.

Hunger March 1934 (1934)
Workers' Film and Photo League.

HUNTED (1952)
Independent Artists. D: Charles Crichton.
P: Julian Wintle. S: Jack Whittingham, Michael McCarthy. C: Dirk Bogarde, Kay
   Walsh, Jon Whiteley.
US title: *The Stranger in Between*.

HYSTERIA (1964)
Hammer. D: Freddie Francis.
P/S: Jimmy Sangster. C: Robert Webber, Leila Goldoni.

I COULD GO ON SINGING (1962)
Barbican. Col/Sc. D: Ronald Neame.
P: Stuart Millar, Lawrence Turman. S: Mayo Simon, Robert Dozier. C: Judy
   Garland, Dirk Bogarde.

I KNOW WHERE I'M GOING (1945)
The Archers. D/P/S: Michael Powell, Emeric Pressburger.
C: Roger Livesey, Wendy Hiller.

I'M ALL RIGHT JACK (1959)
Charter. D: John Boulting.
P: Roy Boulting. S: John Boulting, Frank Harvey, Alan Hackney, from Hackney's
   novel. C: Ian Carmichael, Peter Sellers, Terry-Thomas.

THE IMITATION GAME (TV) (1980)
BBC. Col. D: Richard Eyre.
P: Eyre. S: Ian McEwan. C: Harriet Walter.

THE IMPORTANCE OF BEING EARNEST (1952)
BFM/Javelin. Col. D: Anthony Asquith.
P: Teddy Baird. S: Asquith, from play by Oscar Wilde. C: Michael Redgrave,
   Michael Denison, Edith Evans.

INADMISSIBLE EVIDENCE (1968)
Woodfall. D: Anthony Page.
P: Ronald Kinnoch. S: John Osborne, from his own play. C: Nicol Williamson, Jill
   Bennett.

INDISCREET (1958)
Grandon. Col. D: Stanley Donen.
P: Donen, Cary Grant. S: Norman Krasna, from his own play. C: Cary Grant,
   Ingrid Bergman.

Industrial Britain (1931)
Empire Marketing Board. D/S: Robert Flaherty.
P: John Grierson.

THE INFORMER (1929)
BIP. D: Arthur Robison.

S: Benn Levy, Rolfe E. Vanlo, from play by Liam O'Flaherty. C: Lya de Putti, Lars Hansen.

INN FOR TROUBLE (1959)
Film Locations. D: C.M. Pennington-Richards.
P: Norman J Hyams, Edward Lloyd. S: Fred Robinson, from his own TV series *The Larkins*. C: Peggy Mount, David Kossoff.

THE INNOCENTS (1961)
Achilles. Sc. D: Jack Clayton.
P: Albert Fennell, Clayton. S: William Archibald, Truman Capote, John Mortimer, from story *The Turn of the Screw* by Henry James. C: Deborah Kerr, Michael Redgrave.

INSIGNIFICANCE (1985)
Zenith. Col. D: Nicolas Roeg.
P: Jeremy Thomas. S: Terry Johnson, from his own play. C: Michael Emil, Theresa Russell, Tony Curtis, Gary Busey.

IN THE FOREST (1978)
BFI. D/P/S: Phil Mulloy.
C: Barrie Houghton, Ellen Sheean, Nick Burton.

Invisibility (1909)
Hepworth. D: Cecil Hepworth, Lewin Fitzhamon.
C: Fitzhamon.

INVITATION TO THE DANCE (1956)
MGM British. Col. D/S: Gene Kelly.
P: Arthur Freed. C: Gene Kelly.

IN WHICH WE SERVE (1942)
Two Cities. D: David Lean, Noël Coward.
P/S: Coward. C: Coward, Celia Johnson, Bernard Miles, John Mills, Richard Attenborough.

Irene Latour – Contortionist (1901)
Warwick. C: Irene Latour, Zaza (dog).

ISLAND IN THE SUN (1957)
20th Century-Fox. Col/Sc. D: Robert Rossen.
P: Darryl F. Zanuck. S: Alfred Hayes, from novel by Alec Waugh. C: James Mason, Harry Belafonte, Joan Fontaine.

IT ALWAYS RAINS ON SUNDAY (1947)
Ealing. D: Robert Hamer.
P: Michael Balcon, Henry Cornelius. S: Hamer, Cornelius, Angus Macphail, from novel by Arthur La Bern. C: Googie Withers, John McCallum, Jack Warner.

I THANK YOU (1941)
Gainsborough. D: Marcel Varnel.
P: Edward Black. S: Howard Irving Young, Val Guest, Marriott Edgar. C: Arthur Askey, Richard Murdoch, Lily Morris.

IT'S A GRAND LIFE (1953)
Mancunian. D/P: John E. Blakeley.
S: H.F. Maltby, Frank Randle. C: Frank Randle, Diana Dors.

IVANHOE (1913)
Independent Moving Pictures. D: Herbert Brenon.

S: Brenon, from novel by Walter Scott. C: King Baggot.

IVANHOE (1913)
Zenith. D: Leedham Bantock.
S. Bantock, based on stage adaptation of Scott's novel by Walter and Frederick
Melville.

IVANHOE (1952)
MGM British. Col. D: Richard Thorpe.
P: Pandro S. Berman. S: Aeneas Mackenzie, Noel Langley, from novel by Walter
Scott. C: Robert Taylor, Elizabeth Taylor, George Sanders.

JACK THE RIPPER (1959)
Mid-Century. D: Robert S. Baker.
P: Baker, Monty Berman. S: Jimmy Sangster. C: Lee Patterson, Eddie Byrne.

JAMAICA INN (1939)
Mayflower. D: Alfred Hitchcock.
P: Erich Pommer. S: Sidney Gilliat, Joan Harrison, J.B. Priestley. C: Charles
Laughton, Maureen O'Hara, Robert Newton.

JANE EYRE (1970)
Omnibus/Sagittarius. Col. D: Delbert Mann.
P: Frederick H. Brogger. S: Jack Pulman, from novel by Charlotte Brontë.
C: George C. Scott, Susannah York.

JASSY (1947)
Gainsborough. Col. D: Bernard Knowles.
P: Sydney Box. S: Dorothy and Campbell Christie, Geoffrey Kerr, from novel by
Norah Lofts. C: Margaret Lockwood, Patricia Roc, Dennis Price.

JERICHO (1937)
Buckingham. D: Thornton Freeland.
P: Walter Futter, Max Schach. S: Frances Marion, Walter Futter. C: Paul Robeson,
Henry Wilcoxon, Princess Kouka.
US title: *Dark Sands*.

Jewel in the Crown (TV) (1983)
Granada, 14 part serial (film). Col. D: Christopher Morahan, Jim O'Brien.
P: Morahan. S: Ken Taylor, from the novels *The Raj Quartet* by Paul Scott. C: Tim
Pigott-Smith, Peggy Ashcroft, Geraldine James, Charles Dance.

JEW SÜSS (1934)
Gaumont-British. D: Lothar Mendes.
P. Michael Balcon. S: A.R. Rawlinson, from novel by Lion Feuchtwanger.
C: Conrad Veidt, Benita Hume, Cedric Hardwicke.
US title: *Power*.

John Bull's Animated Sketch Book series (1915–16)
Cartoon Film Company. D/Anim: Dudley Buxton, Anson Dyer.

JOURNEY TOGETHER (1945)
RAF Film Unit. D: John Boulting.
S: John Boulting, Terence Rattigan. C: Richard Attenborough, Edward G.
Robinson, Bessie Love.

Jubilee (1935)
North London Film Society Film Unit. D: Herbert A. Green, R. Green.

JUNO AND THE PAYCOCK (1930)

BIP. D: Alfred Hitchcock.

S: Hitchcock, Alma Reville, Sean O'Casey, from play by O'Casey. C: Sara Allgood, Edward Chapman.

US title: *The Shame of Mary Boyle.*

The Kaiser Catches Pimple (1915)

Piccadilly. D/S: Fred Evans, Joe Evans.

C: Fred Evans.

KIDNAPPED (1971)

Omnibus. Col. D: Delbert Mann.

P: Frederick H. Brogger. S: Jack Pulman, from novels by Robert Louis Stevenson. C: Michael Caine, Trevor Howard, Jack Hawkins.

THE KIDNAPPERS (1953)

Rank. D: Philip Leacock.

S: Sergei Nolbandov, Leslie Parkyn. S: Neil Paterson. C: Duncan Macrae, Adrienne Corri, Jon Whiteley.

THE KILLING FIELDS (1984)

Enigma/Goldcrest. Col. D: Roland Joffé.

P: David Puttnam. S: Bruce Robinson. C: Sam Waterston, Dr Haing S. Ngor.

KIND HEARTS AND CORONETS (1949)

Ealing. D: Robert Hamer.

P: Michael Balcon, Michael Relph. S: Hamer, John Dighton, from novel by Roy Horniman. C: Alec Guinness, Dennis Price, Joan Greenwood, Valerie Hobson.

A KIND OF LOVING (1962)

Vic. D: John Schlesinger.

P: Joseph Janni. S: Willis Hall, Keith Waterhouse, from novel by Stan Barstow. C: Alan Bates, June Ritchie, Thora Hird.

King John (1899)

Mutoscope/Biograph.

From play by Shakespeare. C: Beerbohm Tree.

KING SOLOMON'S MINES (1937)

Gaumont. D: Robert Stevenson.

P: Michael Balcon, Geoffrey Barkas. S: Michael Hogan, Roland Pertwee, from novel by H. Rider Haggard. C: Paul Robeson, Cedric Hardwicke.

KING'S RHAPSODY (1955)

Everest. Col/Sc. D/P: Herbert Wilcox.

S: Pamela Bower, Christopher Hassall, A.P. Herbert, from play by Ivor Novello. C: Anna Neagle, Errol Flynn.

The King with a Terrible Temper (1937)

Anson Dyer for Bush Radio. Col. D: Anson Dyer.

KIPPS (1941)

20th Century. D: Carol Reed.

P: Edward Black. S: Frank Launder, Sidney Gilliat, from novel by H.G. Wells. C: Michael Redgrave, Diana Wynyard, Phyllis Calvert.

US title: *The Remarkable Mr Kipps.*

THE KNACK (1965)

Woodfall. D: Richard Lester.

P: Oscar Lewenstein. S: Charles Wood, Richard Lester, from play by Ann Jellicoe. C: Rita Tushingham, Ray Brooks, Michael Crawford.

KNIGHTS OF THE ROUND TABLE (1954)
MGM British. Col/Sc. D: Richard Thorpe.
P: Pandro S. Berman. S: Talbot Jennings, Jan Lustig, Noel Langley, based on Sir Thomas Malory. C: Robert Taylor, Ava Gardner.

THE LADYKILLERS (1955)
Ealing. Col. D: Alexander Mackendrick.
P: Michael Balcon, Seth Holt. S: William Rose. C: Alec Guinness, Katie Johnson, Cecil Parker, Peter Sellers.

THE LADY VANISHES (1938)
Gainsborough. D: Alfred Hitchcock.
P: Edward Black. S: Frank Launder, Sidney Gilliat, from novel by Ethel Lina White. C: Margaret Lockwood, Michael Redgrave, Dame May Whitty.

The Larkins (TV) (1958–63)
ATV serial.
P: Bill Ward. S: Fred Robinson. C: David Kossoff, Peggy Mount.

LAUGHTERHOUSE (1984)
Greenpoint for Film Four International. Col. D: Richard Eyre.
P: Ann Scott. S: Brian Glover. C: Ian Holm, Penelope Wilton, Bill Owen.

Lautrec (1975)
Dragon in association with the Arts Council of Great Britain. Col. D/S/Des: Geoff Dunbar.
Anim: Dunbar, Oscar Grillo, Jill Brooks, Ginger Gibbons, Len Lewis, Janet Archer.

THE LAVENDER HILL MOB (1951)
Ealing. D: Charles Crichton.
P: Michael Balcon, Michael Truman. S: T.E.B. Clarke. C: Alec Guinness, Stanley Holloway.

LAW AND ORDER (TV) (1978)
BBC, quartet of films. Col. D: Leslie Blair.
P: Tony Garnett. S: G.F. Newman. C: Derek Martin, Alan Ford, Ken Campbell.

LAXDALE HALL (1953)
Group 3. D: John Eldridge.
P: John Grierson, Alfred Shaughnessy. S: Eldridge, Shaughnessy, from novel by Eric Linklater. C: Ronald Squire, Kathleen Ryan.

LEFT RIGHT AND CENTRE (1959)
Vale. D: Sidney Gilliat.
P: Frank Launder, Gilliat. S: Gilliat, Val Valentine. C: Ian Carmichael, Alastair Sim.

LET GEORGE DO IT (1940)
Ealing. D: Marcel Varnel.
P: Michael Balcon, Basil Dearden. S: Dearden, John Dighton, Angus Macphail, Austin Melford. C: George Formby, Phyllis Calvert.

LIBEL (1959)
MGM. D: Anthony Asquith.
P: Anatole de Grunwald. S: De Grunwald, Karl Tunberg, from play by Edward

Wooll. C: Dirk Bogarde, Olivia de Havilland, Paul Massie.

THE LIFE AND DEATH OF COLONEL BLIMP (1943)
The Archers D/P/S: Michael Powell, Emeric Pressburger.
C: Roger Livesey, Anton Walbrook, Deborah Kerr.
US title: *Colonel Blimp*.

The Lincolnshire Poacher (1949)
W.M. Larkins for Central Office of Information for British Council.

THE LION HAS WINGS (1939)
London. D: Michael Powell, Brian Desmond Hurst, Adrian Brunel.
P: Alexander Korda. S: Brunel, Ian Dalrymple, E.V.H. Emmett. C: Merle Oberon,
   Ralph Richardson.

Listen to Britain (1942)
Crown. D: Humphrey Jennings, Stewart McAllister.
P: Ian Dalrymple.

The Little Island (1958)
Richard Williams. P/D/S: Richard Williams. Col.

Little Red Riding Hood (a Kiddiegraph) (1922)
Hepworth. Anim: Anson Dyer.

LOCAL HERO (1983)
Enigma/Goldcrest. Col. D/S: Bill Forsyth.
P: David Puttnam. C: Burt Lancaster, Peter Riegert, Fulton Mackay.

THE LODGER (1926)
Gainsborough. D: Alfred Hitchcock.
P: Michael Balcon. S: Hitchcock, Eliot Stannard, from play by Mrs Belloc Lowndes.
   C: Ivor Novello, June, Malcolm Keen.

THE LONELINESS OF THE LONG-DISTANCE RUNNER (1962)
Woodfall. D: Tony Richardson.
P: Richardson, Michael Holden. S: Alan Sillitoe, from his own short story. C: Tom
   Courtenay, Michael Redgrave.

THE LONG MEMORY (1953)
Europa. D: Robert Hamer.
P: Hugh Stewart. S: Hamer, Frank Harvey, from novel by Howard Clewes. C: John
   Mills, Elisabeth Sellars.

LOOK BACK IN ANGER (1959)
Woodfall. D: Tony Richardson.
P: Harry Saltzman, Gordon Scott. S: Nigel Kneale, John Osborne, from Osborne's
   play. C: Richard Burton, Claire Bloom, Mary Ure.

THE LOST CONTINENT (1968)
Hammer. Col. D: Michael Carreras.
P: Anthony Hinds, Carreras. S: Michael Nash, from novel by Dennis Wheatley.
   C: Eric Porter, Hildegarde Neff.

LOVE ON THE DOLE (1941)
British National. D/P: John Baxter.
S: Walter Greenwood, Barbara K. Emery, Rollo Gamble, from novel by Green-
   wood. C: Deborah Kerr, Clifford Evans, Geoffrey Hibbert.

Love on the Wing (1938)
GPO Film Unit. D/Anim: Norman McLaren.

The Lovers (TV) (1970-1)
Granada, comedy series.
P/S: Jack Rosenthal. C: Paula Wilcox, Richard Beckinsale.

THE LOVERS! (1972)
Gildor. D: Herbert Wise.
P: Maurice Foster. S: Jack Rosenthal, based on his own Granada TV series.
   C: Richard Beckinsale, Paula Wilcox.

LOVE STORY (1944)
Gainsborough. D: Leslie Arliss.
P: George Black. S: Arliss, Doreen Montgomery, Rodney Ackland, from novel by
   J.W. Drawbell. C: Margaret Lockwood, Stewart Granger, Patricia Roc.
US title: *A Lady Surrenders.*

LOYALTIES (1933)
ATP. D/P: Basil Dean.
S: W.P. Lipscomb, from play by John Galsworthy. C: Basil Rathbone, Heather
   Thatcher.

MACBETH (1971)
Playboy. Col/Sc. D: Roman Polanski.
P: Andrew Brannsberg. S: Polanski, Kenneth Tynan, from play by Shakespeare.
   C: Jon Finch, Francesca Annis, Martin Shaw.

MADONNA OF THE SEVEN MOONS (1944)
Gainsborough. D: Arthur Crabtree.
P: Edward Black. S: Roland Pertwee, Brock Williams, from novel by Margery
   Lawrence. C: Phyllis Calvert, Stewart Granger, Patricia Roc.

MAEVE (1981)
BFI/Radio Telefis Eireann. Col. D: Pat Murphy, John Davies.
S: Pat Murphy. C: Mary Jackson, Mark Mulholland, Brid Brennan.

THE MAGGIE (1954)
Ealing. D: Alexander Mackendrick.
P: Michael Balcon, Michael Truman. S: William Rose. C: Paul Douglas, Alex
   Mackenzie.

Magic Canvas (1948)
Halas & Batchelor. D/S: John Halas, Joy Batchelor.
P: Halas, Batchelor. Anim: Wally Crook.

THE MAGISTRATE (1921)
Samuelson. D: Bannister Merwin.
S: Merwin, from play by A.W. Pinero. C: Tom Reynolds, Maudie Dunham.

The Maid of Cefn Ydfa (1902)
D: William Haggar.

MAJOR BARBARA (1941)
Pascal. D/P: Gabriel Pascal.
S: George Bernard Shaw, Anatole de Grunwald, from play by Shaw. C: Wendy
   Hiller, Rex Harrison.

THE MAN BETWEEN (1953)
London. D/P: Carol Reed.
S: Harry Kurnitz, Eric Linklater, from novel by Walter Ebert. C: James Mason, Claire Bloom.

MANDY (1952)
Ealing. D: Alexander Mackendrick.
P: Michael Balcon, Leslie Norman. S: Jack Whittingham, Nigel Balchin, from novel by Hilda Lewis. C: Phyllis Calvert, Jack Hawkins, Terence Morgan, Mandy Miller.
US title: *The Crash of Silence.*

THE MAN IN GREY (1943)
Gainsborough. D: Leslie Arliss.
P: Edward Black. S: Arliss, Margaret Kennedy, Doreen Montgomery, from novel by Eleanor Smith. C: Margaret Lockwood, Phyllis Calvert, James Mason.

THE MAN IN THE WHITE SUIT (1951)
Ealing. D: Alexander Mackendrick.
P: Michael Balcon, Sidney Cole. S: Roger Macdougall, John Dighton, Mackendrick, from Macdougall's play. C: Alec Guinness, Joan Greenwood, Cecil Parker.

MAN OF ARAN (1934)
Gainsborough. D: Robert Flaherty.
P: Michael Balcon. S: Robert and Frances Flaherty. C: Maggie Dirane, Colman King, Pat Mullen.

MAN OF THE MOMENT (1955)
Group. D: John Paddy Carstairs.
P: Hugh Stewart. S: Carstairs, Vernon Sylvaine. C: Norman Wisdom, Belinda Lee.

MAN ON THE RUN (1949)
ABPC. D/P/S: Lawrence Huntington.
C: Derek Farr, Joan Hopkins, Laurence Harvey.

THE MAN WHO COULD WORK MIRACLES (1936)
London. D: Lothar Mendes.
P: Alexander Korda. S: Lajos Biro, from story by H.G. Wells. C: Roland Young, Ralph Richardson.

THE MAN WHO KNEW TOO MUCH (1934)
Gaumont. D: Alfred Hitchcock.
P: Michael Balcon, Ivor Montagu. S: Charles Bennett, D.B. Wyndham-Lewis, A.R. Rawlinson. C: Leslie Banks, Edna Best, Peter Lorre, Nova Pilbeam.

MAN WITHOUT A SOUL (1916)
London. D: George L. Tucker.
S: Tucker, Kenelon Foss. C: Milton Rosmer.
US title: *I Believe.*

A MARRIED MAN (TV) (1982)
London Weekend Television/Lionhead Associates, series of films. D: Charles Jarrott.
P: John Davies. S: Derek Marlowe, from novel by Piers Paul Read. C: Anthony Hopkins, John Le Mesurier, Linda Hilboldt.

MASKS AND FACES (1917)
Ideal. D: Fred Paul.
S: Benedict James, from play by Tom Taylor and Charles Reade. C: Johnston

Forbes-Robertson, Irene Vanbrugh, H.B. Irving, Gerald du Maurier, Gladys Cooper, Ben Webster.

MASTER AND MAN (1929)
British Screen. D: George A. Cooper.
S: Edward Dryhurst. S: Cooper, from play by Henry Pettitt and G.R. Sims.
  C: Humberstone Wright, Anne Grey.

Matches Appeal (c. 1899)
D/P: Arthur Melbourne-Cooper. For Bryant & May.

A MATTER OF LIFE AND DEATH (1946)
The Archers. Col. D/P/S: Michael Powell and Emeric Pressburger.
C: David Niven, Roger Livesey, Kim Hunter.

Max Beeza and the City in the Sky (1977)
National Film School. Col. D: Derek Hayes, Phil Austin.
Anim: Hayes, Austin, Ginny D'Santos.

MEET MR LUCIFER (1953)
Ealing. D: Anthony Pelissier.
P: Michael Balcon, Monja Danischewsky. S: Danischewsky, Peter Myers, Alec
  Graham, from a play by Arnold Ridley. C: Stanley Holloway, Peggy Cummins,
  Joseph Tomelty.

The Memoirs of Miffy series (1920)
D: Dudley Buxton.

THE MERCHANT OF VENICE (1916)
Broadwest. D/P: Walter West.
S: from play by Shakespeare. C: Matheson Lang.

A MIDSUMMER NIGHT'S DREAM (1968)
Royal Shakespeare Enterprises/Filmways. Col. D: Peter Hall.
P: Martin Ransohoff, Michael Birkett. S: from play by Shakespeare. C: David
  Warner, Diana Rigg, Judi Dench.

MILLIONS LIKE US (1943)
Gainsborough. D/S: Frank Launder, Sidney Gilliat.
P: Edward Black. C: Eric Portman, Anne Crawford, Patricia Roc, Gordon Jackson.

THE MILL ON THE FLOSS (1937)
Morgan. D: Tim Whelan.
P: John Clein. S: John Drinkwater, Garrett Weston, Austin Melford, Whelan, from
  novel by George Eliot. C: Frank Lawton, Victoria Hopper, Geraldine Fitzgerald.

THE MIND BENDERS (1962)
Novus. D: Basil Dearden.
P: Michael Relph. S: James Kennaway. C: Dirk Bogarde, Mary Ure, Michael
  Bryant.

MINE OWN EXECUTIONER (1947)
London/Harefield. D: Anthony Kimmins.
P: Kimmins, Jack Kitchen. S: Nigel Balchin, from his own novel. C: Burgess
  Meredith, Dulcie Gray, Kieron Moore.

THE MINIVER STORY (1950)
MGM British. D: H.C. Potter.
P: Sidney Franklin. S: Ronald Millar, George Froeschel. C: Greer Garson, Walter
  Pidgeon.

MIRANDA (1948)
Gainsborough. D: Ken Annakin.
P: Betty Box. S: Peter Blackmore, Denis Waldock, from Blackmore's play.
C: Googie Withers, Glynis Johns, Griffith Jones.

MISTER QUILP (1974)
Reader's Digest. Col. D: Michael Tuchner.
P: Helen M. Strauss. S: Louis and Irene Kamp, from novel by Charles Dickens.
C: Anthony Newley, David Hemmings, Jill Bennett, David Warner.

Mistletoe Bough (1904)
Clarendon. D: Percy Stow.
From poem by E.T. Bayley.

MOBY DICK (1956)
Moulin. Col. D: John Huston.
P: Huston, Vaughan N. Dean. S: Huston, Ray Bradbury, from novel by Herman
Melville. C: Gregory Peck, Richard Basehart.

MODESTY BLAISE (1966)
Fox. Col. D: Joseph Losey.
P: Joseph Janni, Norman Priggen, Michael Birkett. S: Evan Jones, based on comic
strip by Peter O'Donnell. C: Dirk Bogarde, Monica Vitti, Terence Stamp.

Momma Don't Allow (1955)
BFI Experimental Film Fund. D/S: Karel Reisz, Tony Richardson.

THE MONKEY'S PAW (1948)
Kay. D: Norman Lee.
P: Ernest G. Roy. S: Norman Lee, Barbara Toy, from play by W.W. Jacobs.
C: Milton Rosmer, Megs Jenkins.

Monorail (1898)
R.W. Paul. Actuality footage.

MONTY PYTHON'S LIFE OF BRIAN (1979)
HandMade. Col. D: Terry Jones.
P: John Goldstone. S/C: Graham Chapman, John Cleese, Terry Gilliam, Eric Idle,
Terry Jones, Michael Palin.

MOTHER RILEY MEETS THE VAMPIRE (1952)
Fernwood/Renown. D/P: John Gilling.
S: Val Valentine. C: Arthur Lucan, Bela Lugosi, Dora Bryan.

MOULIN ROUGE (1928)
BIP. D/P/S: E.A. Dupont.
C: Olga Tschechowa, Eve Gray, Jean Bradin.

THE MOUNTAIN EAGLE (1926)
Gainsborough-Emelka. D: Alfred Hitchcock.
P: Michael Balcon. S: Eliot Stannard, Charles Lapworth. C: Nita Naldi, Malcolm
Keen, Bernhard Goetzke.
US title: *Fear o' God*.

THE MUPPET MOVIE (1979)
ITC. Col. D: James Frawley.
P: Jim Henson. S: Jerry Juhl, Jack Burns. C: The Muppets, voices of Jim Henson
and others.

MURDER! (1930)
BIP. D: Alfred Hitchcock.
S: Hitchcock, Alma Reville, Walter Mycroft, from play by Clemence Dane and
Helen Simpson. C: Herbert Marshall, Norah Baring.

MURDER BY DECREE (1978)
Saucy Jack/Decree/Canadian Film Development Corporation. Col. D: Bob Clark.
P: Clark, René Dupont. S: John Hopkins, from BBC TV series on Jack the Ripper
by John Lloyd, Elwyn Jones. C: Christopher Plummer, James Mason, Anthony
Quayle, David Hemmings.

MURDER IN SOHO (1939)
ABPC. D: Norman Lee.
P: Walter Mycroft. S: F. McGrew Willis. C: Jack la Rue, Sandra Storme.
US title: *Murder in the Night.*

MURDER ON THE ORIENT EXPRESS (1974)
EMI. Col. D: Sidney Lumet.
P: John Brabourne, Richard Goodwin. S: Paul Dehn, from novel by Agatha
Christie. C: Albert Finney, Ingrid Bergman, John Gielgud, Wendy Hiller.

Musical Paintbox series (1948–9)
G-B Animation (Rank). Col. Exec. P/D: David Hand.
Series D: C. Henry Stringer. S: Nicholas Spargo, Graeme Phillips, R.A.G. Clarke.

MY BROTHER'S KEEPER (1948)
Gainsborough. D: Alfred Roome, Roy Rich.
P: Anthony Darnborough. S: Frank Harvey, Maurice Wiltshire. C: Jack Warner,
Jane Hylton, David Tomlinson.

N or N.W. (1937)
GPO Film Unit. D/Anim: Len Lye.

THE NANNY (1965)
Hammer/Seven Arts. D: Seth Holt.
P/S: Jimmy Sangster. C: Bette Davis, Wendy Craig.

NELSON (1918)
International Exclusives. D: Maurice Elvey.
P: Low Warren. S: Eliot Stannard, from biography by Robert Southey. C: Donald
Calthrop, Malvina Longfellow, Ernest Thesiger.

News and Comment (1978)
D: Frank Abbott.

NICHOLAS NICKLEBY (1947)
Ealing. D: Alberto Cavalcanti.
P: Michael Balcon, John Croydon. S: John Dighton, from novel by Charles Dickens.
C: Derek Bond, Cedric Hardwicke, Stanley Holloway, Bernard Miles.

NIGHT AND THE CITY (1950)
20th Century Productions. D: Jules Dassin.
P: Samuel G. Engel. S: Jo Eisinger, from novel by Gerald Kersh. C: Richard
Widmark, Gene Tierney, Googie Withers.

NIGHT BEAT (1948)
BLPA. D/P: Harold Huth.
S: T.J. Morrison, Roland Pertwee, Robert Westerby. C: Anne Crawford, Maxwell
Reed.

NIGHT JOURNEY (1938)
British National. D: Oswald Mitchell.
P: John Corfield. S: Jim Phelan, Maisie Sharman, from Phelan's novel. C: Geoffrey Toone, Patricia Hilliard.

Night Mail (1935)
GPO Film Unit. D: Harry Watt, Basil Wright.
P: John Grierson. S: Grierson, Wright, Watt (verse: W.H. Auden).

NINE MEN (1943)
Ealing. D: Harry Watt.
P: Michael Balcon, Charles Crichton. S: Watt, Gerald Kersh. C: Jack Lambert, Gordon Jackson.

1984 (TV) (1954)
BBC drama. D: Rudolph Cartier.
S: Nigel Kneale, from novel by George Orwell. C: Peter Cushing, Yvonne Mitchell, André Morell.

1984 (1956)
Holiday. D: Michael Anderson.
P: N. Peter Rathvon. S: William Templeton, R.G. Bettinson, from novel by George Orwell. C: Edmond O'Brien, Michael Redgrave.

1984 (1984)
Virgin. Col. D/S: Michael Radford.
From novel by George Orwell. P: Simon Perry. C: John Hurt, Richard Burton.

NO LIMIT (1935)
ATP. D: Monty Banks.
P: Basil Dean. S: Walter Greenwood, Tom Geraghty, Fred Thompson. C: George Formby, Florence Desmond.

NO ORCHIDS FOR MISS BLANDISH (1948)
Tudor/Alliance. D: St John L. Clowes.
P: A.R. Shipman, Oswald Mitchell. S: Clowes, from novel by James Hadley Chase. C: Linden Travers, Hugh McDermott.

NOOSE (1948)
Edward Dryhurst. D: Edmond T. Greville.
P: Edward Dryhurst. S: Richard Llewellyn, Dryhurst, from Llewellyn's play. C: Derek Farr, Carole Landis, Stanley Holloway.

North Sea (1938)
GPO Film Unit. D: Harry Watt.
P: Alberto Cavalcanti. S: Cavalcanti, Watt.

The Nose Has It (1942)
Gainsborough. D/S: Val Guest.
P: Edward Black. C: Arthur Askey.

NOWHERE TO GO (1958)
Ealing. D: Seth Holt.
P: Michael Balcon, Eric Williams. S: Holt, Kenneth Tynan. C: George Nader, Maggie Smith.

Now is the Time... (1951)
National Film Board of Canada and BFI for Festival of Britain. P/D/Anim: Norman McLaren. Col.

NUMBER 17 (1932)
BIP. D: Alfred Hitchcock.
S: Hitchcock, Alma Reville, Rodney Ackland, from play by Jefferson Farjeon.
C: John Stuart, Anne Grey, Leon M. Lion.

OBSESSION (1949)
Independent Sovereign. D: Edward Dmytryk.
P: Nat Bronstein. S: Alec Coppel, from his own novel. C: Robert Newton, Sally Gray.

THE OCTOBER MAN (1947)
Two Cities. D: Roy Baker.
P: Eric Ambler. S: Ambler, from his own novel. C: John Mills, Joan Greenwood.

ODD MAN OUT (1947)
Two Cities. D/P: Carol Reed.
S: F.L. Green, R.C. Sheriff, from Green's novel. C: James Mason, Robert Newton, Kathleen Ryan.

O Dreamland (1953)
Sequence. D/S: Lindsay Anderson.

Often During the Day (1979)
Four Corner. Col. D: Joanna Davis.

OH! WHAT A LOVELY WAR (1969)
Accord/Paramount. D: Richard Attenborough.
P: Brian Duffy, Attenborough. S: Len Deighton, from musical play by Joan Littlewood. C: Ralph Richardson, Meriel Forbes, Kenneth More, John Mills.

OI FOR ENGLAND (TV) (1982)
Central TV. Col. D: Tony Smith.
P: Sue Birtwistle. S: Trevor Griffiths. C: Adam Kotz, Neil Pearson, Richard Platt.

O-KAY FOR SOUND (1937)
Gainsborough. D: Marcel Varnel.
P: Edward Black. S: Marriott Edgar, Val Guest. C: The Crazy Gang (Bud Flanagan and Chesney Allen, Jimmy Nervo and Teddy Knox, Charlie Naughton and Jimmy Gold), Enid Stamp-Taylor.

OLD MOTHER RILEY JOINS UP (1939)
British National. D: Maclean Rogers.
P: John Corfield. S: Jack Marks, Con West. C: Arthur Lucan, Kitty McShane.

OLD MOTHER RILEY'S GHOST (1941)
British National. D/P: John Baxter.
S: Con West, Geoffrey Orme, Arthur Lucan. C: Arthur Lucan, Kitty McShane.

OLIVER! (1968)
Warwick/Romulus. Col/Sc. D: Carol Reed.
P: John Woolf. S: Vernon Harris, from musical version of Dickens' novel by Lionel Bart. C: Ron Moody, Oliver Reed, Shani Wallis, Mark Lester.

OLIVER TWIST (1948)
Cineguild. D: David Lean.
P: Anthony Havelock-Allan. S: Lean, Stanley Haynes, from novel by Charles Dickens. C: Robert Newton, Alec Guinness, John Howard Davies.

OLIVER TWIST (1982)
Claridge/Trident TV. Col. D: Clive Donner.
P: Ted Child, Norton Romsey. S: James Goldman, from novel by Charles Dickens.
  C: George C. Scott, Tim Curry, Cherie Lunghi.

ON APPROVAL (1944)
I.P. D: Clive Brook.
P: Brook, Sydney Box. S: Brook, Terence Young, from play by Frederick Lonsdale.
  C: Clive Brook, Beatrice Lillie.

ON DUTY (1984)
On Duty for Channel 4 TV. Col. D: Cassie MacFarlane.
C: Pearl Wilson, Michael Hamilton, Sylvester Williams.

ONE DAY IN THE LIFE OF IVAN DENISOVICH (1971)
Leontes/Norsk. Col. D: Caspar Wrede.
P: Wrede. S: Ronald Harwood, from novel by Alexander Solzhenitsyn. C: Tom
  Courtenay, Espen Skjønberg.

ONE WAY PENDULUM (1964)
Woodfall. D: Peter Yates.
P: Oscar Lewenstein, Michael Deeley. S: N.F. Simpson, from his own play. C: Eric
  Sykes, George Cole, Julia Foster.

ON THE BUSES (TV) (1969–75)
London Weekend Television, comedy series.
P: Stuart Allen. S: Ronald Wolfe, Ronald Chesney. C: Reg Varney, Bob Grant,
  Doris Hare.

ON THE BUSES (1971)
EMI/Hammer. Col. D: Harry Booth.
P/S: Ronald Wolfe, Ronald Chesney. C: Reg Varney, Doris Hare.

ON THE NIGHT OF THE FIRE (1939)
G & S. D: Brian Desmond Hurst.
P: Josef Somlo. S: Hurst, Terence Young, Patrick Kirwan. C: Ralph Richardson,
  Diana Wynyard.
US title: *The Fugitive.*

OTHELLO (1965)
BHE. Col/Sc. D: Stuart Burge.
P: Anthony Havelock-Allan, John Brabourne. S: from play by Shakespeare.
  C: Laurence Olivier, Maggie Smith, Frank Finlay.

OUR MAN IN HAVANA (1960)
Kingsmead. Sc. D: Carol Reed.
P: Reed, Raymond Anzarut. S: Graham Greene, from his own novel. C: Alec
  Guinness, Burl Ives, Maureen O'Hara.

The Owl and the Pussycat (1952)
Halas & Batchelor. Col. D/S: John Halas, Brian Borthwick.
P: Halas. Anim: Borthwick.

Painter and Poet series (1951)
Halas & Batchelor for BFI for Festival of Britain.
P: John Halas in association with Joan Maude and Michael Warre.

PANDORA AND THE FLYING DUTCHMAN (1951)
Dorkay/Romulus. Col. D/P/S: Albert Lewin.

C: James Mason, Ava Gardner.

PARANOIAC (1963)
Hammer. Sc. D: Freddie Francis.
P: Anthony Hinds. S: Jimmy Sangster. C: Oliver Reed, Janette Scott.

A PASSAGE TO INDIA (1984)
GW. Col. D: David Lean.
P: John Brabourne, Richard Goodwin. S: Lean, based on novel by E.M. Forster and play by Santha Rami Rau. C: Judy Davis, Victor Bannerjee, Peggy Ashcroft, Alec Guinness, James Fox.

THE PASSIONATE FRIENDS (1922)
Stoll. D: Maurice Elvey.
S: Leslie Howard Gordon, from novel by H.G. Wells. C: Milton Rosmer, Valia.

PASSPORT TO PIMLICO (1949)
Ealing. D: Henry Cornelius.
P: Michael Balcon, E.V.H. Emmett. S: T.E.B. Clarke. C: Stanley Holloway, Hermione Baddeley, Margaret Rutherford.

PAYROLL (1961)
Independent Artists. D: Sidney Hayers.
P: Norman Priggen. S: George Baxt, from novel by Derek Bickerton. C: Michael Craig, Billie Whitelaw.

Peace and Plenty (1939)
Progressive Film Institute for Communist Party of Great Britain. D/P/S: Ivor Montagu.

PEEPING TOM (1960)
Michael Powell (Theatre). Col. D: Michael Powell.
P: Powell, Albert Fennell. S: Leo Marks. C: Carl Boehm, Anna Massey, Moira Shearer.

Phillips Philm Phables series (1919)
Phillips Film Co. D/Anim: Anson Dyer, Dudley Buxton, 'Poy', J.A. Shepherd.

Photographing a Ghost (1898)
G.A.S. D: G.A. Smith.

PICCADILLY (1929)
BIP. D/P: E.A. Dupont.
S: Arnold Bennett. C: Gilda Grey, Anna May Wong, Jameson Thomas, Charles Laughton.

PICKWICK PAPERS (1952)
Renown. D: Noel Langley.
P: George Minter, Langley. S: Langley, from novel by Charles Dickens. C: James Hayter, James Donald, Nigel Patrick.

Pimple Does the Turkey Trot (1912)
Ecko (Cosmo). D: W.P. Kellino. C: Fred Evans.

Pimple's Inferno (1913)
Folly. D/S: Fred Evans, Joe Evans. C: Fred Evans.

THE PLEASURE GARDEN (1926)
Gainsborough-Emelka. D: Alfred Hitchcock.

P: Michael Balcon. S: Eliot Stannard, from novel by Oliver Sandys. C: Virginia Valli, Carmelita Geraghty, Miles Mander, John Stuart.

PLENTY (1985)
Edward R. Pressman for RKO. Col. D: Fred Schepisi.
P: Edward R. Pressman, Joseph Papp. S: David Hare, from his own play. C: Meryl Streep, Charles Dance, John Gielgud, Sting.

THE PLOUGHMAN'S LUNCH (1983)
Greenpoint/Goldcrest. Col. D: Richard Eyre.
P: Simon Relph. S: Ian McEwan. C: Jonathan Pryce, Tim Curry, Frank Finlay.

Plucked from the Burning (1900)
R.W. Paul. D: Walter Booth.

Pocket Cartoon (1940)
Halas & Batchelor. In collaboration with Alexander Mackendrick.

POOL OF LONDON (1951)
Ealing. D: Basil Dearden.
P: Michael Balcon, Michael Relph. S: Jack Whittingham, John Eldridge. C: Bonar Colleano, Susan Shaw, Renee Asherson.

POOR COW (1967)
Vic. Col. D: Kenneth Loach.
P: Joseph Janni. S: Nell Dunn, Loach, from Dunn's novel. C: Carol White, Terence Stamp.

THE PRICE OF COAL (TV) (1977)
BBC, 2-part drama (film). Col. D: Kenneth Loach.
P: Tony Garnett. S: Barry Hines. C: Bobby Knutt, Jackie Shinn.

The Prince of Wales in Edinburgh (1900)
Newsreel footage.

PRINCESS CHARMING (1934)
Gainsborough. D: Maurice Elvey.
P: Michael Balcon. S: L. DuGarde Peach, Arthur Wimperis, Lauri Wylie, from play by F. Martos. C: Max Miller, Evelyn Laye.

THE PRISON BREAKER (1936)
George Smith. D: Adrian Brunel.
S: Frank Whitty, from novel by Edgar Wallace. C: James Mason.

A PRIVATE FUNCTION (1984)
HandMade. Col. D: Malcolm Mowbray.
P: Mark Shivas. S: Alan Bennett. C: Michael Palin, Maggie Smith, Denholm Elliott.

THE PRIVATE LIFE OF HENRY VIII (1933)
London. D: Alexander Korda.
P: Korda, Ludovico Toeplitz. S: Arthur Wimperis, Lajos Biro. C: Charles Laughton, Elsa Lanchester, Robert Donat, Merle Oberon.

PRIVATES ON PARADE (1983)
HandMade. Col. D: Michael Blakemore.
P: Simon Relph. S: Peter Nichols, from his own play. C: John Cleese, Denis Quilley.

PROPERTY RITES (1984)
Birmingham Film and Video Workshop. D: Heather Powell, Carola Klein.

THE PROUD VALLEY (1940)
Ealing. D: Penrose Tennyson.
P: Michael Balcon, Sergei Nolbandov. S: Roland Pertwee, Louis Golding, Jack Jones, Herbert Marshall, Alfredda Brilliant. C: Paul Robeson, Edward Chapman.

Put People First (video) (1983)
Birmingham Film Workshop for NALGO.

Put Una Money for There (1958)
W.M. Larkins Studio in association with the Film Producers' Guild for Barclays Bank DCO. Col. D: Denis Gilpin.
Anim: Beryl Stevens.

Quatermass (TV) (1953)
BBC serial, six ½-hour episodes (with sequels in 1955, 1958 and 1979). D: Rudolph Cartier.
S: Nigel Kneale.

THE QUATERMASS XPERIMENT (1955)
Hammer. D: Val Guest.
P: Anthony Hinds. S: Guest, Landau, from TV series by Nigel Kneale. C: Brian Donlevy, Jack Warner, Richard Wordsworth.
US title: *The Creeping Unknown.*

QUATERMASS 2 (1957)
Hammer. D: Val Guest.
P: Anthony Hinds. S: Nigel Kneale, Guest, from the TV series by Kneale. C: Brian Donlevy, Sidney James.

QUEEN OF SPADES (1949)
ABPC. D: Thorold Dickinson.
P: Anatole de Grunwald. S: Rodney Ackland, Arthur Boys, from novel by Pushkin. C: Edith Evans, Anton Walbrook.

QUIET WEDDING (1941)
Conqueror. D: Anthony Asquith.
P: Paul Soskin. S: Terence Rattigan, Anatole de Grunwald, from play by Esther McCracken. C: Margaret Lockwood, Derek Farr, Peggy Ashcroft.

RADIO PARADE OF 1935 (1934)
BIP. Part col. D: Arthur Woods.
P: Walter Mycroft. S: Jack Davies, Reginald Purdell, John Watt. C: Will Hay, Lily Morris.
US title: *Radio Follies.*

Rainbow Dance (1936)
GPO Film Unit. Col. D/Anim: Len Lye.
P: Basil Wright, Alberto Cavalcanti.

RAISE THE TITANIC (1980)
ITC. Col. D: Jerry Jameson.
P: William Frye. S: Adam Kennedy, from novel by Clive Cussler. C: Jason Robards, Alec Guinness.

THE RANK AND FILE (TV) (1971)
BBC drama (film). D: Kenneth Loach.

P: Graeme McDonald. S: Jim Allen. C: Peter Kerrigan, Billy Dean, Tommy Summers.

RASPUTIN THE MAD MONK (1965)
Hammer/Seven Arts. Col/Sc. D: Don Sharp.
P: Anthony Nelson Keys. S: Anthony Hinds. C: Christopher Lee, Barbara Shelley.

The Ratcatcher's Daughter (?1904)
Hepworth. D: Lewin Fitzhamon.

THE REAL THING AT LAST (1916)
British Actors. D: L.C. Macbean.
S: James Barrie (satirical Americanisation of Shakespeare's *Macbeth*). C: Edmund Gwenn, Godfrey Tearle, Gladys Cooper.

THE RED SHOES (1948)
The Archers. Col. D/P: Michael Powell, Emeric Pressburger.
S: Pressburger, Keith Winter, based on story by Hans Andersen. C: Anton Walbrook, Marius Goring, Moira Shearer.

RED SKIRTS ON CLYDESIDE (1984)
Sheffield Film Co-op. Col. D: Jenny Woodley, Christine Bellamy.
P/S: Sheffield Film Co-op.

Red, White and Blue (1938)
Publicity Films for Samuel Hanson's Red, White and Blue Coffee Essence. Col.

REPULSION (1965)
Compton/Tekli. D: Roman Polanski.
P: Gene Gutowski. S: Polanski, Gerard Brach, David Stone. C: Catherine Deneuve, Ian Hendry.

Rescued By Rover (1905)
Hepworth. D: Lewin Fitzhamon.
S: Mrs Hepworth. C: Hepworth, Mrs Hepworth, Barbara Hepworth, Sebastian Smith, Mrs Smith.

RICH AND STRANGE (1931)
BIP. D: Alfred Hitchcock.
S: Hitchcock, Alma Reville, from novel by Dale Collins. C: Henry Kendall, Joan Barry, Percy Marmont.
US title: *East of Shanghai*.

RICHARD III (1911)
Cooperative Cinematograph Co.
S: from play by Shakespeare. C: Frank Benson, Constance Benson, Violet Farebrother.

RICHARD III (1955)
London. Col. D/P: Laurence Olivier.
S: Alan Dent, from play by Shakespeare. C: Laurence Olivier, John Gielgud, Claire Bloom.

RIDDLES OF THE SPHINX (1977)
BFI. Col. D/P/S: Laura Mulvey, Peter Wollen.
C: Dinah Stabb, Clive Merrison.

THE RING (1927)
BIP. D: Alfred Hitchcock.
S: Hitchcock, Alma Reville. C: Carl Brisson, Lillian Hall Davies, Ian Hunter.

Robbing the Hen Roost (?1904)
Hepworth. D: Lewin Fitzhamon.

ROB ROY THE HIGHLAND ROGUE (1953)
Walt Disney. Col. D: Harold French.
P: Perce Pearce. S: Lawrence E. Watkin. C: Richard Todd, Glynis Johns, James
  Robertson Justice.

ROMEO AND JULIET (1968)
BHE/Verona/Di Laurentiis. Col. D: Franco Zeffirelli.
P: Anthony Havelock-Allan, John Brabourne. S: Franco Brusati, Masolino
  d'Amico, from play by Shakespeare. C: Leonard Whiting, Olivia Hussey.

ROOKERY NOOK (1930)
B & D. D: Tom Walls, Byron Haskin.
P: Herbert Wilcox. S: W.P. Lipscomb, Ben Travers, from play by Travers. C: Ralph
  Lynn, Tom Walls, Mary Brough.
US title: *One Embarrassing Night.*

ROOM AT THE TOP (1959)
Remus. D: Jack Clayton.
P: John and James Woolf. S: Neil Paterson, from novel by John Braine. C: Laurence
  Harvey, Simone Signoret.

Ruddigore (1967)
Halas & Batchelor and WBC, New York. Col. D: Joy Batchelor.
P: John Halas, Batchelor. Anim D: Harold Whitaker. From the opera by W.S.
  Gilbert and Arthur Sullivan.

Rupert and the Frog Song (1984)
Grand Slamm Animation. Col. P/D: Geoff Dunbar.
Exec P: Paul and Linda McCartney. Based on the Alfred Bestall characters.

SABOTAGE (1936)
Gaumont. D: Alfred Hitchcock.
P: Michael Balcon, Ivor Montagu. S: Charles Bennett, Alma Reville, Helen
  Simpson, from novel *The Secret Agent* by Joseph Conrad. C: Sylvia Sidney, Oscar
  Homolka, John Loder.

SAILOR BEWARE! (1956)
Remus. D: Gordon Parry.
P: Jack Clayton. S: Philip King, Falkland Cary, from their own play. C: Peggy
  Mount, Shirley Eaton.

SALLY IN OUR ALLEY (1931)
Associated Radio. D: Maurice Elvey.
P: Basil Dean. S: Miles Malleson, Alma Reville, Archie Pitt, from play by Charles
  McEvoy. C: Gracie Fields, Ian Hunter, Florence Desmond.

Sam and His Musket (1935)
Anglia. Col. D: Anson Dyer.
Anim: Sid Griffiths, Jorgen Myller. Incorporating the Stanley Holloway/Marriott
  Edgar monologue.

SAN DEMETRIO LONDON (1943)
Ealing. D: Charles Frend.
P: Robert Hamer. S: F. Tennyson Jesse. C: Walter Fitzgerald, Mervyn Johns,
  Gordon Jackson.

SANDERS OF THE RIVER (1935)
London. D: Zoltan Korda.
P: Alexander Korda. S: Lajos Biro, Jeffrey Dell, Arthur Wimperis, from novel by
Edgar Wallace. C: Paul Robeson, Leslie Banks.

SAPPHIRE (1959)
Artna. Col. D: Basil Dearden.
P: Michael Relph. S: Janet Green, Lukas Heller. C: Nigel Patrick, Yvonne Mitchell,
Paul Massie.

SARABAND FOR DEAD LOVERS (1948)
Ealing. Col. D: Michael Relph, Basil Dearden.
P: Michael Balcon, Relph. S: John Dighton, Alexander Mackendrick. C: Stewart
Granger, Joan Greenwood, Flora Robson.

SATURDAY NIGHT AND SUNDAY MORNING (1960)
Woodfall. D: Karel Reisz.
P: Harry Saltzman, Tony Richardson. S: Alan Sillitoe, from his own novel.
C: Albert Finney, Rachel Roberts, Shirley Ann Field.

SCROOGE (1935)
Twickenham. D: Henry Edwards.
P: Julius Hagen, Hans Brahm. S: Seymour Hicks, H. Fowler Mear, from novel
A Christmas Carol by Charles Dickens. C: Seymour Hicks, Donald Calthrop.

SCROOGE (1951)
Renown. P/D: Brian Desmond Hurst.
S: Noel Langley, from novel *A Christmas Carol* by Charles Dickens. C: Alastair Sim,
Kathleen Harrison, Jack Warner.

SCROOGE (1970)
Waterbury. Col/Sc. D: Ronald Neame.
P: Leslie Bricusse, Robert Solo. S: Bricusse, from novel *A Christmas Carol* by
Charles Dickens. C: Albert Finney, Alec Guinness.

Seaside Woman (1980)
Borewald/Dragon. Col. D: Oscar Grillo.
Song: Linda McCartney.

THE SEA SHALL NOT HAVE THEM (1954)
Apollo. D: Lewis Gilbert.
P: Daniel Angel. S: Gilbert, Vernon Harris, from novel by John Harris. C: Michael
Redgrave, Dirk Bogarde.

THE SEA URCHIN (1926)
Gainsborough. D: Graham Cutts.
P: Michael Balcon. S: Cutts, Charles Lapworth, from play by John Hastings Turner.
C: Betty Balfour.

SCREAM AND SCREAM AGAIN (1969)
Amicus. Col. D: Gordon Hessler.
P: Milton Subotsky, Louis Heyward, Max Rosenberg. S: Chris Wicking, from novel
by Peter Saxon. C: Vincent Price, Christopher Lee, Peter Cushing.

THE SECOND MRS TANQUERAY (1916)
Ideal. D: Fred Paul.
S: Benedict James, from play by A.W. Pinero. C: George Alexander, Hilda Moore.

THE SECRET AGENT (1936)
Gaumont-British. D: Alfred Hitchcock.
P: Michael Balcon, Ivor Montagu. S: Charles Bennett, from play by Campbell
Dixon and story by Somerset Maugham. C: Peter Lorre, Madeleine Carroll,
Robert Young.

SECRET CEREMONY (1968)
Universal. Col. D: Joseph Losey.
P: John Heyman, Norman Priggen. S: George Tabori. C: Elizabeth Taylor, Mia
Farrow.

SECRET PEOPLE (1952)
Ealing. D: Thorold Dickinson.
P: Michael Balcon, Sidney Cole. S: Dickinson, Wolfgang Wilhelm. C: Valentina
Cortese, Serge Reggiani, Audrey Hepburn.

Secrets of Nature series (1922–33)
British Instructional. D: Percy Smith, Mary Field, Martin Duncan, and others.
P: Bruce Woolf.

Sensational Fire Engine Collision (1898)
Actuality footage.

THE SERVANT (1963)
Springbok/Elstree. D: Joseph Losey.
P: Losey, Norman Priggen. S: Harold Pinter, from novel by Robin Maugham.
C: Dirk Bogarde, James Fox, Sarah Miles.

SERVICE FOR LADIES (1932)
Paramount British. D/P: Alexander Korda.
S: Eliot Crashay-Williams, Lajos Biro, from novel by Ernst Vaida. C: Leslie
Howard, George Grossmith, Benita Hume.
US title: *Reserved for Ladies.*

THE SEVENTH VEIL (1945)
Theatrecraft/Ortus. D: Compton Bennett.
P: John Sutro, Sydney Box. S: Muriel and Sydney Box. C: James Mason, Ann Todd,
Herbert Lom.

SHE (1916)
Barker. D: Will Barker, H. Lisle Lucoque.
S: Nellie E. Lucoque, from novel by Rider Haggard. C: Alice Delysia, Henry Victor.

SHE (1925)
Reciprocity. D: Leander de Cordova.
P: G.B. Samuelson. S: Walter Summers, from novel by Rider Haggard. C: Betty
Blythe.

SHE (1965)
Hammer. Col. D: Robert Day.
P: Michael Carreras. S: David Chantler, from novel by Rider Haggard. C: Ursula
Andress, Peter Cushing.

SHE WAS ONLY A VILLAGE MAIDEN (1933)
Sound City. D: Arthur Maude.
P: Ivar Campbell. S: John Cousins, N.W. Baring-Pemberton, from play by Fanny
Bowker. C: Anne Grey, Lester Matthews.

THE SHIP THAT DIED OF SHAME (1955)
Ealing. D: Basil Dearden.
P: Michael Balcon, Michael Relph. S: Relph, Dearden, John Whiting, from short
story by Nicholas Monsarrat. C: George Baker, Richard Attenborough, Virginia
McKenna.

SHOOTING STARS (1928)
British Instructional. D: Anthony Asquith, A.V. Bramble.
P: H. Bruce Woolf. S: Asquith, J.O.C. Orton. C: Annette Benson, Brian Aherne,
Donald Calthrop.

THE SHOP AT SLY CORNER (1947)
Pennant. D/P: George King.
S: Katherine Strueby, from play by Edward Percy. C: Oscar Homolka, Derek Farr,
Muriel Pavlow.

THE SHOW GOES ON (1937)
ATP. D/P: Basil Dean.
S: Dean, Austin Melford, Anthony Kimmins. C: Gracie Fields, Owen Nares, John
Stuart.

The Silent Village (1943)
Crown. D/P/S: Humphrey Jennings.

SIMON AND LAURA (1955)
Group. Col. D: Muriel Box.
P: Teddy Baird. S: Peter Blackmore, from play by Alan Melville. C: Kay Kendall,
Peter Finch, Muriel Pavlow.

SING AS WE GO (1934)
ATP. D/P: Basil Dean.
S: J.B. Priestley, Gordon Wellesley. C: Gracie Fields, John Loder, Stanley
Holloway.

THE SINGER NOT THE SONG (1961)
Rank. Col/Sc. D: Roy Baker.
P: Baker, Jack Hanbury. S: Nigel Balchin, from novel by Audrey Erskine Lindop.
C: Dirk Bogarde, John Mills.

THE SKIN GAME (1931)
BIP. D: Alfred Hitchcock.
S: Hitchcock, Alma Reville, from play by John Galsworthy. C: Edmund Gwenn,
Frank Lawton, Jill Esmond.

SLAVE GIRLS (1966)
Hammer. Col/Sc. D/P/S: Michael Carreras.
C: Martine Beswick, Michael Latimer.

THE SMALL BACK ROOM (1949)
The Archers/London. D/P/S: Michael Powell and Emeric Pressburger.
From novel by Nigel Balchin. C: David Farrar, Kathleen Byron.

SOMEWHERE IN ENGLAND (1940)
Mancunian. D/P: John E. Blakeley.
S: Arthur Mertz, Roney Parsons. C: Frank Randle.

Song of Ceylon (1934)
GPO Film Unit. D/S: Basil Wright.
P: John Grierson.

THE SONG OF FREEDOM (1936)
Hammer. D: J. Elder Wills.
P: H. Fraser Passmore. S: Claude Wallace, Dorothy Holloway. C: Paul Robeson, Elizabeth Welch.

SONG OF THE SHIRT (1979)
Film and History Project (Royal College of Art/Polytechnic of Central London/ Cinema Action). D/S: Susan Clayton, Jonathan Curling.
C: Martha Gibson, Geraldine Pilgrim.

SONS AND LOVERS (1960)
20th Century-Fox. Sc. D: Jack Cardiff.
P: Jerry Wald. S: Gavin Lambert, T.E.B. Clarke, from novel by D.H. Lawrence.
C: Trevor Howard, Wendy Hiller, Dean Stockwell.

SORROWS OF SATAN (1917)
G.B. Samuelson. D: Alexander Butler.
S: Harry Engholm, from novel by Marie Corelli. C: Gladys Cooper, Owen Nares.

SOUTH RIDING (1938)
London. D: Victor Saville.
P: Saville, Alexander Korda. S: Ian Dalrymple, Donald Brill, from novel by Winifred Holtby. C: Ralph Richardson, Edna Best, Ann Todd, John Clements.

THE SPANISH GARDENER (1956)
Rank. Col. D: Philip Leacock.
P: John Bryan. S: Bryan, Lesley Storm, from novel by A.J. Cronin. C: Dirk Bogarde, Jon Whiteley, Michael Hordern.

SPARE A COPPER (1940)
Ealing. D: John Paddy Carstairs.
P: Michael Balcon, Basil Dearden. S: Roger Macdougall, Austin Melford, Dearden.
C: George Formby, Dorothy Hyson.

Spare Time (1939)
GPO Film Unit. D: Humphrey Jennings.
P: Alberto Cavalcanti. S: Jennings, (commentary) Laurie Lee.

THE SPONGERS (TV) (1978)
BBC, film. Col. Dir: Roland Joffé.
P: Tony Garnett. S: Jim Allen. C: Christine Hargreaves, Bernard Hill, Peter Kerrigan.

Sport and Interest in a Fresh Light (1926)
D/P: John Betts.

Squadron 992 (1940)
GPO Film Unit. D: Harry Watt.
P: Alberto Cavalcanti.

THE SQUARE RING (1953)
Ealing. D: Basil Dearden.
P: Michael Balcon, Michael Relph. S: Robert Westerby, Peter Myers, Alec Grahame, from play by Ralph Peterson. C: Jack Warner, Bill Owen, Joan Collins.

STAGE FRIGHT (1950)
Warner. D/P: Alfred Hitchcock.
S: Whitfield Cook, Alma Reville, James Bridie, from novel by Selwyn Jepson.
C: Jane Wyman, Marlene Dietrich, Michael Wilding.

THE STARS LOOK DOWN (1939)
Grafton. D: Carol Reed.
P: Isadore Goldschmidt. S: J.B. Williams, A.J. Cronin, from Cronin's novel.
  C: Michael Redgrave, Margaret Lockwood, Emlyn Williams.

STEAMING (1984)
World Film Services. Col. D: Joseph Losey.
P: Paul Mills. S: Patricia Losey, from play by Nell Dunn. C: Vanessa Redgrave, Sara
  Miles, Diana Dors, Patti Love, Brenda Bruce.

Steptoe and Son (TV) (1964-73)
BBC ½-hour series.
S: Alan Simpson, Ray Galton. C: Harry H. Corbett, Wilfred Brambell.

STEPTOE AND SON (1972)
Associated London Films. Col. D: Cliff Owen.
P: Aida Young. S: Ray Galton, Alan Simpson, from their BBC TV series. C: Wilfred
  Brambell, Harry H. Corbett.

The Story of the Flag (1927)
Nettlefold. D: Anson Dyer. P: Archibald Nettlefold.

STRANGLERS OF BOMBAY (1959)
Hammer. Sc. D: Terence Fisher.
P: Anthony Hinds. S: David Z. Goodman. C: Guy Rolfe, Allan Cuthbertson.

STRAW DOGS (1971)
Talent Associates/Amerbroco. Col. D: Sam Peckinpah.
P: Daniel Melnick. S: Peckinpah, David Zelag Goodman, from novel by Gordon M.
  Williams. C: Dustin Hoffman, Susan George, David Warner, Colin Welland.

A STUDY IN SCARLET (1914)
G.B. Samuelson. D: George Pearson.
S: Harry Engholm, from novel by Arthur Conan Doyle. C: Fred Paul, Agnes
  Glynne.

THE SUICIDE CLUB (1914)
B & C. D: Maurice Elvey.
From stories by R.L. Stevenson. C: Montagu Love, Elisabeth Risdon.

Summer Travelling (1945)
W.M. Larkins Studio for Ministry of Information for Ministry of War Transport.
  D: W.M. Larkins.

Sunbeam (1980)
Speedy Cartoons for the Arts Council of Great Britain and Christian Gandon
  Productions. Col. D: Paul Vester.
Anim: Vester, John Challis, Alistair McIlwain, Franco Milia.

SuperTed series (1983-)
Siriol for Sianel Pedwar Cymru. Col. D: Dave Edwards.
P: Mike Young. S: Robin Lyons.

T for Teacher (1949)
W.M. Larkins Studio for the Tea Bureau. Anim: Peter Sachs. Verse: Roger
  MacDougall.

TAKE MY LIFE (1947)
Cineguild. D: Ronald Neame.

P: Anthony Havelock-Allan. S: Winston Graham, Valerie Taylor, Margaret Kennedy. C: Hugh Williams, Greta Gynt, Marius Goring.

TAKING A PART (1979)
Jan Worth/Royal College of Art. Col. D: Jan Worth.
C: Lucy, Debbie, Jan Worth.

A TALE OF TWO CITIES (1958)
Rank. D: Ralph Thomas.
P: Betty Box. S: T.E.B. Clarke, from novel by Charles Dickens. C: Dirk Bogarde, Dorothy Tutin, Cecil Parker.

TARGET FOR TONIGHT (1941)
Crown Film Unit. D/S: Harry Watt.
P: Ian Dalrymple.

TASTE OF FEAR (1961)
Hammer. D: Seth Holt.
P/S: Jimmy Sangster. C: Susan Strasberg, Ann Todd, Ronald Lewis, Christopher Lee.

A TASTE OF HONEY (1961)
Woodfall. D/P: Tony Richardson.
S: Shelagh Delaney, Richardson, from Delaney's play. C: Rita Tushingham, Murray Melvin, Dora Bryan.

TELLING TALES (1978)
Yorkshire Arts Association. Col. D/S: Richard Woolley.
C: Bridget Ashburn, Stephen Trafford.

TELL ME LIES (1968)
Ronorus. Col. D: Peter Brook.
P: Peter Sykes, Brook. S: Brook, from play by Dennis Cannan. C: Glenda Jackson.

THE TEMPEST (1979)
Boyd's Company. Col. D/S: Derek Jarman, from play by Shakespeare.
P: Don Boyd. C: Heathcote Williams, Toyah Wilcox, Elizabeth Welch.

TEMPTATION HARBOUR (1947)
ABPC. D: Lance Comfort.
P: Victor Skutezky. S: Skutezky, Frederic Gotfort, from novel by Georges Simenon. C: Robert Newton, William Hartnell.

Terminus (1961)
British Transport. D: John Schlesinger.
P: Edgar Anstey. S: Schlesinger.

TERRITORIES (1984)
St. Martin's College of Art/Sankofa. D: Isaac Julien.

THE TERROR (1938)
ABPC. D: Richard Bird.
P: Walter Mycroft. S: William Freshman, from play by Edgar Wallace. C: Wilfred Lawson, Linden Travers.

THERE AIN'T NO JUSTICE (1939)
Ealing. D: Penrose Tennyson.
P: Michael Balcon, Sergei Nolbandov. S: Tennyson, Nolbandov, James Curtis, from novel by Curtis. C: Jimmy Hanley, Edward Rigby.

THEY DRIVE BY NIGHT (1938)
Warner. D: Arthur Woods.
P: Jerome Jackson. S: Derek Twist, from novel by James Curtis. C: Emlyn Williams, Ernest Thesiger, Anna Konstam.

THEY MADE ME A FUGITIVE (1947)
Gloria/Alliance. D: Alberto Cavalcanti.
P: Nat Bronstein, James Carter. S: Noel Langley, from novel by Jackson Budd. C: Trevor Howard, Griffith Jones, Sally Gray.

THEY WERE SISTERS (1945)
Gainsborough. D: Arthur Crabtree.
P: Harold Huth. S: Roland Pertwee, Katherine Strueby, from novel by Dorothy Whipple. C: Phyllis Calvert, Anne Crawford, James Mason.

THINGS TO COME (1936)
London. D: William Cameron Menzies.
P: Alexander Korda. S: H.G. Wells. C: Raymond Massey, Ralph Richardson.

THE THIRD MAN (1949)
London. D: Carol Reed.
P: David O. Selznick, Alexander Korda. S: Graham Greene. C: Trevor Howard, Joseph Cotten, Orson Welles.

THE 39 STEPS (1935)
Gaumont. D: Alfred Hitchcock.
P: Michael Balcon, Ivor Montagu. S: Charles Bennett, Alma Reville, from novel by John Buchan. C: Robert Donat, Madeleine Carroll.

THIS ENGLAND (1941)
British National. D: David Macdonald.
P: John Corfield. S: A.R. Rawlinson, Bridget Boland, Emlyn Williams. C: Emlyn Williams, John Clements, Constance Cummings.

THIS HAPPY BREED (1944)
Two Cities/Cineguild. Col. D: David Lean.
P: Noël Coward, Anthony Havelock-Allan. S: Lean, Havelock-Allan, Ronald Neame, from play by Coward. C: Celia Johnson, Robert Newton.

THIS SPORTING LIFE (1963)
Independent Artists. D: Lindsay Anderson.
P: Albert Fennell, Karel Reisz. S: David Storey, from his own novel. C: Richard Harris, Rachel Roberts.

This Wonderful World (TV) (1957–66)
Scottish TV. Documentary series edited and presented by John Grierson.

Those Were the Days (1946)
Butcher. D/S: James M. Anderson.
P: Henry W. Fisher.

THREE CASES OF MURDER (1955)
Wessex. D: David Eady, George More O'Ferrall, Wendy Toye.
P: Ian Dalrymple, Alexander Paal, Hugh Perceval. S: Dalrymple, Sidney Carroll, Donald Wilson, from stories by Somerset Maugham and others. C: Orson Welles, Alan Badel, John Gregson.

Three Ha'pence a Foot (1937)
Anglia. Col. D: Anson Dyer.

Anim: Sid Griffiths, Jorgen Myller. S: incorporating the Stanley Holloway/Marriott Edgar monologue.

THREE SISTERS (1970)
Alan Clare. Col. D: Laurence Olivier.
P: Alan Clare, John Goldstone. S: Moura Budberg, from play by Anton Chekhov. C: Joan Plowright, Alan Bates.

Thriller (1979)
Sally Potter/Arts Council of Great Britain. D/P/S: Sally Potter.
C: Colette Laffont, Rose English.

THROUGH AN UNKNOWN LAND (1984)
Spectre for Channel 4. Col. D: Phil Mulloy.
P: Michael Whyte. S: Mulloy. C: Iain Anders, Julia Watson, Max Hafler.

Till Death Us Do Part (TV) (1964–74)
BBC ½-hour series.
S: Johnny Speight. C: Warren Mitchell, Dandy Nichols.

TILL DEATH US DO PART (1968)
British Lion/Associated London. Col. D: Norman Cohen.
P: Jon Pennington. S: Johnny Speight, from his BBC TV series. C: Warren Mitchell, Dandy Nichols.

TIME BANDITS (1981)
HandMade. Col. D/P: Terry Gilliam.
S: Gilliam, Michael Palin. C: Ralph Richardson, John Cleese, Michael Palin, Ian Holm, Shelley Duvall, Sean Connery.

TIME WITHOUT PITY (1957)
Harlequin. D: Joseph Losey.
P: Leon Clore, from play by Emlyn Williams. C: Michael Redgrave, Ann Todd.

THE TITFIELD THUNDERBOLT (1953)
Ealing. Col. D: Charles Crichton.
P: Michael Balcon, Michael Truman. S: T.E.B. Clarke. C: Stanley Holloway, Naunton Wayne, John Gregson.

The Tocher (1938)
GPO Film Unit. D/Anim: Lotte Reiniger.

TOM BROWN'S SCHOOLDAYS (1916)
Windsor. D: Rex Wilson.
S: Wilson, from novel by Thomas Hughes. C: Jack Hobbs, Wilfred Benson.

TOM JONES (1963)
Woodfall. Col. D/P: Tony Richardson.
S: John Osborne, from novel by Henry Fielding. C: Albert Finney, Susannah York, Hugh Griffith, Edith Evans.

TO SIR WITH LOVE (1966)
Columbia British. Col. D: James Clavell.
S: Clavell, from novel by E.R. Braithwaite. C: Sidney Poitier, Judy Geeson, Lulu.

Trade Tattoo (1937)
GPO Film Unit. P: John Grierson. D/Anim: Len Lye.

TRAITOR SPY (1939)
Rialto. D: Walter Summers.

P: John Argyle. S: Summers, Argyle, Jan van Lusil, Ralph Gilbert Bottinson.
C: Bruce Cabot, Marta Labarr.
US title: *The Torso Murder Mystery.*

TRELAWNY OF THE WELLS (1916)
Hepworth. D: Cecil Hepworth.
S: Blanche McIntosh, from play by A.W. Pinero. C: Alma Taylor, Stewart Rome.

TRIUMPH OF THE RAT (1926)
Gainsborough. D: Graham Cutts.
P: Michael Balcon, Carlyle Blackwell. S: Cutts, Reginald Fogwell. C: Ivor Novello,
Isabel Jeans.

TROUBLE IN STORE (1953)
Two Cities. D: John Paddy Carstairs.
P: Maurice Cowan. S: Carstairs, Cowan, Ted Willis. C: Norman Wisdom, Margaret
Rutherford, Moira Lister.

The True Story of Lili Marlene (1944)
Crown Film Unit. D/S: Humphrey Jennings.
P: J.B. Holmes.

THE TUNNEL (1935)
Gaumont. D: Maurice Elvey.
P: Michael Balcon. S: Kurt Siodmak, L. du Garde Peach, from novel by Bernhard
Kellerman. C: Richard Dix, Leslie Banks.
US title: *Transatlantic Tunnel.*

Tusalava (1929)
The Film Society and Robert Graves, in association with Publicity Pictures.
D/Anim: Len Lye.

Typical Budget (1925)
Gainsborough. D: Adrian Brunel.
P: Michael Balcon. S: Brunel, Edwin Greenwood, J.O.C. Orton. C: Jack Buchanan
(part of *Gainsborough Burlesques* series).

Ubu (1979)
Grand Slamm Animation for the Arts Council of Great Britain. Col. D/P/S: Geoff
Dunbar. From play by Alfred Jarry.

ULTUS, THE MAN FROM THE DEAD (1915)
Gaumont. D: George Pearson.
S. Pearson, Thomas Welsh. C: Audrey Sydney.

UNDERGROUND (1928)
British Instructional. D/S: Anthony Asquith.
P: H. Bruce Woolf. C: Elisia Landi, Brian Aherne, Norah Baring.

UNITED KINGDOM (TV) (1981)
BBC drama (film). Col. D: Roland Joffé.
P: Kenith Trodd. S: Jim Allen. C: Colin Welland, Val McLane, Bill Paterson.

Upstairs, Downstairs (TV) (1971–6)
LWT, drama series. Col. D: Bill Bain and others.
P: John Hawkesworth. S: Hawkesworth, Alfred Shaughnessy, Rosemary Anne
Sisson. C: Gordon Jackson, Angela Baddeley, Jean Marsh, David Langton.

THE UPTURNED GLASS (1947)
Triton. D: Lawrence Huntington.
P: Sydney Box, James Mason. S: J.P. Monaghan, Pamela Kellino. C: James Mason, Rosamund John, Pamela Kellino.

The U-Tube (1917)
Jury. D/Anim: Lancelot Speed.

THE VAMPIRE LOVERS (1970)
Hammer. Col. D: Roy Ward Baker.
P: Harry Fine, Michael Style. S: Fine, Style, Tudor Gates, based on story by Sheridan le Fanu. C: Ingrid Pitt, Peter Cushing, George Cole.

VICTIM (1961)
Parkway. D: Basil Dearden.
P: Michael Relph. S: Janet Green, John McCormick. C: Dirk Bogarde, Sylvia Syms, Peter McEnery.

VICTORIA THE GREAT (1937)
Imperator. D/P: Herbert Wilcox.
S: Robert Vansittart, Miles Malleson, from play by Laurence Houseman. C: Anna Neagle, Anton Walbrook.

View from an Engine Front (1900)
Hepworth. Actuality footage.

THE VIRGIN AND THE GYPSY (1970)
Kenwood. Col. D: Christopher Miles.
P: Dmitri de Grunwald, Kenneth Harper. S: Alan Plater, from story by D.H. Lawrence. C: Joanna Shimkus, Franco Nero, Honor Blackman.

THE VOLUNTEER (1943)
The Archers. D/P/S: Michael Powell and Emeric Pressburger.
C: Ralph Richardson, Pat McGrath.

THE VORTEX (1927)
Gainsborough. D: Adrian Brunel.
P: Michael Balcon. S: Eliot Stannard, from play by Noël Coward. C: Ivor Novello, Willette Kershaw, Bunty Mainwaring.

Voyage of the 'Arctic' (1903)
R.W. Paul.

Wakefield Express (1952)
'Wakefield Express' Ltd. D/S: Lindsay Anderson.
P: Michael Robinson.

WALTZES FROM VIENNA (1934)
Tom Arnold. D: Alfred Hitchcock.
P: Tom Arnold. S: Alma Reville, Guy Bolton, from play by Heinz Reichart, Ernst Marischka and D.A. Willner. C: Jessie Matthews, Edmund Gwenn, Esmond Knight.
US title: *Strauss's Great Waltz*.

WALTZ TIME (1933)
Gaumont. D: William Thiele.
P: Herman Fellner. S: A.P. Herbert, from operetta *Die Fledermaus* by Johann Strauss. C: Evelyn Laye, Fritz Schultz.

WANTED FOR MURDER (1946)
Excelsior. D: Lawrence Huntington.
P: Marcel Hellman. S: Emeric Pressburger, Rodney Ackland, Maurice Cowan, from
  play by Percy Robinson and Terence de Marney. C: Eric Portman, Dulcie Gray.

War Cartoons (1914)
H. Tress. D/Anim: Dudley Buxton.

War in the Wardrobe (1945)
W.M. Larkins for Ministry of Information for Board of Trade. D: W.M. Larkins.

Water for Firefighting (1948)
Halas & Batchelor for the Central Office of Information for the Home Office. D/S:
  Allan Crick, Bob Privett.
P/Des: John Halas, Joy Batchelor.

WATERLOO ROAD (1945)
Gainsborough. D: Sidney Gilliat.
P: Edward Black. S: Val Valentine, Gilliat. C: John Mills, Stewart Granger, Alastair
  Sim.

THE WAY AHEAD (1944)
Two Cities. D: Carol Reed.
· P: John Sutro, Norman Walker. S: Eric Ambler, Peter Ustinov, David Niven.
  C: David Niven, Stanley Holloway, James Donald, Raymond Huntley.

THE WAY TO THE STARS (1945)
Two Cities. D: Anthony Asquith.
P: Anatole de Grunwald. S: Terence Rattigan, Richard Sherman. C: Michael
  Redgrave, John Mills, Rosamund John.

We Are the Lambeth Boys (1959)
Graphic. D: Karel Reisz.
P: Leon Clore.

WENT THE DAY WELL? (1942)
Ealing. D: Alberto Cavalcanti.
P: Michael Balcon, S.C. Balcon. S: Angus Macphail, John Dighton, Diana Morgan,
  from short story by Graham Greene. C: Leslie Banks, Basil Sydney, Valerie
  Taylor.
US title: *48 Hours*.

WESTERN APPROACHES (1944)
Crown. Col. D: Pat Jackson. P: Ian Dalrymple.

Whacko! (TV) (1959–60)
BBC, comedy series.
S: Frank Muir, Denis Norden. C: Jimmy Edwards.

What the Curate Really Did (1905)
Hepworth. D: Lewin Fitzhamon.
C: Claude Whitton, Florence Nelson.

WHEN DINOSAURS RULED THE EARTH (1970)
Hammer. Col. D: Val Guest.
P: Aida Young. S: Guest, J.B. Ballard. C: Victoria Vetri, Patrick Allen.

WHEN THE BOUGH BREAKS (1947)
Gainsborough. D: Lawrence Huntington.
P: Betty Box. S: Muriel and Sydney Box, Peter Rogers. C: Patricia Roc, Rosamund
  John.

WHISKY GALORE! (1949)
Ealing. D: Alexander Mackendrick.
P: Michael Balcon, Monja Danischewsky. S: Compton Mackenzie, Angus Macphail, from novel by Mackenzie. C: Basil Radford, James Robertson Justice, Joan Greenwood.

WHITE CORRIDORS (1951)
GFD/Vic. D: Pat Jackson.
P: Joseph Janni, John Croydon. S: Jan Read, Jackson, from novel by Helen Ashton. C: James Donald, Googie Withers, Petula Clark, Jack Watling.

Who Needs Nurseries? We Do! (1978)
Leeds Animation Workshop. Col. D/P/S/Anim: Leeds Animation Workshop.

THE WICKED LADY (1945)
Gainsborough. D: Leslie Arliss.
P: R.J. Minney. S: Leslie Arliss, Aimee Stuart, Gordon Glennon, from novel by Magdalen King-Hall. C: Margaret Lockwood, James Mason, Patricia Roc.

Widdicombe Fair (1949)
W.M. Larkins for Central Office of Information for British Council.

Wil Cwac Cwac series (1984–)
Siriol for Sianel Pedwar Cymru. D: Beth McFall.
P: Robin Lyons. S: Urien Williams.

THE WIND CANNOT READ (1958)
Rank. Col. D: Ralph Thomas.
P: Betty Box. S: Richard Mason, from his own novel. C: Dirk Bogarde, Yoko Tani.

The Wind in the Willows (1982)
Cosgrove Hall for Thames Television. Col. D: Mark Hall.
P: Brian Cosgrove, Hall. S: Rosemary Anne Sisson from book by Kenneth Grahame. Voices: Ian Carmichael, Michael Hordern, Beryl Reid.

A WINDOW IN LONDON (1939)
G & S. D: Herbert Mason.
P: Josef Somlo, Richard Norton. S: Ian Dalrymple, Brigid Cooper. C: Michael Redgrave, Sally Gray.
US title: *Lady in Distress.*

WINGS OF THE MORNING (1937)
New World. Col. D: Harold Schuster.
P: Robert T. Kane. S: Tom Geraghty, John Meehan, Brinsley Macnamara, from story by Donn Byrne. C: Annabella, Henry Fonda, Leslie Banks.

THE WINTER'S TALE (1968)
Cressida/Hurst Park. Col. D: Frank Dunlop.
P: Peter Snell. S: play by Shakespeare. C: Laurence Harvey, Jane Asher.

WITCHFINDER GENERAL (1968)
Tigon. Col. D: Michael Reeves.
P: Tony Tenser, Arnold Miller, Louis Heyward. S: Reeves, Heyward, Tom Baker, from novel by Ronald Bassett. C: Vincent Price, Ian Ogilvy, Rupert Davies.

WOMAN IN A DRESSING GOWN (1957)
Godwin. D: J. Lee Thompson.
P: Frank Godwin, Thompson. S: Ted Willis, from his own TV play. C: Yvonne

Mitchell, Sylvia Syms, Anthony Quayle.

THE WOMAN IN QUESTION (1950)
Javelin. D: Anthony Asquith.
P: Teddy Baird. S: John Cresswell. C: Jean Kent, Dirk Bogarde.

WOMEN IN LOVE (1969)
Brandywine. Col. D: Ken Russell.
P: Larry Kramer. S: Kramer, from novel by D.H. Lawrence. C: Alan Bates, Glenda
   Jackson, Oliver Reed.

**The Wonderful Adventures of Pip, Squeak and Wilfred, the Famous 'Daily
   Mirror' Pets** (1921)
D: Lancelot Speed. Drawings: A.B. Payne.

THE WONDERFUL STORY (1922)
Graham/Wilcox. D: Graham Cutts.
P: Herbert Wilcox. S: Patrick L. Mannock, from novel by I.A.R. Wylie. C: Lillian
   Hall Davies.

Words for Battle (1941)
Crown Film Unit. D/S: Humphrey Jennings.
P: Ian Dalrymple.

Workers' Topical News (1930)
Atlas. Newsreel footage of Unemployment Day (6 March 1930) and of the National
   Hunger March (1 May 1930), edited by Ralph Bond.

XTRO (1982)
Ashley. Col. D: Harry Bromley Davenport.
P: Robert Shaye. S: Iain Cassie, Robert Smith. C: Bernice Stegers, Philip Sayer.

A YANK AT OXFORD (1938)
MGM British. D: Jack Conway.
P: Michael Balcon. S: Leon Gordon, Roland Pertwee, Sidney Gilliat, Michael
   Hogan. C: Robert Taylor, Vivien Leigh, Maureen O'Sullivan.

Yellow Submarine (1968)
Apple/King Features/Suba. Col. D: George Dunning.
P: Al Brodax. S: Lee Minoff, Brodax, Jack Mendelsohn, Erich Segal, from songs by
   John Lennon and Paul McCartney.

YIELD TO THE NIGHT (1956)
Kenwood. D: J. Lee Thompson.
P: Kenneth Harper. S: Joan Henry, John Cresswell, from Henry's novel. C: Diana
   Dors, Yvonne Mitchell, Michael Craig.

THE YOUNG MR PITT (1942)
20th Century. D: Carol Reed.
P: Edward Black. S: Frank Launder, Sidney Gilliat. C: Robert Donat, Robert
   Morley, Phyllis Calvert.

YOU'RE ONLY YOUNG TWICE! (1952)
Group 3. D: Terry Bishop.
P: John Grierson, Barbara K. Emary. S: Reginald Beckwith, Lindsay Galloway,
   Terry Bishop, from play by James Bridie. C: Duncan Macrae, Joseph Tomelty,
   Ronnie Corbett.

You're Telling Me (1937)
GB Screen Services for W.D. & H.O. Wills. D: A.G. Jackson.
Anim: Spud Murphy, Ron Giles.

YOUNG AND INNOCENT (1938)
Gaumont. D: Alfred Hitchcock.
P: Edward Black. S: Charles Bennett, Alma Reville, from novel by Josephine Tey.
  C: Nova Pilbeam, Derrick de Marney.
US title: *The Girl Was Young.*

Z Cars (TV) (1960–78)
BBC, police series. D: Ken Loach, John McGrath, many others.
S: John Hopkins, Alan Plater, Elwyn Jones, many others. C: Stratford Johns, Frank
  Windsor.

SELECT BIBLIOGRAPHY

Books

Edgar Anstey, Roger Manvell, Ernest Lindgren, Paul Rotha (eds.), *Shots in the Dark,* London, Allan Wingate, 1951.

Roy Armes, *A Critical History of British Cinema,* London, Secker & Warburg, 1978.

Martyn Auty and Nick Roddick (eds.), *British Cinema Now,* London, BFI, 1985.

Michael Balcon, Ernest Lindgren, Forsyth Hardy, Roger Manvell, *Twenty Years of British Films 1925–45,* London, Falcon, 1947.

Charles Barr, *Ealing Studios,* London, Cameron & Tayleur/David & Charles, 1977.

Geoff Brown, *Launder and Gilliat,* London, BFI, 1977.

Michael Chanan, *The Dream That Kicks: the Prehistory and Early Years of Cinema in Britain,* London, Routledge & Kegan Paul, 1980.

Ian Christie (ed.), *Powell, Pressburger and Others,* London, BFI, 1978.

James Curran and Vincent Porter (eds.), *British Cinema History,* London, Weidenfeld and Nicolson, 1983.

David Curtis and Deke Dusinberre (eds.), *A Perspective on English Avant-Garde Film,* London, Arts Council, 1978.

Margaret Dickinson and Sarah Street, *Cinema and State: the Film Industry and the British Government 1927–1984,* London, BFI, 1985.

Raymond Durgnat, *A Mirror for England,* London, Faber, 1970.

Kenneth Easthaugh, *The Carry On Book,* Newton Abbot, David & Charles, 1978.

Jane Fleugel (ed.), *Michael Balcon: the Pursuit of British Cinema,* New York, Museum of Modern Art, 1984.

Denis Gifford, *The British Film Catalogue 1895–1970,* Newton Abbot, David & Charles, 1973.

Forsyth Hardy (ed.), *Grierson on Documentary,* London, Faber 1966.

Forsyth Hardy (ed.), *Grierson on the Movies,* London, Faber, 1981.

William Hunter, *Scrutiny of Cinema,* London, Wishart, 1932.

Geoff Hurd (ed.), *National Fictions: World War Two in British Films and Television,* London, BFI, 1984.

Alan Lovell and Jim Hillier, *Studies in Documentary,* London, Secker & Warburg/BFI, 1972.

Rachael Low and Roger Manvell, *The History of the British Film 1896–1906*, London, Allen & Unwin, 1948.

Rachael Low, *The History of the British Film 1906–1914*, London, Allen & Unwin, 1948.

Rachael Low, *The History of the British Film 1914–1918*, London, Allen & Unwin, 1950.

Rachael Low, *The History of the British Film 1918–1929*, London, Allen & Unwin, 1971.

Rachael Low, *The History of the British Film 1929–1939: Documentary and Educational Films of the 1930s*, London, Allen & Unwin, 1979.

Rachael Low, *The History of the British Film 1929–1939: Films of Comment and Persuasion of the 1930s*, London, Allen & Unwin, 1979.

Rachael Low, *Film-Making in 1930s Britain*, London, Allen & Unwin, 1985.

Don Macpherson (ed.), *Traditions of Independence: British Cinema in the Thirties*, London, BFI, 1980.

Roger Manvell, *New Cinema in Britain*, London, Studio Vista, 1969.

J.P. Mayer, *British Cinemas and their Audiences: Sociological Studies*, London, Dobson, 1948.

Colin McArthur (ed.), *Scotch Reels: Scotland in Cinema and Television*, London, BFI, 1982.

Eva Orbanz (ed.), *Journey to a Legend and Back: the British Realistic Film*, Berlin, Volker Spiess, 1977.

PEP (Political and Economic Planning), *The British Film Industry*, London, PEP, 1952.

Penguin Film Review, issues 1–9, August 1946–May 1949, London, Penguin, 1949.

George Perry, *The Great British Picture Show*, London, Hart-Davis, MacGibbon, 1974.

David Pirie, *A Heritage of Horror*, London, Gordon Fraser, 1973.

David Quinlan, *British Sound Films: The Studio Years 1928–59*, London, Batsford, 1984.

Jeffrey Richards and Anthony Aldgate, *Best of British: Cinema and Society 1930–1970*, Oxford, Blackwell, 1983.

Jeffrey Richards, *The Age of the Dream Palace: Cinema and Society in Britain 1930–39*, London, Routledge and Kegan Paul, 1984.

Paul Rotha, *Documentary Diary: an Informal History of the British Documentary Film 1926–1939*, London, Secker & Warburg, 1973.

John Spraos, *The Decline of the Cinema*, London, Allen & Unwin, 1962.

Elizabeth Sussex, *The Rise and Fall of British Documentary*, London, University of California Press, 1975.

Frances Thorpe and Nicholas Pronay (eds.), *British Official Films in the Second World War*, Oxford, Clio Press, 1980.

John Trevelyan, *What the Censor Saw*, London, Michael Joseph, 1973.

François Truffaut, *Hitchcock*, London, Paladin, 1978.

Alexander Walker, *Hollywood, England: The British Film Industry in the Sixties*, London, Michael Joseph, 1974.

John Walker, *The Once and Future Film: British Cinema in the Seventies and Eighties*, London, Methuen, 1985.

David Wilson (ed.), *Sight and Sound: A Fiftieth Anniversary Selection*, London, Faber/BFI, 1982.

Richard Winnington, *Film Criticism and Caricatures* 1943–53, London, Elek, 1975.

Alan Wood, *Mr Rank: A Study of J. Arthur Rank and British Films*, London, Hodder & Stoughton, 1952.

Linda Wood, *British Films 1971–81*, London, BFI, 1983.

Chapters in Books

Lindsay Anderson, 'Get Out and Push' in Tom Maschler (ed.), *Declaration*, London, MacGibbon, 1957.

'Cinema: the Screen Holds the Eye' in *The British Imagination: A Critical Survey from the Times Literary Supplement*, London, Cassell, 1961.

Alex Comfort, 'Social Conventions of the Anglo-American Film', in Denys Val Baker (ed.), *Little Reviews Anthology*, London, Allen & Unwin, 1943.

John Hill, 'Ideology, Economy and British Cinema', in Michele Barrett *et al* (eds.), *Ideology and Cultural Production*, London, Croom Helm, 1979.

Pauline Kael, 'Commitment and the Straitjacket', in *I Lost It At The Movies*, London, Cape, 1966.

Alexander Korda, '*British Films: Today and Tomorrow*', in Charles Davy (ed.), *Footnotes to the Film*, London, Lovat Dickson, 1937.

Harry Alan Potamkin, 'The English Cinema' (1929) and 'The Cinema in Great Britain' (1930) in *The Compound Cinema*, New York, Teachers College Press, 1977.

Satyajit Ray, 'Thoughts on the British Cinema', in *Our Films Their Films*, Bombay, Orient Longman, 1976.

Articles

Lindsay Anderson, 'British Films: the Descending Spiral', *Sequence*, no. 7, Spring 1949.

Lindsay Anderson, 'Only Connect: Some Aspects of the Work of Humphrey Jennings', *Sight and Sound*, vol. 20, no. 1, May 1951.

Lindsay Anderson, 'Stand Up! Stand Up!', *Sight and Sound*, vol. 26, no. 2, Autumn 1956.

Charles Barr, '*Straw Dogs, A Clockwork Orange* and the Critics', *Screen*, vol. 13, no. 2, Summer 1972.

Tony Bennett, 'Text and Social Process: the Case of James Bond', *Screen Education*, no. 41, Winter/Spring 1982.

Geoff Brown, 'Which Way to the Way Ahead?', *Sight and Sound*, vol. 47, no. 4, Autumn 1978.

Robert Colls and Philip Dodd, 'Representing the Nation: British Documentary Film 1930–45', *Screen*, vol. 26, no. 1, Jan/Feb. 1985.

Raymond Durgnat, 'Movie Crazy, or the Man(iac) with a Movie Camera', *Framework*, no. 9, 1979 (on *Peeping Tom*).

Richard Dyer, '*Victim:* Hermeneutic Project', *Film Form*, no. 2, 1977.

John Ellis, 'Made in Ealing', *Screen*, vol. 16, no. 1, Spring 1975.

John Ellis, 'Art, Culture and Quality – Terms for a Cinema in the Forties and Seventies', *Screen*, vol. 19, no. 3, Autumn 1978.

Thomas Elsaesser, 'Between Style and Ideology', *Monogram*, no. 3, 1972.

Philip French, 'The Alphaville of Admass', *Sight and Sound*, vol. 35, no. 3, Summer 1966.

Stuart Hall, 'Jimmy Porter and the Two-and-Nines', *Definition*, no. 1, February 1960 (on *Look Back in Anger*).

Andrew Higson, 'Critical Theory and British Cinema', *Screen*, vol. 24, no. 4–5, July–October 1983.

John Hill, 'The British "Social Problem" Film: *Violent Playground* and *Sapphire*', *Screen*, vol. 26, no. 1, Jan/Feb. 1985.

Claire Johnston and Paul Willemen, 'Brecht in Britain: the Independent Political Film', *Screen*, vol. 16, no. 4, Winter 1975–6.

Annette Kuhn, '*Desert Victory* and the People's War', *Screen*, vol. 22, no. 2, Summer 1981.

Gavin Lambert, 'Free Cinema', *Sight and Sound*, vol. 25, no. 4, Spring 1956.

Alan Lovell, 'The Unknown Cinema of Britain', *Cinema Journal*, Spring 1972.

Alan Lovell, 'Notes on British Film Culture', *Screen*, vol. 13, no. 2, Summer 1972.

Richard Dyer MacCann, 'Subsidy for the Screen: Grierson and Group 3, 1951–55', *Sight and Sound*, vol. 46, no. 3, Summer 1977.

Steve McIntyre, 'National Film Cultures: Policies and Peripheries', *Screen*, vol. 26, no. 1, Jan/Feb. 1985.

Andy Medhurst, '*Victim*: Text as Context', *Screen*, vol. 25, no. 4–5, July–Oct. 1984.

Andy Medhurst, 'Can Chaps Be Pin-Ups? The British Male Film Star in the 1950s', *Ten-8*, no. 17, February 1985.

Robert Murphy, 'Fantasy Worlds: British Cinema Between the Wars', *Screen*, vol. 26, no. 1, Jan/Feb. 1985.

Steve Neale, '*Chariots of Fire*, Images of Men', *Screen*, vol. 23, no. 3–4, Sept/Oct. 1982.

V.F. Perkins, 'The British Cinema', *Movie*, no. 1, 1962.

Carrie Tarr, '*Sapphire*, *Darling* and the Boundaries of Permitted Pleasure', *Screen*, vol. 26, no. 1, Jan/Feb. 1985.

Gerry Turvey, 'The Moment of *It Always Rains on Sunday*', *Framework*, no. 9, 1979.

Robin Wood, 'In Memoriam Michael Reeves', *Movie*, no. 17, 1966.

Notes on contributors

Charles Barr did postgraduate research with Thorold Dickinson at London University. After working in secondary education, teacher training, and adult education, he now lectures on film and television at the University of East Anglia. His published work includes books on *Laurel and Hardy* and *Ealing Studios*, and he is currently writing the World War 2 volume in the *History of the British Film* series.

Geoff Brown writes regularly on cinema for *The Times*, and was co-author of the MOMA volume on Michael Balcon, *The Pursuit of British Cinema*.

Elaine Burrows works for the National Film Archive and has been closely involved in organising the MOMA retrospective on British cinema. She is a member of the Board of the Cambridge Animation Festival.

John Caughie lectures on film at the University of Glasgow, and edited *Theories of Authorship*.

Jim Cook is Adult Education Adviser at the British Film Institute, and has edited a number of publications about film and television.

Pam Cook is Assistant Editor of the *Monthly Film Bulletin*, and edited *The Cinema Book*.

Christine Geraghty is a full-time trade union official, and has written extensively on film and television in *Screen* and other journals.

Denis Gifford is author of *The British Film Catalogue 1895–1970* and of other works on British cinema, and on comics.

Sylvia Harvey lectures on film at Sheffield Polytechnic. She is author of *May 68 and Film Culture* and wrote about independent cinema in *British Cinema History*.

Andrew Higson has taught film at Leicester and Sunderland Polytechnics, and was co-editor of a special issue of *Screen* on British cinema.

Peter Hutchings is a research student at the University of East Anglia, working on post-war British horror films.

Brian McFarlane teaches literature at Chisholm College of Technology in Melbourne. He is the author of *Word and Image*, a study of film adaptations of Australian novels, and has edited a *Sequence* anthology (1986).

Andy Medhurst is Research Fellow in British Cinema at the University of East Anglia, preparing the first post-World War 2 volume in the *History of the British Film* series.

Alastair Michie, a Scottish-born schoolteacher, has an M.A. in Film from the University of East Anglia.

Robert Murphy has written widely on British cinema. He is currently based at the University of Kent, researching the final volumes in the *History of the British Film* series.

Geoffrey Nowell-Smith is Head of Publishing at the British Film Institute.

Julian Petley is a freelance writer on film and television, and author of *Capital and Culture: German Cinema 1933-45.*

Jeffrey Richards lectures in History at the University of Lancaster. His many publications on the cinema include *Visions of Yesterday, The Age of the Dream Palace,* and (with Anthony Aldgate) *The Best of British* and *Britain Can Take It.*

Jen Sansom did postgraduate research on the Film Society at the University of Kent, and is now Assistant Television Acquisitions Officer at the National Film Archive.

GENERAL INDEX

445